Born to Grill

Other Cookbooks
by Cheryl Alters Jamison and Bill Jamison

The Rancho de Chimayó Cookbook
Texas Home Cooking
Smoke & Spice
The Border Cookbook
Sublime Smoke

BORN TO GRILL

AN AMERICAN CELEBRATION

CHERYL ALTERS JAMISON AND BILL JAMISON

ILLUSTRATIONS BY SARA LOVE

THE HARVARD COMMON PRESS
BOSTON, MASSACHUSETTS

THE HARVARD COMMON PRESS
535 Albany Street
Boston, Massachusetts 02118

Printed in the United States of America
Printed on acid-free paper

Library of Congress Cataloging-in-Publication Data

Jamison, Cheryl Alters.
Born to grill : an American celebration / by Cheryl Alters
Jamison and Bill Jamison ; illustrations by Sara Love.
p. cm.
Includes index.
ISBN 1-55832-111-X (hardcover)
1. Barbecue cookery. 2. Cookery, American. I. Jamison,
Bill. II. Title.
TX840.B3J35 1998
641.5'784—dc21

Special bulk-order discounts are available on this
and other Harvard Common Press books.
Companies and organizations may purchase books
for premiums or for resale, or may arrange a custom edition,
by contacting the Marketing Director at the address above.

FRONT COVER ILLUSTRATION BY NANCY STAHL
JACKET AND TEXT DESIGN BY KATHLEEN HERLIHY-PAOLI, INKSTONE DESIGN
TEXT ILLUSTRATIONS BY SARA LOVE
BACK COVER PHOTOGRAPHS BY RITA MAAS (LOWER LEFT AND LOWER RIGHT)
AND © TSM/GERALD ZANETTI (UPPER RIGHT)

10 9 8 7 6 5 4 3 2

For Riley Jamison Neale,
our grandson who was born to grill
almost the same day we finished
Born to Grill

CONTENTS

THANKS

To several generations of backyard cooks in Illinois and Texas, our parents included, who fired up our initial enthusiasm for grilling.

To chefs, cookbook authors, food scientists, and other culinary professionals who gave us advice or inspired our efforts in other ways: Marlys Bielunski, Arch and Shirley Corriher, Jennifer Cuccia, Robin Kline, Harold McGee, Mark Miller, Stephan Pyles, Chris Schlesinger, and John Willoughby.

To friends who opened their personal cookbook libraries to us: Rob Coffland, Craig Smith, and Wayne Whitworth.

To archivists and librarians who aided our research at Kraft Foods, the Girl Scouts of America, the Schlesinger Library of Radcliffe College, *Sunset* magazine, and Texas Woman's University.

To our cheerful local suppliers at The Forager, Kaune's, Kokoman Circus, and The Market Place, who came through for us no matter how weird the request.

And most especially to publisher Bruce Shaw and editor Dan Rosenberg for years of support and friendship that have always kept us fired up.

The Open Sky, the Open Flame

Americans didn't invent outdoor cooking, but they can take much of the credit for making it fun. People started cooking outdoors even before they had an indoors, as soon as they tamed flame, and the advance marked one of the earliest and most significant steps ever in human social development. For many millennia, fireside cooking remained the only kind on earth, but it was more of a routine necessity than a pleasure, at least until the victuals reached the mouth.

By the time most people around the globe had successfully moved the cooking fire inside, with huge sighs of self-satisfaction, Americans took the old practice out the back door and made it into a party. They discovered that you could keep the chores in the kitchen and play with the flame in the forest, at a park, or on the patio.

They went to the woods originally. With inspiration from their Native American neighbors, early English, French, and Spanish colonists in the New World found they could tenderize and flavor wild game and other meat through slow smoking over smoldering wood embers. They improvised several methods of doing it, but typically they cut a few trees, dug a long pit in the ground, filled the trench with logs, and cooked whole animals overnight above a smoky fire. The Spanish named the technique *barbacoa*, a term that transmuted in English into *barbecue*.

One of Martha Stewart's predecessors proclaimed the idea perfect for entertaining and it became the party of choice long before Democrats and Republicans existed. From New York City to the Texas frontier, the young country staged barbecues to celebrate weddings, births, religious revivals, and anything else worth a good shout. Margaret Mitchell stoked up one in *Gone With the Wind* to bring together Scarlett O'Hara and Rhett Butler, and the sure sign of an American institution, George Washington probably slept at one.

The love of outdoor feasting survived and thrived through the following centuries, though the original style of cooking gradually died out in most areas except the South and Midwest. When Americans began flocking to cities and suburbs, they left behind their woodsy ways, including the old slow-smoked barbecue. They couldn't very well dig up their streets to make underground pits or cut the trees in their lawns for log fires. Longing for a backyard and balcony alternative, urban Americans jumped into charcoal grilling as soon as the fuels and tools started becoming widely available in the 1940s. In the national euphoria following the end of the Great Depression and World War II, the new method of outdoor cooking took off quicker than a Hollywood scandal.

Fans even called the craze "barbecue," despite vast differences from the historical version, because it offered the same combination of flavor and fun in an open-air setting. In direct contrast to the old art, grilling starts with small, tender ingredients and cooks them quickly over high heat. The methods and results couldn't be more different between the two techniques, but each is naturally suited to the outdoors and boasts the same kind of pleasures, particularly of the palate. Whether the succulence comes in the form of barbecued ribs basted in a pit for hours or a juicy steak seared on a grate in minutes, both ways of cooking bring out the best in America's favorite foods.

In the years since the first grills (or "barbecues") popped up across the country, the patio passion has spawned a huge industry. Within five decades, by the 1990s, more than 80 percent of American households owned at least one grill and some 12 million people bought a new one each year. Charcoal manufacturers sold about 800,000 tons of briquettes annually, twice as much as during the 1960s, even though gas grills were rapidly challenging charcoal models in popularity.

With success came marketing departments, as in all industries, and they in turn drove the introduction of new products. The simple, cheap grills of yesteryear—barely more than a cooking grate on spindly legs—evolved into sophisticated appliances capable of doing anything short of a back rub. Virtually all grills today can roast a turkey or bake a potato, and many of them can simmer beans, steam broccoli, and fry fish, attributes intended to broaden the appeal of the equipment and encourage aficionados to upgrade to fancier models. Compared to their counterparts from the past, every one of these modern all-purpose outdoor cookers looks and operates like a dream machine.

Therein lies the rub. Contemporary grills are so versatile and easy to use that they've led us to neglect real grilling, an earthy and primal process based at its best on human touch rather than mechanical prowess. Too often these days we think we're grilling just because we're using a grill. In fact, much of the time we're actually cooking the food in quite a different way and losing much of the grill flavor that brought us into the backyard originally, a matter that we address more fully in the next chapter.

The issue is not charcoal versus gas, as it is frequently presented. Either fuel can produce high heat and that's its critical role in grilling. Charcoal sometimes adds nuances of taste to food, unlike gas, but it's a controversial contribution because its character comes as much from the industrial plant as from anything that grows in the great outdoors. Ultimately, the two fuels yield comparable results at similar heat levels and neither is more authentic than the other—both briquettes and propane would have bewildered George Washington and Scarlett O'Hara. Which serves your needs best depends on other factors we discuss later.

It's time to remind ourselves why we went outside to cook in the first place. Most modern home kitchens are not set up for smoking or grilling. Both belong outdoors, and they are the only forms of cooking that provide new potentials in that setting which we can't realize inside. Few people really care about backyard baking, but many of us do it when we think we're grilling. We cut to the basics in this book, focusing on genuine grilling in the same straightforward way that we've dealt with smoke cooking in two previous books, *Smoke & Spice* (1994) and *Sublime Smoke* (1996).

Our goal is to capture the rapture of the open sky and the open flame, to celebrate the elemental glories of grilling and the deliciously unpretentious foods that form the roots of the craft. The recipes take a fresh, hearty look at the foods Americans love to cook outdoors, reveling in full grill flavor and the creative fun of working directly with fire. Join us for some hot times ahead.

HONEST-TO-GOODNESS GRILLING

Grilling with a grill sounds as automatic as sawing with a saw or partying at a party. You light the fire, put on your dinner, and cook until done. You're using a grill, after all, so it's going to grill the food.

Not always. Contemporary outdoor grills actually cook in many different ways, some of which have little to do with grilling. They usually bake, roast, and smoke, among their various functions, and these capabilities in particular frequently get confused with grilling, even in owner's manuals that come with new equipment.

Grilling is a specific form of cooking, like frying, boiling, or steaming, and it produces its own distinctive flavor, as do other methods. You're not frying just because you're using a frying pan—we bake cornbread in one of our skillets—and you're not grilling just because you're using a grill. The taste tells. French fries taste different from baked potatoes, even if you start from the same spuds, and in many cases the better you've accomplished the cooking technique, the more pronounced the difference.

Grill flavor comes, first and foremost, from the high-heat browning of the food's surface that scientists call the Maillard reaction. The dean of kitchen science, Harold McGee, explains the transformations that occur in his classic *On Food and Cooking* (Collier Books, 1984), detailing the lively interactions of carbohydrates and amino acids at elevated temperatures that produce "a brown coloration and full, intense flavor." In our own simplistic terms, a hot fire rapidly sears the outer surface of food, concentrating the juices of shrinking muscle fibers in meat into a potently delicious, crisp coating of crust. When you combine that effect with an interior that's cooked through but still juicy, you've got great grill taste and texture.

By the nature of the cooking method, the desired result is only possible with relatively small, naturally tender ingredients. Grilling works wonderfully with steaks and chops, but will turn the surface of a roast into soot long before the interior cooks. You can expertly grill half a chicken but not a whole one, a whole trout but not a big bass, a green onion but not a softball-size Vidalia, a pizza crust but not a loaf of bread.

Some people say there's more than high-heat browning to grill flavor, claiming that it's enhanced by the smoke that results from fat and juices dripping into the fire. We believe this is an overrated factor, given undue

importance perhaps in confusion with barbecue smoking, the original American style of outdoor cooking, which adds an intense wood-smoke flavor to food in a slow, low-temperature cooking process.

Not all smoke tastes the same, of course, as anyone can tell by lighting a cigar. Wood smoke often embellishes food delightfully, but fat smoke sometimes leaves a sooty tang, particularly in excess amounts, and it's also known to carry carcinogens that cling to your meal. For both of these reasons, we make an effort to diminish the effects of fat smoke in the way we grill. In the following discussion of techniques, we focus on using a grill to achieve a clean, crisp grill taste, a hearty balance of crustiness and juiciness.

OPEN AND COVERED GRILLING

Grilling began in the open air, in the United States and elsewhere, and that's still how it's practiced in most of the world. Contemporary American outdoor grills generally provide another option, gaining their versatility as multipurpose cookers by adding a cover over the grate that traps heat inside and reflects it back on the food. In contrast with older braziers and hibachis that came without lids, a covered cooker functions as a combination grill and oven, capable of roasting a turkey or baking a potato as well as grilling a steak.

The cover is clearly an important innovation, expanding the range of outdoor cooking, but its contribution to grill flavor is subject to serious question. When you use the cover in true grilling, as has become common in this country, you cook in two different ways at once. The direct heat of the fire sears the bottom of the food while the reflected heat of the lid roasts or bakes the top side.

The approach offers some definite advantages in convenience and ease of grilling. Employing the cover reduces flare-ups, which can char food badly, and helps to level the cooking temperature across the entire grate. The method also saves a little time and fuel, because of the dual sources of heat, and makes grilling possible on windy and rainy days.

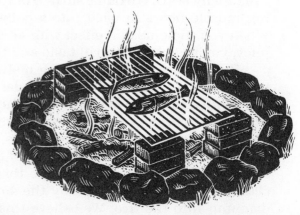

The issue is flavor, particularly the optimum searing of all the food's surface. We experimented for months in the early stages of creating this book, contrasting the taste of dozens of different dishes grilled covered and uncovered at the same time on the same kind of equipment. We enjoyed the covered versions, but found them consistently short of the uncovered versions in full grill flavor.

When we added wood chips to the fire, we got more smoky tang using the cover, but not nearly to the same degree as we enjoy in real smoked barbecue, which absorbs more wood smoke over its longer, slower cooking time. The results seemed a weak compromise of flavors, not completely satisfying a desire for either grilled or smoked taste.

Just as the lid trapped and circulated a modicum of wood smoke from the chips, it did the same with smoke from dripping fat. Removing the cover dissipated both kinds of smoke, producing a cleaner, crisper grill flavor. We assume that some of the fat-smoke carcinogens disappeared into the air as well, instead of sticking to the food, but we had no way to measure that.

Our recipes reflect these testing conclusions, stating a preference for open-air cooking without a lid. We don't ignore the advantages of covered grilling, however, describing how to adjust for it as an alternative method in all appropriate recipes. Most of the charcoal and gas grills we own have a cover, which we always use in roasting large cuts of meat and occasionally use in grilling, especially in cold or stormy weather.

The flavor difference is the main reason we usually grill without the cover, but there's another consideration as well. Even if taste didn't matter, open grilling is just more fun.

Playing with Fire

Covered cooking is almost foolproof, one of the reasons that many grill manufacturers and other authorities recommend the method. You put on food, close the cover, and let the grill do the rest. You cook on auto-pilot, avoiding flare-ups and even the need to turn the food in many cases. It's a perfect system if you don't enjoy cooking.

Open grilling requires careful control of the fire, which makes it both more challenging and rewarding. Some say it's just too difficult for home cooks like ourselves, a sentiment that reeks of the condescension of the culinary academy. In the words of A. Cort Sinnes in *The Grilling Encyclopedia*

OLD MASTERS OF GRILLING

American cookbooks rarely spoke of grilling or barbecuing before the 1930s and '40s. In earlier years, the closest authors usually came to the subject was a discussion of broiling in a regular kitchen stove, often fired in those days by wood or charcoal. They clearly understood the key principles behind grilling, but didn't deal with it as a special technique or an outdoor art.

Across the Atlantic, however, British and French authorities defined the territory decades earlier. An eight-volume English culinary opus from 1890, *The Encyclopedia of Practical Cookery*, identified barbecuing as a festive American specialty that involved cooking whole animals over an outdoor fire, an accurate depiction of the original practice. Grilling, on the other hand, was presented as akin to open-air broiling and perfectly suited to steaks and chops. Author Theodore Francis Garrett described the technique briefly, but focused much of his attention on disparaging French heresies about the cooking style. While admitting the slim possibility that France might be the birthplace of "modern grilling,"

he rejected all Gallic approaches to the craft, including the seasoning of meat in advance with salt and pepper and the use of butter for basting. In conclusive proof of the superiority of English ways, he pointed out that his countrymen turn the meat frequently, "whereas the French cook declares that the meat should only be turned once, in which he decidedly is in error."

The famed French chef Auguste Escoffier didn't deign to respond a decade later in his *Guide Culinare*, an authoritative compilation of classic techniques and dishes. Ignoring any conceivable British influence on the subject, he spoke of open-air grilling as "the first culinary method ever employed," the distant inspiration in the past when "cooking was launched forth upon that highroad along which it has not yet ceased steadily to advance." In advice that often remains relevant a century later, Escoffier emphasized the importance of searing red meat thoroughly over high heat, using a two-level fire for some foods (such as Châteaubriand), and avoiding the "very disagreeable taste" of fat smoke in the process of grilling.

(Atlantic Monthly Press, 1992): "Professional chefs will argue that some foods, such as steaks, chops and certain kinds of fish, are better cooked on an open grill with an adjustable fire grate, preferably with the coals up close to the cooking surface. This may be so, but most home cooks find the expertise and precise timing this cooking method requires to be overly demanding, especially for an activity that's supposed to be relaxing."

Nonsense. Golf and bridge don't become less relaxing because you strive to improve your skills and neither does grilling. As in most enjoyable activities, success depends on mastering a few basic techniques, gaining talent with experience, and improvising with individual flair. As long as you exercise proper caution, open grilling makes playing with fire both gratifying and creative.

All the necessary skills revolve around the fire—how you build it, how you use it, and how you regulate the cooking temperature. Most of the essential principles go back for decades, to the early years of outdoor grills, when simple charcoal braziers and hibachis dominated the market. With some small modifications, the old techniques apply equally well to contemporary grills, including gas models.

PRINCIPLE 1: GETTING FRIENDLY WITH YOUR FIRE. Fire isn't always a friend, of course, but it can be if you're constantly conscious of its power to burn. Beware its bite, and treat it with respect, and it becomes an indispensable ally in grilling. For specific safety tips on using your grill, refer to the owner's manual.

The size and intensity of an open fire determine most of its cooking capability. Good grillers learn the maximum and minimum temperatures possible with their equipment and fuel, and figure out how to make adjustments up and down all along the range. The following general guidelines should help in that effort, but no one can tell you exactly how to regulate the heat on your particular equipment—grills vary substantially in style today, even within brands, and each functions somewhat differently in different conditions, depending on factors such as outside temperature and wind. A little experience goes a long way in tweaking open-grilling techniques for your own needs.

Charcoal grills have a greater heat range than most outdoor gas grills, providing the potential for both higher and lower temperatures. The main variable is the amount of charcoal you use, which is always relative to the size of the grill (particularly the size of the cooking grate) and the quantities and types of food you're fixing. Don't skimp on the fuel because it's much easier to reduce the heat, if necessary, than to raise it, and always start with more charcoal than the manufacturer recommends for covered cooking. On a standard 22.5-inch kettle-style grill on a sunny summer day, we light about seventy briquettes—between four and five pounds, or a full charcoal-chimney load—to cook four chicken breasts over medium heat. For the same number of thick steaks on the same grill the same day, we would increase the amount of charcoal by 50 percent or more to get a much hotter fire under part of the grate. Always preheat the grate for a few minutes before cooking, preferably with the cover on the grill.

Other heat factors in an open charcoal fire include the readiness of the briquettes or lump hardwood for cooking, the spacing of the coals, the level of air circulation provided by bottom or side vents, and the distance between the charcoal and the food. Briquettes reach a prime cooking temperature when they are covered in gray ash, usually about thirty to forty minutes after you light them, and they slowly decrease in heat beyond that point. Lump hardwood charcoal ignites faster, gets hotter, and burns more quickly. With either kind of charcoal, you can bump up the heat by bunching the coals together, opening vents fully, or moving the food closer to the fire. To reduce the temperature, spread the coals apart, dampen the draft, or increase the distance between the food and the fire.

Heat adjustments on gas grills are far simpler, requiring little more than the turn of a knob, but you're often restricted to a narrower range of temperature options. Because they surged into popularity during the years when covered cooking had become the norm in American backyards, most models are engineered to reach their highest temperatures with the lid down. We find this odd because it's in direct contrast with most indoor gas grills, particularly restaurant versions, which are never covered and usually cook hotter overall than their outdoor cousins.

The most powerful gas grills, whether inside or outside, produce open-air temperatures approaching those of a good charcoal fire and they do it with less fuss. With models designed primarily for covered cooking, you'll probably need to turn all burners to their highest setting just to reach a medium temperature for open grilling (that is, four to five seconds with the hand test described next). That's hot enough for many recipes, though you might want to talk to your manufacturer or gas supplier about the possibility of increasing the heat for serious searing. If your grill won't go beyond low, we'd reserve it for covered cooking and get an inexpensive charcoal model for open grilling. Even when you're cooking with the cover up, preheat most outdoor gas grills with the lid lowered.

PRINCIPLE 2: THE HAND TEST. Grilling requires a fire that's blazing hot but doesn't burn, that cooks quickly but thoroughly. The proper temperature varies with different types of food, so you need a means to gauge the heat. The hand test is the time-honored method, easier and more reliable than mea-

TOOLS OF THE TRADE

To listen to some people, you need a second kitchen to store all the tools and utensils required for successful grilling. We've bought most of the gadgets over time and frequently allowed them to rust away from lack of use. Now we stick with just a few essentials beyond such everyday cooking implements as hot pads or oven mitts, bamboo and metal skewers, and an instant-read meat thermometer.

First, you should have tools for moving food on the grate and removing it from the fire. For most items, tongs work best, especially the heavy-duty, spring-loaded type that lift anything quickly and easily. You'll also want a big-bladed spatula—preferably the offset kind with a bent neck—for handling burgers, fish, and similar fare in danger of crumbling. As a supplement to the spatula, consider a small-mesh grill rack for small delicate items, or a hinged wire grill basket that holds fragile food in place and lets you turn it by simply flipping the contraption. In each case, look for long handles to keep your fingers away from the fire.

The only other tools you really need are brushes. To oil the cooking grate before grilling—always important—we use a basting, pastry, or paint brush dedicated solely to that purpose. Keep it separate from other kitchen brushes. To clean the grate after grilling, a critical chore if you want the right results in the future, a wire brush does the job as effectively and effortlessly as possible. Scrub well without any soap to eliminate all the food residue, which will otherwise flavor your next meal.

surements with most grill thermometers. You hold your hand a certain distance from the fire and count the seconds ("one thousand-one," and so on) until the heat forces you to pull your hand away.

In our recipes we apply a standard that assumes the cooking grate is four to six inches above the fire. Place your hand palm down an inch or two above the grate, being careful not to touch it. If you have to pull back in one to two seconds, the fire is hot. Three seconds indicates medium-high heat, four to five seconds is medium, six seconds is medium-low, and seven seconds or longer is low. The measurements are relative only to other grilling temperatures, not to the settings on an indoor stove, because you always grill on higher heat than you simmer, steam, or smoke.

The hand test works on all types of open grills, whether charcoal or gas. It gauges the temperature on the grilling surface, unlike the built-in thermometers on grill lids, which measure the inside air temperature for baking or roasting purposes. The method may not be exact, but it is effective and certainly handy.

PRINCIPLE 3: THE TWO-LEVEL FIRE. Many foods benefit from grilling at two different temperatures, usually starting at a relatively high level and then finishing at a reduced level, a tactic we employ in a number of our recipes. The old rule in charcoal grilling was to spread the hot coals in a single layer, just touching each other, directly under the food. That approach still works when you want steady, even heat, but it gives you less flexibility and cooking capability than a two-level fire.

On gas grills you can change cooking temperatures with a turn of the control dial, making the two-level technique a breeze. With single- or dual-burner models, you simply change the heat setting, usually speeding the transition between higher and lower temperatures by moving food at the same time to a cooler edge of the grate. On grills with three or more burners, you can also adjust the heat level by varying the number of burners in use, perhaps starting a two-level fire with all in operation and then turning off one to finish the cooking.

Charcoal grills with adjustable grates or fireboxes function in a similar way. To reduce the heat during cooking, you increase the distance between the food and the fire, using the hand test to guide the fine tuning. Some grills adjust more easily than others, but the principle—if not the mechanism—is always straightforward.

Non-adjustable charcoal grills, the most common kind, pose a slightly bigger challenge. If you have no means of raising the cooking grate or lowering the firebox, you fiddle with the fire itself to achieve variable temperatures. Basically, you stack and spread the heated coals in a manner that gives you two different cooking surfaces on the same grate, one somewhat hotter than the other with the hand test.

To build a fire with both hot and medium ranges—the levels we recommend for steaks and many other foods—most people pile coals two or three deep on one side of the firebox and then scatter others in a single layer elsewhere. They sear the food well over the hot

A two-level charcoal fire.

8

section and then move it to the medium area to finish cooking through without burning. For a fire with lower levels, you simply use less fuel in both zones.

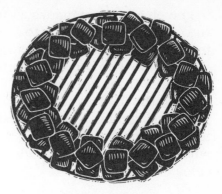

As an alternative method, we sometimes construct a "ring of fire" around a cooler center, akin to the way many people arrange the coals for indirect cooking on a covered grill. We stack all the charcoal along the outer wall of the firebox, leaving an empty doughnut hole in the middle. The center gets ample heat for the last stage of grilling without any coals

A "ring-of-fire."

directly underneath, virtually eliminating flare-ups and fat smoke.

Try the "ring of fire" or invent a technique of your own for achieving variable heat. That's part of the fun of playing with fire, and it not only improves results with many foods but also allows you to cook different items at the same time at different temperatures.

PRINCIPLE 4: CONTROLLING FLARE-UPS. Excessive heat scorches food and so do flare-ups caused by fat and food particles falling in the fire. For optimum flavor in open grilling, you must tame the flame with a combination of prevention and fireman duty.

Building a two-level fire, with little or no direct heat in one area, helps immensely. If a flare-up occurs, you move food temporarily to the cooler spot on the grate while the fat burns away. In some cases, when medium or lower temperatures are desirable in a recipe, you can cook the food completely with indirect heat. Grilling inside a "ring of fire," as just described, works well for that purpose on a charcoal grill. The method consumes larger quantities of fuel than normally needed to produce medium heat, but it averts almost all flare-ups and fat smoke. On today's multiple-burner gas grills, you often get equally good results cooking over a central burner that's turned off.

Even with a single-level fire, you can prevent many flare-ups in two simple ways, by regularly cleaning the cooking grate and exercising caution about oils and fat that can drip in the fire. Scrub the grate well when the metal is hot, preferably right after you finish grilling or at least when you fire up again the next time. Cut excess fat from meat before cooking it and, in a similar vein, go light on vegetable oils used in grilling. It's important to coat the heated grate thoroughly with a little oil before putting on food, especially fish, and some items benefit from an oil spritz prior to cooking, but the amounts should be below levels that will cause flare-ups. We also avoid adding

9

too much oil to marinades, cutting back significantly on the quantities often recommended. Contrary to some popular notions, very little oil is necessary to keep lean food moist during grilling.

If a flare-up occurs despite all your prevention efforts, you need to stop the flame from burning the food. In many cases that's simply a matter of moving the food around on the grate, keeping it away from fiery spots. With a charcoal grill you can also extinguish the flare-up with a small squirt of water, but don't try the old trick on a gas grill. As a last resort, cover the grill with its lid temporarily, which cuts back on the oxygen supply and suffocates the flame.

THE ONLY OTHER THINGS YOU REALLY NEED TO KNOW AND SHOULD NEVER FORGET

○ **START WITH TOP-QUALITY INGREDIENTS.** More than any other cooking method, grilling accentuates the natural flavor of food. When you cook something fast with dry heat, you cook it true, and nothing you can do with seasoning or techniques will change the essential quality. The choice of ingredients is so important in grilling that we include extensive shopping advice in the recipe chapters, identifying ways that anyone, anywhere can find premium products.

○ **SEASON FOOD WITH BOLD SUBTLETY.** The crusted, browned flavor of grilled food gains heft and dimension from many assertive seasonings, but your touch has to be gentle enough to protect the inherent taste of your main ingredient. Go intense but easy, hearty but not heavy-handed, striving to add layers of savor that enrich both the character of the food and its grill flavor. If you mask the underlying tastes by piling on the spices or sauce, you've achieved nothing by grilling. It's better to tilt toward simplicity—some fine ingredients don't need much more than salt and pepper anyway—but the optimum end is balanced complexity.

○ **ORGANIZE YOUR GRILLING IN ADVANCE.** The cooking goes so quickly, it's important to have everything in place before you start. Prepare yourself by going through each step in your mind, reviewing what you'll need as you proceed. Line up ingredients, seasonings, and cooking utensils, placing them within easy reach. Know your projected cooking time and any other useful recipe details. If you intend to serve the food hot off the grill, when it's usually at its best, set the table well ahead. Grilling is easy when you're ready, but not when you're not.

    ☯ **THINK GRATE.** That's what you grill on, and it should always be clean, hot, and lightly oiled before you begin. Preheat the grate with the grill covered while the charcoal or gas heating element reaches cooking temperature. Right before you put on the food, brush the warm surface with a thin coat of oil to prevent sticking, and when you're done, scrub the grate with a wire brush to remove anything that didn't make it to the plate.

    ☯ **SERVE COOKED FOOD.** Sounds simple, but checking for doneness can be a little tricky in grilling. An instant-read meat thermometer is seldom practical because grill cuts are usually too small to allow accurate measurements. The recipe chapters provide general guidance on doneness for different types of food, but also watch the clock carefully while you grill and pay attention to the suggested cooking times for each dish. The times given in any grill recipe are always approximate, because of the many factors that can affect a quick, high-heat cooking process, but we've devoted a lot of time to getting our cooking times as close as possible. Even so, you'll often need to cut into meat, poke a fork into fish, or nibble on a vegetable to get the irrefutable inside evidence. Whatever anyone says, it's better for you to do the checking at the grill than to leave the job to your guests at the table.

FUELING THE FIRE

Often portrayed as the critical issue in grilling, the choice of fuels is actually far less important in your results than the cooking principles we have discussed. The decision whether to use charcoal briquettes, lump hardwood charcoal, gas, wood, or other appropriate fuels may say something about your personality—the real reason people love to debate the subject—but in the end, when the food reaches the table, the basics of the cooking method are the primary factor in flavor. You may like to credit special vine cuttings from Bordeaux, or that rare brand of mesquite coals you found in Arizona, but you won't be bragging about much if you've neglected your part of the art.

BASIC CHARCOAL FIRE BUILDING

Charcoal briquettes can be stubborn to light, an attribute that has spawned an industry of corrective products, sold in any store offering a decent selection of grills. The choices of fire starters today range from electric gadgets to built-in propane burners, from that old flammable fluid to new cubes of non-petroleum gel, from natural kindling to factory-fabricated or homemade "chimneys." We find the chimneys and electric coils the easiest and safest methods for ourselves, but in a pinch we'll use anything that works except dangerous products like gasoline. Lump hardwood coals light more readily than briquettes, often with only a little newspaper.

The fun starts after the charcoal reaches an optimum cooking temperature, usually when it's covered in gray ash. The way you lay your bed of coals determines the heat level(s) of the fire, which in turn becomes one of the major success factors in your grilling that day. You plan your approach according to the food going on the grate. If you're cooking something that does best at a steady temperature, as noted in the recipes, spread the coals evenly below and just beyond the area needed for the food. A single layer of charcoal briquettes bunched together in contact with each other usually produces medium to medium-high heat in a non-adjustable, kettle-style grill. For a hotter fire, build a higher bed.

If the food grills best on a two-level fire, or you're cooking different items at different temperatures, combine the approaches. Stack some of the coals on top of each other in one area, as much as three or four deep for a very hot spot, and spread the others in a single layer, just touching or spaced apart depending on the heat desired. Alternatively, experiment with the "ring of fire" we describe in this chapter in "Principle 3: The Two-Level Fire," or any other arrangement that suits your fancy and yields the right results. The hand test serves as the draftsman's tool in all cases, guiding the architecture.

A few fuels—particularly real wood—contribute a distinctive aroma to food, but the quickness of the cooking time in grilling limits the influence on flavor. Charcoal briquettes and gas, the most common fuels, make almost no difference in taste. Gas is completely neutral in impact and briquettes come close, losing their wood character in the manufacturing process without gaining anything savory in return. When charcoal leaves a lingering tang, as sometimes happens, the effect is usually faint compared to other flavor factors, especially in open grilling.

The fuels differ mainly in other ways, with each offering its own set of advantages and disadvantages. Gas claims the crown for convenience. In both propane and natural forms, it ignites with the turn of a knob, heats quickly, and cleans up readily. On the down side, good gas grills cost considerably more than good charcoal grills, and even top models often don't have the temperature ranges of their charcoal counterparts. If you've had wimpy results from gas, it's likely because the grill baked the food at a heat level too low for true grilling.

When we're cooking with charcoal, we prefer the lump hardwood version to briquettes. It fires up almost as easily as gas, burns hotter than any other fuel, contains none of the industrial additives used to make briquettes, and retains some of its original wood character. The primary drawbacks are scarcity and expense. You can find briquettes anywhere, usually at a good price, but the irregular-shaped lump hardwood coals cost more to ship and stock, reducing the demand and the supply. If we strike out locally, we often mail-order from Hasty-Bake (800-4AN-OVEN) or another dealer.

Wood chips and chunks are sold primarily to enhance flavor, but large chunks can also serve as a fuel, along with hardwood logs, fruit-tree trimmings, and grapevine cuttings. You take a step back in time to the primal roots of grilling, and add a much stronger hint of smoke to food than you can ever manage with a few chips. It takes time and patience, however, because you have to burn the wood down to hot, glowing embers and you frequently get a fire with fluctuating cooking temperatures. Always use hardwood from a nut or fruit tree, not construction scraps or a resinous soft wood like pine.

Ultimately, any appropriate fuel you like will light your fire. What really counts is how you grill on it.

THE GRILL OF YOUR DREAMS

When Americans began grilling with a passion, right after World War II, you could go to your local lawn and garden store and check out every grill on the market in a single stop. The most expensive model on the floor cost barely more than a pocketful of change and it came complete with a bag of newfangled charcoal briquettes. The only dilemma was how to get the goods home in the back of the family station wagon.

Judging by the proliferation of manufacturers and models since then, you might think that money grows on grills. Today, hundreds of companies make outdoor cooking equipment, and each touts its own special features with devoted bravado. You couldn't see all the choices in a year of searching the country, and even if you could, you would probably be more bewildered than ever by the diverse BTUs, side burners, built-in shelves, grate designs, and other decision factors. To make the quandary worse, some of the options push the price well beyond that old station wagon.

We can't solve the problem by recommending particular models that everyone will love, but we can offer some general guidelines for buying grills that apply to a wide range of equipment. We'll focus first on broad criteria we use in selecting any kind of grill—charcoal, gas, or other—and then deal separately with important characteristics of the different generic types.

The main consideration to us is a clear capability for both open grilling and covered cooking. That means the grill comes with a lid designed to facilitate roasting, baking, and smoking, and that it also has the firepower for high-heat searing with the cover off. Most contemporary charcoal grills meet this criterion easily, but some gas grills don't. American manufacturers often engineer their outdoor gas grills exclusively for covered cooking, providing them with plenty of energy for high-temperature roasting—what the built-in thermometer measures—but less searing power. At the highest heat setting you can generally grill open at medium temperatures (four to five seconds with the hand test discussed in the preceding chapter, "Honest-to-Goodness Grilling"), which is fine for many dishes, but you can't always reach the optimum heat level for foods such as fajitas or shrimp (one to two seconds with the hand test). When we're spending hundreds of dollars on a gas grill, we insist on a money-back guarantee that it'll produce the same intensity of open fire as a cheap charcoal model.

The second thing we look for is ample grate space. What matters isn't the girth of the grill overall, which can grow geometrically according to the number of gadgets installed, but the size of the cooking area. You want enough room to grill burgers or chicken breasts for your full family or a small party without crowding the food, plus a little extra to allow you to move the victuals around as necessary to change cooking temperatures or stop flare-ups. You would never know it from the advertising, but grate space is far more important than shelf space, which is never adequate for everything anyway.

As a final overall consideration, we pay careful attention to the quality of workmanship and materials relative to price. Some grills will last a lifetime, some a season: get what you pay for. Buy as much as you can afford of heavy metal construction, sturdy legs and wheels, tight-fitting parts, easy-ignition features, and clean-up conveniences. Beware of loose and flimsy elements, a shaky structure, poor assembly and operation information, and doodads that do nothing.

If the big buying issue for you is charcoal versus gas, we offer a variety of tips in the following sections, but also suggest one flexible general rule. The more you plan to cook on your grill, the more you'll love gas. For year-round, frequent use, a gas grill pays for itself in dozens of saved hours and quick amortization of the extra investment. Someone who cooks outside a few days a summer should stick with charcoal in most cases. We consider the rule flexible because the choice has to fit your personality. If you hated the Boy or Girl Scouts, go for gas regardless of how often you grill.

CHARCOAL GRILLS

People just don't gather around a gas fire. When a family or home magazine runs one of those familiar photos of the clan cooking and laughing together on the patio, you can bet the folks are arrayed around a charcoal grill. Charcoal feels more "authentic" than gas because it conjures pleasant associations with childhood campfires, blazing logs in a winter fireplace, and other convivial times. It doesn't actually add a woodsy taste to food, but that's easy to imagine because it does evoke warm, woodsy feelings. If you cook outdoors only on special occasions, you may never want more than your old tried-and-true charcoal grill.

Any version purchased in the last twenty years or so is probably still close to state-of-the-art. All the popular shapes and sizes go back for decades to the early days of grilling, and most recent enhancements are limited to fine-tuning details, such as hinged grates (making it easier to add charcoal), closed ash-catchers, and convenient lid holders. You might want to upgrade an hibachi—too small for most home purposes—or an aging brazier that wobbles when you walk by, but most types of charcoal grills remain as proficient today as they were yesteryear. The ubiquitous kettle-style grills and other covered cookers may never go out-of-date, despite their frequent lack of something as simple and useful as an adjustable firebox or grate.

Just as long-established designs dominate the market, so do long-established manufacturers. Char-Broil, Kingsford, Sunbeam, and Weber continue to lead the field, primarily because they still do a sound job of combining quality and value. Their products are widely available in home and hardware shops, discount stores, and warehouse clubs, but you may also find it worthwhile to shop farther afield for specialty brands with custom features.

If you want a combination charcoal grill and smoker with an easily adjustable firebox for any level of heat, you simply can't do better than a Hasty-Bake (800-4AN-OVEN), made by a small Oklahoma company since 1948. If you cook a lot for big parties, check out the Fajita Grill from Pitt's & Spitt's (800-521-2947) in Houston, hefty enough to sizzle a steak for every cowboy in Texas. If you're looking for a solid portable grill that also comes with a substantial stand for home use, the Lodge Manufacturing Company (423-837-8279) in Tennessee produces clever cast-iron versions. Someone somewhere makes something in charcoal for every need.

A Hasty-Bake charcoal grill.

GAS GRILLS

Nothing in the great outdoors is easier than cooking with gas. You start your fire with a turn of a knob and you're ready for grilling before your neighbor has even washed the charcoal soot from his hands. You can raise and lower temperatures in a snap, significantly broadening the range of how and what you cook. The fire goes out when you stop grilling, unlike charcoal and wood embers, and the spent fuel leaves no residue to clean up. If your neighbor is actually having more fun with charcoal, he's probably retired and looking for ways to keep busy.

The advantages of gas have sent sales soaring in recent years, producing a market as competitive as the Olympics. Some of the same manufacturers that dominate the charcoal grill industry also hold sway in the gas field, but a bevy of aggressive rivals keep the leaders on the run. Ducane challenges on quality, Thermos attacks on price, and scores of other companies compete on custom craftsmanship.

When we requested product information from every manufacturer we could identify, we wound up with a full closet of costly four-color brochures, each boasting of unique and exemplary features just introduced with the new year's models. Metal plates, triangular bars, and ceramic briquettes now replace messy lava rocks as heat distributors and juice vaporizers. Regulators come with quick-release devices and fuel tanks flaunt accurate gauges. You can choose sure-searing cast-iron grates, brass burners, a deep fryer, a wok ring, or a built-in ice chest for your beer. No one offers a slide-out waterbed yet, but the sleep-in version can't be far away.

We enjoy and seek out many of the options available today, but when we're buying a new gas grill, the only factor that matters to us in the end is how well it grills. If it won't produce high heat uncovered (one to two seconds with the hand test), no amount of gilding can compensate. Fortunately, an increasing number of manufacturers are grasping the point. Weber (800-446-1071), the industry leader, developed its powerful Summit grills in the early 1990s for the Australian market, where open grilling thrives, and then introduced the model several years later in the United States. About the same time, an Australian retailer that became a premier American chain, Barbeques Galore (800-GRILL-UP), started importing and selling sophisticated Australian and Canadian grills that were always engineered to be capable of high-heat uncovered grilling. Cook-On, Capt'n Cook, and Turbo, among others, are sear-serious models.

Several smaller domestic companies also offer choice products. The Thermal Engineering Corporation (800-331-0097) makes amazing infra-red gas grills that heat almost instantly to appropriate open-grilling temperatures. Broilmaster (800-255-0403) and MHP (847-395-6556) grills are in or near the right range, and other U.S. manufacturers should be on board soon. If you can't find what you want today in this rapidly changing market, waiting may be rewarded tomorrow.

OTHER GRILLS

Unlike charcoal, gas works indoors too. Though most grills on home cooktops and ranges don't produce sufficient heat for serious searing, there are a few exceptions among high-end appliances. We haven't found any electric grills that perform consistently well, even the most advanced, but some gas grills can reach the same temperatures as any outdoor fire. Check out the professional-style cooktops from Viking (601-455-1200), among other companies. You pay a lofty price to grill inside, and need a heavy-duty ventilation system, but it's a definite blessing in colder parts of the country.

Indoor gas grilling isn't novel, of course—restaurants have been doing it for years. The vast majority of grill establishments cook with gas, using vented open-air systems heftier than any home product. When chefs go another direction with fuel, it's usually toward wood. Influenced by venerable European traditions promoted by Berkeley and San Francisco grilling pioneers, a small but dedicated band of professionals across the country won't grill with anything except real wood embers.

It's difficult to emulate their methods—and success—at home, but it can be done. Experiment first on your charcoal grill outside, substituting hardwood chunks for the regular fuel and burning down several large handfuls into hot coals. When the fire is ready, spread and bank the embers to get as steady a cooking temperature as possible at the desired level(s). Be sure you start with hardwood (such as hickory, oak, mesquite, pecan, or a fruit wood) and not a soft, resinous wood like pine or spruce, which produces an acrid, tarry smoke.

If you find that you like the flavor and challenges of working with wood, consider buying one of the several styles of Tuscan grills made to fit inside a patio, kitchen, or living room fireplace. Chef Alice Waters, of Chez Panisse fame, located a version in Italy that a friend of hers sometimes imports and sells at The Gardener (510-548-4545) in Berkeley. We've seen other models as well in scattered fireplace and kitchen stores, the best places to check locally for a source. In case the contractor forgot the hearth in your home, you can usually improvise other ways to use a Tuscan grill outside on a bed of dirt or gravel.

Whether we're shopping for a wood, charcoal, or gas grill, we try to focus on a single, simple principle that we apply to all aspects of grilling. Forget the frills, we tell ourselves, and savor the flavor, a goal that guides us in everything from buying equipment to trying recipes. Grilling may not be as elementary as a Sherlock Holmes deduction, but it is elemental, an earthy craft rather than a mechanical process. Grills don't grill, after all, people do.

A Tuscan grill.

An American
Grill
Pantry

An American Grill Pantry

ALL-'ROUND RUB

If your goal in grilling is simplicity of preparation and complexity of flavor, no seasoning technique works as well as dry spice rubs. An approach inherited from slow-smoked barbecue, rubs add new dimensions to the taste of food and help crust the surface for great grill texture. This is our basic, all-purpose grill rub, a blend that we always have on hand for a quick, easy makeover of any meal. The optional cayenne adds a little heat to the mild mixture.

MAKES ABOUT 3/4 CUP

6 tablespoons paprika
2 tablespoons coarse-ground black pepper
2 tablespoons kosher salt or other coarse salt
1 tablespoon chili powder
2 teaspoons packed brown sugar
Pinch or 2 of cayenne pepper, optional

Mix the spices in a small bowl. Store the rub covered in a cool, dark pantry or freezer.

TECHNIQUE TIP: Be cautious about using the same spice rubs in grilling that you use in slow smoke cooking. The lighter, more sprightly savor of grilled food benefits from fresher, subtler seasonings than those often found in traditional barbecue rubs. We cut back significantly on sugar—which tends to burn at the much higher grill temperatures—and on salt, a balancing accent in smoke flavor that can overwhelm the cleaner taste of grilled dishes. We also avoid bland products such as garlic and onion powder, common in the older rubs, in favor of fresher ingredients that maintain a clear, independent character in the quick cooking process.

CHILE RUB ROJO

The Wall Street Journal reported in 1997 that Americans now consume an average of over three pounds of spice per person annually, up more than a pound for each of us in the last decade. Some of the growth comes from the rising popularity of dried chile, a prime ingredient in many great rubs. We like to combine two or more varieties to layer the flavors, using pods of moderate heat to keep the firepower in check.

MAKES ABOUT 3/4 CUP

¼ cup paprika
2 tablespoons kosher salt or other coarse salt
2 tablespoons ground chipotle chile
2 tablespoons ground dried mild to medium-hot red
　　chile, such as New Mexican, ancho, or pasilla, or a
　　combination of these chiles
2 teaspoons ground cumin
1½ teaspoons sugar

Mix the spices in a bowl. (Wear rubber gloves when handling this chile-based rub, or be sure to wash your hands well before touching your eyes or other sensitive body parts.) Store the rub covered in a cool, dark pantry or freezer.

TECHNIQUE TIP: Dry rubs get sticky on the grill. When you're using one, be sure to oil the cooking grate well to prevent fusion between the food and the metal. As further insurance, don't move the food during the first minute of grilling, giving the spices time to singe into the surface.

A Little Spice Would Be Nice

Much of life, the pundits say, is about being prepared. For a griller that means keeping the pantry stocked with your favorite flavorings. When you come home from work and need to unwind outdoors, when a conversation with a neighbor turns into dinner, when nothing will do but a great steak, you want to be ready to grill.

An ample supply of store-bought seasonings is the starting point for any pantry. For a griller interested in the American favorites featured in this book, the basics include peppercorns for fresh-ground pepper, salt (preferably kosher because of its coarser texture), Worcestershire sauce, Tabasco or similar hot sauce, prepared horseradish, soy sauce, chili powder, brown sugar or molasses, ketchup, at least a couple of mustards, fresh garlic, and a well-stocked spice shelf. Other common ingredients on our shelves include olive oil and various flavored oils, infused and aged vinegars, canned chipotle chiles in adobo sauce, ground dried New Mexican red chile, Caribbean and Mexican hot sauces, Asian fish sauce, hoisin sauce, and beer, wine, tequila, and rum. If we can't make something good out of that pantry, we'll turn in our spatula.

Most of these seasonings hold up well in long-term storage, but dry spices are an exception, losing their character in months, especially if they sit anywhere near the stove or in bright sunlight. Plan to replenish supplies regularly. Buy in small quantities, easy to do today with the growing numbers of markets that sell in bulk. If you suspect your grocer's spices don't turn over regularly, order by mail. Two good sources are Penzey's (414-574-0277), in southern Wisconsin, and Vanns (800-584-1693), in Baltimore.

Beyond the staples, most grillers will want to stock a variety of homemade, down-home condiments, special types of seasonings that are always on hand to add an individual touch to food. The possibilities in this chapter start with spice rubs and range from there through sauces, pickles, and robust variations on popular commercial products, all tailored for grilled food. Each works well in multiple dishes, and, because of the versatility, appears with some regularity in our outdoor cooking, as you'll see in later chapters. Feel free to appropriate any of the condiments for your own, or use them as inspiration for developing different signature flavorings. Whatever you stock, the more your pantry brims, the more you'll relish your grilling.

SUGAR AND SPICE

Sweet and fragrant, this rub flavors some of our favorite grilled pork dishes. Turbinado sugar—a crystallized, lighter version of brown sugar—contributes a coarse texture to the mix that enhances its crusting effect.

MAKES ABOUT 3/4 CUP

3 tablespoons ground allspice
2 tablespoons turbinado sugar or 1 tablespoon sugar
1½ tablespoons kosher salt or other coarse salt
1 tablespoon ground dried mild red chile, such as New Mexican
1 tablespoon ground cinnamon
1 tablespoon fresh-ground black pepper
1½ teaspoons ground white pepper

Mix the spices in a small bowl. Store the rub covered in a cool, dark pantry or freezer.

TECHNIQUE TIP: In spite of the conventional wisdom, sugar and fire don't always equal incineration. Sugar and naturally sweet foods such as oranges or tomatoes will burn over time at high temperatures, but when you use them properly in a dry rub, marinade, or glaze, they can produce a delightful caramelized crunch on grilled foods. If you keep the quantities proportionately small, cook the food only briefly, or grill over moderate heat, the sweetening contributes to a chewy, lightly charred, deeply flavored crust. The effect is similar to what happens with crème brûlée, where the sugar topping melts down to a rich, brown caramel under a direct flame.

TRIPLE-PLAY PEPPER RUB

Pink peppercorns, actually berries from a rose plant, join their black and white namesakes in this hearty rub, great for steaks.

MAKES ABOUT 3/4 CUP

¼ cup whole black peppercorns
2 tablespoons whole white peppercorns
2 tablespoons whole pink peppercorns
2 tablespoons kosher salt or other coarse salt
1½ teaspoons yellow mustard seeds
1 tablespoon dried onion flakes, optional

Place the spices in a blender or spice mill and grind coarsely. Store the rub covered in a cool, dark pantry or freezer.

RED-EYE RUB

You won't be rubbing your eyes awake after trying this coffee-bean blend. It's assertive, but still makes a good team player with other seasonings such as cinnamon, allspice, ginger, sugar, or chile. We like it on game birds, particularly quail, as well as on pork, the long-term Southern mate of red-eye flavor.

MAKES ABOUT 3/4 CUP

½ cup coarse-ground coffee beans
¼ cup coarse-ground black pepper
1½ tablespoons kosher salt or other coarse salt

Mix the spices in a small bowl. Store the rub covered in a cool, dark pantry or freezer.

TECHNIQUE TIP: When you find yourself rushed, and don't have the time to marinate food for as long as a recipe suggests, a dry rub offers significant advantages over other seasoning methods, contributing the greatest amount of flavor in a short span of time. If necessary, you can apply a rub right before grilling and still get much of its savor.

MIXED MUSTARD PLASTER

A wet version of a dry rub, a paste both seasons and moistens food, helping to protect delicate, lean items from drying out during the cooking process. We plaster this multi-mustard version over and under the skin of poultry, or sometimes on pork tenderloin. The mixture sounds stout, but it mellows on the grill.

MAKES ABOUT 1 CUP

6 tablespoons Honey-Beer Mustard (page 37) or other
    sweet hot mustard
6 tablespoons coarse-ground Dijon mustard or other
    mild coarse mustard
3 tablespoons yellow ballpark mustard
1 to 2 teaspoons malt vinegar or cider vinegar, optional

In a small bowl, combine the three mustards. The paste can be used immediately or covered and refrigerated indefinitely. If the paste gets too thick to spread easily, stir in a teaspoon or more of vinegar to get the right consistency.

Lemon Rosemary Paste

Pastes make a fine way of adding fresh herb flavors to grilled food. Here we spotlight a current American favorite, rosemary, which boasts an earthy, robust perfume perfect for many dishes, from steak to trout. Plan to use any herb paste within a couple of days for optimum taste.

Makes about 1 cup

⅔ cup olive oil
½ cup packed fresh rosemary sprigs
Zest and juice of 2 lemons
¼ cup chopped onion
3 plump garlic cloves
2 teaspoons kosher salt or other coarse salt

In a blender, preferably, or a food processor, purée the rosemary with the oil. Let the rosemary steep in the oil for 5 to 10 minutes, then strain the mixture to remove the tough little leaves. Return the oil to the blender, add the remaining ingredients, and purée until fairly smooth. The paste will be somewhat soupy. It is ready to use immediately or can be covered and refrigerated for up to two days.

Technique Tip: Many of our recipes call for lemon, lime, or orange zest. This is the colored outer peel of the fruit, without the bitter white pith found immediately under it. Loaded with fragrant oils, zest provides the concentrated essence of citrus without the tangy acid or liquid of the fruit juice. You can remove the zest with a paring knife or sharp vegetable peeler, but the most effective tool is an inexpensive citrus zester, available in cookware stores. Any extra shreds can be air-dried for future use.

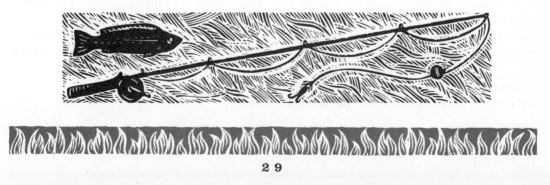

DOG SAUCE MARINADE

A more subtle flavoring method than rubs and pastes, marinades can still pack a wallop, as in our variation on the *sauce chien* popular in the French Caribbean. We seldom make up marinades more than a day in advance of grilling, but this one retains its punch for as long as a week and works well on a variety of foods, including fish, shellfish, chicken, and pork. It's also a terrific table sauce, the role it usually serves so splendidly in the West Indies.

MAKES ABOUT 2 CUPS

. . . .

1 large onion, chopped very fine by hand
1 small carrot, chopped very fine by hand
3 green onions, chopped very fine by hand
2 tablespoons minced fresh thyme
½ to 1 fresh Scotch bonnet or habanero chile, minced
    fine, or ½ to 1½ teaspoons Caribbean hot sauce
½ teaspoon salt, or more to taste
½ teaspoon fresh-ground black pepper
Juice of 2 medium limes
2 tablespoons white vinegar
2 tablespoons water
⅓ cup vegetable oil

. . . .

Make sure the vegetables and herbs are cut in very small bits to release their flavor fully. In a medium bowl, stir together all the ingredients, whisking in the oil at the end. The sauce is ready to use immediately as a marinade, but for a table sauce, let it sit for at least 30 minutes at room temperature. It can be kept covered and refrigerated for up to a week.

TECHNIQUE TIP: The Scotch bonnet or habanero chile, one of the hottest edibles on earth, looks a bit like a tam-o'-shanter, hence the popular name. Use the chile in small quantities, always wear rubber gloves to cut them, and as you chop, avoid taking any deep breaths of the intoxicating aroma. Since most bottled Caribbean hot sauces are based on the pod, they make an adequate substitute for the fresh chile. Season to taste carefully in either case.

Zesty Lemon Pepper

Once so valuable that it inspired global expeditions and the European discovery of the Americas, pepper is one of the world's most potent seasonings. Don't just shake it for granted; grind your peppercorns fresh to bring out the full flavor. The bantam berries, native to Asia, are harvested at different stages and processed in different ways to produce black, white, and green varieties. We like to mix two or more types, coarsely ground in this case, and for a fragrant citrus complement we add fresh lemon zest. If your pepper mill doesn't have a coarse-grind option, place the peppercorns in a freezer-weight plastic bag and crack them with a rolling pin or other heavy object. Use this blend—with the respect pepper deserves—on chicken, lamb, and steaks.

Makes about 1/2 cup

¼ cup coarse-ground black peppercorns, preferably
    Tellicherry, Lampong, or Malabar variety, or a mix
    of two of these
3 tablespoons minced lemon zest
2 teaspoons ground white peppercorns
2 teaspoons kosher salt or other coarse salt

Mix the spices in a small bowl. Store the pepper covered in a cool, dark pantry or freezer.

Technique Tip: It's easy to make superior homemade versions of many commercial seasonings, though what you gain in flavor is sometimes sacrificed in shelf life. If you want a full-bodied garlic salt, for example, just mash a whole head of peeled, roasted garlic cloves together with about ½ cup kosher salt or other coarse salt. The mixture will be moister than the supermarket product, which is fine for most rubs, pastes, and marinades. Plan to use the roasted garlic salt within a week or so, and keep it covered and refrigerated in the meantime.

QUINTESSENTIAL KETCHUP

More richly seasoned and fresher in flavor than store-bought brands, this ketchup puts a personal seal of approval on anything it covers. The sweetness complements rather than overwhelms the tomato taste, which comes from the canned fruit in this case to provide year-round availability.

MAKES ABOUT 2 CUPS

14- to 15-ounce can chopped or crushed tomatoes, undrained
6-ounce can tomato paste
⅛ small onion, minced
⅛ small red bell pepper, minced
⅛ cup water
¼ cup cider vinegar
3 tablespoons corn syrup
1 tablespoon packed brown sugar
1 cinnamon stick
1 teaspoon ground allspice
1 teaspoon salt
¾ teaspoon fresh-ground black pepper
¼ teaspoon ground cloves

In a large, nonreactive saucepan, combine all the ingredients. Bring to a boil over high heat, reduce the heat to medium-low, and cook the mixture for 45 to 50 minutes, stirring occasionally at first and more frequently near the end. The ketchup is the proper consistency when it's a little thinner than store-bought versions. Use the ketchup warm or chilled. It keeps, covered and refrigerated, for several weeks.

A Little Catch-Up

That old American favorite, ketchup, had an unlikely origin in China as a spicy pickled-fish condiment. Seventeenth-century British sailors grew fond of the *ke-tsiap*, brought the idea home, and started making it with the ingredients at hand, including oysters, walnuts, and mushrooms. These versions crossed the Atlantic to the colonies and quickly became kitchen staples.

Colonists may have introduced tomatoes as a base before the turn of the eighteenth century, but it took two hundred years for that to become standard. Early American cookbooks usually featured several kinds of ketchup, demonstrating both its budding popularity and its original versatility. In her 1847 *The Carolina Housewife*, Sarah Rutledge offered four different preparations, ranging from a version made with home-pressed walnut oil to a tomato concoction that gets its tang from port wine instead of vinegar. The mushroom ketchup was the simplest of the recipes: "Gather your mushrooms early in the morning, wipe them very clean, break them into pieces, and lay them in a dry stone, or earthen vessel, with a good deal of fine salt, for twelve or fifteen hours; then squeeze them very dry in a cloth, and give the liquor one or two good boils, with a few cloves, a little mace, and allspice, let it cool and bottle it."

No wonder the first commercial ketchup was advertised as "Blessed Relief for Mother and Other Women of the Household." The man who flaunted the slogan, Henry J. Heinz, began his career growing horseradish in his backyard in Sharpsburg, Pennsylvania. He found an eager market for his crop locally, branched out into pickles, and then took on ketchup along the way toward his fifty-seven varieties. When Heinz introduced his tomato-based product in 1876, other forms of ketchup began to disappear from the American pantry. We gained relief from the once-complicated labor of making our own, but also lost many of the flavoring potentials of a once-creative condiment.

SPICY MUSHROOM KETCHUP

Even after the appearance of commercial tomato ketchup, homemade mushroom variations lingered as an American favorite into the early decades of the twentieth century. Two of the most popular cookbooks of the period—*Marian Harland's Complete Cook Book* and *Mrs. Rorer's New Cook Book*—presented spiced-up recipes, flavored in one case or the other with ground ginger, mustard seeds, cloves, port, onions, and paprika. We take inspiration from these seminal versions, hoping to show why the old idea shouldn't be allowed to die.

MAKES ABOUT 2 CUPS

1 pound portobello mushrooms, caps halved and caps
    and tender stems sliced thin
1 tablespoon kosher salt or other coarse salt
2 large shallots, cut into chunks
2 garlic cloves
2 cups water
1 cup red wine vinegar
1 tablespoon paprika
1 teaspoon dry mustard
½ teaspoon ground ginger
⅛ teaspoon ground allspice
¼ teaspoon ground cloves
3 tablespoons port or sweet red wine

Plan to make the mushroom ketchup over 2 days. Place the mushrooms in a large ceramic, glass, or stainless steel bowl. Mix the salt with the mushrooms, cover with a clean dish towel, and set them aside in a cool spot for 12 hours or up to 24 hours. We normally do this step one evening and let the bowl sit out overnight.

In a blender, preferably, or a food processor, combine the mushrooms and accumulated liquid with the shallots, garlic, and enough of the water to purée it easily. You will probably need to do this in two batches. Spoon the purée into a nonreactive saucepan and pour in any remaining water, the vinegar, and the spices. Bring to a boil over high heat, reduce the heat to low, and cook the mixture for 45 to 50 minutes,

stirring occasionally at first and more frequently near the end. The ketchup is the proper consistency when it's a little thinner than store-bought tomato ketchup. Add the port and cook for 3 to 5 additional minutes. Use the ketchup warm or chilled. It keeps, covered and refrigerated, for several weeks.

Classic Kansas City Sauce

Many tomato-based barbecue sauces, developed originally for smoked food, smother the taste of grilled dishes. We lighten the tone in this rendition, but retain the essence of the Kansas City style that dominates supermarket brands everywhere today.

Makes about 2 1/2 cups

- 1 tablespoon vegetable oil
- 1 medium onion, chopped fine
- 2 garlic cloves, minced
- 1 cup canned tomato purée
- ¾ cup cider vinegar
- ¾ cup water
- ½ cup tomato paste
- 3 tablespoons Super Wooster Sauce (page 39) or other Worcestershire sauce
- 3 tablespoons molasses
- 3 tablespoons packed brown sugar
- 2 tablespoons chili powder
- 1 tablespoon yellow ballpark mustard
- 1 tablespoon fresh-ground black pepper
- 1 tablespoon pure liquid hickory smoke, optional

In a nonreactive saucepan, warm the oil over medium heat. Add the onion and sauté until translucent, about 5 minutes, then add the garlic and cook an additional minute. Mix in the remaining ingredients, reduce the heat to low, and cook the mixture until it thickens, approximately 30 minutes. Stir frequently. If the consistency is thicker than you prefer, add a little water. Use the sauce warm or chilled. It keeps, covered and refrigerated, for several weeks.

GEORGIA GRILLING SAUCE

Among traditional barbecue sauces—which we cover in detail in *Smoke & Spice* (Harvard Common Press, 1994)—the ones based on mustard often contribute more to grilled flavor than those that start with tomato or vinegar foundations. This blend has deep roots in Georgia, but we've modified the mix to make it a grilling sauce.

MAKES ABOUT 2 CUPS

¼ cup butter
1 medium onion, minced
¼ cup yellow ballpark mustard
¼ cup water
Juice of 2 large lemons
2 tablespoons chili sauce (the ketchup-style sauce)
1 tablespoon white vinegar
¼ teaspoon cayenne pepper
¼ teaspoon salt, or more to taste

In a nonreactive saucepan, warm the butter over medium heat. Add the onion and sauté until translucent and very soft, about 5 to 7 minutes. Mix in the remaining ingredients, reduce the heat to low, and cook the mixture for 10 additional minutes. Use the sauce warm. It keeps, covered and refrigerated, for several weeks, but reheat before using.

Honey-Beer Mustard

We enjoy sweet mustards, but too often the sugar overrides the other flavors. Here we use a dollop of honey and the yeastiness of a good brew to balance the robust mustard blend, which also features a slightly coarse texture and a hint of heat.

Makes about 2 cups

½ cup plus 2 tablespoons yellow mustard seeds
¼ cup dry mustard
½ cup malt vinegar, preferably, or cider vinegar
1 cup light- to medium-bodied beer
3 tablespoons honey
2 teaspoons salt
¼ teaspoon cayenne pepper

In a small bowl, combine the mustard seeds and mustard with the vinegar and cover it. Let the thick mixture sit at room temperature for at least 1 hour and up to several hours, during which time its pungency mellows a bit.

In a blender, preferably, or a food processor, combine the mustard mixture with the remaining ingredients and blend to a coarse purée. Refrigerate the mustard for at least a day, then taste and adjust the seasoning if you wish. It keeps indefinitely covered and refrigerated.

ENRICHED MAYONNAISE

Fears of salmonella poisoning and cholesterol keep most people from making mayonnaise from scratch with egg yolks, but that doesn't mean you have to live with the blandness of commercial brands. Just add a splash of extra-virgin olive oil to any mayonnaise, even a low-fat version, and the taste soars. From that dead-simple starting point, we make the Hot Shot Tartar Sauce below and several flavored mayos that we use in dishes in later chapters.

MAKES ABOUT 1 CUP

1 cup store-bought mayonnaise
1½ tablespoons extra-virgin olive oil
¼ teaspoon fresh lemon juice
¼ teaspoon minced garlic
2 to 6 drops Tabasco sauce or other hot pepper sauce

In a medium bowl, whisk the ingredients together. Use the mayo immediately or refrigerate. It keeps, covered and refrigerated, for up to several weeks.

HOT SHOT
TARTAR SAUCE

European in origin, like its mayonnaise base, tartar sauce began sinking American roots the first time someone—undoubtedly a Southern cook—added sweet pickle relish. We replace that regional innovation with another, this time from the Southwest.

MAKES ABOUT 1 1/2 CUPS

1 cup Enriched Mayonnaise (page 38) or other
    mayonnaise
1 tablespoon minced pickled jalapeño
2 teaspoons small capers or minced large capers
2 teaspoons minced fresh dill or 1 teaspoon dried dill
1 teaspoon fresh lemon juice
¼ teaspoon Dijon mustard

. . . .

In a small bowl, combine the ingredients and refrigerate for at least 30 minutes. The sauce keeps, covered and refrigerated, for several days.

Super Wooster Sauce

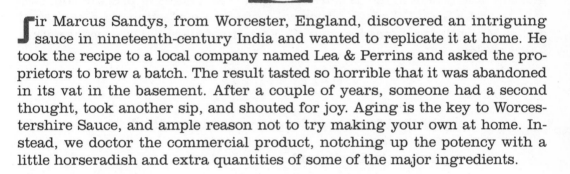

Sir Marcus Sandys, from Worcester, England, discovered an intriguing sauce in nineteenth-century India and wanted to replicate it at home. He took the recipe to a local company named Lea & Perrins and asked the proprietors to brew a batch. The result tasted so horrible that it was abandoned in its vat in the basement. After a couple of years, someone had a second thought, took another sip, and shouted for joy. Aging is the key to Worcestershire Sauce, and ample reason not to try making your own at home. Instead, we doctor the commercial product, notching up the potency with a little horseradish and extra quantities of some of the major ingredients.

Makes about 2 cups

. . . .

15-ounce bottle commercial Worcestershire sauce
¾ cup water
½ medium onion, chopped
2 tablespoons unsulphured molasses
2 tablespoons balsamic vinegar
1 tablespoon chopped anchovies
2 teaspoons grated fresh horseradish root or 4
    teaspoons prepared horseradish
2 plump garlic cloves, chopped
1 teaspoon dried red chile flakes

. . . .

In a heavy, nonreactive saucepan, bring the ingredients to a boil over high heat. Reduce the heat to medium-low and cook for 50 to 60 minutes. The sauce will be thin with some texture to it. Cool the sauce to room temperature, then spoon it into a blender and purée. Refrigerate for at least 1 day for the flavor to develop. The sauce keeps for months covered and refrigerated.

Sage Oil

Flavored oils abound today, offering everything from chile zip to fruit fragrances worthy of an Arabian Nights bath. Some of the oils are great marinades, such as the porcini variety that we pour over mushrooms before grilling, and others shine as a seasoning at later stages of preparation. Our easy-to-make Sage Oil plays either role, often to perfection, in a variety of dishes. As with any home-blended oil, keep it refrigerated and use it within a few weeks.

Makes 1/2 Cup

¼ cup packed fresh sage leaves, washed and dried before using
½ cup extra-virgin olive oil

Place both ingredients in a blender. Purée for about 30 seconds, then let the oil sit for 10 minutes. Strain the oil through cheesecloth or a fine strainer into a jar. Use the oil immediately or refrigerate. The oil keeps for several weeks covered and refrigerated, gradually losing its fresh potency.

PEACH VINEGAR

When a recipe calls for fruit vinegar, this is the one we usually grab from the shelf. Like many of the similar specialty products on the market today, it's made by steeping fruit in mild vinegar rather than fermenting juice, the traditional way. Because of the process, full-flavored, height-of-the-season peaches produce the best results, but even frozen peaches will work.

MAKES ABOUT 2 CUPS

2 large peaches, peeled and sliced
2 cups rice vinegar or champagne vinegar

Place the peaches into a large ceramic, glass, or stainless steel bowl and pour the vinegar over them. With the back of a fork, mash the peaches enough to release more juice. Let the mixture sit at room temperature for 6 to 12 hours. Pour through cheesecloth or a fine strainer into a jar, pushing down with a spoon on the peaches to release more of their flavor. Use the vinegar immediately or store covered at room temperature. It keeps for at least several weeks.

PEPPERED SHERRY

A splash of peppered sherry adds dash to many a dish, from grilled shrimp to black-bean soup. Another steeped condiment, like our previous vinegar, it flaunts its flavoring by displaying the guilty chiles in the bottle.

MAKES ABOUT 1 1/2 TO 2 CUPS

1 to 2 tablespoons small hot dried red chiles, such as
    chiltepíns or chiles pequíns
8 to 12 long, slim medium-hot to hot dried red chiles,
    such as chiles de árbol
1½ to 2 cups dry sherry

You don't need a real recipe for this, just a few ingredients and a tall, slim decorative bottle. Drop the chiles into the bottle, adding more if you wish while leaving room for the pods to expand. Wear rubber gloves or make sure to wash your hands very well before touching your eyes or other sensitive body parts. Pour the sherry over the chiles and let the mixture stand for at least 1 day before using. It lasts indefinitely stored covered at room temperature.

MUSTARD RELISH

A simple combo of mustard, sweet gherkins, and pickled vegetables, this dresses a dog like it's going to a debutante ball. We also like the relish with other grilled sandwiches, particularly chicken and turkey.

MAKES ABOUT 1 1/2 CUPS

One-half 16-ounce jar mixed pickled vegetables
    (carrots, cauliflower, celery, and onions are good)
    such as Italian giardiniera, drained, rinsed, and
    drained again
10-ounce jar sweet gherkin pickles, drained and 3
    tablespoons of syrup reserved
½ cup yellow ballpark mustard
1 tablespoon sugar

Chop the vegetables and the pickles into small bite-size pieces, but avoid mincing them as in a commercial relish to maintain texture. Place the vegetables and pickles in a medium bowl and stir in the reserved syrup, mustard, and sugar. The relish keeps indefinitely covered and refrigerated.

James Beard and a Bunch of Browns

Americans didn't need a lot of encouragement to jump into outdoor grilling in the 1940s and '50s, but they did seek inspiration on how to do it well. Many professional cooks, home economists, and food writers volunteered help—through cookbooks, TV shows, newspapers, and magazines—but the advice was often more ephemeral than enduring.

Among the pioneers who truly added to our knowledge, a handful stand out as genuine masters. The first on the scene were an almost forgotten trio of great home cooks, Cora, Rose, and Bob Brown. They wrote numerous magazine articles and books, but their 1940 *Outdoor Cooking* (Greystone Press) remains a classic on the subject. Sophisticated in their understanding of food and seasoning, but down-home in their love of eating, the Browns ranged in their recipes from Bordeaux Brandied Crawfish to this simple steak sauce: "Dump plenty chili sauce out of the bottle into the frying pan and heat it up on a good bed of embers and ashes with the juice of a whole lemon, a lump of butter about the size of your pipe bowl and a few shakes of zigzag Tabasco lightning."

Far better known than the Browns, in his day and today, James Beard took an outdoor approach to becoming the contemporary virtuoso of American cooking. His second cookbook—after one on happy-hour hors d'oeuvres—introduced a lifelong call to *Cook It Outdoors* (M. Barrows and Company, 1941). Perhaps more than anyone before or since, he appreciated the place of outdoor cooking and flavors in the mainstream of American cuisine. Beard's field of vision ultimately encompassed much more than grilling and barbecuing, but he returned to those topics in his cookbooks far more than any others and wrote about them with unsurpassed passion.

One of his finest works, *The Complete Book of Outdoor Cookery* (Doubleday, 1955), was co-authored by another great grilling pioneer, Helen Evans Brown. A talented cook who celebrated the joy of patio and backyard dining, she brought a sunny California perspective to the collaboration with Beard and to several books of her own. Brown talked about deferring to men when it came to outdoor cooking, but in fact she had a major influence on the main man himself and a whole generation of male grillers.

OLIVE OIL DILLS

We combine two old and tasty ideas here. Everyone loves dill pickles, long an American favorite, but most of us have forgotten olive oil pickles, popular a century ago when cooks used the oil for little else. The two approaches together turn a cucumber into a humdinger treat.

MAKES 7 TO 8 PINTS

4 pounds 3- to 4-inch pickling cucumbers
1 pound white onions
½ cup pickling salt
1 quart white vinegar
¾ cup olive oil
⅛ cup sugar
3 tablespoons yellow mustard seeds
2 tablespoons celery seeds
6 fresh dill "heads" with seeds
6 plump garlic cloves

Plan to make the pickles over 2 days. Slice the cucumbers and onions about ¼-inch thick. Place the cucumber slices and onion slices in a large ceramic, glass, or stainless steel bowl. Mix the salt throughout the vegetables, cover with a clean dish towel, and set them aside in a cool spot for 8 to 12 hours. We normally do this step one evening and let the bowl sit out overnight.

Drain and rinse the vegetables and then rinse the bowl itself. Return the vegetables to the bowl and pour the vinegar over them. Let stand again at room temperature, this time for at least 4 hours and up to 12 hours.

Prepare pint canning jars according to the manufacturer's directions.

Drain the vinegar into a large, nonreactive saucepan and add the oil, sugar, mustard seeds, and celery seeds. Bring the mixture to a full, rolling boil, stirring occasionally. While the mixture comes to a boil, spoon the cucumbers and onions equally in jars, and with clean hands insert a dill head and garlic clove in each. Carefully pour the hot liquid into each jar, spooning some of the spices into each. Leave ½ inch of head space in each jar, and discard any syrup that doesn't end up fitting.

Process the jars in a water bath according to the manufacturer's directions, generally about 10 minutes. For peak flavor, store at least one week before using, and serve chilled.

All-Star Pickled Starfruit

Still exotic enough to elicit *oohs* and *ahhs*, the starfruit, or carambola, makes a superb sweet pickle, on a par with the watermelon-rind version. Freezing the fruit, a technique we learned from pickling pro Jeanne Lesem, provides some of the crispness that came in old recipes from long soaks in pickling lime. That ingredient is no longer recommended for home preserving. Serve the pickles on a relish tray or alongside sandwiches, but certainly for any all-star game.

Makes about 2 Pints

2 pounds starfruit (carambolas), about 6 medium fruit
½ cup loosely packed thin-sliced onion rings
1½ teaspoons kosher salt or other coarse salt
3 tablespoons water
1⅓ cups sugar
⅔ cup cider vinegar
1 teaspoon whole allspice

At least a day before you plan to serve the pickles, begin preparations. Cut any brown edges from the ribs of the starfruit. Slice the fruits into ¼- to ⅓-inch stars. Mix the starfruit, onions, salt, and water together in a nonreactive medium bowl and let stand at room temperature for about 1 hour. Drain the liquid off and discard it.

In a heavy medium saucepan, combine the sugar, vinegar, and allspice, and warm over medium heat until the sugar has dissolved. Pour the hot liquid over the starfruit and let it cool to room temperature. Spoon the fruit and syrup into freezer containers and freeze, at least overnight, to firm the pickles.

Defrost the pickles as needed, storing any leftovers in the refrigerator. The pickles keep in the freezer for several months.

PICKLED PEPPER HASH

A technicolor cross between chow chow and relish, this bell pepper mixture enlivens the look and the taste of anything from a burger to a premier pork chop.

MAKES ABOUT 2 CUPS

3 cups chopped red bell peppers
1 cup chopped onion
3 green onions, sliced
¾ cup white vinegar
½ cup sugar
1 tablespoon paprika
1½ teaspoons yellow mustard seeds
1½ teaspoons salt
¾ teaspoon ground cinnamon

In a heavy, nonreactive saucepan, combine all the ingredients. Bring the mixture to a boil over high heat. Reduce the heat to low and cook for 25 to 30 minutes, stirring frequently, until thick. The pepper hash keeps, covered and refrigerated, for a couple of weeks.

DRIED FRUIT CHUTNEY

Most chutneys gain their zest from fresh seasonal fruit, but this one thrives year-round on dried produce. Like many chutneys, it goes great with game.

MAKES 2 CUPS

1 large onion, minced
½ cup dried apricots or dried peaches, cut in quarters
½ cup prunes, cut in quarters
¼ cup golden raisins
¼ cup dried cranberries, cherries, or blueberries
1½ cups water
6 tablespoons sherry vinegar
3 tablespoons sugar
1 teaspoon salt
½ teaspoon dry mustard
½ teaspoon ground coriander

In a heavy saucepan, combine all the ingredients and bring the mixture to a boil over high heat. Reduce the heat to low and cook for 25 to 30 minutes, stirring frequently, until thick. The chutney keeps, covered and refrigerated, for a couple of weeks.

Happy-Hour Skewers and Spreads

HAPPY-HOUR SKEWERS AND SPREADS

MARGARITA SHRIMP SKEWERS

A happy hour in themselves, these kebobs flaunt a breezy, south-of-the-border spirit. We usually flavor shrimp with rubs or thick pastes, which help crisp the surface quickly during the brief grilling time, but the marinade manages the same job here because the orange juice concentrate fosters a light, crusty singe. Be careful to avoid overcooking the shrimp, though, because the coating will burn unpleasantly. Serve the skewers with margaritas, *por favor*.

MAKES ABOUT 2½ DOZEN KEBOBS

MARGARITA MARINADE
½ cup tequila
¼ cup fresh lime juice
One-half 6-ounce can frozen orange juice concentrate, thawed
2 teaspoons vegetable oil

1½ pounds medium shrimp, peeled and, if you wish, deveined
Soaked bamboo skewers
3 fresh jalapeños, each cut into 8 small pieces
1 large red bell pepper, cut into ½-inch squares
Kosher salt or other coarse salt
Minced fresh cilantro
Lime wedges

Prepare the marinade, combining the ingredients in a small bowl. Place the shrimp in a plastic bag or shallow dish, pour the marinade over them, and refrigerate for 30 minutes.

Fire up the grill, bringing the temperature to high (1 to 2 seconds with the hand test).

While the grill preheats, drain the shrimp, discarding the marinade.

Skewer the shrimp with the jalapeños and bell pepper pieces, avoiding crowding. Slide one end of the first shrimp on a skewer, add a piece of jalapeño and bell pepper to rest in the curve of the shrimp, and then slide the other end of the shrimp over the skewer. Repeat on the same skewer with a second shrimp and the jalapeño and bell pepper pieces. Assemble the remaining kebobs and sprinkle them lightly with the salt.

Grill the kebobs uncovered over high heat for 1½ to 2 minutes per side, until the shrimp are just opaque with lightly browned edges. The jalapeño and bell pepper should remain a bit crisp. If grilling covered, cook the kebobs the same amount of time, turning once midway.

When done, sprinkle the kebobs lightly with cilantro and serve them hot, with lime wedges for squeezing.

As a variation from serving the shrimp on the skewer, we sometimes pile them in margarita glasses with salted rims and lime wedges.

TECHNIQUE TIP: When you're serving kebobs hot off the grill as finger food, always cook on bamboo skewers, much easier and safer to handle than hot metal skewers. Even after soaking, the bamboo itself can scorch during grilling, so place the exposed handles near the cooler edges of the fire. We like skewers nine inches or longer, simply because they look better to us for entertaining, not because we're trying to cram a lot of food on them. As you may notice in later chapters, where we present some main-course kebobs, we usually switch to metal skewers when grilling large pieces of food.

MARINER'S HARPOON

This simple seafaring treat strings together scallops, shrimp, and a choice of other seafood on a lemon-laced skewer. We prefer seafood sausage to complete the trio, when we can find it readily, but strips of squid or cubes of swordfish also wrap up the package smartly.

MAKES 1 1/2 DOZEN KEBOBS

MARINER'S MARINADE
½ cup white wine Worcestershire sauce
1 tablespoon juice from a jar of pickled jalapeños
6 garlic cloves, minced

18 sea scallops, no larger in diameter than a
    50-cent coin
18 large to jumbo shrimp, peeled and, if you wish,
    deveined
Three 4- to 5-ounce uncooked seafood sausages, each
    cut into 6 chunks, or ¾ pound squid tubes or squid
    steak cut into 18 long strips, or 1 small ¾-inch-thick
    swordfish steak cut into 18 cubes

5 slices thin bacon, cut in half horizontally, and then
    cut again lengthwise
Soaked bamboo skewers, preferably 2 for each kebob
    (see Technique Tip)
1 to 1½ large lemons, cut into bite-size chunks with
    some skin and flesh attached to each
Vegetable oil spray
Hot Shot Tartar Sauce (page 38) or other tartar sauce,
    optional

Prepare the marinade, combining the ingredients in a small bowl. Place the scallops, shrimp, and seafood sausage in a plastic bag, pour the mari-nade over the seafood, and refrigerate for 30 to 45 minutes.

Fire up the grill, bringing the temperature to high (1 to 2 seconds with

the hand test).

While the grill preheats, par-cook the bacon in a small skillet for about 2 minutes per side, until it loses its raw look and browns lightly but is still quite limp. Drain the bacon.

Drain the shrimp and scallops of accumulated liquid. Avoiding crowding, thread the scallops, shrimp, sausage, and lemon chunks onto the skewers (preferably using 2 skewers per kebob to hold the ingredients securely while cooking). Start each kebob with a lemon, skewered so that the skin faces the handle. Wrap a strip of bacon around the edge of a scallop and skewer the scallop through from side to side, holding the bacon in place. (You will have a couple of extra bacon strips to work with, in case any shriveled unexpectedly during the earlier par-cooking.) Repeat with the remaining scallops and bacon on the other skewers. Add a shrimp to each kebob, pierced through the center with its U-shaped arch pointed downward. Thread on a chunk of sausage, and add another lemon wedge to finish each kebob, this time with the skin facing upward to the skewer's point. Spray the kebobs lightly with oil.

Transfer the kebobs to a well-oiled grate. Grill them uncovered over high heat for 2 to 2½ minutes per side, until the scallops and shrimp are just opaque with lightly browned edges. Be careful not to overcook or the seafood will become dry and tough. If grilling covered, cook for the same amount of time per side, turning once midway.

Serve the kebobs immediately, accompanied by tartar sauce if you wish.

TECHNIQUE TIP: Using two side-by-side skewers per kebob, rather than one, prevents the swirling-dervish problem, where scallops and other ingredients twist around at supernatural volition. We suggest the approach in several recipes in the chapter, when a single skewer won't hold the food securely. We don't usually cook different items on separate skewers, however, in the manner currently fashionable, because we want to serve the food together on the same stick(s). It doesn't take much energy to figure out how to get a variety of ingredients to the same degree of doneness at the same time, the potential problem usually cited as the rationale for separate skewers. In the case of the Mariner's Harpoon, for example, we start with slightly larger shrimp than we usually grill, to balance the cooking time needed for the sea scallops. Even with a brief total cooking time of 4 to 5 minutes, medium shrimp on the same skewer as the scallops would begin to dry out.

FIRING UP A PARTY

You need a nibble with a drink. Any time you invite friends over for a pre-dinner libation—whether or not they are staying for a full meal—you want to offer some kind of finger food. Two of the best options for the grill are skewered tidbits, cooked after the guests arrive to serve hot, and cold spreads or dips prepared ahead so you can devote your time to hosting rather than tending the fire.

Pizzas and quesadillas, featured in the following chapter, also work well as hot hors d'oeuvres, but we present them separately because they can double as a main course. The same is true to some degree of the "Flame-Kissed Salads, Pastas, and Other Delights" presented later in the book, but when they are served as starters instead of entrées, they function better as sit-down appetizers than as stand-around drink food. We limit our focus in this chapter to simple, hands-on treats meant for happy hour. They can suffice alone as cocktail snacks, lead off a grilled or non-grilled meal, or become the core of a grazing dinner, but in any situation they provide solid booster fuel for a party.

If you intend to move on to a grilled main course, plan your cooking strategy in advance, particularly for a charcoal grill. With gas, it's relatively simple to grill two or more courses at different times on the same evening, shutting down and starting up again with the turn of a knob. A charcoal fire takes longer to reach grilling temperature and then burns out slowly at a lower heat. If you want to cook twice on charcoal an hour or two apart, cover the grill after the first round, cut air circulation by closing the vents, and add more pre-ignited coals shortly before you plan to grill again. In some cases you may find it easier to grill the starter course in advance and serve it cold, as we do with dips and spreads. Either way, hot or chilled, goodies from the grill always spark up an outdoor happy hour.

SCALLOP AND MELON KEBOBS

The essence of sweet succulence, a combo of sea scallops and jewel-toned melon balls keeps friends coming back to the grill for more nibbles. Look for firm, plump scallops, and any kind of melon, from the familiar options to the more unusual varieties showing up these days.

MAKES ABOUT 2 DOZEN KEBOBS

2 pounds sea scallops, halved if larger in diameter than
    a 50-cent coin
½ cup Peach Vinegar (page 41) or other fruit vinegar
    such as raspberry
1½ teaspoons kosher salt or other coarse salt
1 teaspoon sugar
3 to 4 cups melon balls or bite-size cubes, from at least
    two types of melon

Soaked bamboo skewers, preferably 2 for each kebob
Vegetable oil spray

Fire up the grill, bringing the temperature to high (1 to 2 seconds with the hand test).

Place the scallops in a plastic bag or shallow bowl and pour the vinegar over them. Let the scallops sit in the vinegar at room temperature for 10 to 20 minutes (much longer and you'll have ceviche). Drain the scallops and discard the vinegar.

Stir the salt and sugar together and sprinkle them lightly over the scallops. Avoiding crowding, skewer 2 to 3 scallops interspersed by balls of different types of melon (preferably using 2 skewers per kebob to hold the ingredients securely while cooking). Assemble the remaining kebobs and spray them lightly with oil.

Transfer the kebobs to a well-oiled grate. Grill them uncovered over high heat for 2 to 2½ minutes per side, until the scallops are just opaque with lightly browned edges. Be careful not to overcook or the scallops will become dry and tough. If grilling covered, cook for the same amount of time, turning once midway.

Serve the kebobs immediately.

TECHNIQUE TIP: In threading skewers for the grill, generally avoid squash-

ing foods together on the stick. In most cases, you want the heat to reach and crisp all the edges, and that won't happen unless the individual pieces have some breathing room.

OYSTER-SAUCED OYSTERS

Briny fresh oysters get a jolt from their own juice and other seasonings, doubling the pleasure of their company at a skewer party.

MAKES 12 KEBOBS

OYSTER MARINADE
¼ cup oyster liquor (juice), bottled clam juice, or
    seafood stock
¼ cup Chinese oyster sauce
¼ cup minced fresh cilantro
2 garlic cloves, minced
2 large shallots, chopped
2 teaspoons packed brown sugar
½ teaspoon crushed dried hot red chile

2 dozen fresh medium oysters, shucked but liquor
    (juice) reserved
Soaked bamboo skewers, preferably 2 for each kebob
Minced fresh cilantro, for garnish

Prepare the marinade, first pouring the liquor from the oysters into a measuring cup and adding bottled clam juice or seafood stock if needed to measure ¼ cup. Pour the liquid into a small bowl and add the rest of the marinade ingredients. Place the oysters in a plastic bag or shallow dish, pour the marinade over them, and refrigerate for 30 to 45 minutes.

Fire up the grill, bringing the temperature to high (1 to 2 seconds with the hand test).

Thread 2 oysters onto each skewer (preferably using 2 skewers per kebob to hold the oysters securely while cooking).

Grill the oysters uncovered over

high heat for 2 to 3 minutes, turning occasionally, until the edges curl and the oysters become firm but are still moist. If grilling covered, cook for the same amount of time, turning once midway.

Sprinkle the kebobs with cilantro and serve immediately.

DOWNSIZING THE GRILL, REVVING UP THE PARTY

The hibachi isn't a practical everyday grill for many people today, because of the limited cooking surface, but it can be perfect for a skewer party. String together a variety of kebobs, fire up the hibachi, and invite your guests to choose and grill their own. You free your time for your friends and, at the same time, make them feel right at home.

The Japanese creators of the hibachi always intended it for small, thin cuts of meat, more common in Asian cooking than thick steaks or roasts. For those purposes, the bantam outdoor grill provided the right combination of high heat and maximum fuel efficiency. Americans adopted it for different reasons—because it fit on urban balconies and offered on-the-go portability—but in skewer cooking, you are returning to the roots, using the hibachi in the way it was originally designed.

Hibachis have made a minor comeback in the United States in recent years, partially due to their party potential. The plain, clunky style of the past is out of fashion now, though still available in some places. Newer, upscale models feature everything from sleek recycled-aluminum shells to cast-iron grates made to resemble a log burning on a fire. The innovations boost the price, of course, without really improving the cooking capacity. In a pinch, follow some old advice from *Better Homes and Gardens*, which devised an inexpensive alternative to the hibachi. The editors suggested lining a flower pot with foil, firing up charcoal inside, and suspending skewers across the rims. Whatever works, as long as it's fun.

BASIL BOUNTY KEBOBS

Seafood sausage and meaty tuna make a stalwart kebob, particularly with a dab of basil-infused olive oil.

MAKES ABOUT 2 DOZEN KEBOBS

BASIL OIL
⅔ cup extra-virgin olive oil
⅓ cup packed minced fresh basil
½ teaspoon kosher salt or other coarse salt

1-pound tuna steak, preferably yellowfin, approximately 1 inch thick, cut into 1-inch chunks
Four 4- to 5-ounce fresh uncooked seafood sausages, each cut into 5 to 6 chunks, or a small ¾-inch-thick swordfish or halibut steak, cut into ¾-inch chunks
Soaked bamboo skewers
Fresh basil leaves, optional, for garnish

Prepare the basil oil, puréeing the oil with the basil and salt in a blender. Let the oil stand at room temperature for 30 minutes for the herb flavor to infuse the oil. Divide the oil equally into two ramekins or small bowls.

Fire up the grill, bringing the temperature to high (1 to 2 seconds with the hand test).

Thread a tuna chunk and sausage chunk onto each skewer, avoiding crowding. Brush the skewers with enough oil from one bowl to coat them lightly, avoiding drips. Discard any of the oil remaining in this bowl, which could have picked up bacteria from the raw seafood.

Transfer the kebobs to a well-oiled grate. Grill the kebobs uncovered over high heat for 4 to 6 minutes, turning to sear on all sides, for tuna with a distinctly pink center. If grilling covered, cook for the same amount of time, turning the kebobs once midway.

Serve the kebobs hot with additional drizzles of the basil oil, garnished if you wish with basil leaves.

TECHNIQUE TIP: The usual rule about grilling fish 8 to 10 minutes per inch of thickness doesn't apply to kebobs. When you cube the fish, even into big chunks, it cooks more quickly because of the increased surface area.

CLAM RUMAKI

Given our comfortable familiarity today with many Asian flavors, it's stunning to realize that our parents and grandparents considered soy sauce an exotic condiment. Nothing illustrates the situation better than rumaki, perhaps the most popular cocktail snack of the 1950s. Cooks took the idea of tidbits wrapped in bacon, an old American and British favorite, and created a rage with the simple addition of a water chestnut and a soy marinade. Chicken livers usually completed the ingredients for the toothpick-bound morsel, but grillers also experimented with a variety of seafood substitutes. Our favorite version features clams, bundled under the bacon by a skewer. Once remarkably novel, rumaki remains remarkably good.

MAKES ABOUT 2 DOZEN KEBOBS

RUMAKI MARINADE
½ cup soy sauce, preferably a reduced-salt variety
1 tablespoon minced fresh ginger
2 teaspoons packed brown sugar
1 teaspoon Asian-style sesame oil
½ teaspoon curry powder

24 small to medium clams, shucked
12 thin bacon slices, halved crosswise
8-ounce can water chestnuts, drained
Soaked bamboo skewers

Prepare the marinade, stirring together the ingredients in a small bowl. Place the clams in a plastic bag or bowl, pour the marinade over them, and refrigerate for 30 to 60 minutes.

In a small skillet, par-cook the bacon for about 2 minutes per side, until it loses its raw look and colors lightly but is still quite limp. Drain the bacon and reserve it.

Fire up the grill, bringing the temperature to medium (4 to 5 seconds with the hand test).

Drain the clams, reserving the marinade.

If your water chestnuts taste tinny, like their can, blanch them in boiling water for about 1 minute. Avoiding crowding, skewer a water chestnut and a clam. Wrap them with bacon,

making sure it covers the clam in particular, and secure the bacon with the skewer. Dip the kebob in the reserved marinade and then drain it. Repeat with the remaining ingredients.

Grill the rumaki uncovered on medium heat until the bacon is crisp and the clams are tender, about 4 to 6 minutes, turning them several times to cook evenly. If grilling covered, cook for the same amount of time, turning once midway.

Serve the rumaki hot, preferably with mai tais.

TECHNIQUE TIP: Use any kind of small to medium clams for rumaki, but avoid really tiny littlenecks, which resist skewering. Pick the freshest clams you can find, either hard-shells or the soft-shell "gapers" that are partially open and relatively easy to shuck at home with a paring knife. If you prefer to get clams shucked at your seafood market, plan to grill them the same day and keep them refrigerated in the meantime wrapped in a clean, damp dish towel. Live, unshucked clams should also be eaten soon, but can be kept overnight in the refrigerator in an uncovered dish of cool, salted water, with a heaping tablespoon of cornmeal to purge them of accumulated grit.

TERIYAKI TWINS

Another soy-flavored favorite from the same grill era as rumaki, teriyaki sauce retains its spry and sassy appeal. Fast to make and easy to fine-tune for a particular dish, it starts with soy, sugar, sake, and ginger, and ends at the limits of your fancy. We make it a couple of ways here for a two-fisted treat starring salmon and beef on separate skewers. Tangerine scents the beef marinade and baste, and hot mustard and cayenne add spark to the salmon teriyaki. Bet you can't eat just one.

MAKES ABOUT 2½ DOZEN KEBOBS

. . . .

BEEF TANGERINE TERIYAKI SAUCE
½ cup fresh tangerine juice (about 1 medium tangerine)
¼ cup regular soy sauce, *not* a reduced-salt variety
5 tablespoons sugar
1 tablespoon sake or dry sherry
1 garlic clove, minced
⅛ teaspoon five-spice powder or ground star anise

SALMON FIREWORKS TERIYAKI SAUCE
½ cup regular soy sauce, *not* a reduced-salt variety
¼ cup sake or dry sherry
2 tablespoons minced fresh ginger
1 tablespoon prepared sweet hot mustard
1 tablespoon sugar
⅛ teaspoon cayenne pepper

1 pound top sirloin steak, sliced across the grain into
    ¼-inch-thick strips
1 pound salmon fillet, skin removed and sliced into
    ½-inch-thick strips
Soaked bamboo skewers
2½ dozen kumquats, optional

Prepare the teriyaki sauces. In a small bowl, combine the beef teriyaki sauce ingredients and stir until the sugar dissolves. In another small bowl, combine the salmon teriyaki sauce ingredients. (Both sauces can be made up to several days ahead, kept covered and refrigerated, and returned to room temperature before use.)

Just before heating the grill, divide the sauces evenly into 2 bowls each, one for basting and one for the table. Baste the beef and salmon with their respective basting sauces.

Fire up the grill, bringing the temperature to high (1 to 2 seconds with the hand test). While the grill preheats, thread each beef and salmon strip onto individual skewers. If you are using kumquats, add them to the tips of the skewers.

Grill the kebobs uncovered on high heat for 30 to 45 seconds on one side. Turn them and baste the cooked side, using a clean brush. Repeat the process for the second side. Continue grilling the kebobs without additional turning about 1 minute, until the beef is medium-rare and the salmon is just barely opaque pink at the center. The sugar in the marinade will create a crispy surface and help develop a few singed edges on both the beef and salmon, but the brief cooking time prevents burning. Because of the quick grilling and the risks in overcooking, we don't recommend covered grilling for these skewers.

Serve the kebobs hot with the remaining teriyaki sauces.

TECHNIQUE TIP: We once made all our teriyaki sauces with brown sugar, assuming its deeper flavor would work best for grilled foods. After some recent comparative testing, we realized that white sugar gives greater rein to the other flavors, especially ingredients such as the fresh tangerine juice used in the beef teriyaki.

SOUTH SEAS SOY

Soy sauce fueled the Polynesian passion that blazed its way through American cooking in the 1940s and '50s. One of the zaniest and most lovable of the many culinary fads in our past, the craze peaked in the career of San Francisco native Victor Bergeron, better known as Trader Vic.

A P.T. Barnum of food and drink, Bergeron deserves more credit than he usually gets for broadening mainstream tastes in the country. Prior to the founding of his Trader Vic chain in 1938, true Cantonese cooking seldom moved out of Chinese neighborhoods, and other Asian cuisines rarely surfaced anywhere. Bergeron believed Americans wouldn't like the fare straight and authentic—"their taste buds aren't educated enough to take foreign dishes first hand with appreciation"—so he toned down unfamiliar flavors, called the food "Polynesian," and served it in a kitschy South Seas setting designed to make people dream of tropical escapes and "pretty women without any clothes on." The restaurants offered plenty of dishes that were different and exciting at the time, but, more important in the end, they made it adventuresome and romantic to explore Asian and pan-Pacific flavors.

Nothing appeared more often in Bergeron's cooking than soy sauce. In his 1946 *Trader Vic's Book of Food and Drink* (Doubleday), he acknowledges that the uninitiated call the condiment "bug juice," but says "the little-known ingredient" deserves to be as common a seasoning as salt and pepper. In a chapter on grilling, soy flavors almost every recipe, from Steak Hawaiian to Barbecued Chicken Livers. Within a decade millions of outdoor cooks followed suit, wowing their friends and neighbors with exotic "South Seas" specialties such as rumaki and teriyaki. The Polynesian posture faded about the same time as polyester, but it left us the lasting gift of soy.

LACQUERED SATAY

Another keeper from the "Polynesian" period of American grilling, satay secured its roots in this country gradually as grillers gained the courage to serve the marinated meat on a stick with a spicy peanut dipping sauce. We add a second sauce in this case, giving you a choice of one or both, and also boost the flavor of the chicken and pork strips with a strange-smelling marinade that produces a scrumptious, lacquered crust.

MAKES ABOUT 2 1/2 DOZEN KEBOBS

PEANUT SAUCE
2 tablespoons peanut oil
⅛ large onion, minced
2 plump garlic cloves, minced
14- to 15-ounce can unsweetened coconut milk
1 cup peanut butter
3 tablespoons Asian fish sauce
3 tablespoons packed brown sugar
1 tablespoon tamarind concentrate
1½ teaspoons curry powder
2-inch cinnamon stick
2 bay leaves
Zest and juice of ½ lemon
Zest and juice of ½ lime

FIRE-AND-ICE SAUCE
1 cup plain yogurt
1 fresh jalapeño, minced
⅛ cup minced fresh cilantro
⅛ cup minced fresh mint

LACQUER MARINADE
6 tablespoons sugar
¼ cup Asian fish sauce
2 tablespoons peanut oil
Juice of 1 lime
1 teaspoon curry powder

1 pound boneless, skinless chicken breast, sliced into
⅛-inch-thick strips
1 pound pork loin, sliced into ½-inch-thick strips
Soaked bamboo skewers

Prepare the peanut sauce, first warming the oil over medium-low heat in a large, heavy saucepan. Cook the onions and garlic until very soft, about 10 minutes, lowering the heat further if any edges begin to brown. Stir in the rest of the peanut sauce ingredients and raise the temperature to medium. Simmer the sauce for 25 to 30 minutes, stirring occasionally at first and more often as it thickens. Remove the cinnamon stick and bay leaves. For a smoother sauce, purée in a blender before serving. (The peanut sauce can be made several days ahead and kept covered and refrigerated. Reheat or bring back to room temperature before serving. Add a little water if the sauce is too stiff for dunking.)

Prepare the fire-and-ice sauce, combining the ingredients in a small bowl. Cover and refrigerate until needed.

Prepare the marinade, first spooning the sugar and fish sauce into a small, heavy saucepan and stirring together. Melt the sugar over medium-low heat, stirring occasionally, and continue cooking for a few minutes until the mixture forms a thick, bubbling syrup. Remove the pan from the heat and immediately stir in the oil, lime juice (watch out for the steam), and curry powder. While you allow the marinade to cool for a few minutes, place the chicken and pork strips in separate plastic bags or shallow dishes. Spoon equal amounts of the thick caramelized marinade over the chicken and pork, rub it thoroughly over all the strips, and refrigerate for 30 to 60 minutes.

Fire up the grill, bringing the temperature to medium (4 to 5 seconds with the hand test). While the grill preheats, drain the chicken and pork strips and thread each strip onto a skewer.

Grill the skewered strips uncovered over medium heat for 4 to 5 minutes, turning at least once. If grilling covered, cook for the same amount of time, turning once midway.

Serve the satay hot off the grill with the peanut and yogurt sauces. Leftovers of either sauce are great with grilled shrimp or as a dip for carrot and celery sticks.

CHAMPIONSHIP SATAY

Almost every diner at the original Trader Vic's in Oakland, California, wanted to sample the "Javanese Saté." It sounded and looked exotic at the time, even though it was just marinated meat grilled on a skewer and served without a sauce, peanut or otherwise. The popularity of the dish inspired the restaurant to begin bottling its "saté spice," a proprietary blend of dry seasonings that flavored the marinade.

No records exist of how many grillers used the spice blend in homemade satays, but the basic dish became a staple of outdoor cooking over the following decade. When the mother of all grilling contests rolled around in 1959, satay went on parade. Kaiser Aluminum sponsored the annual national cookoff, awarding the winner $10,000 and the title of "America's Cookout Champion of the Year." Open to men only, the competition attracted thousands of recipe entries, eventually weeded down to twenty-five top choices. Kaiser flew the lucky finalists to Hawaii with their wives, all expenses paid, to grill their specialties for celebrity judges.

Helen Evans Brown and her husband, Philip, documented the first two years of the contest in *The Cookout Book* (Ward Ritchie Press, 1961), providing each recipe of the fifty finalists. Four satay-style preparations made the cut, easily claiming more places than any other dish with foreign roots. The Singapore Satays featured beef, the others pork, and two came with a peanut sauce.

The Browns, experts on grilling, praised the food and the inventive cooks behind it. "No conformists here! Like their recipes, the men themselves had distinction. All were individualists—some really characters, but charming ones—and all were equipped with brains. But this figures, as professional men, executives, and intellectuals have often turned to one of the arts for a creative outlet. Now many have discovered The Art of Cookery."

SOUTHERN HAM AND SHRIMP SKEWERS

Nuggets of country ham, watermelon pickles, and shrimp—true Southern comforts—make a sweet and tangy trio. Unlike most kebobs, which usually taste best right off the grill, these can be served chilled, perhaps with a cool mint julep.

MAKES ABOUT 2 DOZEN KEBOBS

SOUTHERN COMFORT MARINADE
½ cup juice from a jar of watermelon rind pickles, either homemade or store-bought
Juice of 1 lemon
1 tablespoon Peppered Sherry (page 41) or other dry sherry

2 dozen large shrimp, peeled and, if you wish, deveined
8 green onions
½ cup minced country ham or other smoky, somewhat salty ham
½ cup watermelon rind pickles
Soaked bamboo skewers
Kosher salt or other coarse salt to taste
Vegetable oil spray

Additional Peppered Sherry (page 41) or other dry sherry, optional

At least 1 hour and up to 3 hours before you plan to grill the shrimp, prepare the marinade, combining the ingredients in a medium bowl. Place the shrimp in a plastic bag, pour the marinade over them, and refrigerate.

Fire up the grill, bringing the temperature to high (1 to 2 seconds with the hand test).

While the grill preheats, finish preparing the kebobs. Drain the shrimp and discard the marinade. Slice off the full length of the green onion tops and reserve them. Mince the white portions

of half the green onions and cut the remaining white portions into ¾-inch sections. In a small bowl, mix the ham with the minced green onions. Make a slit into the back of each shrimp, just wide and deep enough for about 1 teaspoon of the ham mixture. With your fingers, stuff each shrimp with the filling and then wrap a section of green onion top around the shrimp to help hold the filling in place. Thread each shrimp onto a skewer, with its U-shaped arch toward the skewer's point.

Avoiding crowding, thread a couple of watermelon pickle chunks and a green onion section onto each skewer. Sprinkle the kebobs with salt and spritz them lightly with oil.

Grill the kebobs uncovered over high heat for 3 to 4 minutes, turning once, until the shrimp are just opaque with lightly charred edges. If grilling covered, cook for the same amount of time, turning once midway.

Serve the kebobs hot or chilled, perhaps with a sprinkling of sherry.

PORK IN THE GARDEN

Lushly laced with tropical seasonings, these pork balls are meant to be tucked in a lettuce leaf and eaten by hand. You can also munch them directly from the skewer or serve them like other meatballs, but the garden wrap and the toppings add a crunchy, festive touch.

SERVES 4 TO 6

PORK MEATBALLS
1½ pounds ground pork
¾ cup minced green onions
¾ cup dry bread crumbs
3 tablespoons Pickapeppa sauce or mild Jamaican jerk
  sauce
Juice of 1 lime
1 egg, lightly beaten
2 teaspoons minced crystallized ginger
1 fresh jalapeño or serrano chile, minced
½ teaspoon salt

Soaked bamboo skewers
Bibb lettuce or other soft leaf lettuce
Pickapeppa sauce or mild Jamaican jerk sauce
Shredded carrots
Mint, basil, or cilantro leaves
Chopped peanuts

• • • • • • • • • • • • • • • • • •

Prepare the meatballs, combining the ingredients in a large bowl. Mold the meatballs into an elongated oval shape, using 2 to 3 teaspoons of the pork mixture for each.

Fire up the grill, bringing the temperature to medium (4 to 5 seconds with the hand test).

Avoiding crowding, thread 2 balls lengthwise per skewer. If the pork mixture seems very soft, refrigerate it briefly.

Transfer the skewers to a well-oiled grate. Grill them uncovered over medium heat for 5 to 6 minutes, turning as often as necessary for even cooking. If grilling covered, cook for the same amount of time, turning once midway.

Present the skewers of pork on a platter with the lettuce and remaining ingredients. Fold a leaf of lettuce around a skewer and slide the meatballs off onto the lettuce. Add sprinklings of the remaining ingredients and serve warm.

POLISH AND POTATOES ON A STICK

Look for a robust, well-seasoned version of Polish sausage for this kebob, perfect fare for a crisp fall weekend. To make these a main course, for a football party perhaps, switch to metal skewers, add more meat and potatoes plus a few pearl onions and bay leaves, and serve the grilled tidbits over sautéed cabbage enriched with a bit of cream and some juniper berries.

MAKES 2 DOZEN KEBOBS

• • • • • • • • • • • • • • • • • •

¼ cup butter

2 tablespoons Mixed Mustard Plaster (page 28) or
brown mustard

1½ pounds waxy red potatoes, well scrubbed and cut
into bite-size chunks

Four 6-ounce fully cooked Polish sausages, such as
kielbasa, sliced into ½- to ¾-inch rounds

Soaked bamboo skewers

All-'Round Rub (page 23) or kosher salt or other coarse
salt

Mixed Mustard Plaster (page 28) or brown mustard

· · · · · · · · · · · · · · · · · ·

In a small saucepan, melt the butter over low heat and stir in the mustard.

Par-cook potato chunks by steaming or boiling them until they can be easily pierced with a skewer but are not completely tender. (The potatoes can be cooked several hours ahead and refrigerated. Bring them to room temperature before proceeding.)

Fire up the grill, bringing the temperature to medium (4 to 5 seconds with the hand test).

Thread 2 sausage chunks onto a skewer, interspersed with a potato chunk, avoiding crowding. Thread the sausage chunks through their casing-covered sides so that the cut surfaces will face the fire during grilling. Brush the kebobs with the mustard butter. Sprinkle moderately with the dry rub or lightly with salt.

Grill the kebobs uncovered over medium heat for 5 to 7 minutes, turning the skewers regularly to sear all sides. The sausage and potatoes should be a little crusty on the surface but still juicy. If grilling covered, cook for 5 to 6 minutes, turning once midway.

Serve the kebobs hot with a cold beer and more mustard for dunking.

TECHNIQUE TIP: Instead of bamboo or metal skewers, try sturdy herb stalks. Rosemary and mint in particular add a hint of their scent and look wonderful with a tuft of leaves emerging from the top of a kebob. Consider other interesting possibilities too, such as stripped-down sugar-cane skewers, now beginning to pop up in supermarket produce sections, or slim bay tree branches. Avoid cuttings from soft resinous woods like pine, and anything that may have been sprayed with chemicals or that grows close to a road where it can collect exhaust. With any plant stalks, soak them as you would bamboo.

VENISON AND RED ONION SKEWERS

A century and longer ago, back when most beef was tough and fresh venison was plentiful, some cookbooks suggested ways to make the former taste as good as the latter. It's easier to start with the real thing, which can be better than beef even today in many dishes.

MAKES ABOUT 2 DOZEN KEBOBS

1½ pounds venison backstrap or tenderloin, cut into
 ¾-inch cubes
1 to 2 tablespoons Sugar and Spice (page 26) or
 1 teaspoon kosher salt or other coarse salt
Soaked bamboo skewers
1 medium red onion, cut into chunks slightly smaller
 than the venison
About 2 dozen red or green seedless grapes
3 tablespoons currant liqueur
2 tablespoons coarse-ground Dijon mustard
1 teaspoon vegetable oil

Coat the venison with the dry rub or sprinkle lightly with salt, place it in a plastic bag, and refrigerate for at least 30 minutes.

Fire up the grill, bringing the temperature to high (1 to 2 seconds with the hand test).

Thread 2 venison chunks onto a skewer, interspersed with an onion chunk and grape, avoiding crowding. Mix together the currant liqueur, mustard, and oil, and brush the mixture lightly over the kebobs just before grilling.

Grill the kebobs uncovered over high heat for 4 to 6 minutes, turning the skewers regularly to sear all sides. The venison should be a little crusty on the surface but still pink and juicy inside, the onions just crisp-tender, and grapes soft. If grilling covered, cook for the same amount of time, turning once midway.

Serve the kebobs hot.

TOTALLY SKEWERED

A survey conducted at the 1996 annual meeting of the International Association of Culinary Professionals came to the conclusion that kebobs were one of the foods now out of fashion. We doubt a similar poll of backyard chefs would get the same results, but certainly skewer cooking has lost a lot of ground since its heyday as a craze in the 1950s and '60s.

James Beard and Helen Evans Brown devoted a whole chapter to the subject in their 1955 classic, *The Complete Book of Outdoor Cookery* (Doubleday). The masters led off with traditional shish kebob and shashlik recipes, but then went on to recommend several dozen other creative combos, including duck and green olives, turkey cubes with oysters, and banana slices rolled in chopped peanuts. The respected Time-Life cooking series matched the bounty in its later treatise on outdoor cooking, adding skewer suggestions for eel, shark, tripe, goose liver, and pumpkin.

The most common kebobs didn't stray so far from the supermarket shelf. No one in the era knew more about popular possibilities than *Better Homes and Gardens*, the publisher of many best-selling cookbooks. The company's 1963 *Barbecues and Picnics* featured Pig-in-a-Poke (bacon-wrapped wieners, bologna, and dill pickles), Mandarin Dinner (canned luncheon meat, canned crab apples, and preserved kumquats), and to give "your patio dinner a touch of sophistication," the Western Starter (canned artichoke hearts, water chestnuts, and chicken livers).

As the country became more worldly in its tastes, so did *Better Homes and Gardens*, taking the kebob to new continents in the 1977 *All-Time Favorite Barbecue Recipes*. The editors encouraged us to go Japanese with chicken, zucchini, and mushrooms, to satisfy a Korean craving with pork and green bell peppers, and to toast Hawaiian tastes with sirloin, tomatoes, and peppers. If you weren't ready to head so far overseas, the cookbook also covered the home bases, offering everything from a cheese sandwich on a stick to a mustard-brushed bologna and pineapple treat.

GOLD AND ORANGE CHICKEN KEBOBS

Colorful and crispy, these kebobs get much of their character from the marinade and baste. The egg in the mayonnaise and the sugar in the orange juice in the mixture combine forces to create a delicious crust on the chicken. Saffron adds its bright fragrance and a rich golden hue.

MAKES ABOUT 2 DOZEN KEBOBS

GOLD AND ORANGE MARINADE
1 medium to large orange
6 tablespoons Enriched Mayonnaise (page 38) or other
    mayonnaise
1 teaspoon minced fresh thyme or savory or ½ teaspoon
    dried thyme or savory
1 plump garlic clove, minced
1 teaspoon crumbled saffron threads
½ teaspoon salt

1½ pounds boneless, skinless chicken breasts, cut into
    1-inch cubes
2 medium to large oranges
Soaked bamboo skewers
4 to 5 green onions, limp tops trimmed, cut on the
    diagonal into 1-inch sections

At least 1½ hours and up to 4 hours before you plan to grill, prepare the marinade, first zesting the orange and mincing its peel. Place the minced zest in a small bowl and squeeze the orange's juice into it. To the orange juice and zest add the other marinade ingredients and stir well. Place the chicken chunks in a plastic bag or shallow dish, pour the marinade over them, and refrigerate.

Peel the additional oranges and pull into individual sections. Set these aside.

Fire up the grill, bringing the temperature to medium (4 to 5 seconds with the hand test).

Remove the chicken from the

refrigerator and drain the marinade from it into a small saucepan. Avoiding crowding, thread a piece of chicken onto a skewer, followed by an orange section, another piece of chicken, and a section of green onion. Repeat with the remaining ingredients and skewers. Let the kebobs sit covered at room temperature for about 15 minutes.

Bring the marinade to a vigorous boil, boiling for several minutes until reduced to a creamy sauce, stirring occasionally.

Transfer the kebobs to a well-oiled grate. Grill them uncovered over medium heat for 8 to 10 minutes, until the chicken is opaque throughout but still juicy. Turn the kebobs 3 to 4 times, brushing the cooked chicken lightly with the cooked sauce each time. If grilling covered, cook for 7 to 9 minutes, turning once midway and basting the kebobs; baste the second side of the kebobs just before removing them from the grill.

Serve the kebobs immediately.

CHEESE IN A BLANKET

A crunchy crumb blanket envelops warm, soft cheese in these simple skewers. Though easy to make, they must be watched carefully and shouldn't be attempted in a covered grill. Be ready to take them off the fire as soon as the coating turns a light brown and the cheese begins to melt. If you miss by even a minute, the molten mess will give new meaning to those old lava rocks you're cooking on. Serve the skewers warm, before the gooey cheese centers harden again.

MAKES ABOUT 1 1/2 DOZEN KEBOBS

1 tablespoon butter
½ cup dry bread crumbs
½ cup walnut or pecan pieces, chopped fine
1 egg

1 pound semi-firm cheese, such as a flavorful cheddar,
provolone, Manchego, or kasseri, cut into ½-inch-
diameter batons, at room temperature
Soaked bamboo skewers

Dried Fruit Chutney (page 46) or mango chutney,
optional

In a small skillet, melt the butter over medium heat. Stir in the bread crumbs and nuts and continue cooking until they are toasted, about 5 minutes. Scrape the crumb mixture onto a plate and let it cool.

In a small bowl, whisk the egg until frothy. Thread a cheese baton onto a skewer lengthwise, repeating with the remaining cheese and skewers. Brush each skewer with the beaten egg, coating the cheese thoroughly. Reserve the remaining egg. Place the cheese skewers in the freezer for 15 to 30 minutes while you heat up the grill.

Fire up the grill, bringing the tem-perature to medium (4 to 5 seconds with the hand test).

Just before you're ready to grill, brush each skewer again with the egg and then roll them in the bread crumb mixture, coating the cheese thorough-ly. Transfer the cheese skewers to a well-oiled grate. Grill them uncovered over medium heat for 3 to 4 minutes, turning them on all four sides. Cook until the cheese is soft and just starting to melt under a crisp and lightly browned crumb coating.

Serve the kebobs immediately, ac-companied by chutney if you wish.

Jade and Alabaster Skewers

Chinese- and Japanese-Americans have made tofu in the United States for over a century, but it took the rest of us a long time to catch up to the concept. As interest in vegetarian cooking surged in the 1970s, grillers began substituting the soybean curd for the meat on kebobs, juxtaposing it with water chestnuts, onions, and other wholesome foods. The idea was solid, but too often the veggie flavors ended up drowned in a sea of super-sweet teriyaki or hoisin sauce. We give the primary ingredients some elbow room in this case and add savory dimensions to the Oriental sauce.

Makes about 12 kebobs

Two 12-ounce packages extra-firm, preferably, or firm
    tofu, well drained and blotted with paper towels

Oriental Sauce
2 garlic cloves
3 tablespoons chopped fresh cilantro
¼ cup soy sauce
3 tablespoons peanut butter
2 tablespoons honey
1 tablespoon dry sherry
1 tablespoon peanut oil, preferably a roasted variety
    such as Loriva
¼ teaspoon Chinese chile paste or chile-garlic paste or
    pinch of cayenne

4 asparagus spears, cut into 1½-inch pieces on the
    diagonal
12 crisp snow peas
Soaked bamboo skewers, preferably 2 for each kebob
Vegetable oil spray

Cut the tofu into cubes, 12 per package, and place them in a plastic bag or shallow bowl.

Prepare the sauce, combining the ingredients in a blender. Pour about two-thirds of the sauce over the tofu

cubes and marinate them at room temperature for 30 minutes to 1 hour.

Fire up the grill, bringing the temperature to medium (4 to 5 seconds with the hand test).

Drain the tofu. Avoiding crowding, skewer the tofu and vegetables (preferably using 2 skewers per kebob to hold the ingredients securely while cooking). Start with a tofu cube. Follow with an asparagus section and snow pea speared crosswise, followed by another tofu cube. Repeat with remaining ingredients and skewers. Spritz each kebob with oil.

Transfer the kebobs to a well-oiled grate. Grill them uncovered over medium heat for 8 to 10 minutes, turning on all sides. If grilling covered, cook for 7 to 9 minutes, turning the skewers midway.

Baste the kebobs with the remaining sauce and serve hot or at room temperature. For a variation, the kebobs, served on a bed of chive-flecked rice, make a light main dish for 2 or 3 people.

TECHNIQUE TIP: Tofu tends to stick to the grill even more than fish. Be sure to oil both the food and the grate. If you have a grill basket, you might want to get it out for these kebobs, making sure that its wire mesh is well oiled too.

WILD MUSHROOM BROCHETTES

While flavored oils sometimes provide a great contrast in flavors, they also can pump up the natural essence of a similar ingredient. Here a porcini-flavored oil, such as the kind marketed nationally by Consorzio, enhances succulent portobellos.

MAKES 2 DOZEN KEBOBS

Three 6-ounce portobello mushroom caps, cut into 8
    thick slices each
⅛ cup white wine Worcestershire sauce
¼ cup porcini-flavored oil, other mushroom-flavored oil,
    or olive oil
Soaked bamboo skewers
Kosher salt or other coarse salt to taste

Arugula or watercress, for garnish

About 45 minutes to an hour before you plan to grill, place the portobello slices in a plastic bag or shallow dish. Pour the Worcestershire sauce and oil over the portobellos and let them marinate at room temperature. (Allowing the mushrooms to sit in the marinade much longer makes the Worcestershire flavor too pronounced.)

Fire up the grill, bringing the temperature to medium (4 to 5 seconds with the hand test).

Thread each portobello slice lengthwise on a skewer. Repeat with the remaining mushrooms and skewers. Salt the brochettes lightly.

Grill the brochettes uncovered over medium heat for 5 to 6 minutes per side, until the mushrooms are juicy and soft. If grilling covered, cook for about 10 minutes, turning once midway.

Serve the brochettes hot on a platter garnished with arugula or watercress.

GILROY ARTICHOKE KEBOBS

Gilroy, California, is famous for two crops—artichokes and garlic—that pair beautifully together. Black olives add hearty tones to these handsome skewers.

MAKES 1 1/2 DOZEN KEBOBS

GARLIC MAYONNAISE SAUCE
½ cup Enriched Mayonnaise (page 38) or other
    mayonnaise
¼ cup extra-virgin olive oil
1 tablespoon fresh lemon juice
1 plump garlic clove, minced
Kosher salt or other coarse salt to taste

MUSTARD-LEMON MARINADE
Juice of 2 lemons
¼ cup extra-virgin olive oil
2½ tablespoons Dijon mustard

1 tablespoon sherry vinegar
2 garlic cloves, minced
½ teaspoon kosher salt or other coarse salt

18 baby artichokes, toughest exterior leaves removed
Soaked bamboo skewers
1 cup pitted briny black olives

Prepare the mayonnaise sauce, whisking together the ingredients in a small bowl. Refrigerate covered for at least 1 hour. (Reblend the sauce if it separates.)

Prepare the marinade, combining the ingredients in a broad, shallow dish. Trim any remaining tough edges from the artichoke leaves and slice them in half vertically. Using a small spoon, remove the tiny fuzzy choke near the base of each half. Place each artichoke in the marinade promptly to avoid discoloration. Cover loosely and let sit at room temperature for 30 to 45 minutes.

Fire up the grill, bringing the temperature to medium (4 to 5 seconds with the hand test).

While the grill heats, drain the artichokes, reserving the marinade. Thread an artichoke half on a skewer, followed by two olives and then another artichoke half, avoiding crowding. Repeat with the remaining ingredients and skewers.

Grill the kebobs uncovered over medium heat for 15 to 18 minutes, turning to cook on all sides and brushing with the reserved marinade at the same time. When done, the artichokes should be tender and darkened with a few crisp edges. If grilling covered, cook for 12 to 15 minutes, turning once midway and brushing then with the marinade.

Serve the kebobs hot accompanied by the mayonnaise sauce.

SWANKY NEW POTATOES WITH CAVIAR CREAM

If you know any people who look down their noses at grilling, the dunk for these skewers is certain to raise their eyebrows. If you want to make them beg for a bite, tell them you used true sturgeon caviar in the sauce—but don't really do it. Golden whitefish caviar and pale orange salmon roe are almost as fancy, much cheaper, and sturdy enough in flavor to stand up to the lightly crusted potatoes.

MAKES 2 DOZEN

24 small new potatoes
Olive oil
2 teaspoons Zesty Lemon Pepper (page 31) or other
    lemon pepper
Kosher salt or other coarse salt

CAVIAR CREAM SAUCE
1 tablespoon butter
1 large shallot, minced
2 cups whipping cream
¼ teaspoon kosher salt or other coarse salt
Pinch of white pepper

Soaked bamboo skewers
2 ounces whitefish or salmon caviar
Minced chives, for garnish

Steam or boil the potatoes until tender. Drain the potatoes. When cool enough to handle, halve the potatoes and place them in a medium bowl. Drizzle the oil over them and toss gently. Sprinkle them with the lemon pepper and salt to taste and toss again. Reserve the potatoes at room temperature.

Prepare the sauce, first melting the butter over medium heat in a heavy saucepan. Stir in the shallot and cook just to soften it, about 1 to 2 minutes. Pour in the cream, add the salt and white pepper, and raise the heat until

the cream boils. Adjust the heat as needed to get a steady low boil, with small bubbles breaking around the edges. Reduce the sauce by half. (The sauce can be prepared to this point a day ahead and kept covered and refrigerated. Reheat it before proceeding, adding a little water if it is no longer easily pourable.)

Fire up the grill, bringing the temperature to medium (4 to 5 seconds with the hand test).

Thread two potato halves on each skewer, avoiding crowding. Turn one cut-side up and the other cut-side down for a most attractive presentation.

Transfer the kebobs to a well-oiled grate. Grill them uncovered over medium heat for 8 to 10 minutes, turning regularly, until crusty and very soft. If grilling covered, cook for 7 to 9 minutes, turning once midway.

Stir the caviar into the sauce, sprinkle it with the chives, and serve it alongside the hot kebobs, for dunking or spooning.

TECHNIQUE TIP: It's becoming possible to find bite-size new potatoes, at least in the late spring or early summer. If you come across them at a farmers' market or other source, double the number of potatoes in the recipe and don't bother to halve them. A combination of brown- and red-skinned baby spuds looks particularly swanky.

PIQUANT SNAPPER SPREAD

It looks as delicate as a fish mousse, but it barks back when you take a bite. The yelp comes from the Dog Sauce Marinade, kept on a short leash here by the mildness of snapper and the mellowness of cream cheese.

MAKES ABOUT 1 1/2 CUPS

DOG SAUCE MARINADE
1 small onion, chopped very fine by hand, rinsed and
    drained
1 small carrot, chopped very fine by hand
2 green onions, limp tops removed, chopped very fine
    by hand
1 tablespoon minced fresh thyme
¼ to ½ fresh Scotch bonnet or habanero chile, finely
    minced, or ¼ to 1 teaspoon Caribbean hot sauce

¼ teaspoon salt, or more to taste
¼ teaspoon fresh-ground black pepper
Juice of 1 medium lime
1 tablespoon white vinegar
1 tablespoon water
3 tablespoons vegetable oil

8-ounce snapper or other white fish fillet
3 ounces cream cheese, at room temperature
3 tablespoons crème fraîche, preferably,
    or sour cream
Salt to taste

Caribbean hot sauce, optional

* * * * * * * * * * * * * * * * * * *

Prepare the marinade. In a medium bowl, combine all the ingredients, whisking in the oil at the end.

Place the fish in a plastic bag or shallow dish. Set aside ⅓ cup of the marinade. Pour the rest of the marinade over the fish and refrigerate for 45 to 60 minutes.

Fire up the grill, bringing the heat to medium-high to high heat (2 to 3 seconds with the hand test).

Drain the fish, discarding the used marinade. Transfer the fillet to a well-oiled grate or, preferably in this case, to a well-oiled small-mesh grill rack or hinged grill basket. Grill it uncovered over medium-high to high heat for 2 to 2½ minutes per side per half inch of thickness. Rotate the fillet 180° once on each side. The fish is done when opaque throughout and flaky. If grilling covered, cook for the same amount of time, turning and rotating in a similar manner.

Break the fish into chunks. Place the fish, at least half of the reserved Dog Sauce Marinade, and the remaining ingredients in a food processor and process just until well mixed. Taste and add more or all of the marinade, if you like. Pack the spread into a small serving bowl and refrigerate, covered, for at least 30 minutes.

Serve the chilled spread, accompanied by hot sauce for bolder eaters, with crackers or cucumber rounds.

GRILLED CHICKEN SPREAD WITH HERBS AND MORELS

Earthy morel mushrooms team up with other woodsy tastes in this subtle pâté-like spread.

MAKES ABOUT 2 CUPS

5- to 6-ounce boneless, skinless individual chicken
    breast, pounded to ¼ to ½ inch thickness
Olive oil
Kosher salt or other coarse salt

¼ cup butter
1 tablespoon olive oil
1 medium leek, chopped
1 celery stalk, minced
1½ tablespoons brandy
1½ teaspoons minced fresh tarragon, preferably,
    or ¾ teaspoon dried tarragon
⅛ teaspoon ground nutmeg
Pinch of white pepper
⅓ cup dried morel mushrooms, soaked in ⅔ cup hot
    water until soft
4 plump garlic cloves, roasted (see Technique Tip)
Salt

Thyme sprigs, for garnish

Fire up the grill, bringing the temperature to medium (4 to 5 seconds with the hand test).

Coat the chicken breast lightly with oil and sprinkle with salt. Cover the chicken and let it sit at room temperature for about 15 minutes.

Grill the chicken uncovered over medium heat for 3½ to 5 minutes per side, until opaque throughout but still

juicy. If grilling covered, cook the chicken for 6 to 8 minutes, turning once midway. Set the chicken aside to cool.

In a small skillet, warm the butter and oil over medium-low heat. Add the leek and celery and cook until both are very tender but not brown, about 10 minutes. Stir in the brandy, tarragon, nutmeg, white pepper, and morels and their soaking liquid, pouring the liquid carefully to leave behind any grit. Raise the temperature to medium and simmer the mixture until the liquid has reduced but the mixture is still very moist from the butter.

When the chicken is cool enough to handle, shred it.

In a food processor, purée the garlic, the vegetable mixture, and the chicken until nearly smooth. Add salt to taste. Pack the spread into a small bowl, cover, and refrigerate for at least 4 hours for the flavors to mingle.

Remove the spread from the refrigerator about 20 minutes before serving. Offer crisp toasts, crackers, or country bread on the side.

TECHNIQUE TIP: To roast individual cloves of garlic quickly, pull them from a larger head. With the papery skin still on, place the cloves in a small heavy skillet. Cook over medium heat, turning the cloves occasionally, until they are squeezably soft and the skin is lightly browned. Pull the skin from the cloves and chop or mash the soft garlic as needed. The flavor of roasted garlic is much milder and mellower than fresh.

TOASTED ONION AND JACK CHEESE DIP

Every American outdoor cook needs at least one good onion dip. We offer our two favorite grill variations, which differ so substantially you might want to double-dip with both. Close to the classic model, this is a deeply caramelized rendition accented with sharp dry cheese.

MAKES ABOUT 2 CUPS

1 large onion, sliced ⅛ inch thick
Olive oil
¾ cup sour cream
¼ cup grated dry jack cheese, Pecorino Romano, or
    other pecorino cheese
½ teaspoon salt, or more to taste

Fire up the grill, bringing the temperature to medium-low (6 seconds with the hand test).

Coat the onion slices with oil.

Grill the onion uncovered over medium-low heat for 18 to 20 minutes, turning several times. The onion rings are ready when very soft with caramelized edges. If grilling covered, cook for 15 to 18 minutes, turning once midway.

Purée the onions in a food processor, then add the remaining ingredients and continue processing until nearly smooth. Chill the dip for at least 30 minutes and up to a day.

Serve the dip chilled with potato chips or crisp zucchini rounds.

TECHNIQUE TIP: When you're grilling for a party anyway, add some firepower to store-bought potato chips. Place the chips in a popcorn basket or on a small mesh cooking grate and warm them over the coolest edge of the grill. Then shake on salt or other seasonings, and toss the chips with a little grated dry jack cheese. Enhance tortilla chips in a similar way, topping them with chili powder.

GREEN ONION DIP

The garden-green color suggests the flavor of this onion dip, fresher and more sprightly in taste than the previous version.

MAKES ABOUT 2 1/2 CUPS

16 to 18 medium-size green onions, with tops
Olive oil
2 cups sour cream, or a mix of sour cream and plain
    yogurt
2 chopped green onion tops
¾ teaspoon minced lemon zest
¾ teaspoon salt, or more to taste

Additional green onion tops, sliced in thin rings,
    optional, for garnish

Fire up the grill, bringing the temperature to medium (4 to 5 seconds with the hand test).

Coat the onions with oil and transfer them to the grill, with their tops positioned away from the hottest part of the fire. Grill uncovered over medium heat for 6 to 8 minutes, rolling the onions frequently. When done, the onions will be tender with some browned spots. Avoid getting blackened edges, though, or the dip becomes bitter. If grilling covered, cook for 5 to 7 minutes, turning once midway.

When the onions are cool enough to handle, chop them coarsely.

In a blender, purée the grilled onions with the sour cream, raw green onion tops (to deepen the color), lemon zest, and ¾ teaspoon salt. If you taste the dip at this point, it may taste a bit harsh or out of balance. Refrigerate it for at least 30 minutes and up to a day, then taste and adjust the seasoning if necessary.

Serve the dip chilled with sweet potato chips, regular potato chips, or crisp carrot strips.

Farmers' Market Red Bell Pepper Dip

Imagine squeezing a bell pepper like a lemon to extract its essence. That's what you get here, a robust concentration of the sweet, mellow spirit.

Makes about 2 cups

2 red bell peppers
Olive oil

1 to 2 teaspoons fresh lemon juice
2 garlic cloves, roasted (see Technique Tip, page 84)
½ teaspoon kosher salt or other coarse salt
⅛ teaspoon cayenne pepper
¼ cup extra-virgin olive oil

Fire up the grill, bringing the heat to medium (4 to 5 seconds with the hand test).

Coat the peppers lightly with oil. Grill them uncovered over medium heat for 12 to 15 minutes, turning every 3 to 5 minutes, until well softened with somewhat charred skins. If grilling covered, cook the peppers for 10 to 12 minutes, turning them once midway.

Transfer the peppers to a plastic bag and close it to let the peppers steam, loosening the skin. When they are cool enough to handle, pull off loose, blackened pieces of skin, but don't get zealous in removing every little bit. Chop the peppers coarsely, transfer them to a food processor, and add 1 teaspoon of lemon juice, the garlic, salt, and cayenne. Purée the mixture. With the motor running, pour in the oil in a thin stream and continue processing until well blended. Refrigerate for at least 30 minutes, taste, and add more lemon juice or otherwise adjust the seasonings as you wish.

Serve the dip chilled with other grilled vegetables, crackers, or spooned over toasted bread.

FIRED-UP TOMATO SALSA

Using a hotter fire than normal for vegetables, we grill the tomatoes, onion, and jalapeño in this salsa to blacken their skins and intensify their natural flavor. If you already have a favorite salsa recipe, try the technique with it. In your own blend or ours, you'll definitely notice the difference from grilling key ingredients.

MAKES ABOUT 2 CUPS

½ medium onion, cut through its "equator," in one piece
1 to 2 fresh jalapeños
Vegetable oil
1½ pounds whole small tomatoes, preferably Italian
    plum, unpeeled
3 tablespoons chopped fresh cilantro
2 garlic cloves, roasted (see Technique Tip, page 84)
1 to 1½ teaspoons salt
Juice of ½ to 1 lime

Fire up the grill, bringing the temperature to high heat (1 to 2 seconds with the hand test).

Coat the onion and jalapeño with oil. Grill the onion, jalapeño, and tomatoes over high heat, turning occasionally until the surfaces of each are deeply brown with some black spots. The jalapeño will be ready in about 5 to 6 minutes, and the onion and tomatoes in about 10 to 12 minutes. The tomato skins will split as they cook and the onion and jalapeño will become crisp-tender. If grilling covered, cook the jalapeño for the same amount of time and the onion and tomatoes for about 8 to 10 minutes, turning each once midway.

Trim and discard the stem end from the onion and remove the stem and seeds from the jalapeño. Place them in a blender with the tomatoes (skins, cores, and all), cilantro, garlic, salt, and lime juice and purée. Adjust the seasoning if needed.

Serve the salsa warm or refrigerate it for use later. Eat it with fresh tortillas, chips, on a burger, in Salsa-Sassy Chicken Salad, or as a second salsa accompaniment to Olvera Street Fish Tacos.

CHARRED EGGPLANT SPREAD

In the same way that everything with soy sauce used to be "Polynesian" a few decades ago, these days everything with olive oil is "Mediterranean." An Aegean delight that goes swimmingly on any party table, this dish deserves the tag.

MAKES 2 TO 2½ CUPS

. . . .

1-pound eggplant, peeled and cut into ½-inch-thick
    slices
Kosher salt or other coarse salt
6 tablespoons extra-virgin olive oil
2 teaspoons red wine vinegar
½ large red bell pepper
3 tablespoons mayonnaise (a low-fat variety is fine but
    avoid the nonfat style)
3 tablespoons fresh lemon juice, or more to taste
1 to 2 garlic cloves, minced
2 tablespoons minced fresh parsley
¼ heaping teaspoon ground cumin
Additional kosher salt or other coarse salt

Mixed greens
Minced fresh parsley

. . . .

At least 2 hours and up to the day before you plan to serve the spread, rub the eggplant slices generously with the salt. Transfer them to a colander and drain in the sink or over a plate for 30 minutes.

Fire up the grill, bringing the temperature to medium heat (4 to 5 seconds with the hand test).

Rinse the eggplant slices well and pat them dry. In a small bowl mix to-gether 3 tablespoons of the oil with the vinegar and brush the eggplant slices and bell pepper with about ⅔ of the mixture, reserving the rest.

Grill the eggplant and bell pepper uncovered over medium heat. Cook the bell pepper 8 to 10 minutes, until tender, turning once. Cook the eggplant for 12 to 14 minutes, until soft and juicy, turning the slices once. If the slices begin to look dry, brush them

with the reserved oil and vinegar. If grilling covered, cook the bell pepper for 7 to 9 minutes and the eggplant for 10 to 12 minutes, turning each once midway.

When the pepper is cool enough to handle, pull off any loose bits of charred skin, but otherwise leave the browned skin on for extra flavor. Cut the pepper into fine dice and reserve it.

Transfer the eggplant to a food processor, and chop it coarsely. Add the remaining olive oil, mayonnaise, 3 tablespoons of lemon juice, and as much garlic as you like, and combine again. The mixture should be fairly smooth, but have a little texture remaining. Spoon the spread into a bowl and fold in the bell pepper, parsley,

cumin, and salt to taste. Refrigerate for at least 30 minutes for the flavors to blend. Taste and add more lemon or otherwise adjust the seasoning if you wish.

Arrange the greens on a plate or shallow bowl, mound the chilled spread over the greens, and sprinkle with parsley. Serve the spread with toasted pita wedges or other toasts for dunking or spreading.

TECHNIQUE TIP: Small, tender eggplants, the multicolored orbs seen more frequently today, need no salting to draw out bitter juices. Cut them into half-inch-thick slices and skip right to the oil rubdown, adding just a touch of salt for flavor if you wish.

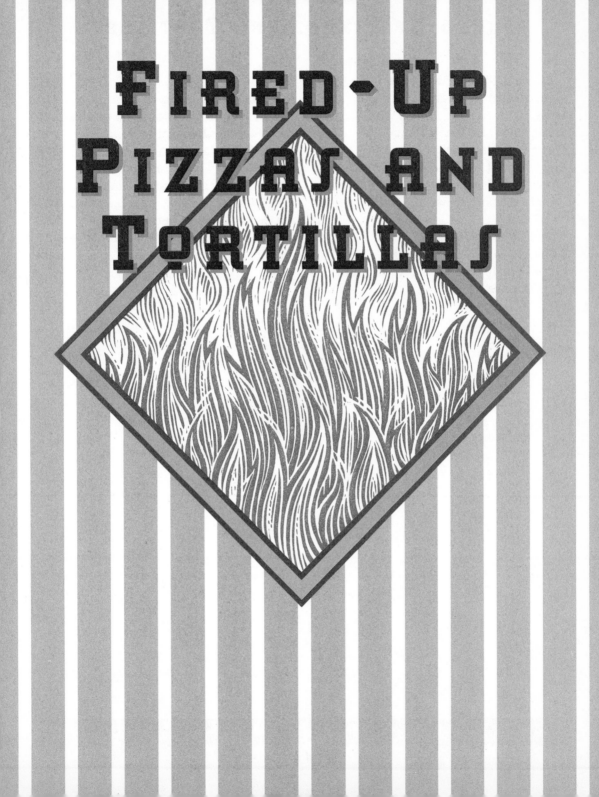

Fired-Up Pizzas and Tortillas

FIRED-UP PIZZAS AND TORTILLAS

LEAN-AND-MEAN PIZZA CRUST

In Italy and elsewhere, the best pizzas come out of wood-burning ovens that cook at a very high temperature. Open grilling over a hot fire emulates the approach better at home than oven baking or the closely related practice of covered cooking on a grill. Keep the crust thin, as they do in Italy, and grill it quickly directly above the fire, without a baking sheet or other container. The goal is a crust good enough to eat on its own, a crisp, crunchy bread that provides much of the ultimate flavor in the pizza rather than serving as a puffy, bland base for the toppings. This is how we prepare a trim and tasty crust, the foundation for most of the following pizza recipes.

MAKES TWO THIN 10- TO 11-INCH PIZZA CRUSTS

. . . .

1 envelope active dry yeast (about 2½ teaspoons)
½ teaspoon sugar
⅔ cup lukewarm water, 105° F to 115° F
About 2 cups bread flour (see Technique Tip)
¼ cup stone-ground cornmeal
1½ teaspoons kosher salt or other coarse salt
2 tablespoons olive oil
1 garlic clove, minced, optional

. . . .

Combine the yeast and sugar with the water in a small bowl and let sit for a few minutes until foamy. With a heavy-duty mixer or in a food processor, mix the yeast with a scant 2 cups of flour and the rest of the dough ingredients for several minutes, until the dough becomes smooth and elastic.

Transfer the dough to a floured pastry board or counter, and knead at least 2 more minutes, adding in another tablespoon or two of flour if needed to get a mass that is no longer sticky. Dough on the dry side is a bit more challenging to work with, but yields a crisper crust. Form the dough into a ball, then place it in a greased bowl and cover with a damp cloth. Set the dough in a warm, draft-free spot and let it rise until doubled in size, about 1 hour. Punch the dough down on the floured pastry board and let it rest for 10 minutes. Roll out the dough into two thin disks, about ⅛ inch thick and 10 to 11 inches in diameter, stretching and prodding it with your fingers, too. (A lip isn't necessary on the dough because when you're grilling

YOU WON'T FALL FLAT

Pizzas and tortillas are America's favorite types of flatbread, a style of bread common throughout the world in multiple forms, from Middle Eastern pitas to Indian *chapatis*. We focus in this chapter on the flatbreads most popular in the United States, but also include a couple of other varieties to illustrate the range of ways that grilling can enhance foods made with wheat and corn crusts.

Flatbreads derive their generic name from the lack or scantiness of leavening. With little or no baking powder, baking soda, or yeast, they stay flat instead of rising like other breads. Traditionally, they are usually baked in a wood oven or fried above a wood fire on some type of griddle, such as the Mexican *comal* or the Indian *tava*. Versions with a firm dough that's rolled thin can also be grilled directly on the grate without a griddle or other supporting pan because the hot fire instantly stiffens the dough and pulls it away from the cooking surface to prevent sticking. With pizzas in particular, the method adds a layer of flavor to the crust that's difficult to achieve at home in any other way.

The appropriate temperature level in the grilling varies with the thickness and density of the bread. We make thin flour tortillas from scratch on high heat, but crank down to medium-high for corn tortillas, which start from a more compressed dough. Both set quickly and will remain supple if removed from the fire at that point, but can be cooked further at the same temperature to a crusty, chip-like stage. Slightly thicker pizzas benefit from a two-level fire. We begin the grilling on high, to crisp the surface of the crust, and then alternate between high and medium-low to cook the dough through and warm the toppings. Chewier breads with a bit of leavening, such as the cornmeal cake at the end of the chapter, grill best at a steady medium or medium-low heat, browning spots on the surface while retaining some softness in the center. Experiment with other flatbreads on your own. As long as the dough is firm and the cooked thickness doesn't exceed ½ to ¾ inch, grilling offers a new dimension of flavor and fun in bread making.

a pizza, you don't want to pile it with toppings that might spill off the side.) The dough is ready to use at this point, but also can be saved for later in the refrigerator or freezer. To carry the crusts from your pastry board to the grill, stack them on a baking sheet covered with waxed paper, with more

waxed paper layered between the crusts. Do the same if you plan to refrigerate or freeze the crusts. If freezing, first chill the crusts on the baking sheet for about 30 minutes to firm the dough, wrap the crusts, and freeze. Bring the crusts back to room temperature before proceeding.

TECHNIQUE TIP: Standard all-purpose flour is designed to cover a broad range of culinary needs. It works well in many dishes, but the higher gluten content of bread flour ensures stronger, more elastic dough for the thin, crisp pizza crusts and flour tortillas we favor for the grill. For rolling the dough, an inexpensive flour-tortilla roller—a simple fat dowel the thickness of a broomstick—is easier to use than a conventional rolling pin. .

CAPRI SUMMER PIZZA

When you start with a crisp, flavorful crust, pizzas don't need a truckload of toppings. A light coating of good cheese and a few summer-fresh garden ingredients bring out the best in the bread, as in this treat based on the popular Italian salad, the *insalata caprese*.

MAKES TWO 10- TO 11-INCH PIZZAS

· · · · · · · · · · · · · · · · · · ·

CHEESE TOPPING
1 cup grated mozzarella cheese, at room temperature
¼ cup fresh-grated Parmesan cheese, at room temperature
2 tablespoons minced fresh basil
1 garlic clove, minced
¾ teaspoon crushed dried hot red chile
½ teaspoon dried oregano

1 to 2 tablespoons extra-virgin olive oil
½ cup whole basil leaves
3 small red-ripe tomatoes, preferably Italian plum, sliced thin
Lean-and-Mean Pizza Crust (page 93)

· · · · · · · · · · · · · · · · · · ·

Fire up the grill for a two-level fire capable of cooking at the same time on both high heat (1 to 2 seconds with the hand test) and medium-low heat (6 seconds with the hand test).

Prepare the cheese topping, combining the ingredients in a medium bowl.

Place the cheese mixture, the oil, an oil brush, the basil, and the tomatoes within easy reach of the grill. The process needs to go quickly once you begin cooking. Place a baking sheet near the grill on a convenient work surface and have your largest spatula handy too.

Transfer the first crust to the grill, laying it directly on the cooking grate. Grill uncovered over high heat for 1 to 1½ minutes, until the crust becomes firm yet still flexible. (Don't be alarmed if it puffs up; you'll flatten it when you flip it over.)

Flip the crust onto the baking sheet cooked side up. Immediately brush with half of the oil, sprinkle with half of the cheese mixture, and top with half of the basil and tomatoes. Quickly remove the pizza from the baking sheet and return it to the grill, uncooked side down, arranging the pie so that half of it is over high heat and the other half is over medium-low. Cook the pizza another 3 to 4 minutes, rotating it in quarter turns about once a minute. With the spatula, check the bottom during the last minute or two, rotating a bit faster or slower if needed to get a uniformly brown, crisp crust.

Slice the pizza into wedges and serve immediately. Repeat the process for your second pizza.

TECHNIQUE TIP: Until you develop an instinctive feel for the doneness of pizza crust, use a timer as back-up support to follow the timing guidelines in the recipes. Cookware and grilling shops sell small, portable models, some with magnetic backs that attach to metal grill shelves. You'll find the timer an asset in grilling any new dish.

COOL PIZZA

This pizza boasts a refreshing contrast between the hot crust, bubbling with melted cheese, and the cold and tangy salad topping.

MAKES TWO 10- TO 11-INCH PIZZAS

SALAD TOPPING
3 cups arugula or watercress, any gangly stems pinched off
2 small red-ripe tomatoes, preferably Italian plum, chopped
¼ cup diced red onion, soaked for several minutes in hot water and drained
¼ cup capers, rinsed if you prefer a milder flavor
1 tablespoon extra-virgin olive oil
Splash or two of red wine vinegar

CHEESE TOPPING
¾ cup grated mozzarella cheese, at room temperature
½ cup fresh-grated Parmesan cheese, at room temperature
2 tablespoons minced fresh basil
1 garlic clove, minced
½ teaspoon crushed dried hot red chile
½ teaspoon dried oregano

1 tablespoon extra-virgin olive oil
Lean-and-Mean Pizza Crust (page 93)

Fire up the grill for a two-level fire capable of cooking at the same time on both high heat (1 to 2 seconds with the hand test) and medium-low heat (6 seconds with the hand test).

Prepare the salad topping, mixing together the ingredients in a medium bowl. Refrigerate until needed. Prepare the cheese topping, combining the ingredients in a medium bowl.

Place the toppings, the oil, and an oil brush within easy reach of the grill. The process needs to go quickly once you begin cooking. Place a baking

sheet near the grill on a convenient work surface and have your largest spatula handy too.

Transfer the first crust to the grill, laying it directly on the cooking grate. Grill uncovered over high heat for 1 to 1½ minutes, until the crust becomes firm yet still flexible. (Don't be alarmed if it puffs up; you'll flatten it when you flip it over.)

Flip the crust onto the baking sheet cooked side up. Immediately brush with half of the oil and sprinkle with half of the cheese mixture. Quickly remove the pizza from the baking sheet and return it to the grill, uncooked side down, arranging the pie so that half of it is over high heat and the other half is over medium-low. Cook the pizza another 3 to 4 minutes, rotating it in quarter turns about once a minute. With the spatula, check the bottom during the last minute or two, rotating a bit faster or slower if needed to get a uniformly brown, crisp crust. Near the end of the cooking, with about 1 minute left, top the pizza with half of the salad topping.

Slice the pizza into wedges and serve immediately. Repeat the process for your second pizza.

TECHNIQUE TIP: Porous pizza dough absorbs wood smoke more readily than most grilled food, even in a quick cooking process. You can taste the difference in commercial pizzas baked in wood ovens, and you can replicate much of that flavor at home by grilling over real wood embers or adding wood chips to the fire.

ARTICHOKE AND LEEK PIZZA

The light, pleasant saltiness of pecorino, an aged cheese made from sheep's milk, complements the mild sweetness of sautéed artichokes and leeks on this pizza. You can substitute good, grated Parmesan for the pecorino, but the result won't be as robust. Frozen artichokes work fine on the pizza, saving the extra preparation effort needed for the fresh ingredient.

MAKES TWO 10- TO 11-INCH PIZZAS

VEGETABLE TOPPING
3 tablespoons olive oil
2 cups chopped leeks
9-ounce package frozen artichoke hearts, thawed and
    sliced thin (about 2 cups)
Juice of ½ lemon
½ teaspoon salt, or more to taste

CHEESE TOPPING
¾ cup grated mozzarella or fontina cheese, at room
    temperature
½ cup grated pecorino, preferably Pecorino Romano, or
    fresh-grated Parmesan cheese, at room temperature
1 garlic clove, minced
½ to 1 teaspoon crushed dried hot red chile
½ teaspoon dried oregano
½ teaspoon dried thyme

1 tablespoon extra-virgin olive oil
¼ cup slivered drained oil-packed sun-dried tomatoes or
    1 medium red bell pepper, roasted, peeled, and sliced
    into thin strips
¼ cup pine nuts, optional
Lean-and-Mean Pizza Crust (page 93)

• • • • • • • • • • • • • • • • • •

Prepare the vegetable topping, first warming the oil in a heavy, nonreactive skillet over medium heat. Sauté the leeks several minutes until limp. Add the artichoke hearts and continue cooking an additional few minutes until both the leeks and artichokes are tender. Stir in the lemon juice and salt and reserve the mixture.

Fire up the grill for a two-level fire capable of cooking at the same time on both high heat (1 to 2 seconds with the hand test) and medium-low heat (6 seconds with the hand test).

Prepare the cheese topping, combining the ingredients in a medium bowl.

Place the vegetable and cheese mixtures, the oil, an oil brush, the tomatoes, and, if you wish, the pine nuts within easy reach of the grill. The process needs to go quickly once you begin cooking. Place a baking sheet near the grill on a convenient work surface and have your largest spatula handy too.

Transfer the first crust to the grill, laying it directly on the cooking grate. Grill uncovered over high heat for 1 to

1½ minutes, until the crust becomes firm yet still flexible. (Don't be alarmed if it puffs up; you'll flatten it when you flip it over.)

Flip the crust onto the baking sheet cooked side up. Immediately brush with half of the oil, sprinkle with half of the cheese mixture, and top with half of the vegetable topping and other remaining ingredients. Quickly remove the pizza from the baking sheet and return it to the grill, uncooked side down, arranging the pie so that half of it is over high heat and the other half is over medium-low. Cook the pizza another 3 to 4 minutes, rotating it in quarter turns about once a minute. With the spatula, check the bottom during the last minute or two, rotating a bit faster or slower if needed to get a uniformly brown, crisp crust.

Slice the pizza into wedges and serve immediately. Repeat the process for your second pizza.

PIZZA POINTERS FOR THE GRILL

Our recipe instructions call for rotating a pizza, after its initial quick toasting on high heat, between the hot and medium-low areas of a two-level fire. It's easier than it may sound, and, from our experience, it makes an important difference in the results. We've tried a variety of approaches, but nothing else has worked as well as alternating between periods of high-heat crisping and low-heat finishing. Some large and powerful grills provide other means than rotation to accomplish the goal, but none of the methods is any more simple or sure than turning the pizza as you cook.

The hands-on nature of the process requires an open grill, as is also true of other flatbreads, so we don't include directions for covered cooking in this chapter. Some people do bake pizzas in a covered grill, usually on medium heat, but the outcome is considerably different and, we think, not nearly as good.

Because of the attention needed with the rotation method, we always grill one pizza at a time, serving each as it's ready and continuing to cook until the last one is done. Be sure to have all the ingredients ready and handy when you start to work. The grilling goes so quickly you won't have time to run back to the kitchen for anything missing. Unless a recipe specifically calls for cold toppings, as in our Cool Pizza, the ingredients should be warm or at room temperature before you begin. With all the necessities in place, apply your showman's touch, adding a bit of this and a bunch of that with Neapolitan flair.

TECHNIQUE TIP: When you've mastered pizza basics, tell your spouse you want a peel for a graduation present. No telling what your reward may be, but eventually you can explain you meant a baker's peel, the broad, flat paddle professionals use to move pizzas and other breads in and out of ovens. A shovel-size hardwood spatula sold in restaurant supply stores, it allows you to handle a whole crust fully and simply, making a dramatic opening act of the moment you plop the crust on the grate.

PIZZA SURF-'N'-TURF

When pizza immigrated to the United States, the toppings sometimes went over the top. In contrast to the few fresh, local ingredients favored in southern Italy, Americans piled on a cornucopia of products, including tomato sauce, sausage, pepperoni, bell peppers, mushrooms, mussels, and much more. In a nod to both traditions, this pizza features a bounty of flavors starring clams and Italian pork sausage, but keeps the toppings in balance with the bread underneath.

MAKES TWO 10- TO 11-INCH PIZZAS

VERMOUTH SAUCE
3 tablespoons olive oil
3 tablespoons minced shallots
½ cup vermouth
¼ cup clam juice or seafood stock
1 small red-ripe tomato, preferably Italian plum, chopped

CHEESE TOPPING
¾ cup grated mozzarella cheese, at room temperature
½ cup fresh-grated Parmesan cheese, at room temperature
1 garlic clove, minced
½ to 1 teaspoon crushed dried hot red chile
½ teaspoon dried oregano
½ teaspoon dried thyme

Two 4- to 5-ounce sweet or hot Italian sausage links,
    grilled or otherwise cooked and sliced thin, warm
¾ cup shelled cooked small clams, such as littlenecks,
    or mussels, warm
¼ cup minced fresh parsley
Lean-and-Mean Pizza Crust (page 93)

Prepare the sauce, first warming the oil in a small skillet over medium heat. Stir in the shallots and sauté them for several minutes until very soft. Pour in the vermouth and the clam juice, add the tomato, and raise the heat to medium-high. Boil the sauce briefly until reduced to about 6 tablespoons and reserve.

Fire up the grill for a two-level fire capable of cooking at the same time on both high heat (1 to 2 seconds with the hand test) and medium-low heat (6 seconds with the hand test).

Prepare the cheese topping, combining the ingredients in a medium bowl.

Place the cheese mixture, the sauce, a spoon for the sauce, the sausage, clams, and parsley within easy reach of the grill. The process needs to go quickly once you begin cooking. Place a baking sheet near the grill on a convenient work surface and have your largest spatula handy too.

Transfer the first crust to the grill, laying it directly on the cooking grate. Grill uncovered over high heat for 1 to 1½ minutes, until the crust becomes firm yet still flexible. (Don't be alarmed if it puffs up; you'll flatten it when you flip it over.)

Flip the crust onto the baking sheet cooked side up. Immediately spoon on half of the sauce, sprinkle with half of the cheese mixture, and top with half of the remaining ingredients. Quickly remove the pizza from the baking sheet and return it to the grill, uncooked side down, arranging the pie so that half of it is over high heat and the other half is over medium-low. Cook the pizza another 3 to 4 minutes, rotating it in quarter turns about once a minute. With the spatula, check the bottom during the last minute or two, rotating a bit faster or slower if needed to get a uniformly brown, crisp crust.

Slice the pizza into wedges and serve immediately. Repeat the process for your second pizza.

PEPPERONI PIZZA PICCOLA

The popular American toppings of pepperoni and a basic tomato sauce taste best, perhaps, in small doses, such as in these Frisbee-size mini-pizzas.

MAKES 6 MINI-PIZZAS,
EACH ABOUT 5 INCHES IN DIAMETER

QUICK TOMATO SAUCE
2 tablespoons extra-virgin olive oil
1 garlic clove, minced
1½ cups canned tomato purée or crushed tomatoes with
    purée
2 tablespoons minced fresh basil
½ teaspoon dried oregano
Salt, optional

CHEESE TOPPING
¾ cup grated mozzarella cheese, at room temperature
½ cup fresh-grated Parmesan cheese, at room
    temperature
2 tablespoons minced fresh basil
1 garlic clove, minced
½ to 1 teaspoon crushed dried hot red chile
½ teaspoon dried oregano

2 tablespoons extra-virgin olive oil
3 ounces pepperoni, sliced very thin, at room
    temperature
¼ cup sliced briny black or green olives
Lean-and-Mean Pizza Crust (page 93), formed into six
    5-inch mini-crusts

Prepare the sauce, first warming the oil in a heavy skillet over medium heat. Add the garlic and sauté it about 1 minute, then stir in the remaining ingredients. Bring the sauce to a simmer over high heat and cook for 5 minutes. Keep the sauce warm. (The sauce can be made a day ahead and

kept covered and refrigerated. Rewarm before proceeding.)

Fire up the grill for a two-level fire capable of cooking at the same time on both high heat (1 to 2 seconds with the hand test) and medium-low heat (6 seconds with the hand test).

Prepare the cheese topping, combining the ingredients in a medium bowl.

Place the cheese mixture, the sauce, a spoon for the sauce, the oil, an oil brush, the pepperoni, and the olives within easy reach of the grill. The process needs to go quickly once you begin cooking. Place a baking sheet near the grill on a convenient work surface and have your largest spatula handy too. You'll be making two small pizzas at a time.

Transfer the first two crusts to the grill, laying them directly on the cooking grate. Grill uncovered over high heat for 1 to 1½ minutes, until the crusts become firm yet still flexible. (Don't be alarmed if they puff up; you'll flatten them when you flip them over.)

Flip the crusts onto the baking sheet cooked side up. Immediately brush them with one-third of the oil,

spoon on one-third of the sauce, top with one-third of the pepperoni and olives, and sprinkle with one-third of the cheese mixture. Quickly remove the pizzas from the baking sheet and return them to the grill, uncooked side down, arranging the pies so that half of their crusts are over high heat and the other half are over medium-low. Cook the pizzas another 3 to 4 minutes, rotating them in quarter turns about once a minute. With the spatula, check the bottoms during the last minute or two, rotating a bit faster or slower if needed to get uniformly brown, crisp crusts.

Slice the pizzas into wedges and serve immediately. Repeat the process for the rest of your pizzas.

TECHNIQUE TIP: For fast pizza-type snacks on the grill, use ready-made bread for the base. Grill the split side of a bagel, focaccia square, or baguette, or one side of a flour tortilla or pita round. When toasted, flip it over, cover with toppings, and grill the bottom side to heat through. Since you're just heating the "crust" rather than cooking it, grill these "pizzas" at medium heat or lower.

STEAMING STUFFED PIZZA WITH WILD MUSHROOMS, BACON, AND BLUE CHEESE

When you fold a pizza during cooking to create a calzone, it steams a bit inside and the crust becomes slightly doughier. The hefty turnover makes a wonderful fall supper, bursting in this case with the hearty aroma of freshly picked mushrooms and melted blue cheese.

MAKES 2 LARGE STUFFED PIZZAS

CHUNKY TOMATO SAUCE
2 tablespoons extra-virgin olive oil
3 slices uncooked thin bacon, chopped
1½ cups diced wild mushrooms, such as porcini or portobello
¼ cup diced red onion
1 garlic clove, minced
¾ cup canned tomato purée or crushed tomatoes with purée
¼ cup dry red wine
½ teaspoon dried oregano
½ teaspoon crushed dried hot red chile

CHEESE FILLING
¾ cup grated mozzarella cheese, at room temperature
6 tablespoons crumbled Maytag blue or other creamy blue cheese, at room temperature

Water
1 tablespoon extra-virgin olive oil
Lean-and-Mean Pizza Crust (page 93)

Prepare the sauce, first warming the oil in a heavy skillet over medium heat. Add the bacon and cook until crisp. Remove the bacon with a slotted spoon, drain it, and reserve. Add the mushrooms, onion, and garlic to the

skillet, and sauté a few minutes until the mushrooms give up their moisture and become tender. Stir in the tomatoes, wine, oregano, and chile and bring the mixture to a simmer. Reduce the heat to low and cook for about 15 minutes, stirring occasionally, until the sauce is thick but spoonable. Keep the sauce warm. (The sauce can be made a day or two ahead and refrigerated. Rewarm before proceeding.)

Fire up the grill for a two-level fire capable of cooking at the same time on both high heat (1 to 2 seconds with the hand test) and medium-low heat (6 seconds with the hand test).

Prepare the cheese filling, combining the ingredients in a medium bowl.

Place the filling, the sauce, a spoon for the sauce, the reserved bacon, a small bowl of water, the oil, and an oil brush within easy reach of the grill. The process needs to go quickly once you begin cooking. Place a baking sheet near the grill on a convenient work surface and have your largest spatula handy too.

Transfer the first crust to the grill, laying it directly on the cooking grate. Grill uncovered over high heat for just 30 seconds, no longer. The crust will have only begun to cook, and still will be quite flexible. (Don't be alarmed if it puffs up; you'll flatten it when you flip it over.)

Flip the crust onto the baking sheet cooked side up. Immediately spoon on half of the sauce, avoiding the edges. Sprinkle on half of the bacon and half of the cheese mixture, and fold one side of the crust over the other, creating a half-moon turnover. Pinch the edge together firmly, using a bit of the water to help it stick together. Brush both sides of the stuffed pizza with oil.

Quickly remove the stuffed pizza from the baking sheet and return it to the grill, arranging it so that half is over high heat and the other half is over medium-low. Grill the pizza another 1½ to 2 minutes, until lightly browned, rotating it a half turn one time. Turn the stuffed pizza over and cook for a similar amount of time, rotating it again. With the spatula, check the crust regularly to make sure it is browning uniformly.

Repeat the process for your second stuffed pizza. Serve the pizzas whole for two hungry diners or cut into wedges for a crowd.

TECHNIQUE TIP: For this turnover-style pizza or calzone, it's important that your pizza crust be as close to round as you can make it, to facilitate pinching together the edges when the crust is folded over. Cut off uneven edges if necessary to shape it properly before you begin cooking.

THE PIZZA EPIDEMIC

Ben Franklin bemoaned his inability to make the Parmesan cheese he loved in Italy, and Thomas Jefferson developed such a passion for pasta overseas that he brought back a machine for producing it at home. Today's dandy among Italian foods, the ubiquitous pizza, lagged much further behind in acceptance on American shores. What James Beard called "the pizza epidemic" didn't hit until after World War II, when returning veterans spurred demand and fast-food marketers began providing a national supply.

The servicemen discovered pizza in Naples, the only place in Italy where the dish thrived at the time. Neapolitan cooks created the treat centuries ago as a peasant bread, subsistence fare for the poor people of the area. Tomatoes became an early topping, soon after their introduction from the New World, because they grew well in nearby fields, and other local products such as mozzarella, basil, and oregano gradually joined the standard ingredients, which always remained simple and lightly spread on a thin crust.

When Neapolitans began immigrating to the United States in large numbers, in the 1880s, most went to Eastern cities, particularly New York, where America's first pizzerias opened around the turn of the twentieth century. Everything was different in the new land, from the flour to the abundance of the marketplace, and the style of the dish evolved accordingly, becoming bigger, deeper, meatier, and more heavily sauced. The Americanized version swept across the country during the "epidemic" as another form of a fast-food sandwich, competing effectively with burgers and dogs, and then hopscotched around the globe, even returning to Italy to inspire interest in pizza in parts of the nation that had ignored it before.

Recently, a few Americans and many Italians have begun to urge a return to the roots, a renewed emphasis on the flavor of the crust and the freshness of elemental toppings. That's the kind of pizza that works well on the grill, as we learned originally from Johanne Killeen and George Germon, the talented twosome behind Al Forno restaurant in Providence, Rhode Island. Our recipes are far from being totally traditional, but they do honor the earthy Neapolitan notion of a pizza.

FIRED ONION FLATBREAD

This and the following flatbread are made from the same dough as our pizzas, but they don't rely on cheese or tomatoes for flavor. Here we top the crisp rounds of bread with caramelized onions punctuated with bits of black olive.

MAKES TWO 10- TO 11-INCH FLATBREADS

ONION TOPPING
6 tablespoons olive oil
2 medium to large onions, sliced thin
2 tablespoons minced fresh marjoram, or 1 teaspoon
    dried crumbled marjoram
1 teaspoon sugar
1 teaspoon salt, or more to taste

Coarse-ground black pepper
1 to 2 tablespoons extra-virgin olive oil
Lean-and-Mean Pizza Crust (page 93)

Prepare the onion topping, first warming the oil in a heavy, large skillet over medium-low heat. Stir in the onions, sprinkle them with the marjoram, sugar, and salt, and cook them covered for 6 to 8 minutes, until they begin to turn golden, shaking them occasionally. Remove the cover and continue cooking the onions, stirring occasionally until the liquid evaporates and the onions are medium brown and chewy, another 10 to 15 minutes. (The topping can be prepared a day ahead and refrigerated. Rewarm it before proceeding.)

Fire up the grill for a two-level fire

capable of cooking at the same time on both high heat (1 to 2 seconds with the hand test) and medium-low heat (6 seconds with the hand test).

Place the onion topping, pepper, oil, and an oil brush within easy reach of the grill. The process needs to go quickly once you begin cooking. Place a baking sheet near the grill on a convenient work surface and have your largest spatula handy too.

Transfer the first crust to the grill, laying it directly on the cooking grate. Grill uncovered over high heat for 1 to 1½ minutes, until the crust becomes firm yet still flexible. (Don't be alarmed

if it puffs up; you'll flatten it when you flip it over.)

Flip the crust onto the baking sheet cooked side up. Immediately brush with half of the oil and top with half of the onions and a good sprinkling of pepper. Quickly remove the bread from the baking sheet and return it to the grill, uncooked side down, arranging it so that half is over high heat and the other half is over medium-low. Cook the bread another 2 to 3 minutes, rotating it in quarter turns about once a minute. With the spatula, check the bottom during the last minute, rotating a bit faster or slower if needed to get a uniformly brown, crisp crust.

Slice the bread into wedges and serve immediately. Repeat the process for your second flatbread.

LEMON-PARSLEY FLATBREAD

A simple aromatic duo of sunny citrus and heady herbs accent this crisp crust. Be sure to use Italian flat-leaf parsley for its deeper flavor. If you have a garden full of fresh herbs, add others such as basil or rosemary to the lemon-parsley base.

MAKES TWO 10- TO 11-INCH FLATBREADS

LEMON-PARSLEY TOPPING
Zest of 3 lemons
½ cup chopped Italian flat-leaf parsley
1 garlic clove
1 teaspoon kosher salt or other coarse salt

1 to 2 tablespoons extra-virgin olive oil
Lean-and-Mean Pizza Crust (page 93)

Fire up the grill for a two-level fire capable of cooking at the same time on both high heat (1 to 2 seconds with the hand test) and medium-low heat (6 seconds with the hand test).

Prepare the topping, combining the ingredients in a food processor. Spoon the mixture into a small bowl.

Place the topping, the olive oil, and an oil brush within easy reach of the

grill. The process needs to go quickly once you begin cooking. Place a baking sheet near the grill on a convenient work surface and have your largest spatula handy too.

Transfer the first crust to the grill, laying it directly on the cooking grate. Grill uncovered over high heat for 1 to 1½ minutes, until the crust becomes firm yet still flexible. (Don't be alarmed if it puffs up; you'll flatten it when you flip it over.)

Flip the crust onto the baking sheet cooked side up. Immediately brush with oil and sprinkle with about half of the lemon mixture. Quickly remove the bread from the baking sheet and return it to the grill, uncooked side down, arranging it so that half is over

high heat and the other half is over medium-low. Cook the bread another 3 to 4 minutes, rotating it in quarter turns about once a minute. With the spatula, check the bottom during the last minute or two, rotating a bit faster or slower if needed to get a uniformly brown, crisp crust.

Slice the bread into wedges and serve immediately. Repeat the process for your second flatbread.

GREEN CHILE AND CHICKEN MEXICAN PIZZA

The national colors of both Italy and Mexico—red, green, and white—highlight this vibrant Southwestern pizza, covered with tomatoes, a bright cilantro pesto, and molten cheese. The cross-cultural seasonings sit on a crunchy blue-cornmeal crust, blended with shredded chicken and chopped mild green chiles. You can use chicken cooked in any way, but we prefer it smoked or grilled, and flavored with a rub such as All-'Round Rub (page 23) or Chile Rub Rojo (page 24).

MAKES TWO 10-INCH PIZZAS

MEXICAN PIZZA CRUST
1 envelope active dry yeast (about 2½ teaspoons)
1 teaspoon sugar
¾ cup lukewarm water, 105° F to 115° F
About 1½ cups bread flour
½ cup stone-ground blue cornmeal, or other cornmeal
1 teaspoon salt
1 tablespoon olive oil
1 garlic clove, minced

CILANTRO PESTO
1 cup chopped fresh cilantro
1 garlic clove
¼ cup grated dry jack, Cotija, pecorino, or fresh-grated
    Parmesan cheese
2 tablespoons *pepitas* (hulled pumpkin seeds) or
    slivered almonds
6 tablespoons extra-virgin olive oil
Salt and fresh-ground black pepper

1¼ cup grated asadero, Monterey jack, or pepper jack
    cheese, at room temperature
1 cup shredded grilled or smoked chicken breast
2 small red-ripe tomatoes, preferably Italian plum,
    diced
½ to ¾ cup chopped fresh or frozen mild green chile,
    such as New Mexican or Anaheim, at room
    temperature
Crushed dried red chile

. . . .

Prepare the pizza crust, first combining the yeast and sugar with the water in a small bowl and letting the mixture sit until foamy. With a heavy-duty mixer or in a food processor, mix the yeast with 1½ cups of flour and the rest of the dough ingredients for several minutes, until the dough becomes smooth and elastic.

Transfer the dough to a well-floured pastry board or counter and knead at least 2 more minutes, adding in another tablespoon or two of flour if needed to get a mass that is no longer sticky. Place the dough in a greased bowl and cover with a damp cloth. Set the dough in a warm spot and let it rise until doubled in size, about 1 hour.

Punch the dough down on the floured pastry board and let it rest for 10 minutes. Roll the dough into two thin disks, about 10 inches in diameter, stretching and prodding it with your fingers too. (The dough is ready to use, but can be refrigerated or frozen at this point. Bring it back to room temperature before proceeding.)

Fire up the grill for a two-level fire capable of cooking at the same time on both high heat (1 to 2 seconds with the hand test) and medium-low heat (6 seconds with the hand test).

Prepare the cilantro pesto. In a food processor, combine the cilantro, garlic, cheese, and *pepitas*. With the machine still running, add the oil in a steady drizzle. Add salt and pepper, and combine again.

Place the pesto, a spoon for the pesto, and remaining ingredients within easy reach of the grill. The process needs to go quickly once you begin cooking. Place a baking sheet near the grill on a convenient work surface and have your largest spatula handy too.

Transfer the first crust to the grill, laying it directly on the cooking grate. Grill uncovered over high heat for 1 to 1½ minutes, until the crust becomes firm yet still flexible. (Don't be alarmed if it puffs up; you'll flatten it when you flip it over.)

Flip the crust onto the baking sheet cooked side up. Immediately top with half of the pesto, sprinkle with half of the cheese, chicken, tomatoes, and green chile, and finish with a sprinkling of dried red chile. Quickly remove the pizza from the baking sheet and return it to the grill, uncooked side down, arranging the pie so that half is over high heat and the other half is over medium-low. Cook the pizza another 3 to 4 minutes, rotating it in quarter turns about once a minute. With the spatula, check the bottom during the last minute or two, rotating a bit faster or slower if needed to get a uniformly brown, crisp crust.

Slice the pizza into wedges and serve immediately. Repeat the process for your second pizza.

TUCSON TORTILLAS

Americans took to the flour tortilla in the 1980s the way they took to pizza a generation earlier. In both cases, curiously, we made the bread thicker and doughier than the original. In the Mexican state of Sonora and in adjoining Arizona, the home of the first flour tortillas, cooks roll the dough almost paper-thin. Tortillas taste better that way in most dishes, we think, and they also cook better on the grill. Don't even think about using a cover over the grate because the cooking is done in a flash, before you have time to position and remove the lid.

MAKES TEN 8-INCH TORTILLAS

. . . .

2 cups bread flour, preferably, or all-purpose flour
¾ teaspoon salt
3 tablespoons vegetable shortening
¾ cup warm water

. . . .

Stir together the flour and salt in a large bowl. With your fingertips, mix in the shortening. Add the water, working the liquid into the dough until a sticky ball forms.

Dust a counter or pastry board with flour and knead the dough vigorously for 1 to 2 minutes. The mixture should be soft but no longer sticky. Let the dough rest, covered with a damp cloth, for about 15 minutes. Divide the dough into 10 balls, cover them again with the damp cloth, and let them rest again for at least 45 minutes. (The dough can be made up to 12 hours in advance, oiled lightly and refrigerated. Bring back to room temperature before proceeding.)

Fire up the grill, bringing the tem-perature to high (1 to 2 seconds with the hand test).

Cover the counter or pastry board with waxed paper, place a ball of dough in the center of it, and top with another piece of waxed paper. An inexpensive tortilla roller (much like a short section of broomstick) is easier to use than a conventional rolling pin. Roll the dough from the center outward, then turn the tortilla a few inches and roll again, attempting to keep the growing circle even. For grilling, roll the tortillas about ⅛ inch thick. Remove the waxed paper and pull on the dough with your fingertips too, being careful to avoid tearing it. Trim off any ragged edges and discard them. Stack the tortillas with more waxed paper or

plastic wrap between them.

Grill the tortillas uncovered, one at a time, over high heat. Cook each tortilla 10 seconds per side, then flip back and forth for about 10 more seconds on each side, cooking just until the dough looks slightly dry and wrinkled, and a few brown speckles form on both surfaces.

Fold each tortilla in quarters and serve warm in a napkin-lined basket, with butter and salsa, or reserve for another use. The tortillas taste best the day they are made.

QUESADILLA DORADA

If a pizza isn't complete without cheese, a quesadilla can't even claim the name without *queso*, the Spanish word for cheese. The *queso* in this case comes from goats, domesticated for centuries in the borderlands between Mexico and the United States, and the gilding comes from golden squash blossoms, one of the oldest foods in the region. As with most flour-tortilla quesadillas, we serve these open-faced, sliced into wedges like a pizza for eating by hand.

MAKES 2 LARGE QUESADILLAS

QUESO TOPPING
2 ounces creamy fresh goat cheese, at room
    temperature
4 ounces asadero, Chihuahua, Monterey jack, or
    Muenster cheese, at room temperature
½ teaspoon ground cumin
Pinch of salt

2 thin flour tortillas, approximately 8 inches in
    diameter, either Tucson Tortillas (page 113) or
    store-bought
Green onion slivers
10 squash blossoms, sliced lengthwise into quarters,
    steamed or microwaved until limp
2 whole squash blossoms

Fire up the grill, bringing the temperature to medium-high (3 seconds with the hand test).

Prepare the cheese topping, combining the ingredients in a small bowl.

Place the topping, the green onion slivers, the steamed and whole squash blossoms, and a baking sheet near the grill on a convenient work surface. The process needs to go quickly once you begin cooking.

Transfer the tortillas to the grill, laying them directly on the cooking grate. Grill uncovered over medium-high heat for about 1½ minutes, until the tortillas become firm and semi-crisp.

Flip the tortillas onto the baking sheet, grilled side up. Immediately scatter the cheese over the tortillas and arrange green onions and the steamed squash blossoms over the cheese. Quickly remove the quesadillas from the baking sheet and return them to the grill, uncooked side down. Grill an additional 1½ to 2 minutes, until the tortillas are crisp and the cheese is gooey. In the last 30 seconds or so, place a whole squash blossom in the middle of each quesadilla.

Transfer the quesadillas to a platter whole and serve immediately, slicing them after your guests have had a chance to admire the whole blossoms.

Riata Ranch Cowboy Quesadilla

I n a delightful study of Texas film folklore, *Cowboys and Cadillacs* (Texas Monthly Press, 1983), Don Graham calls *Giant* "the archetypal Texas movie," replete with all the elements of the state stereotype, "cowboys, wildcatters, cattle empire, wealth, crassness of manners, garish taste, and barbecue." The setting was the mythic ranch called Riata, in far west Texas near the town of Marfa, home of the first Tex-Mex restaurant. We beef up these yellow-cheese quesadillas in Riata style, leaving out little except the garish taste, and serve them as a giant sandwich.

MAKES 2 LARGE DOUBLE-DECKER QUESADILLAS

STEAK FILLING

1 tablespoon butter

⅛ small onion, sliced thin

1 to 2 fresh jalapeño or serrano chiles, sliced in very
thin strips

⅛ teaspoon ground cumin

4 ounces grilled or smoked flank steak, sliced very
thin, or other shredded cooked beef

QUESO FILLING

4 ounces mild cheddar cheese, grated, at room
temperature

2 ounces asadero, Chihuahua, Monterey jack, or
Muenster cheese, grated, at room temperature

4 thin flour tortillas, approximately 8 inches in
diameter, either Tucson Tortillas (page 113) or
store-bought

Fired-Up Tomato Salsa (page 88) or other favorite
tomato-based salsa

Fire up the grill, bringing the temperature to medium-high (3 seconds with the hand test).

Prepare the steak filling, first melting the butter in a small skillet over medium heat. Add the onion, jalapeño, and cumin and sauté several minutes until the vegetables are soft. Stir in the flank steak, heat it through, and reserve.

Prepare the cheese filling, combining the cheeses in a bowl.

Place the filling mixtures and a baking sheet near the grill on a convenient work surface. The process needs to go quickly once you begin cooking.

Transfer the tortillas to the grill, laying them directly on the cooking grate. Grill uncovered over medium-high heat for 1 to 1½ minutes, until the tortillas become firm and semi-crisp.

Flip the tortillas onto the baking sheet, grilled side up. Immediately scatter equal portions of the cheese and steak mixtures over two of the tortillas. Place the other two tortillas on top, grilled side toward the cheese. Quickly remove the quesadillas from the baking sheet and transfer them back to the grill. Grill an additional 1½ to 2 minutes per side, until the tortillas are crisp and the cheese is gooey.

Transfer the quesadillas to a platter and cut into wedges. Serve the quesadillas immediately accompanied by salsa.

TECHNIQUE TIP: Like a conventional sandwich, a quesadilla can serve as a vehicle for almost anything in the refrigerator or garden. Start with a cheese that melts well and add other compatible flavors, from seafood to meat, from a sprinkling of a favorite spice to a bounty of seasonings. Keep the combinations down-to-earth, in sync with the medium, but let the imagination soar.

CRAB-OLIVE QUESADILLA

Mild mozzarella and cream cheese allow the crab to shine in this flour-tortilla treat. The recipe calls for the common pimento-stuffed green olives, but you may want to substitute the ones tucked with jalapeños or onions for a special touch.

MAKES 2 LARGE QUESADILLAS

CILANTRO SAUCE
½ cup chopped fresh cilantro
½ fresh jalapeño or serrano chile
½ cup crème fraîche or Mexican *crema*, preferably, or
    sour cream (see Technique Tip)
⅛ teaspoon salt

CRAB-OLIVE TOPPING
2 ounces cream cheese, at room temperature
½ cup grated mozzarella cheese, at room temperature
4 ounces lump crabmeat, at cool room temperature
⅓ cup chopped pimento-stuffed green olives
1 to 2 fresh jalapeño or serrano chiles, minced

2 thin flour tortillas, approximately 8 inches in
    diameter, either Tucson Tortillas (page 113) or
    store-bought

Prepare the sauce, first puréeing the cilantro and the jalapeño in a food processor. Spoon in the crème fraîche and salt and process again until well blended. Spoon the sauce into a medium bowl, cover, and refrigerate until needed. (The sauce can be made 1 to 2 hours ahead, but the cilantro's sparkle and vibrancy begin to fade after that point.)

Fire up the grill, bringing the temperature to medium-high (3 seconds with the hand test).

Prepare the topping, combining the ingredients in a medium bowl and using the back of a fork to mash the mixture together.

Place the topping and a baking sheet near the grill on a convenient work surface. The process needs to go quickly once you begin cooking.

Transfer the tortillas to the grill, laying them directly on the cooking grate. Grill uncovered over medium-high heat for about 1½ minutes, until the tortillas become firm and semi-crisp.

Flip the tortillas onto the baking sheet, grilled side up. Immediately scat-ter equal portions of the cheese mixture over the tortillas. Quickly remove the tortillas from the baking sheet and transfer them back to the grill, uncooked side down. Cook an additional 1½ to 2 minutes, until the tortillas are crisp and the cheese is gooey.

Transfer the quesadillas to a platter, cut into wedges, and serve immediately with a drizzle of cilantro sauce.

TECHNIQUE TIP: Crème fraîche, a silky, thickened cream, costs an outlandish amount in most supermarkets. It's essentially the same product as Mexican *crema*, which you may find cheaper. Whatever you call it and pay for it, you can make it at home easily for less. Just combine a cup of whipping cream with 2 tablespoons of buttermilk in a nonreactive container. Cover the mixture and let it stand at room temperature for 8 to 12 hours until it's very thick, then refrigerate and use as needed. The crème fraîche or *crema* tastes richer than sour cream and melts into delightful rivulets on the warm quesadillas.

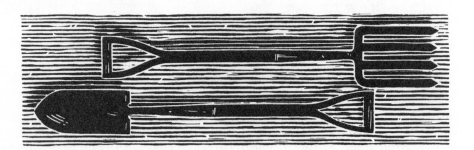

CORN TORTILLAS ROJO

Even if you live in an area where you can buy freshly made corn tortillas, you can make better ones at home. Most supermarkets across the country now carry dried *masa harina*, the key ingredient. If you happen to have access to fresh corn *masa*, use it instead of the dried version and eliminate the water and salt in the recipe. Generations of cooks have patted out corn tortillas by hand, but unless you do it regularly, you'll find a tortilla press eases the task considerably. We tint our homemade version red with a mild chile that adds more fragrance than heat.

MAKES TWELVE 5-INCH TO 6-INCH TORTILLAS

2 cups *masa harina*
1 tablespoon ground dried mild red chile, or more to
    taste
½ teaspoon salt
1¼ cups warm water, or more as needed

Fire up the grill, bringing the temperature to medium-high (3 seconds with the hand test). Find a steady surface near the grill to place your tortilla press.

In a large bowl, mix the ingredients with a sturdy spoon or your hands until the dough is smooth and forms a ball. A food processor can speed up this step, but we typically use it only when doubling or tripling the recipe. The dough should be quite moist, but no longer sticky, and hold its shape. Add a little more water or *masa harina*, if needed, to achieve the

proper consistency.

Form the dough into 12 balls approximately 1½ inches in diameter. Cover the balls with plastic wrap to keep them from drying out. If any of the balls do dry out before cooking, knead more water into them. Unlike the dough for flour tortillas, this dough can be reworked.

Place one ball of dough in the tortilla press between the two sheets of plastic sometimes sold with the press, or use two plastic sandwich bags. Press the ball until it is flattened to the desired thickness, generally about ⅛

inch. Carefully pull the plastic from the round of dough and lay the dough on the hot grill.

Grill the tortilla uncovered over medium-high heat for 30 seconds. Flip it and cook it for 1 minute on its second side. Then flip it back over to cook about 30 seconds longer on the first side. The tortilla should be speckled lightly brown.

Cover the cooked tortilla to keep it warm while the remaining balls of dough are shaped and cooked. Serve the tortillas warm in a napkin-lined basket with butter and salsa or reserve for another use. The tortillas taste best the day they are made.

PROPOSING A TOAST

A grill makes a great toaster. In addition to being a fine way to cook flatbreads, grilling can enhance other breads and similar dishes that you want to warm and crisp before serving.

From thick slabs of Texas toast to bite-size Tuscan bruschetta, slices of white yeast breads gain a new dimension when heated over fire. Top the toast with butter in the Lone Star fashion, brush it with fresh garlic in the Italian manner, or combine the two approaches for a crusty version of the old grill favorite, garlic bread. We also like the toast with a drizzle of extra-virgin olive oil, a sliver of smoked mozzarella, diced mushrooms and garbanzo beans flavored with cumin, or a halved tomato rubbed over the surface until it disintegrates.

If that sounds too corny for your neighborhood, try toasting cornmeal mush, better known today in trendy restaurant circles as polenta. First, cook a cup of coarse cornmeal or non-instant grits in the same way your grandmother did, or prepare the same amount of polenta according to the instructions on the package. Let the mush sit until firm, cut it into triangles or other manageable pieces, brush the slices with oil, and grill them on high heat until each side is crisp and lightly brown. It's delicious alone or even better topped with chow chow or shavings of Italian Parmesan cheese. You get a tasty treat and at the same time, you make Grandma proud and impress the local connoisseurs.

VEGETABLES VERDE QUESADILLA

We prefer two kinds of cheese in this corn-tortilla sandwich, one that melts and one that stays crumbly. Skip the second, if you wish, but you lose a little complexity in the flavor. The greens cut the richness of the cheese and the chunky avocado-zucchini salsa enlivens both.

MAKES 4 QUESADILLAS

CHUNKY AVOCADO-ZUCCHINI SALSA
½ cup diced zucchini
¼ cup diced onion, soaked in hot water several minutes
    and drained
1 small fresh jalapeño or serrano chile, minced
1 tablespoon olive oil
2 teaspoons fresh lime juice
1 teaspoon white vinegar
¼ teaspoon salt
1 small Hass avocado, diced

QUESO **FILLING**
6 ounces asadero, Chihuahua, Monterey jack, or
    Muenster cheese, grated, at room temperature
2 ounces manchego or panela cheese, or queso fresco,
    crumbled, or more of the cheese you chose above
1 to 1½ cups fresh dandelion greens, arugula, spinach,
    or chard, steamed until tender and chopped
2 slices cooked bacon, crumbled

8 corn tortillas, either Corn Tortillas Rojo (page 119) or
    store-bought

Prepare the salsa, combining all the ingredients except the avocado in a medium bowl. Cover and refrigerate until needed. Reserve the avocado to mix into the salsa just before serving time.

Fire up the grill, bringing the temperature to medium-high (3 seconds with the hand test).

Prepare the cheese filling, combining the ingredients in a medium bowl.

Place the filling, a shallow bowl of water, a baking sheet, and a spatula near the grill on a convenient work surface. The process needs to go quickly once you begin cooking.

Dunk the tortillas quickly in water. Transfer the tortillas immediately to the grill, laying them directly on the cooking grate. Grill uncovered over medium-high heat for 1 to 1½ minutes, until the tortillas become semicrisp. Press down on them with the spatula if any edges start to turn up oddly.

Flip the tortillas onto the baking sheet, grilled sides up. Immediately scatter equal portions of the cheese mixture over half of the tortillas. Place the remaining tortillas on top, grilled sides toward the cheese. Quickly remove the quesadillas from the baking sheet and transfer them back to the grill. Grill an additional 1½ to 2 minutes per side, until the tortillas are crisp and the cheese is gooey.

Transfer the quesadillas to a platter and cut them into wedges. Mix the reserved avocado into the salsa and serve the quesadillas immediately with the salsa.

TECHNIQUE TIP: Our recipes call for dunking corn tortillas in water before grilling them. The quick bath gives a bit of extra crunch to the texture. A broad, shallow pasta bowl makes a perfect-size dunking container. For superior crispness, always start with the freshest tortillas you can buy or make.

POTATO-CHORIZO QUESADILLA

Grated skin-on potatoes are a homey quesadilla filling in Mexico, particularly tasty when spiced with chorizo.

MAKES 4 QUESADILLAS

POTATO-CHORIZO FILLING
4 ounces bulk chorizo sausage or other spicy sausage
Vegetable oil
½ small onion, sliced thin
1 small well-scrubbed russet potato, grated with its peel

6 ounces asadero, Chihuahua, Monterey jack, or
    Muenster cheese, grated, at room temperature
8 corn tortillas, either Corn Tortillas Rojo (page 119) or
    store-bought

Fired-Up Tomato Salsa (page 88) or other tomato-based
    salsa

Prepare the filling, first cooking the chorizo in a heavy skillet over medium heat until crisp and brown, breaking it apart with a spatula while it cooks. Remove the chorizo from the skillet with a slotted spoon and drain it. Add oil to the skillet to measure approximately 2 tablespoons of fat. Stir in the onion and potato and sauté for 5 to 10 minutes until the vegetables are soft. Return the chorizo to the skillet. Reserve the mixture, keeping it warm.

Fire up the grill, bringing the temperature to medium-high (3 seconds with the hand test).

Place the filling, cheese, a shallow bowl of water, a baking sheet, a spatula, and a spoon near the grill on a convenient work surface. The process needs to go quickly once you begin cooking.

Dunk the tortillas quickly in water. Transfer the tortillas immediately to the grill, laying them directly on the cooking grate. Grill uncovered over medium-high heat for 1 to 1½ minutes, until the tortillas become firm and semi-crisp. Press down on them with the spatula if any edges start to turn up oddly.

Flip the tortillas onto the baking sheet, grilled sides up. Immediately scatter equal portions of the cheese over

half of the tortillas, and spoon equal portions of the potato-chorizo mixture over them. Place the remaining tortillas on top, grilled sides toward the cheese. Quickly remove the quesadillas from the baking sheet and transfer them back to the grill. Grill an additional 1½ to 2 minutes per side, until the tortillas are crisp and the cheese is gooey.

Transfer the quesadillas to a platter, cut them into wedges, and serve immediately with salsa.

THE "Q" CLUB

A three-story tortilla tower, this quesadilla club sandwich bulges with cheese, chile, corn, and a choice of chicken or turkey.

MAKES 4 TRIPLE-DECKER QUESADILLAS

CORN-CHILE FILLING
1 tablespoon butter
⅔ cup corn kernels, fresh or frozen
½ cup chopped roasted mild green chile, such as New Mexican, preferably fresh or frozen
Salt to taste

3 ounces mild cheddar cheese, grated, at room temperature
3 ounces asadero, Chihuahua, Monterey jack, or Muenster cheese, grated, at room temperature
4 ounces grilled or smoked turkey breast or chicken breast, or other cooked turkey or chicken, shredded
4 slices cooked bacon, crumbled
12 corn tortillas, either Corn Tortillas Rojo (page 119) or store-bought

Your favorite green chile–based salsa, optional, for accompaniment

Fire up the grill, bringing the temperature to medium-high (3 seconds with the hand test).

Prepare the corn-chile filling, first warming the butter over medium heat in a small saucepan. Stir in the corn and green chile and cook for 2 to 3 minutes, adding salt to taste.

Place the filling, cheeses, turkey, bacon, a shallow bowl of water, a baking sheet, and a spatula near the grill on a convenient work surface.

Working quickly, dunk four of the tortillas in water and immediately drain them. Transfer the tortillas immediately to the grill, laying them directly on the cooking grate. Grill them uncovered over medium-high heat until crispy, about 1½ minutes per side. Press down on them with the spatula if any edges start to turn up oddly. This batch of tortillas will be the center of each of the four quesadillas. Put the cooked tortillas on the baking sheet, and prepare the remaining tortillas, dunking and draining them, but cooking them only until they start to crisp, about 1 minute per side.

Flip the less-cooked tortillas onto the baking sheet, grilled sides up. On four of the less-cooked tortillas, scatter equal amounts of the cheddar cheese and the corn-chile filling. Place a crispier tortilla on top, followed by equal amounts of the other cheese, turkey, and bacon. Place the remaining less-cooked tortillas on top, grilled side down.

Return the quesadillas to the grill. Grill uncovered about 1 minute per side, until the outer tortillas are crisp and the cheese is melted. When you flip the quesadillas, do it quickly but carefully with the spatula to avoid losing the filling in the fire.

Transfer the quesadillas to a platter and cut them into quarters. Serve immediately, with a salsa on the side if you wish.

QUESO MASA POCKETS

These corn-flour turnovers hark back to an early form of the quesadilla, prepared directly from *masa harina* without the additional step of forming tortillas. We stuff the dough balls with a combination of cheeses and smoky chipotle chiles, which keep the inside of the corn pockets soft, gooey, and aromatic as the outside crisps over the grill fire.

MAKES 8 QUESADILLAS

QUESO FILLING

4 ounces Oaxacan string cheese (*quesillo* or *queso oaxaca*), chopped, or asadero or Monterey jack cheese, grated, at room temperature (see Technique Tip)

4 ounces smoked mozzarella cheese or smoked cheddar cheese, grated, at room temperature

1 to 2 green onions, minced

1 to 2 canned chipotle chiles, minced

1½ cups *masa harina*
¼ teaspoon salt
1 cup warm water, or more as needed

Fired-Up Tomato Salsa (page 88) or other tomato-based salsa

Prepare the filling, stirring together the ingredients in a small bowl.

Prepare the dough, first combining the *masa harina* and salt in a bowl and then mixing in the water. Working with your hands is easiest. The dough should be quite moist but should hold its shape. Add a little more water if needed to achieve the proper consistency. Form the dough into 8 equal balls and cover them tightly with plastic wrap. (If any of the dough seems too dry by the time you want to form it, just add a little more water.)

Fire up the grill, bringing the temperature to medium-high (3 seconds with the hand test).

With a tortilla press, press the first ball of dough out into a ⅛-inch-thick round (the dough can be rolled out by

hand too, by placing it between sheets of plastic wrap). Spoon about 1½ table-spoons of the filling over the dough round. Fold the dough over turnover style. Seal the edge, being sure to enclose the filling. Using the tines of a fork, crimp the edge of the dough. Transfer the masa pocket to a platter and cover with plastic wrap. Repeat with remaining dough and filling.

Transfer the masa pockets to the grill, laying them directly on the cooking grate. Grill them uncovered over medium-high heat for 2 to 3 minutes per side, until crisp with brown speckles. When you bite into the masa pocket, the flavor should taste of toasted corn, not raw dough. If underdone, leave the remaining quesadillas on a minute or two longer.

Serve them hot with salsa.

TECHNIQUE TIP: The Mozzarella Company in Dallas (800-798-2954 or 214-741-4072 for mail orders) makes an extraordinary version of the milky, mild Oaxacan-style string cheese. It's our first choice for one of the *quesos* in the filling, but other mild cheeses can be used too.

GRILLED CHEDDAR CORNMEAL CAKE

Just as the Aztecs taught the Spanish conquistadors about corn tortillas, Native Americans along the Atlantic coast introduced early British settlers to their own cornmeal breads, which the colonists called by such names as johnnycakes and hoecakes. We developed a variation on the old American classic that contains enough leavening and flour to lighten the dough and thicken the bread slightly. We grill it on medium-low heat to get a contrast of textures between the toasted surface and the chewy interior.

MAKES 18 TO 24 WEDGES

1¾ cups all-purpose flour
½ cup yellow or white stone-ground cornmeal
½ teaspoon sugar
½ teaspoon baking powder
½ teaspoon salt

½ cup chilled butter, cut into 4 to 6 pieces
8 ounces sharp or extra-sharp cheddar cheese, grated
½ cup corn kernels, fresh or frozen
1 tablespoon white vinegar
8 to 10 tablespoons ice water
Chili powder
Kosher salt or other coarse salt

In a food processor, combine the flour, cornmeal, sugar, baking powder, salt, and butter. Add the cheese and corn and combine again. With the processor running, quickly pour in the vinegar and 8 tablespoons of the ice water and process just until the mixture pulls itself together into a dough. If it still feels powdery and dry, add an additional tablespoon or two of water.

Divide the dough into 3 balls and wrap in plastic wrap. Refrigerate the dough for at least 30 minutes.

Fire up the grill, bringing the temperature to medium-low (6 seconds with the hand test).

On a lightly floured surface, roll out the dough into ⅛-inch-thick rounds. It's fine to leave the edges ragged, which looks more rustic and earthy.

Cut each round into 6 or 8 wedges. Sprinkle chili powder and salt on each wedge to taste.

Transfer the wedges to the grill, a few at a time, and cook directly on a well-oiled grate. Grill the bread on medium-low heat for 1½ to 2 minutes per side, until toasted golden brown with medium-brown grill marks on each side. The bread should have a crispy surface and slightly moist interior.

We prefer the bread hot off the grill, but the wedges can be cooked in advance and reheated or served at room temperature. If you wish, accompany the bread with salsa, chopped fresh tomatoes, or a relish of black beans and corn.

TANGY STUFFED FLATBREAD

Bakers in various areas of the world use yogurt in dough to soften the texture of bread, a trick we apply here to a crisp-crusted, cheese-filled flatbread.

MAKES 2 LARGE BREADS, ENOUGH FOR 4 TO 6 SIDE-DISH SERVINGS

. . . .

FLATBREAD FILLING
½ cup grated fontina, gouda, or Monterey jack cheese
3 tablespoons crumbled feta cheese
1 egg yolk
2 tablespoons minced fresh parsley
1 fresh jalapeño or serrano chile, minced

TANGY FLATBREAD
¾ cup plain yogurt
¼ cup water
¼ teaspoon ground cumin
¼ teaspoon salt
About 2 cups all-purpose flour

. . . .

Prepare the filling, mixing together the ingredients in a small bowl.

Prepare the bread dough, first combining the yogurt, water, cumin, and salt in a medium bowl. Add 2 cups of flour, 1 cup at a time, mixing with a sturdy spoon or clean hands into a soft but unsticky dough. Mix in a little more flour if necessary for the proper texture. Divide the dough into two balls, cover, and let sit at room temperature for 15 to 30 minutes.

Fire up the grill, bringing the temperature to medium (4 to 5 seconds with the hand test).

On a floured board, roll the dough into two ⅛-inch-thick rectangles. Spoon half the filling over half of each rectangle. Fold the dough rectangles over to make two turnovers, each roughly square. Press down on all the edges to enclose the filling. Transfer the breads to a baking sheet to carry them to the grill.

Grill the breads uncovered directly on the cooking grate over medium heat for 3 to 4 minutes per side, until crisp and lightly brown. The flatbreads should be moist at the center but not doughy.

Serve the hot breads immediately, cut into sections or torn into pieces.

HOT BURGERS AND HAUTE DOGS

THE OLD-TIMEY BIG 'UN

James Villas was a man on a noble mission in *American Taste* (Arbor House, 1982), celebrating the down-home larder of the land while lancing phony and fop food with needle-like wit. As usual, he had a few opinions on burgers, saying that fast-food chains have made a national disgrace of the sandwich, threatening "an aspect of our background that's as important as liberty itself." In his view, an honest-to-goodness burger has to be "thick as sin" and wide enough to spill out every side of the bun. It should come with a fat slice of raw onion, garden tomatoes, crisp iceberg lettuce, plain American cheese if desired, and gobs of mayonnaise mixed with a little ketchup—"true hamburger lovers *hate* mustard on their patties"—and it must be served with a cold bottle of Coke or Pepsi—some people opt for "milk shakes, root beer, or some other unorthodox soft drink, and I personally wonder why they don't choke." Our Old-Timey Big 'Un doesn't follow Villas to the letter, but he'd definitely put it in the camp of the real McCoy.

SERVES 6 HEARTY EATERS

1 cup Enriched Mayonnaise (page 38) or other
    mayonnaise
3 tablespoons Quintessential Ketchup (page 32) or
    other ketchup

3 to 3½ pounds freshly ground chuck (see "Not a Grind
    At All," page 139)
1½ teaspoons salt
1 teaspoon fresh-ground black pepper

6 large hamburger buns, preferably bakery-made
12 thin slices American or cheddar cheese, at room
    temperature, optional
6 thick slices red onion
6 thick slices large red-ripe tomatoes
Crisp iceberg lettuce leaves

Fire up the grill for a two-level fire capable of cooking first on high heat (1 to 2 seconds with the hand test) and then on medium heat (4 to 5 seconds with the hand test).

In a small bowl, combine the mayonnaise and ketchup. Reserve the mixture at room temperature.

In a bowl, mix together the ground chuck with the salt and pepper. Gently form the mixture into six patties about ¾ inch thick. The patties should hold together firmly, but don't compact them or handle them any longer than necessary.

Grill the burgers uncovered over high heat for 1½ minutes per side. Move the burgers to medium heat and cook for 5 to 6 minutes per side for medium doneness, until crusty and richly brown with a bare hint of pink at the center. If grilling covered, sear both sides of the meat on high heat for 1½ minutes; finish the cooking with the cover on over medium heat for 8 to 10 minutes, turning once midway. Toast the buns at the edge of the grill if you wish. If you plan to make cheeseburgers, place two overlapping slices on each burger a few minutes before you remove the meat from the grill.

Spoon the mayonnaise-ketchup mixture generously on both sides of a bun. Add the burger, an onion slice, a tomato slice, and lettuce, and repeat with the remaining burgers and ingredients. Eat the burgers hot, squeezing the buns firmly to mingle all the juices together. Big 'Uns are messy but worth every drip and dribble.

THE CLASSIC AMERICAN BURGER

ur Old-Timey Big 'Un departs from classic burger tradition in only one way, the thickness of the pattie. People used to pile the meat 1½ inches high, but that's considered risky today. When you grind beef, surface bacteria get mixed throughout the meat, including in the center of a pattie. Heat must reach all areas to kill the bacteria. If a burger is too thick, the outside becomes scorched and dried before the inside cooks adequately. We stay under an inch in thickness, generally around ¾ inch.

The classic pattie is close to the diameter of the bun, and always a little larger in the case of a Big 'Un. Since most buns today are about 3½ inches across, we usually call for patties of that size in the recipes, made with approximately 6 ounces of meat. Adjust the portions upward for bigger buns or spill-over burgers. Bakery-fresh bread enhances the taste of any sandwich.

The burger may be the single worthy use of processed American cheese, a place where its bland milkiness yields a pleasing gooeyness that doesn't compete with the meat flavor. For a stronger cheese tang, substitute sharp cheddar, perhaps something as distinctive as Vermont sage cheddar. Dress the sandwich with a choice of condiments, but you won't get the old, authentic taste and texture without good tomatoes, crisp lettuce, and a slice of onion, usually red or another mild variety.

For a straight-and-narrow stickler, the only proper side dish is a vegetable cooked in oil, either French fries or onion rings, except during the height of the summer season, when fresh corn on the cob joins the acceptable accompaniments. And don't forget the cold cola, drunk direct from the bottle (or even the can) rather than drowned in ice.

GARLIC AND GUAC BURGER

From ground nuts to matzo flour, eggs to cream, jalapeños to celery, American cooks have loaded their hamburger meat at one time or another with almost everything sold in a Safeway. We think when you want to flavor the pattie, you shouldn't mince around. This burger bellows with a load of roasted garlic.

SERVES 6

2 medium to large heads (yes, heads) of garlic
Vegetable oil
⅔ cup Enriched Mayonnaise (page 38) or other
    mayonnaise
2¼ pounds freshly ground chuck (see "Not a Grind At
    All," page 139)
1 tablespoon Super Wooster Sauce (page 39) or other
    Worcestershire sauce
1 teaspoon kosher salt or other coarse salt
½ teaspoon fresh-ground black pepper
2 tablespoons Chile Rub Rojo (page 24), optional

CREAMY GUACAMOLE
1 perfectly ripe Hass avocado
1 tablespoon minced onion
½ to 1 fresh jalapeño or serrano chile, minced
¼ teaspoon salt
Juice of ¼ lime

Watercress or lettuce
6 hamburger buns, preferably bakery-made

Up to a day before you plan to grill the burgers, roast the garlic. Preheat the oven to 350° F. Cut a small slice off the top of each head, just far enough down to expose the tops of the cloves, and rub the heads with oil. Shape a foil

pouch around the garlic, leaving the top of it open. Bake the garlic until soft, about 30 to 40 minutes. (The garlic can be prepared to this point, cooled, wrapped in plastic, and refrigerated.)

Separate the garlic into individual cloves. Squeeze the garlic from the skins (easy now that the garlic is cooked). Mash the garlic with the side of a large knife blade, and add one-half of it to the mayonnaise in a small bowl. Refrigerate the mayonnaise.

Fire up the grill for a two-level fire capable of cooking first on high heat (1 to 2 seconds with the hand test) and then on medium heat (4 to 5 seconds with the hand test).

Place the rest of the garlic in a large bowl and mix it with the ground chuck, Worcestershire sauce, salt, and pepper until just combined. Gently form the mixture into six patties about ½ to ¾ inch thick. The patties should hold together firmly, but don't compact them or handle them any longer than necessary. Coat the patties equally with the dry rub if you wish.

Prepare the guacamole just before grilling. In a small bowl, mash the avocado roughly, leaving some small chunks. Add the remaining ingredients and stir gently to combine.

Grill the burgers uncovered over high heat for 1 minute per side. Move the burgers to medium heat and cook for 4 to 5 minutes per side for medium doneness, until crusty and richly brown with a bare hint of pink at the center. If grilling covered, sear both sides of the meat on high heat uncovered for 1 minute; finish the cooking with the cover on over medium heat for 7 to 9 minutes, turning the burgers once midway. Toast the buns at the edge of the grill if you wish.

Slather mayonnaise on one side of a bun, and top with watercress, a burger, and a big dollop of guacamole. Repeat with remaining burgers and ingredients and serve hot. How about a side of Crispy Cumin Fries or Hoppin' John Salad with Tabasco Dressing?

BURGERS O'BRIEN

If garlic goes too far as a burger filling for you, try sautéed potatoes and bell pepper, a combo as auspicious as a four-leaf clover.

SERVES 6

O'BRIEN FILLING

6 slices uncooked bacon, halved

1 small russet potato or other baking potato
(about ⅓ pound), grated

3 tablespoons chopped green or red bell pepper, or a
combination

3 tablespoons chopped onion

½ fresh jalapeño or serrano chile, minced, optional

2 pounds freshly ground chuck (see "Not a Grind At
All," page 139)

1 egg

1 teaspoon salt

Fresh-ground black pepper to taste

2 to 3 tablespoons All-'Round Rub (page 23) or
additional salt and pepper

6 onion rolls, split, or hamburger buns, preferably
bakery-made

Mild cheddar or colby cheese slices, optional

Red bell pepper rings and onion slices

• • • • • • • • • • • • • • • • • •

Prepare the filling, first frying the bacon over medium heat in a heavy skillet. When the bacon is brown and crisp, remove it with a slotted spoon, drain it, and reserve. Add the potato, bell pepper, onion, and optional chile to the skillet and pat down in a single layer. Cook for several minutes, until the bottom of the mixture is brown and crisp, stirring up and patting back down until well browned on all sides. Cool briefly. (Don't refrigerate the mixture because it loses some of the crispness.)

Fire up the grill for a two-level fire capable of cooking first on high heat (1 to 2 seconds with the hand test) and then on medium heat (4 to 5 seconds with the hand test).

While the grill preheats, place the ground chuck in a large bowl, and mix in the egg, salt, pepper, and the potato filling. Gently form the mixture into six patties about ½ to ¾ inch thick. Coat the patties with equal amounts of the dry rub or sprinkle lightly with salt and pepper.

Grill the burgers uncovered over high heat for 1 minute per side. Move the burgers to medium heat and cook for 4 to 5 minutes per side for medium doneness, until crusty and richly brown with a bare hint of pink at the center. If grilling covered, sear both sides of the meat on high heat uncovered for 1 minute; finish the cooking

with the cover on over medium heat for 7 to 9 minutes, turning once midway. Toast the buns at the edge of the grill if you wish. If you are adding cheese, place a piece on each burger a few min- utes before you remove the meat from the grill.

Top the buns with the burgers, re- served bacon slices, and pepper and onion slices. Serve hot.

NOT A GRIND AT ALL

The key to a great burger is starting with freshly ground beef—nothing extra-lean—pre- pared to order at the meat market or ground at home. Many butchers, even in chain supermarkets, will grind the beef for you, but don't let the meat sit in the refrigerator for more than a few hours afterwards before you cook it.

For the freshest grind, we prefer to do the job ourselves right before we grill. The best tools for the task are a meat grinder or grinding at- tachment on a mixer, but you can also use a food processor, a more common appliance in the modern home kitchen. Take cold meat di- rectly from the refrigerator and cut it into chunks or strips. In an average- size processor, grind the beef one burger at a time, pulsing it with the regular chopping blade. For the best taste and texture, we like a grind slightly coarser than the usual super- market version.

We make burgers from beef chuck, though some people opt for round or a mixture of chuck with sirloin or other cuts. Buy a good grade of meat that contains a fair portion of fat, at least 15 percent and up to 20 percent. Cutting back on the fat simply diminishes the flavor with- out beginning to turn a burger into health food.

Don't compact the beef too tightly in forming patties and never smash it down with a spatula when you're cooking. Some folks refuse to salt the meat before it goes on the grate, saying that it draws out juices, but we think it enhances the taste. Definitely add pepper. Sear burgers briefly at first on high heat and fin- ish the cooking over a medium fire, seeking a crusty but not charred sur- face and a juicy interior.

JUMPING JACKS WITH MOONSHINE SAUCE

A pair of jacks won't win every pot in poker, but a pairing of smoky Jack Daniels and mellow Monterey jack cheese will win a lot of hearts at home.

SERVES 6

MOONSHINE SAUCE
½ cup Classic Kansas City Sauce (page 35) or other
    tomato-based barbecue sauce
3 to 4 tablespoons Jack Daniels or other similar
    American whiskey
1½ teaspoons Super Wooster Sauce (page 39) or other
    Worcestershire sauce
1 teaspoon molasses

2¼ pounds freshly ground chuck (see "Not a Grind At
    All," page 139)
2 tablespoons Jack Daniels or similar American whiskey
4 ounces Monterey jack cheese, grated
1 teaspoon salt
2 tablespoons coarse-ground black pepper

6 hamburger buns, preferably bakery-made
Red onion slices
Lettuce

Fire up the grill for a two-level fire capable of cooking first on high heat (1 to 2 seconds with the hand test) and then on medium heat (4 to 5 seconds with the hand test).

Prepare the sauce, combining the ingredients in a small bowl. Use the greater amount of Jack Daniels for the most robust flavor. Reserve the sauce at room temperature.

In a bowl, mix together the ground chuck with the Jack Daniels, cheese, and salt. Gently form the mixture into six patties about ½ to ¾ inch thick. The patties should hold together firmly, but don't compact them or handle them any

longer than necessary. Rub pepper over the surfaces of the burgers.

Grill the burgers uncovered over high heat for 1 minute per side. Move the burgers to medium heat and cook for 4 to 5 minutes per side for medium doneness, until crusty and richly brown with a bare hint of pink at the center. If grilling covered, sear both sides of the meat on high heat uncovered for 1 minute; finish the cooking with the cover on over medium heat for 7 to 9 minutes, turning once midway. Toast the buns at the edge of the grill if you wish.

Spoon sauce on the buns, top with the burgers, onion slices, and lettuce. Serve immediately. Some Red Pepper Hash would be great on the side.

TECHNIQUE TIP: As in the Jumping Jacks, you can mix cheese in any burger pattie as easily as you can add slices on top. The cheese melts more fully in that case and blends in with the meat and other ingredients. Just keep the amount moderate, in similar proportions as here, to prevent a messy meltdown on the cooking grate.

BERGHOFF'S CHICAGO BEER BURGER

When Americans first started cooking hamburger meat, they frequently served it with a mess of sautéed onions. This recipe from caterer Carlyn Berghoff and chef David Norman takes the old approach a beautiful, beery step further. With it, the imaginative cooks offer a toast to a Chicago institution, The Berghoff, founded by Carlyn's great-grandfather in 1898. Still in the family, the restaurant remains true to its roots, serving robust food with authentic hand-brewed beer. Thanks to Marcel Desaulniers for allowing us to borrow the burger, featured originally in his wonderful *The Burger Meisters* (Simon & Schuster, 1993).

SERVES 4

MUSHROOM-BEER KETCHUP
1 tablespoon unsalted butter
1 small onion, chopped
¼ pound button mushrooms, stems trimmed, sliced
6 tablespoons hot beer

⅓ cup **Quintessential Ketchup** (page 32) or other
  ketchup
1 tablespoon white vinegar
¼ teaspoon sugar
¼ teaspoon salt

BEER-BRAISED ONIONS
1 tablespoon unsalted butter
1 large onion, sliced thin
1 cup beer
1 teaspoon sugar
½ teaspoon salt

1½ pounds freshly ground chuck (see box, page 139)
2 tablespoons beer
½ teaspoon Tabasco sauce or other hot pepper sauce
¼ teaspoon Worcestershire sauce
Salt and fresh-ground black pepper
4 hamburger buns, preferably bakery-made
Four ½-ounce slices brick cheese or other pungent
  cheese such as sharp or extra-sharp Wisconsin
  cheddar, at room temperature

• • • • • • • • • • • • • • • • • •

At least 24 hours before you plan to grill the burgers, prepare the ketchup, first melting the butter in a large, heavy saucepan over medium heat. Add the onion and mushrooms and sauté until just tender, about 3 to 4 minutes. Remove the saucepan from the heat and add the beer, ketchup, vinegar, sugar, and salt. Use a hand-held immersion blender to purée the mixture, or spoon it into a blender or food processor and purée. Return the ketchup to the saucepan (if needed), return the heat to medium, and bring the mixture to a boil. Reduce the ketchup until slightly thickened, about 12 minutes. Remove from the heat and cool.

Spoon the ketchup into a nonreactive container and refrigerate for at least 1 day. (The ketchup can be made to this point several days ahead.)

Prepare the onions, first melting the butter in a large, heavy saucepan over medium-high heat. Add the onions and sauté, stirring frequently, until the onions are very tender, about 5 to 6 minutes. Add ¾ cup of the beer, the sugar, and the salt. Cook until all of the beer has been absorbed by the onions and they begin to brown lightly, about 16 to 18 minutes. Add the remaining ¼ cup of beer and bring to a simmer. Keep the onions warm.

Fire up the grill for a two-level fire

capable of cooking first on high heat (1 to 2 seconds with the hand test) and then on medium heat (4 to 5 seconds with the hand test).

In a large bowl, gently but thoroughly combine the ground chuck, beer, Tabasco sauce, Worcestershire sauce, and salt and pepper to taste. Gently form the mixture into four patties about ½ to ¾ inch thick. The patties should hold together firmly, but don't compact them or handle them any longer than necessary.

Grill the burgers uncovered over high heat for 1 minute per side. Move the burgers to medium heat and cook for 4 to 5 minutes per side for medium doneness, until crusty and richly brown with a bare hint of pink at the center. Toast the buns at the same time at the edge of the grill. If grilling covered, sear both sides of the meat on high heat uncovered for 1 minute; finish the cooking with the cover on over medium heat for 7 to 9 minutes, turning once midway.

Serve the burgers hot on the toasted buns, topped with some of the beer-braised onions and the cheese, with the mushroom-beer ketchup on the side.

TO YOUR HEALTH

Everyone knows that burgers contain more saturated fat than the food police allow. That fact combined with the national love of the sandwich gave rise in the 1970s to the health-food burger, a fad that refuses to fade. You can find tofu and veggie burgers anywhere in the country and, in exotic corners like Hawaii, even such quixotic concoctions as a mashed taro burger. What you may not know is that hamburger meat was actually one of the original health foods.

America's favorite European chef at the mid-twentieth century, Louis P. De Gouy, told an interesting story about the invention of the hamburger. In his magnum opus, *The Gold Cook Book* (Chilton Books, 1947), he put the origin of the idea back to 780 A.D., when he says "Italian physicians prescribed chopped beef fried with onions to cure colds and coughs."

A nineteenth-century physician, Dr. James Henry Salisbury, carried the claims further and left us the enduring legacy of the Salisbury steak, an American staple for generations. He recommended everyone eat ground beef three times a day to prevent and treat colitis, anemia, asthma, rheumatism, tuberculosis, and other ills. Salisbury even thought the diet would relieve hardening of the arteries, a notion we love to mention to doctors.

RUEDI'S CARIBBEAN CURRY BURGER

Chef Ruedi Portmann makes every meal special at the Curtain Bluff resort on Antigua. His classical European training shines at dinner, which crowns an elegant evening of music and merriment, but during the day he drops the pomp, moves the kitchen to the beach, and makes one of the meanest burgers in the Americas. Here's the secret, as simple and sassy as a calypso.

SERVES 6

RUEDI'S CURRY SAUCE
¾ cup mayonnaise
¾ cup sour cream
6 tablespoons chopped mango chutney
1 tablespoon plus 1 teaspoon curry powder

2¼ pounds freshly ground chuck (see "Not a Grind At All," page 139)
2 teaspoons fresh-ground black pepper
1½ teaspoons salt

6 kaiser rolls or other large rolls, split
6 red onion slices
Lettuce leaves
Caribbean Scotch bonnet or habanero hot sauce, optional (see Technique Tip)

Prepare the curry sauce, mixing together the ingredients in a medium bowl. (The sauce can be prepared several days ahead and refrigerated.)

Fire up the grill for a two-level fire capable of cooking first on high heat (1 to 2 seconds with the hand test) and then on medium heat (4 to 5 seconds with the hand test).

In a large bowl, combine the ground chuck, pepper, and salt. Gently form the mixture into six patties about

½ to ¾ inch thick. The patties should hold together firmly, but don't compact them or handle them any longer than necessary.

Grill the burgers uncovered over high heat for 1 minute per side. Move the burgers to medium heat and cook for 4 to 5 minutes per side for medium doneness, until crusty and richly brown with a bare hint of pink at the center. If grilling covered, sear both sides of the meat on high heat uncovered for 1 minute; finish the cooking with the cover on over medium heat for 7 to 9 minutes, turning once midway. Toast the rolls at the edge of the grill if you wish.

Serve the burgers hot on the buns with onion, lettuce, generous spoonfuls of curry sauce, and, if you wish, a little splash of Caribbean hot sauce. Any leftover curry sauce keeps for at least a week, and can enhance chicken or fish as well as beef. Try All-Star Pickled Starfruit on the side.

TECHNIQUE TIP: Simple curry sauces like Ruedi's flavor many meat dishes in the Caribbean, particularly goat. We like most of the curries best with an added splash of a local hot sauce. The most authentic choice in this case would be Susie's Hot Sauce, an Antiguan favorite, but any fiery habanero blend from the islands will fill the bill.

DEVILISH
HORSERADISH BURGER

Devilish here in two ways, we put spicy horseradish directly on this burger and then add some more to a ketchup topping. Beef can take the heat, so plaster the root generously over the patties.

SERVES 6

ROSY HORSERADISH SAUCE
½ cup sour cream
2 tablespoons prepared horseradish (see Technique Tip)
1 tablespoon Quintessential Ketchup (page 32) or other
   ketchup

2¼ pounds freshly ground chuck (see "Not a Grind At
   All," page 139)
2 teaspoons fresh-ground black pepper
1½ teaspoons salt
2 tablespoons prepared horseradish (see Technique Tip)

6 kaiser rolls or other large rolls, split
Onion slices
Romaine or iceberg lettuce leaves

Fire up the grill for a two-level fire capable of cooking first on high heat (1 to 2 seconds with the hand test) and then on medium heat (4 to 5 seconds with the hand test).

Prepare the sauce, combining the ingredients in a small bowl.

In a large bowl, combine the ground chuck, pepper, and salt. Gently form the mixture into six patties about ½ to ¾ inch thick. The patties should hold together firmly, but don't compact them or handle them any longer than necessary. Spread the horseradish on the burgers, slathering it on amply because it does mellow some while cooking.

Grill the burgers uncovered over high heat for 1 minute per side. Move the burgers to medium heat and cook for 4 to 5 minutes per side for medium doneness, until crusty and richly

brown with a bare hint of pink at the center. If grilling covered, sear both sides of the meat on high heat uncovered for 1 minute; finish the cooking with the cover on over medium heat for 7 to 9 minutes, turning once midway. Toast the rolls at the edge of the grill if you wish.

Serve the burgers hot on the buns with dollops of sauce, onion slices, and lettuce. Crispy Cumin Fries really round out the plates.

TECHNIQUE TIP: Prepared horseradish comes in small jars because it loses pungency and flavor fast. If you can't remember how long yours has been in the fridge, it's probably over the hill. We recommend replacing it every six months, if it lasts that long in your house. Fresh horseradish works even better as the flavoring agent applied directly to these burgers. If you can find the root, about the color and shape of fresh ginger, peel and finely grate about 6 ounces to pat into the surface of the patties before grilling. Any remaining root keeps for a few weeks, refrigerated, ready for instant grating for more burgers, various sauces, and many other uses.

BRASSY BRASSERIE BURGER

Studded with juicy shallots and green peppercorns, then topped with creamy goat cheese and a tomato-and-herb relish, this burger prances with panache.

SERVES 6

TOMATO-BASIL RELISH
2 large red-ripe tomatoes, chopped
2 tablespoons minced fresh basil
2 teaspoons olive oil
½ to 1 teaspoon Triple-Play Pepper Rub (page 27) or coarse-ground black pepper and kosher salt or other coarse salt

1 tablespoon olive oil

3 tablespoons minced shallots

2¼ pounds freshly ground chuck (see "Not a Grind At All," page 139)

3 tablespoons minced fresh basil

1 tablespoon drained green peppercorns, rinsed and drained again, chopped

2 tablespoons Triple-Play Pepper Rub (page 27) or coarse-ground black pepper and kosher salt or other coarse salt

6 large squares of focaccia, split, or 12 slices of another specialty bread such as black olive– or tomato-flavored, or onion rolls

6 ounces creamy fresh goat cheese, cut into 6 small rounds, at room temperature

• • • • • • • • • • • • • • • • • •

Prepare the relish, combining the ingredients in a small bowl. Add pepper and salt to taste if you aren't using the dry rub. Let the relish sit at room temperature to marinate.

Fire up the grill for a two-level fire capable of cooking first on high heat (1 to 2 seconds with the hand test) and then on medium heat (4 to 5 seconds with the hand test).

In a small skillet, warm the oil over medium-low heat. Sauté the shallots until very tender, about 5 minutes. Scrape the shallots into a large bowl and add the ground chuck, basil, and green peppercorns and combine. Gently form the mixture into six patties about ½ to ¾ inch thick. The patties should hold together firmly, but don't compact them or handle them any longer than necessary. Coat the patties with the dry rub or sprinkle generously with pepper and salt.

Grill the burgers uncovered over high heat for 1 minute per side. Move the burgers to medium heat to cook for 4 to 5 minutes per side for medium doneness, until crusty and richly brown with a bare hint of pink at the center. If grilling covered, sear both sides of the meat on high heat uncovered for 1 minute; finish the cooking with the cover on over medium heat for 7 to 9 minutes, turning once midway. Toast the focaccia at the edge of the grill if you wish.

Pile the burgers on the focaccia and top them with the cheese. Drain the relish of any accumulated juice, top the burgers with generous spoonfuls, and serve immediately. We like our Fancy Bean Salad on the side.

THE BIRTH OF THE BURGER

A bun makes ground beef into a burger, but who made the first bun? We know a lot more about the meat itself. The German city of Hamburg gave its name by the mid-nineteenth century to a pulverized steak popular among residents at the time. The Hamburgers imported the dish themselves, perhaps from Baltic trading partners or Austro-Hungarian cooks, and then exported it to the New World via German immigrants. The "Hamburg steak" gained fans quickly in the United States, but it was seldom if ever served on a bun until the twentieth century.

Loosely documented stories credit the initial inspiration to several sources. Local boosters in Hamburg, New York, say that county-fair vendors Charles and Frank Menches created the first burger in 1885 when they ran out of pork at their sandwich stand. Dallas journalist Frank X. Tolbert, always true to Texas, gave the recognition to Fletcher "Old Dave" Davis, who ran a lunch counter in the same decade in the Lone Star burg of Athens. Other folks, including the savants at McDonald's Hamburger University, assert the meat didn't hit the bun until an international exposition in St. Louis in 1904, where someone definitely did hawk an early version of the Americanized treat.

It still took years for the burger to reach the American home, however. Judging by popular cookbooks from the first half of the twentieth century, most home cooks stuck with the old Hamburg steak for family meals. The bun seemed superfluous unless you lacked a plate. James Beard recalled seeing burgers at picnics, but they made headway mainly as roadside food in the dawning automobile age. The White Castle chain, founded in Wichita, Kansas, in 1921, spawned a slew of imitators across the country, mostly selling steam-cooked, bite-sized snacks by the sackload. Main-street cafes soon took up the idea, usually frying the meat on the griddle and serving it on grease-sopped bread.

The outdoor grilling revolution finally brought the burger home and solidified its proper place in American life. World War II rationing made ground beef a family favorite and returning veterans made the meat into a snappy, happy backyard meal full of charbroiled flavor. Mom added a salad in the center, wrapped it all in a store-bought bun, and took a night off from washing dishes. After a long gestation, the burger blossomed at last into an institution.

LATROBE LAMB BURGER

L amb has long starred in fancy burgers, ones you could serve even at a dress-up dinner. During the Kennedy years, you might have stuffed the meat with mozzarella and mint, and topped it with a creme de menthe sauce, as one national contest winner did. In the Reagan decade, the Silver Palate duo of Sheila Lukins and Julee Rosso updated the idea for a new generation, filling lamb burgers with creamy goat cheese and flavoring them with mint and raspberry vinegar. Green with envy at those ideas, we take a farm-fresh approach with spinach and dill, refusing to be subdued in ambition by the Clinton era. We named our version in honor of the bountiful pastures near Latrobe, Pennsylvania, where John and Sukey Jamison—noble name but no relation to us—raise lamb naturally on native bluegrass and white clover. If you lack a local source for premium lamb, contact the Jamison Farm at 800-237-5262 for mail-order information.

SERVES 4

ROASTED GARLIC MAYONNAISE
½ cup store-bought mayonnaise
2 teaspoons extra-virgin olive oil
½ head garlic, roasted (see Technique Tip, page 84) and
    mashed
Splash of Tabasco sauce or other hot pepper sauce

FRESH DILL PASTE
2 tablespoons minced fresh dill
1 plump garlic clove, minced
¾ teaspoon paprika
½ teaspoon kosher salt or other coarse salt
½ teaspoon fresh-ground black pepper

1¼ pounds ground lamb
½ cup minced fresh spinach
½ teaspoon kosher salt or other coarse salt
8 slices sourdough bread
Crisp stemmed spinach leaves
Dried Fruit Chutney (page 46) or other chutney, optional

Prepare the mayonnaise, whisking together the ingredients in a medium bowl. Cover and refrigerate until you are ready to serve the burgers.

Fire up the grill, bringing the temperature to medium (4 to 5 seconds with the hand test).

Prepare the dill paste, combining the ingredients in a small bowl.

In a medium bowl, mix together the ground lamb, spinach, salt, and 2 teaspoons of the paste. Gently form the mixture into four patties about ½ to ¾ inch thick. The patties should hold together firmly, but don't compact them

or handle them any longer than necessary. Sprinkle the remaining paste over the burgers, patting it in lightly.

Grill the burgers uncovered over medium heat for a total of 5 to 5½ minutes per side for medium-rare. If grilling covered, cook for 8 to 10 minutes, turning once midway. Toast the bread at the edge of the grill if you wish.

Serve the burgers on the bread, slathered with the garlic mayonnaise, topped with spinach leaves, and, should you like, a bit of chutney. Mixed Herb Tabbouleh mates splendidly with the burgers.

PIEDMONT PORKERS

This burger is inspired by slow-smoked barbecue, the only kind that merits the name in the Piedmont region of North Carolina. Using pork preferably ground from the shoulder, the traditional cut, we cover the meat in Lexington red slaw, as the pitmasters do locally in a real BBQ sandwich.

SERVES 4

RED SLAW
½ cup Enriched Mayonnaise (page 38) or other mayonnaise
1½ tablespoons thin, not too sweet, tomato-based barbecue sauce
1 to 1¼ tablespoons sugar
½ tablespoon Quintessential Ketchup (page 32) or other ketchup
½ tablespoon cider vinegar
¼ teaspoon salt, or more to taste
½ medium head green or red cabbage, shredded

ALL-'ROUND RUB
1½ tablespoons paprika
1½ teaspoons coarse-ground black pepper
1½ teaspoons kosher salt or other coarse salt
¾ teaspoon chili powder
½ teaspoon packed brown sugar
Pinch of cayenne, optional

1½ pounds ground pork, preferably from the shoulder
2 tablespoons buttermilk or milk
8 slices sturdy sourdough bread

Prepare the slaw. In a lidded jar, shake together the mayonnaise, barbecue sauce, sugar, ketchup, vinegar, and salt until well blended. Place the cabbage in a large bowl. Pour the dressing over the cabbage and toss together. For the best flavor, chill the slaw for at least 1 hour. (It can be made several days ahead.)

Fire up the grill, bringing the temperature to medium (4 to 5 seconds with the hand test).

Prepare the dry rub, combining the ingredients in a small bowl.

In a medium bowl, mix together the pork, milk, and 2 teaspoons of the dry rub. Gently form the mixture into four patties, approximately ½ to ¾ inch thick. The patties should hold together firmly, but don't compact them or handle them any longer than necessary. Coat the patties with the rub, using at least two-thirds of it and more if you're a real rub fan.

Grill the burgers uncovered over medium heat for about 6 minutes per side, turning once. The burgers are done when medium-brown and crisp with a fully cooked interior. If grilling covered, cook for about 10 minutes, turning once midway. Toast the bread at the edge of the grill if you wish.

Serve the burgers on the bread, generously topped with the slaw. Lightly squeeze the buns so that the meat juices and sauce mingle. On the side, try some Olive Oil Dills or other crunchy pickles, and Hoppin' John Salad with Tabasco Vinaigrette.

KAREN'S VERY FINE VENISON BURGER

Our friend Karen Berlanti never does anything on a small scale. With her first elk hunting permit, she bagged a 6 x 7 buck on the Carroll Ranch in western Montana, the largest elk ever taken off the ranch. We created this elegant but unfussy open-face burger to help consume her largesse, but you can make it just as well with any properly dressed wild venison or store-bought venison such as red deer, axis deer, or antelope. To prevent the lean meat from drying out on the grill, we add a splash of wine and flavorful bacon drippings to the burgers and cook them no further than medium-rare.

SERVES 4

MUSHROOM TOPPING
4 slices uncooked bacon, chopped
2 tablespoons butter
¾ pound wild mushrooms, sliced thin
1 tablespoon dry red wine
¼ teaspoon ground coriander
¼ teaspoon salt

1½ pounds ground venison
1 tablespoon dry red wine
¾ teaspoon ground juniper berries
½ teaspoon crumbled dried sage
½ teaspoon salt
Fresh-ground black pepper

4 large slices hearty whole-grain bread or herbed
    sourdough bread
Honey-Beer Mustard (page 37) or other honey
    mustard, optional

Prepare the topping, first frying the bacon in a nonreactive medium skillet over medium heat until brown and crisp. Remove the bacon with a slotted spoon and reserve it. Add the butter to the bacon drippings and melt it. Pour 2 tablespoons of the mixed drippings into a medium bowl and reserve it. Add the mushrooms to the skillet and sauté over medium heat until limp. Pour in the wine, add the coriander and salt, and continue cooking briefly until the mushrooms are tender with only a bit of the liquid clinging to them. Keep the topping warm.

Fire up the grill for a two-level fire capable of cooking first on high heat (1 to 2 seconds with the hand test) and then on medium heat (4 to 5 seconds with the hand test).

To the reserved drippings, add the venison, wine, juniper berries, sage, salt, and a good grinding of pepper. Gently form the mixture into four patties, approximately ½ to ¾ inch thick. The patties should hold together firmly, but don't compact them or handle them any longer than necessary.

Grill the burgers uncovered over high heat for 1 minute per side. Move the burgers to medium heat and cook for 2½ to 3 minutes per side, until crusty and richly brown with a pink center. If grilling covered, sear both sides of the meat on high heat uncovered for 1 minute; finish the cooking with the cover on 5 to 6 minutes, turning once midway. Toast the bread at the edge of the grill if you wish.

Spread mustard over the bread slices, if you like, and top each with a burger. Spoon the mushrooms equally over the burgers, then scatter bacon over each. Serve immediately with knives and forks. We like to pair the open-face burgers with Land of the Lakes Wild Rice–Pecan Salad.

TECHNIQUE TIP: To keep venison, buffalo, or even beef burgers juicy, some grillers add a few slivers of frozen butter or chips of ice to the patties prior to cooking. We don't find either essential, especially when burgers are cooked at the proper temperature and for the correct amount of time, but you might want to experiment with these tricks when you're working with lean meat.

TURKEY BURGER WITH CRIMSON CRANBERRY KETCHUP

Turkey always reminds us of Thanksgiving, so we dress these bird burgers in T-Day fashion.

SERVES 4

. . . .

CRIMSON CRANBERRY KETCHUP
1 tablespoon butter
1 tablespoon minced onion
8-ounce can jellied cranberry sauce
2 tablespoons raspberry vinegar, Peach Vinegar (page
    41), or other fruity vinegar
1 tablespoon tomato paste
1 tablespoon water
Pinch of kosher salt

1½ pounds ground turkey
½ cup herb-seasoned stuffing bread crumbs
¼ cup milk
½ teaspoon kosher salt (omit if stuffing crumbs are
    salted)

T-DAY DRY RUB
2 teaspoons dried thyme
1 teaspoon dried sage
1 teaspoon fresh-ground black pepper
1 teaspoon white pepper
1 teaspoon kosher salt

4 onion rolls, split, or hamburger buns, preferably
    bakery-made
Shredded red cabbage, for garnish

. . . .

Prepare the ketchup, first melting the butter in a small saucepan over medium heat. Stir in the onion and cook briefly until translucent. Stir in the remaining ingredients and reduce the heat to low. Cook until thickened to ketchup consistency, about 10 minutes, stirring occasionally. (The ketchup can be made a day or two ahead and kept covered and refrigerated. Serve chilled or reheated, adding a little water if it becomes too thick for easy spooning.)

Fire up the grill, bringing the temperature to medium (4 to 5 seconds with the hand test).

While the grill preheats, prepare the burgers. Combine the ground turkey, bread crumbs, milk, and salt. Gently form the mixture into four patties about ½ to ¾ inch thick. The patties should hold together firmly, but don't compact them or handle them any longer than necessary.

Prepare the dry rub, mixing the ingredients in a small bowl. Sprinkle the rub equally over both sides of the burgers, lightly patting in the spices.

Grill the burgers uncovered over medium heat for 8 to 10 minutes per side, until medium-brown and crisp with a fully cooked interior. If grilling covered, cook for 15 to 18 minutes, turning once midway. Toast the rolls at the edge of the grill if you wish.

Spread ketchup on both sides of the rolls, sprinkle with cabbage, and top with the burgers. Serve immediately.

BIG ISLAND BURGER

Once on a small, remote Pacific island, we ordered fishburgers for lunch. We didn't learn until later that the chef who put the sandwich on the menu had quit the day before, leaving an untrained cook in charge of the kitchen. After a long delay, while the staff pondered our order no doubt, the cheery waitress returned with two plates of bulging buns. Curious about the catch of the day inside, we lifted the lid to discover a regular hamburger pattie covered in a pile of canned tuna—truly a fishy fishburger. No one would make that mistake on the Big Island of Hawaii, where they treat fresh tuna as the prize among Neptune's treasures.

SERVES 4

MUSTARD-GARLIC MAYO
6 tablespoons Enriched Mayonnaise (page 38) or other
    mayonnaise
1 heaping teaspoon hot Chinese mustard or
    1 tablespoon Dijon mustard
2 garlic cloves, roasted (see Technique Tip, page 84)
    and mashed

1½ pounds fresh tuna steak
1½ tablespoons extra-virgin olive oil
2 teaspoons hot Chinese mustard or 1½ tablespoons
    Dijon mustard
2 garlic cloves, minced

BIG ISLAND DRY RUB
2 teaspoons kosher salt or other coarse salt
2 teaspoons fresh-ground black pepper
2 teaspoons paprika
⅛ teaspoon dried ginger

8 slices sourdough bread
Crisp romaine leaves

• • • • • • • • • • • • • • • • • •

Prepare the mustard-garlic mayonnaise, combining the ingredients in a small bowl.

With a large, sharp knife, coarsely chop the tuna into ¼-inch cubes. Hand-chopping is more work than chopping in a food processor, but the texture will be far superior. Transfer the tuna to a medium bowl and toss it with oil, mustard, and garlic.

Fire up the grill, bringing the temperature to medium (4 to 5 seconds with the hand test). While whole tuna steaks can handle high heat, the chopped burger mixture stays juicier over a lower fire.

Gently form the tuna mixture into four patties about ½ to ¾ inch thick. The patties should hold together firmly, but don't compact them or handle them any longer than necessary.

Prepare the dry rub, combining the ingredients in a small bowl. Sprinkle the rub equally over both sides of the burgers, lightly patting in the spices.

Transfer the burgers to a well-oiled grate. Grill the burgers uncovered over medium heat for 3 to 4 minutes per side, until lightly browned with medium-rare centers. If grilling covered, cook for 6 to 7 minutes, turning once midway. Toast the bread at the edge of the grill if you wish.

Spread the mayo on the bread and add the burgers and romaine. Serve hot.

These fishburgers pair especially well with Grant Street Pickled Vegetables.

CONCH REPUBLIC SEAFOOD BURGER

Would-be secessionists in Key West, Florida, only slightly serious, like to call their home the Conch Republic in honor of their favorite native sea creature, a tasty if chewy gastropod. The locals relish conch in so many ways, including in a burger, that they drove it to the verge of extinction. As a spry substitute today in a sandwich, we favor a combination of crab or shrimp with scallops. Even devoted conch fans enjoy the switch, though we haven't found any yet who are willing to proclaim themselves proud citizens of the Crab Republic or Shrimpland.

SERVES 4

12 ounces lump crabmeat
12 ounces bay or sea scallops, chopped
¼ cup minced red bell pepper
2 tablespoons minced fresh parsley
1 medium egg
½ teaspoon salt, or more to taste
Generous splash of Caribbean Scotch bonnet or
     habanero hot sauce

About ¾ cup dry bread crumbs
Vegetable oil spray
8 slices country bread
1 Hass avocado, sliced
Hot Shot Tartar Sauce (page 38) or other tartar sauce

In a medium bowl, combine the crab, scallops, bell pepper, parsley, egg, salt, and hot sauce. Gently form the mixture into four patties about ½ to ¾ inch thick. The patties should hold together, but don't compact them or handle them any longer than necessary.

Place the bread crumbs on a plate. Lay each burger gently on the crumbs, coating both sides well. Cover the burgers and refrigerate them for at least 30 minutes.

Fire up the grill, bringing the temperature to medium (4 to 5 seconds with the hand test).

Spritz the burgers lightly but thoroughly with oil and transfer them to a well-oiled grate. Grill the burgers uncovered over medium heat for 5 to 6 minutes per side, until lightly brown and crisp with opaque centers. If grilling covered, cook for 8 to 10 minutes, turning once midway. Toast the bread at the edge of the grill if you wish.

Arrange avocado slices on half of the bread, and top with the burgers, dollops of the tartar sauce, and the rest of the bread. Serve immediately.

'BELLO BURGER

Meaty and versatile, portobello mushrooms make a great burger. Here we marinate them in equal portions of olive oil, vinegar, and soy, and then slather them with a roasted bell pepper mayo.

SERVES 4

'BELLO MARINADE
¼ cup inexpensive balsamic vinegar
¼ cup soy sauce
¼ cup olive oil
3 garlic cloves, minced

4 portobello mushroom caps (stems reserved for
    another purpose), each about 5 inches in diameter

RED BELL MAYONNAISE
½ medium red bell pepper
⅓ cup Enriched Mayonnaise (page 38) or other
　　mayonnaise
1 teaspoon olive oil
Pinch of cayenne pepper

4 thin slices mozzarella cheese, each large enough to
　　cover a mushroom cap, optional
4 kaiser rolls or other large, crusty rolls
Lettuce leaves
Red-ripe tomato slices
Spicy Mushroom Ketchup (page 34), optional

At least 30 minutes and up to 2 hours before you plan to grill, prepare the marinade, combining the ingredients in a medium bowl. Place the mushrooms in a large plastic bag, pour the marinade over them, and let sit at room temperature. Turn the bag occasionally if needed to saturate the surface with the marinade.

Prepare the mayonnaise, first roasting the bell pepper to blister its skin. Spear it with a fork and hold it skin-side down directly over a gas or electric stove burner briefly until the skin blackens. Transfer the pepper to a plastic bag and let it steam until cool enough to handle. Pull the loose skin from the pepper. Cut the pepper into several chunks and purée with the other ingredients in a small food processor or blender. Refrigerate until serving time.

Fire up the grill, bringing the temperature to medium (4 to 5 seconds with the hand test).

Drain the mushroom caps, discarding the marinade. Transfer the mushrooms to the grate cap-side up so you immediately caramelize some of the accumulated juice on their undersides. Grill uncovered over medium heat for 8 to 10 minutes, turning the mushrooms twice and topping each with a cheese slice, if you wish, when the mushrooms are again cap-side up. Toast the rolls at the same time on the edge of the grill. If grilling covered, cook for 7 to 8 minutes, turning once midway; add the optional cheese to the mushrooms just as you take them off the grill.

Place the mushrooms on the toasted rolls and add the lettuce leaves, tomatoes, and dollops of the mayonnaise. Serve hot. We opt for Grilled Fries on the side.

DOGGONED GOOD CLASSIC DOG

First, you have to start with the kind of dog that's almost gone, a loss that should shame the American meat industry. Once upon a time butchers made wieners by hand, mixing ground—not puréed—beef and pork, stuffing the meat into natural casings, twisting the sausage into strings of links, and smoking the franks lightly. You have to search diligently for these dogs today, but you can find them in scattered meat markets (see "Hot Sources for Dogs and Other Sausages"). The second key to a classic wiener is the topping. You spoon on a heap of pickled relish, add chopped onions if desired, and cover it all with a thin but thorough coat of mustard. We take some liberties with tradition in our preferred brands of relish and mustard, but so did the founders of hot dog art.

SERVES A PARTY

Old-fashioned, casing-stuffed smoked wieners

Hot dog buns, preferably bakery-made
Mustard Relish (page 42), chow chow, or other sweet
    pickle relish with mustard
Chopped onions, optional
Creole mustard or yellow ballpark mustard

Fire up the grill, bringing the temperature to high (1 to 2 seconds with the hand test).

Grill the wieners uncovered for 3 to 5 minutes over high heat until deeply browned, rolling to crisp all surfaces. Toast the buns on the edge of the grill if you wish.

Arrange the dogs on the buns and top with hearty spoonfuls of relish and, if you wish, onions. Add squiggles of mustard to finish them off and serve immediately. Plates aren't necessary, but napkins are.

TECHNIQUE TIP: When you grill a precooked sausage like a hot dog, the goal is to crust the skin and create a bold, contrasting texture between the seared surface and the juicy interior. You don't need to worry about doneness or exact timing, but you do want to roll the

doggie around for a thorough crisping that stops well short of the incineration once popular at wiener roasts. Because of the frequent turning and short cook-ing time, the process works much better on an open rather than covered grill.

HOT SOURCES FOR DOGS AND OTHER SAUSAGES

The O.K. Market in Wahoo, Nebraska, hand-crafts honest-to-goodness dogs daily, using a formula that dates back in inspiration to 1926. Little Rolls Royces of the frankfurter world, Wahoo Wieners combine beef chuck, pork picnic, and a secret spice blend, all wrapped in sheep casings and smoked twice over hickory chips, with a stint of steam-cooking between visits to the smoke-house. Market owner Barb Coenen makes the original dogs in coarse and fine grinds—both a triumph of texture and flavor—and now she also offers garlic, jalapeño, and haba-nero versions that'll make you yelp "wahoo." For a born-again hot dog revelation at a doggoned good value, order by mail from 888-562-8114 or 402-443-3015.

If the mailman doesn't arrive in time, we substitute hefty all-beef hot dogs such as Oscar Mayer Original, Hebrew National, or Vienna Beef, sold in most supermarkets. We avoid low-fat or fat-free wieners for grill-ing. Since there is little or no oil to bind their watery juice, they dry out as fast as a bead of sweat in the Sahara sun.

Beyond dogs, the O.K. Market is a good source for other sausages too, and so is the Aidells Sausage Company. Bruce Aidells and his San Francisco–based business helped fuel the current sausage renaissance, winning justified acclaim for both traditional favorites and inventive flavor combinations. Many of the products make their way to super-market freezer sections, but you'll probably find a broader selection in the mail-order catalog, available by calling 800-546-5795.

CRUNCHY KRAUT DOG

Dressing up a dog is as American as souping up a Chevy. Marlene Dietrich liked her wieners paired with champagne, a combo she called her favorite meal. California cooking pioneer Elena Zelayeta soused her franks with sauterne, mixed in a sauce with mustard and chili or ketchup. Another cookbook author may have imbibed something stronger on the side before developing a hot-dog crown roast, with wieners strung together upright in a circle and the center filled with packaged stuffing mix. For a manly meal—not meant for "a dainty damsel you hope to impress"—*Esquire* offered several suggestions in 1949, including dogs topped with a pile of mashed potatoes. *Better Homes and Gardens* one-upped that notion a decade later in "a new favorite for all ages" called "Nutty Pups," spread with chunky peanut butter and optional pickle relish. We enter this crowded arena with trepidation, sticking with a conservative but sensational blend of bacon, sauerkraut, and thousand island dressing. We make our own dressing for this recipe, but substitute a favorite bottled variety if you wish.

SERVES 4 TO 8

THOUSAND ISLAND DRESSING
½ cup Enriched Mayonnaise (page 38) or other
    mayonnaise
2 tablespoons chili sauce (the ketchup-style sauce),
    Quintessential Ketchup (page 32), or other
    ketchup
1 tablespoon minced onion
1 tablespoon minced green bell pepper
1 tablespoon minced dill pickle, sweet pickle, or drained
    pickle relish
2 teaspoons minced fresh parsley

¾ cup sauerkraut
8 wieners
8 hot dog buns, preferably bakery-made
3 bacon slices, chopped and fried crisp

Prepare the dressing, combining the ingredients in a small bowl. Cover and refrigerate until needed. (The dressing can be made several days in advance if you wish. In that case, don't add the parsley until the day you plan to grill the dogs.)

Fire up the grill, bringing the temperature to high (1 to 2 seconds with the hand test).

In a medium bowl, mix together the sauerkraut with the dressing.

Grill the wieners for about 3 to 5 minutes over high heat until deeply browned, rolling to crisp all surfaces. Toast the buns on the edge of the grill if you wish.

Toss the bacon with the sauerkraut mixture. Place the dogs on the buns and the souped-up sauerkraut over the dogs. Serve immediately. For an accompaniment, try Potluck Macaroni and Cheese Salad.

CHICAGO DOG

Commercial hot dog stands developed some of America's most famous franks. Coney Island vendors concocted various dogs, though the place name stuck on one with a meaty chili or sloppy-Joe sauce. A Texas State Fair stand run by vaudeville entertainers Neil and Carl Fletcher created the corn dog. And Chicago street chefs perfected "the garden on a bun" named for their city, the best of the bunch for grilling at home. Vienna Beef dogs are almost synonymous with this local legend in the Windy City, but substitute your favorite all-beef dog if they're not available.

SERVES 4 TO 8

8 all-beef wieners
8 poppyseed hot dog buns or other hot dog buns,
   preferably bakery-made

Yellow ballpark mustard
Chopped cucumber
Sport peppers, or pepperoncini, chopped
Chopped onion
Chopped red-ripe tomato
Celery salt
Olive Oil Dills (page 44) or other dill pickle spears,
   optional

Fire up the grill, bringing the temperature to high (1 to 2 seconds with the hand test).

Grill the wieners uncovered for 3 to 5 minutes over high heat until deeply browned, rolling to crisp all surfaces. Toast the buns at the same time on the edge of the grill.

Place the dogs on the toasted buns and top each with a good squiggle of mustard. Then pile on, in approximately equal portions, generous spoonfuls of cucumber, peppers, onion, and tomato. Sprinkle celery salt over each bulging bun. Chicago dogs are definitely a two-fisted meal. If the condiments aren't oozing ominously toward your wrists, you haven't heaped them high enough. The side dish of choice is a dill pickle, should you feel the need for anything extra.

THIS DOG'LL HUNT

In 1987 the city of Frankfurt, Germany, celebrated the five hundredth birthday of the hot dog, claiming local wurst meisters developed the popular sausage, appropriately enough, just before Columbus set sail for the New World. The frankfurter party failed to impress descendants of Johann Georghehner, a German butcher from Coburg also given credit for the invention two centuries later, or residents of Wien (Vienna), Austria, who say the term "wiener" clearly establishes the bloodlines of the dog.

Whatever the origin, the sausage found a following in the United States by the late nineteenth century. Probably some enterprising vendors sold their wieners on a bun in that period, perhaps as early as the 1860s or '70s, but the first well-documented instance wasn't until 1904, at the same St. Louis exposition where the hamburger gained budding renown. A Bavarian concessionaire, Anton Feuchtwanger, offered wieners originally as a plain sausage, loaning customers white gloves to hold the piping hot snack. When he found that people walked off with the gloves, and his supply began to get dangerously low, he hired a baker to make long soft rolls as a substitute way of eating the frank.

New Yorkers, as you might expect, won't swallow any baloney about creative hot doggery west of the Hudson. They set their compass on Coney Island as the source of wiener wizardry, maintaining that German butcher Charles Feltman was the real pioneer when he opened a hot dog stand at the amusement park in 1871. It is certain at least that one of Feltman's employees, Nathan Handwerker, made a major contribution to frankfurter frenzy after he started a stand of his own in 1916. The founder of Nathan's Famous cut the price of a Coney dog from a dime to a nickel, and to prove that the cheap franks weren't full of funny stuff, he gave free ones to interns at a nearby hospital on the condition that they would come to his stand in their lab coats.

Today, according to one of America's indefatigable market research firms, 95 percent of all families in the country eat hot dogs at home, at an average rate of approximately eighty per person per year. Consumption reaches a peak between Memorial Day and Labor Day, the main grilling season, when we chow down on five billion franks. As former Texas governor Ann Richards says about such successes, "This dog'll hunt."

NUOVO NORTH END SAUSAGE SANDWICH

Bostonians flock to the city's historic Italian North End for its lively street life, which includes vendors selling hearty sausage sandwiches from carts. This is a zippy home-grilled salute to the street version, overflowing with a crunchy, colorful fennel-and-pepper slaw. For a variation, substitute Portuguese-style linguiça for the Italian sausage.

SERVES 6

FENNEL SLAW
1 large fennel bulb, sliced thin and cut into thin
    matchsticks
1 bell pepper, preferably yellow, cut into thin
    matchsticks
1 carrot, shredded
½ small red onion, cut into thin half-moons
3½ tablespoons olive oil
1 tablespoon red wine vinegar
½ teaspoon Dijon mustard
1 small garlic clove, minced
½ teaspoon kosher salt or other coarse salt

6 fresh uncooked sweet or hot Italian sausages,
    approximately 5 to 6 ounces each
6 Italian rolls or buns or hot dog buns, preferably
    bakery-made
6 thin slices provolone cheese, at room temperature,
    optional

Prepare the slaw, combining the ingredients in a medium bowl. Cover and refrigerate until needed. (The slaw can be made up to 12 hours in advance.)

Fire up the grill for a two-level fire capable of cooking first on high heat (1 to 2 seconds with the hand test) and then on medium heat (4 to 5 seconds with the hand test).

Grill the sausages uncovered for a total of 20 to 25 minutes. First cook the sausages over high heat for 8 to 10 minutes, rolling them every couple of minutes to crisp all sides. Move the sausages to medium heat and continue cooking for 12 to 15 additional minutes. When done, the sausages should be brown, crisp, and thoroughly cooked, but still juicy. If grilling covered, sear all sides of the sausages on high heat uncovered for 3 to 4 minutes; finish the cooking with the cover on over medium heat for 13 to 16 additional minutes. Toast the rolls on the edge of the grill in the last few minutes.

Arrange the sausages in the toasted rolls, tuck cheese in at the side of each if you wish, and top with the slaw. Serve immediately.

TECHNIQUE TIP: Grilling fresh, uncooked sausage is much different from grilling hot dogs or other pre-cooked sausages. You still sear the skin on high heat, but it becomes critical to cook the meat through, which is best accomplished by switching to a moderate temperature. In contrast with dogs, covered grilling works fine with uncooked sausage, but we prefer the results when the initial searing is done open, allowing you to turn the sausage regularly and crisp the entire surface.

BREWED BRATS WITH CARAWAY KRAUT

No town in the country is prepared for the wurst like Sheboygan, Wisconsin, home of a serious sausage festival each August. The king of the encased meats locally is bratwurst, made and consumed in the burg with Wagnerian passion. Our souped-up brats take inspiration from one of the Sheboygan styles.

SERVES 6

BREW MARINADE
12 ounces beer
½ large onion, chopped
3 tablespoons brown mustard
½ teaspoon caraway seed
½ teaspoon ground coriander

Twelve 4- to 5-ounce fresh uncooked bratwursts, halved
lengthwise

Caraway Kraut Relish
2 tablespoons butter
1 small onion, chopped
2 teaspoons caraway seeds
2 teaspoons brown mustard
2 cups drained sauerkraut
Fresh-ground black pepper

6 kaiser rolls or other large rolls, or 6 halved large
slices of rye or sourdough bread
Additional brown mustard
6 thin slices Swiss, provolone, gouda, or Gruyère
cheese
Chopped dill pickle

Prepare the marinade, bringing all the ingredients to a boil in a large saucepan and simmering the mixture for 5 minutes. Add the halved bratwursts to the liquid, reduce the heat to a bare simmer, cover, and cook for 15 minutes. Remove the pan from the heat but leave the brats in the liquid to steep while you heat the grill.

Fire up the grill, bringing the temperature to high (1 to 2 seconds with the hand test).

Prepare the relish, first melting the butter in a medium saucepan over medium heat. Stir in the onion and caraway and cook for 1 to 2 minutes, just until the onion turns translucent. Add the remaining relish ingredients and heat through. Keep the relish warm.

Drain the sausage, discarding the marinade. Split the halved brats in half again, lengthwise, resulting in four sausage spears. Grill the brat pieces uncovered over high heat for about 2 minutes per side, until well browned and crusty but still juicy. Toast the rolls at the same time on the edge of the grill.

Assemble the sandwiches, slathering both sides of each toasted roll with mustard. To the bottom of the roll, add a slice of cheese and build upward, topping each with eight brat pieces and a generous dollop of the relish. Sprinkle chopped dill pickle over all, top with the rest of the roll, and squeeze to mingle juices and ingredients. Repeat with the remaining sandwiches and serve immediately. They are especially good paired with Sprightly Potato Salad.

Technique Tip: In recipes that call for fresh, uncooked sausage, you can usually substitute the same kind of

pre-cooked sausage when available, eliminating the need for a two-level fire and cutting the total grilling time in half. This bratwurst is an exception. Here it's important to start with fresh sausage because of the advance simmering and steeping in beer. Pre-cooked sausage won't absorb the marinade fully and will dry out during the pot-to-grill cooking process.

SPITFIRE SEAFOOD SAUSAGE

Seafood concoctions rank among the top blessings of America's recent rediscovery of sausage. Typically delicate but bountiful in seafaring flavor, the links love a bath in Caribbean spices.

SERVES 6

. . . .

DOG SAUCE MARINADE
2 small onions, chopped very fine by hand, rinsed and
    drained
2 small carrots, chopped very fine by hand
4 green onions, limp tops removed, chopped very fine
    by hand
2 tablespoons minced fresh thyme
½ to 1 fresh Scotch bonnet or habanero chile, minced
    fine, or ½ to 2 teaspoons Caribbean hot sauce
½ teaspoon salt, or more to taste
½ teaspoon fresh-ground black pepper
Juice of 2 medium limes
2 tablespoons white vinegar
2 tablespoons water
6 tablespoons vegetable oil

Six 5- to 6-ounce fresh uncooked mildly seasoned
    seafood sausages
6 long rolls, split, or hot dog buns, preferably
    bakery-made
Shredded lettuce

. . . .

At least 1½ hours and up to 4 hours before you plan to serve the sausages, prepare the marinade, combining the ingredients in a medium

ON A ROLL WITH WIENERS

There really was an Oscar Mayer. A Bavarian immigrant, he got his start in the meat business in 1873 at age fourteen as a "butcher's boy" in Detroit. Over the next ten years Oscar saved enough money to move to Chicago, the slaughterhouse capital of the country, and opened a meat market of his own. He focused at first on Old World sausages and Westphalian ham, but the young entrepreneur soon branched out to bacon and the product that was to turn him into a household name, the wiener. Fame came in the decades ahead through promotion of the skinless hot dog, the common kind today, and clever packaging that extended the shelf life of processed meat and provided opportunities for national distribution.

A frank flair for publicity also helped. Oscar sold his dogs to butcher shops around Chicago out of a "wiener wagon," replete with a German band to attract customer attention. The founder's nephew and advertising manager, Carl Mayer, added a singer to the show, "Little Oscar, the world's smallest chef," who rhapsodized about the "German-style" wieners and then passed out prizes to lucky shop patrons.

Carl topped that trick with a new flourish in 1936 when he replaced the old wagon with the first Wienermobile, destined to develop into an American icon. The original version, a thirteen-foot metal hot dog on wheels, became a familiar sight on the streets of Chicago, and an improved long-distance model soon made a mark throughout the East and Midwest. The company updated the design in the 1950s, incorporating buns for the first time, and eventually increased the fleet to ten, including four on foreign tour.

The contemporary Wienermobile hit the highways in 1995, so aerodognamically sleek that it's theoretically capable of hauling buns at over ninety miles per hour. Weighing in at 100,000 hot dogs (or 10,000 pounds) and now 55 hot dogs (or 27 feet) in length, it features a wiener-shaped dashboard, relish-colored seats, and a complete entertainment system programmed with twenty-one versions of the jingle "Oh, I Wish I Were an Oscar Mayer Wiener." For us at least, it's the Wienie-bago of our dreams.

bowl and whisking in the oil at the end. Place the sausages in a plastic bag. Set aside 1 cup of the marinade to use as a sauce, pour the rest of it over the sausages, and refrigerate.

Fire up the grill, bringing the temperature to medium-high (3 seconds with the hand test).

Drain the sausages, discarding the marinade. Grill the sausages over medium-high heat, rolling them on all sides until lightly browned and just cooked through. Plan on a total cooking time of about 8 to 12 minutes, but it will vary with the density of the sausage. Experiment with one sausage first before you commit yourself to the others, keeping a close eye on it, since such lean sausages can't take overcooking. If grilling covered, cook for about 7 to 10 minutes, or as needed to cook through, turning once midway.

Arrange the sausages on the rolls and top with lettuce. Serve accompanied by the reserved Dog Sauce, allowing each diner to customize the heat.

Aromatic Lamb Sausage Sandwich

Scented with lemon and rosemary, and topped with a medley of grilled veggies, this is a bunful of hearty eating.

SERVES 6

LEMON-ROSEMARY PASTE
½ cup packed fresh rosemary sprigs
⅔ cup olive oil
Zest and juice of 2 lemons
3 tablespoons chopped onion
3 plump garlic cloves
1 tablespoon kosher salt or other coarse salt

Six 5- to 6-ounce fresh uncooked mildly seasoned lamb
    sausages
1 large onion, sliced ⅓ inch thick
1 small eggplant, about 12 ounces, peeled and cut
    lengthwise into ⅓-inch slices
1 large green bell pepper, halved and core removed
6 long rolls, split, or hot dog buns, preferably
    bakery-made
Dijon mustard
Pickled Pepper Hash (page 46), optional, for garnish

· · · · · · · · · · · · · · · · ·

At least 1½ hours and up to 4 hours before you plan to serve the sandwiches, prepare the lemon-rosemary paste. Purée the rosemary with the oil in a blender, preferably, or a food processor. Let the rosemary steep in the oil for 5 to 10 minutes, then strain the mixture to remove the tough little leaves. Return the oil to the blender, add the remaining ingredients, and purée until fairly smooth. The paste will be somewhat soupy. Rub the sausages and vegetables with the paste, place them in a plastic bag, and refrigerate.

Remove the sausages and vegetables from the refrigerator, drain any accumulated liquid, and let them sit covered at room temperature for about 15 minutes.

Fire up the grill for a two-level fire capable of cooking at the same time on both high heat (1 to 2 seconds with the hand test) and on medium heat (4 to 5 seconds with the hand test).

Grill the sausages and vegetables uncovered, starting the sausages on the hot side of the fire for 8 to 10 minutes, rolling them every couple of minutes to crisp all sides. Move the sausages to medium heat and continue cooking for 12 to 15 additional minutes, until brown and crisp but still juicy. Place the vegetables on medium heat while the sausages cook, allowing 16 to 18 minutes for the onions and about 2 minutes less for the eggplant and bell pepper. Turn all the vegetables once. Toast the rolls on the edge of the grill in the last few minutes.

If grilling covered, sear all sides of the sausages on high heat uncovered for 3 to 4 minutes; finish the cooking with the cover on over medium heat for 13 to 16 minutes, turning once midway. Cook the vegetables covered over medium heat, allowing 13 to 15 minutes for the onions and about 2 minutes less for the eggplant and bell pepper.

Take each food off as it is done, slicing the vegetables into thin strips and mixing them together in a medium bowl. Brush each toasted roll with mustard, put the sausages into the rolls, and top each with vegetables. Serve hot, with spoonfuls of Red Pepper Hash on the side if you wish. We like to add Bastille Day Beans, too, for an even heartier meal.

CHICKEN SAUSAGE BURRITO

Southwesterners routinely use flour tortillas to wrap hot dogs, other sausages, and almost anything else edible. We take that notion to one of its natural limits in a spicy twist on franks and beans.

SERVES 6

1½ cups cooked black beans, drained
¾ cup Fired-Up Tomato Salsa (page 88) or other tomato- or tomatillo-based salsa
Six 5- to 6-ounce fresh uncooked chile-laced chicken sausages or similar turkey sausages
Vegetable oil spray
6 Tucson Tortillas (page 113) or other flour tortillas
Minced fresh cilantro, optional

In a small bowl, gently mix together the beans and salsa. Refrigerate the mixture until needed.

Fire up the grill for a two-level fire capable of cooking first on high heat (1 to 2 seconds with the hand test) and then on medium heat (4 to 5 seconds with the hand test).

Spritz the sausages lightly with oil and let them sit covered at room temperature for about 15 minutes.

Grill the sausages uncovered for a total of 20 to 25 minutes. Start the sausages on the hot side of the fire and grill for 5 to 8 minutes, rolling them every couple of minutes to crisp all sides. Move the sausages to medium heat and continue cooking for 15 to 18 additional minutes. When done, the sausages should be brown, crisp, and thoroughly cooked, but still juicy. If grilling covered, sear all sides of the sausages on high heat uncovered for 3 to 4 minutes; finish the cooking with the cover on over medium heat for 12 to 15 minutes, turning once midway.

Place the sausages on the flat tortillas, topping each with some of the beans. Scatter cilantro over the beans if you wish. For eating with your fingers, tuck in one end of the tortilla before rolling and compact it tightly. For serving on plates, roll the tortilla into a tube. Serve hot.

PEANUTS AND CRACKER JACK?
GET REAL.

At every professional baseball park in America, the hometown fans rise to their feet for the seventh-inning stretch and sing about the joys of going out to the ballgame and eating peanuts and Cracker Jack. Silence descends as they sit back down and every mouth in the stadium wraps around another big bite of a dog. Some say that the songwriters had never attended a game, but if that isn't the case they must have followed a vegetarian team. Baseball and hot dogs go together like sin and country music, with season consumption estimated at 26 million franks in 1996 at major-league parks alone. Laid end to end, those dogs would form a mustard-yellow road from Baltimore's Camden Yards to Dodger Stadium in Los Angeles.

Even the name "hot dog" probably owes its debut to baseball. On a chilly April day in 1901 at the New York Polo Grounds, according to the story, catering director Harry Stevens was having trouble selling ice cream and cold sodas. He sent his vendors out to buy dachshund sausages, which they hawked around the park in portable hot water tanks, calling out "Red hot! Get your dachshund sausages while they're red hot!" Up in the press box, sports cartoonist Tad Dorgan found little to inspire him on the field that day, so he drew a caricature of barking dachshund sausages nestled in a roll. Confounded by the German spelling and facing his publication deadline, Dorgan captioned his cartoon "Hot Dogs!" The name stuck on the street and the sausages stayed in the stands.

Humphrey Bogart summed up the gratitude of the nation, saying, "A hot dog at the game beats roast beef at the Ritz." Babe Ruth added a testimony of his own, downing a dozen franks between games of a doubleheader, and another slugger, Boog Powell, sometimes let it all hang out when he came to the plate with his uniform splattered with dog condiments. More recently and respectably, Julia Child went public on the subject, pronouncing the famous Fenway Frank "very good" despite a "wet and soggy" bun.

Even the Japanese can't resist the paired American pastimes. We once got two miniature dogs at a Tokyo baseball game, sold in a cardboard bento-style box labeled in English as a "hot dog set." Proving the fans there have more to learn about the food than the sport, the wienie meal came with a sour sunomono garnish and a fried chicken wing.

SERIOUS STEAKS

PRIMAL PORTERHOUSE

A t a great steakhouse or at your house, steak success starts with shopping. The better you select the meat, the better cook the meat makes you. The country's top steakhouses put extraordinary effort into picking the beef. They insist, of course, on USDA prime grade—almost a no-brainer for a special steak—but they also get obsessive about cattle breeds and crossbreeds, the type of feed, the months on the hoof, the characteristics of the cut, and the process of aging. We review these factors briefly in "Making the Grade" and "Acting Their Age," later in this chapter, but alas, all of us home cooks ultimately have to rely on our meat purveyor to help with the choices. When the shopping goes well, so does the grilling, even in the plainest preparation. We illustrate the point in this simply seasoned prime-grade porterhouse, the American steak lover's favorite cut since the days of the first rowdy chop houses.

SERVES 2 TO 4 OR EVEN MORE

Two 1½-inch-thick prime porterhouse steaks, about 2
    pounds each, preferably dry aged (see "Making the
    Grade," page 185, for shopping advice)
Kosher salt or other coarse salt
Fresh-ground black pepper
4 tablespoons of the highest-quality, freshest butter
    you can locate, such as Plugra (see Technique Tip),
    cut in 4 pats, at room temperature

Generously sprinkle the steaks with salt and pepper and let them sit covered at room temperature for 30 to 45 minutes.

Fire up the grill for a two-level fire capable of cooking first on high heat (1 to 2 seconds with the hand test) and then on medium heat (4 to 5 seconds with the hand test).

When grilling porterhouses, it's important to keep the smaller, more tender section of the steak angled away from the hottest part of the fire. Grill the steaks uncovered over high heat for 2½ to 3 minutes per side. Move the steaks to medium heat, turning them again, and continue grilling for 3 to 4 minutes per side for medium-rare doneness. The steaks should be turned a minimum of three times, more often if juice begins to form on the surface. If grilling covered, sear both sides of the

GRILLING A STEAK

Serious meat loves serious heat. The reason a properly pan-seared steak tastes so great is that the accumulated high heat of the cast-iron or other heavy metal skillet sizzles the steak surface directly, crusting it almost immediately. With a blazing charcoal fire or some fully cranked-up gas grills, you can achieve a similar sear, the first step in transforming a fine steak into a memorable meal. The trick is knowing when and how to cut back the heat to prevent burning the meat.

For superior steaks an inch or more in thickness—cuts such as a porterhouse, T-bone, strip, and rib eye—we suggest a two-level fire capable of cooking on both very high heat (1 to 2 seconds or less with the hand test) and medium heat (4 to 5 seconds with the hand test). Sear the steaks well on each side over high and then move them to medium heat to cook the center through to the desired doneness. You make the temperature transition earlier in some cases than others, like with lean tenderloin medallions that dry out fast over high heat. On the other hand, some thinner, less tender cuts, such as skirt and round steak, thrive over the hot fire and don't need any time at a lower level to cook through. Because buffalo steaks are especially lean, they should never be grilled beyond medium-rare, our strong preference for beef steaks too.

To test for doneness, we cut into the steak and peek. We don't do that randomly, however. We time the cooking precisely as we go along, so we have

meat first on high heat uncovered for 2½ to 3 minutes; finish the cooking with the cover on over medium heat for 5 to 7 minutes, turning the steaks once midway. Transfer the steaks to a platter and immediately top each with butter.

Bring the steaks to the table, slice the meat from the bones in thin strips, and serve hot, making sure to spoon the mingling meat juices and butter on each portion. We nearly always add Steakhouse Tomato Salad and True-Guilt Creamed Spinach, and when in season, buttery corn on the cob.

TECHNIQUE TIP: Well-marbled meat doesn't require added fat for cooking; but a dollop before serving can enhance the taste. Olive oil works fine if you're wary of saturated fat, but good butter is the old home and steakhouse standard. Look for unsalted butter, typically fresher because it doesn't keep well; and try to find a premium brand such as Plugra with low water content and intense flavor. If you need a mail-order source, try Zabar's (800-697-6301) in New York, which carries a variety of superior butters.

a clear sense of when the steak will be ready. There are other, perhaps better ways of checking for doneness, but each presents peculiar problems. The touch test taught to professional chefs works great provided you remember the nuances under fire and your friends don't mind you playing touchy-feely with their food while you talk. A steak is medium-rare when the surface feels like the flesh in the triangle between your thumb and forefinger with your fingers spread apart. You can also check for doneness by inserting an instant-read meat thermometer horizontally through the side of a steak, at least a thick cut. The trouble for us is specifying the right internal temperature to seek. Most authorities today stay safe by saying medium-rare is 145° F, a temperature at which beef looks too done for our tastes. We want to see that a steak is plenty pink, so we peek.

Before grilling, take the chill off all meat. Given current knowledge about the possibility of bacterial contamination, we don't recommend bringing meat fully to room temperature in a home kitchen, but it should sit out for a short spell on the route between the refrigerator and the grill to make sure you don't end up with a cold center. To promote even cooking, we turn steaks at least three times, so that each side gets two periods of direct exposure to the fire. Turn more often as necessary the instant any juice begins to bead on the surface, to keep from losing the flavorful liquid to the fire. Most experts say to let meat sit for a few minutes after cooking and before serving, to allow the juices to settle, but we don't make a point of it in our recipes because it almost always happens anyway in moving food and people to the table.

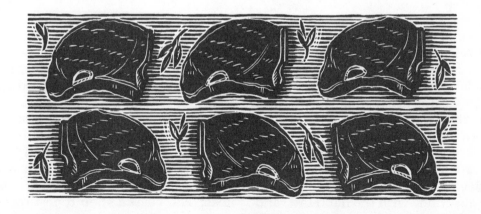

PALE ALE
PORTERHOUSE

A bone-in cut from the back of a steer, combining meat from the top loin and the tenderloin, the porterhouse gained its repute in beery cheer. Eighteenth-century porters in London's Covent Garden market drank ale in taverns that came to be known, in England and America, as "porterhouses." A New York pub owner popularized the steak in the United States during the War of 1812 and gave it a name by association with his porterhouse business. This recipe toasts that legacy with a bit of the brew, added after grilling for a complementary tang.

SERVES 2 TO 4 OR EVEN MORE

Two 1½-inch porterhouse steaks, about 2 pounds each,
    at least choice grade
Kosher salt or other coarse salt

2 tablespoons unsalted butter
1 cup pale ale or other ale-style beer, at room
    temperature
1 to 2 teaspoons Super Wooster Sauce (page 39) or
    other Worcestershire sauce

Generously sprinkle the steaks with salt and let them sit covered at room temperature for 30 to 45 minutes.

Melt the butter in a small saucepan over medium heat. Remove the pan from the heat, stir in the beer and Worcestershire sauce, and reserve the mixture.

Fire up the grill for a two-level fire capable of cooking first on high heat (1 to 2 seconds with the hand test) and then on medium heat (4 to 5 seconds with the hand test).

When grilling porterhouses, it's important to keep the smaller, more tender section of the steak angled away from the hottest part of the fire. Grill the steaks uncovered over high heat for 2½ to 3 minutes per side. Move the steaks to medium heat, turning them again, and continue grilling for 3 to 4 minutes per side for medium-rare doneness. The steaks should be turned a minimum of three times, more often if

juice begins to form on the surface. If grilling covered, sear both sides of the meat first on high heat uncovered for 2½ to 3 minutes; finish cooking with the cover on over medium heat for 5 to 7 minutes, turning the steaks once midway. Transfer the steaks to a platter and immediately top with equal amounts of the beer-butter mixture.

Bring the steaks to the table, slice the meat from the bones in thin strips, and serve hot, making sure to spoon the mingling meat juices, beer, and butter on each portion. Consider Crispy Cumin Fries and St. Louis Italian Salad for sides.

TUSCAN T-BONE WITH FRESH TOMATO RELISH

When you order a *bistecca alla fiorentina* in Italy, the kitchen sends out a giant T-bone for your inspection before the cooking begins, to get your assent to the quality and size of the cut. The chef seasons the meat simply but amply, grills it over hot coals, tops it with fine olive oil, and often serves the steak on a bed of peppery arugula right out of the garden. In our version of the vibrant T-bone, we add a tomato-and-mozzarella relish to round out the Florentine feast.

SERVES 4 OR MORE

TOMATO RELISH
2 cups halved tiny tomatoes, such as yellow and red
    pear tomatoes, Sweet 100s, or cherry tomatoes
6 ounces fresh mozzarella cheese, cut into tiny cubes
3 tablespoons of a premier extra-virgin olive oil
1 tablespoon balsamic vinegar
½ teaspoon kosher salt or other coarse salt, or more to
    taste
2 tablespoons minced fresh basil

Four 1- to 1¼-pound T-bone steaks, 1 to 1¼ inches thick,
   at least choice grade
Kosher salt or other coarse salt
Fresh-ground black pepper

4 to 6 cups arugula
Premier extra-virgin olive oil
Lemon wedges

. . . .

Up to several hours before you plan to grill the steaks, prepare the tomato relish. In a small bowl, combine the tomatoes, mozzarella, oil, vinegar, and salt, and cover and refrigerate the mixture. Reserve the basil for mixing into the relish later.

Generously sprinkle the steaks with salt and pepper and let them sit covered at room temperature for 30 to 45 minutes.

Fire up the grill for a two-level fire capable of cooking first on high heat (1 to 2 seconds with the hand test) and then on medium heat (4 to 5 seconds with the hand test).

Stir the basil into the relish and let it sit at room temperature.

When grilling T-bones, it's important to keep the smaller, more tender section of the steak angled away from the hottest part of the fire. Grill the steaks uncovered over high heat for 2½ to 3 minutes per side. Move the steaks

to medium heat, turning them again, and continue grilling for 2½ to 3 minutes per side for medium-rare doneness. The steaks should be turned a minimum of three times, more often if juice begins to form on the surface. If grilling covered, sear both sides of the meat first on high heat uncovered for 2½ to 3 minutes; finish cooking with the cover on over medium heat for 5 to 6 minutes, turning the steaks once midway.

Transfer the steaks to plates, with the arugula under, over, or on the side, as you wish. Immediately drizzle enough oil over the top of each steak to make it glisten, with little rivers of oil barely pooling on the sides. Accompany with lemons for squeezing over the meat, and sides of the tomato relish, served with a slotted spoon.

TECHNIQUE TIP: Tuscans grill their *bisteccas* over real wood embers, flavoring the meat with a subtle scent of smoke. Partially inspired by the Italian example, a number of American chefs have taken up the technique. Alice Waters, among others, led the way at Chez Panisse in Berkeley, saying she always prefers wood rather than charcoal for a fire when she has really good meat.

MAKING THE GRADE

The U.S. Department of Agriculture inspects all meat sold in the country for safety, a mandatory program financed by taxpayers, and also grades the quality of meat on the request of packers, a voluntary program whose cost gets passed along to consumers. The inspectors grade beef on its anticipated flavor, juiciness, and tenderness, looking in particular at the marbling, or internal distribution of fat. In theory at least and usually in practice, well-marbled steaks taste richer and more complex than leaner ones, and they stay more juicy and tender during cooking.

Only 2 to 3 percent of graded beef ranks as "prime," the top rung of quality, while almost 70 percent falls into the next level of "choice." As meat master Merle Ellis points out in *The Great American Meat Book* (Alfred A. Knopf, 1996), "When most beef is Choice, what choice do you have?" Our answer is choosing where we shop. Savvy, experienced butchers or meat cutters may be able to get you prime steaks on occasion—though most of the best go to restaurants—and they can always guide you toward the most desirable and value-conscious cuts of choice or select meat depending on what you're cooking. As you demonstrate your own seriousness on the subject, you'll find that local pros will help you identify moderately priced choice steaks that rival or even top expensive prime options.

If you don't have that kind of expertise in your neighborhood, consider shopping by mail. Prime Access (800-314-2875) distinguishes itself by shipping dry-aged prime steaks fresh rather than frozen. Balducci's (800-225-3822) dry ages its steaks a little longer than most purveyors, intensifying the beefy flavor. Omaha Steaks International (800-228-9055) provides solid service and value, selecting high-quality choice steaks and wet aging them for mellow taste and tenderness. Check out the company's "private reserve" line, handpicked for superior quality from a vast inventory.

MAYTAG BLUE T-BONE

Blue cheese makes an elegantly traditional topping for a steak, particularly tasty when blended with sweet onions. We favor Iowa's creamy Maytag blue, developed by a washing machine scion whose Holstein hobby got out of hand. If you can't find it locally, go right to the source by calling 800-247-2458, or substitute another domestic or imported blue cheese. The recipe calls for T-bone steaks—much like porterhouses except for a smaller section of tenderloin—but works well with heftier porterhouses or smaller strip steaks, cut like the T-bone from the short loin.

SERVES 4 OR MORE

. . . .

Four 1- to 1¼-pound T-bone steaks, 1 to 1¼ inches thick,
    at least choice grade
Kosher salt or other coarse salt

SWEET ONION TOPPING
2 large sweet onions, such as Vidalia, Maui,
    Texas 1015, or Walla Walla
¼ cup unsalted butter
2 tablespoons vegetable oil
3 tablespoons dry red wine
½ teaspoon kosher salt or other coarse salt

3 ounces Maytag blue cheese or other blue cheese,
    crumbled, at room temperature

. . . .

Sprinkle the steaks lightly with salt, cover them, and let them sit at room temperature for about 30 minutes.

Slice the onions in half from end to end. Slice each half into ¾-inch to 1-inch wedges, cutting through the root end so that the wedges hold together. Melt the butter with the oil in a heavy skillet over medium-low heat. Add the onions to the skillet and gently turn them over in the butter to coat all sides. Cover the skillet and let the onions cook for 12 to 15 minutes, until crisp-tender with some brown edges. Uncover the onions and add the wine and salt. Raise the heat to medium-high and continue cooking until the onions color lightly and the excess liquid evaporates, frequently scraping

up any browned bits from the bottom of the pan. Keep the onions warm.

Fire up the grill for a two-level fire capable of cooking first on high heat (1 to 2 seconds with the hand test) and then on medium heat (4 to 5 seconds with the hand test).

When grilling T-bones, it's important to keep the smaller, more tender section of the steak angled away from the hottest part of the fire. Grill the steaks uncovered over high heat for 2½ to 3 minutes per side. Move the steaks to medium heat, turning them again, and continue grilling for 2½ to 3 minutes per side for medium-rare doneness. The steaks should be turned a minimum of three times, more often if juice begins to form on the surface. If grilling covered, sear both sides of the meat first on high heat uncovered for 2½ to 3 minutes; finish cooking with the cover on over medium heat for 5 to 6 minutes, turning the steaks once midway.

Transfer the steaks to plates, scatter blue cheese over each, top with the warm onions, and serve hot.

BASIL AND SAGE T-BONE

We first tried marinating this hearty T-bone in a fresh basil and sage mixture, but discovered that a dried-herb rub flavored the meat more effectively for grilling. Now we save the fresh seasonings—two of summer's liveliest—for an herb butter that we serve with the steak.

SERVES 4 OR MORE

BASIL AND SAGE DRY RUB
3 tablespoons dried basil
1½ tablespoons dried sage
1 tablespoon kosher salt or other coarse salt
1 teaspoon fresh-ground black pepper

Four 1- to 1¼-pound T-bone steaks, about 1 to 1¼ inches
thick, at least choice grade

BASIL AND SAGE BUTTER
6 tablespoons unsalted butter
2 tablespoons extra-virgin olive oil
¼ cup packed fresh sage leaves
¼ cup packed fresh basil leaves
1 teaspoon mashed anchovy fillet, preferably, or
anchovy paste (see Technique Tip)

Basil and sage sprigs, optional, for garnish

. . . .

At least 2½ hours and up to 12 hours before you plan to grill the steaks, prepare the dry rub, combining the ingredients in a small bowl. Coat the steaks thoroughly with the rub, wrap them in plastic, and refrigerate.

Prepare the herb butter, combining the butter, oil, sage, and basil in a small saucepan. Cook over medium-low heat for about 10 minutes. Let the butter sit for another 10 minutes at room temperature to steep. Strain the butter, and while still hot, mash the anchovy into the butter until dissolved. Reserve the butter.

Remove the steaks from the refrigerator and let them sit at room temperature for about 30 minutes.

Fire up the grill for a two-level fire capable of cooking first on high heat (1 to 2 seconds with the hand test) and then on medium heat (4 to 5 seconds with the hand test).

When grilling T-bones, it's important to keep the smaller, more tender section of the steak angled away from the hottest part of the fire. Grill the steaks uncovered over high heat for 2½ to 3 minutes per side. Move the steaks to medium heat, turning them again, and continue grilling for 2½ to 3 minutes per side for medium-rare doneness. The steaks should be turned a minimum of three times, more often if juice begins to form on the surface. If grilling covered, sear both sides of the meat first on high heat uncovered for 2½ to 3 minutes; finish cooking with the cover on over medium heat for 5 to 6 minutes, turning the steaks once midway.

Spoon the butter over the steaks and serve, garnished with basil and sage if you wish. We like to offer the steaks with Buttermilk Potato Casserole and a crunchy romaine salad.

TECHNIQUE TIP: Having grown up with pungent mass-market anchovies and cheap anchovy paste, the rich and much mellower anchovies common in Italy were a revelation on our first trip there. Salt-packed versions are a particular treat, now available in an

increasing number of American supermarkets or from Zingerman's in Ann Arbor, Michigan (313-769-1625). Italian oil-packed anchovies are our second choice, with fishy anchovy paste coming in dead last. Because the flavor of anchovies becomes harsh under direct high heat, use them in an accompanying butter for steaks rather than in a paste spread on the surface of the meat before cooking.

STEPHAN PYLES'S TEXAS RIB EYE

We've eaten at many great steakhouses, but we've never had a better steak than the chile-crusted gem that Stephan Pyles serves at Star Canyon in Dallas, where it's only one of the specialties. The soft-spoken but outgoing chef attributes the success to prime Texas beef, a roaring hickory fire for grilling, and a robust dry rub. Stephan has kindly provided us with his recipe, but if you prefer a shortcut, he bottles the rub and sells it commercially through the restaurant (214-520-7827). The exuberantly seasoned onion rings are part and parcel of the steak at Star Canyon, and moderately easy to manage on a grill with a side burner, but you won't go hungry or unsatisfied without them.

SERVES 4 OR MORE

COWBOY RUB
¼ cup paprika
¼ cup ground dried medium-hot red chiles, such as a
    mixture of guajillo, pasilla, and chipotle
2 tablespoons kosher salt or other coarse salt
4 teaspoons sugar

Four 1- to 1¼-pound bone-in rib eye steaks, 1 to 1¼
    inches thick, at least choice grade and preferably
    prime grade

RED CHILE ONION RINGS

3 medium onions, cut into ¼-inch slices
Milk
1 cup all-purpose flour
¼ cup paprika
¼ cup ground dried medium-hot red chiles, such as a
    mixture of guajillo, pasilla, and chipotle
¼ cup ground cumin
Kosher salt or other coarse salt
Cayenne pepper
Vegetable oil for deep-frying

At least 2½ hours and up to 12 hours before you plan to grill the steaks, prepare the dry rub, combining the ingredients in a small bowl. Coat the steaks thickly with the mixture. Wrap the steaks in plastic and refrigerate.

About an hour before you plan to grill the steaks, get the onion rings ready for frying. Place the onion rings in a large bowl and cover them with milk. In a paper or plastic sack, combine the flour, paprika, dried chiles, cumin, and salt and cayenne to taste. Pour at least 4 inches of oil in a Dutch oven or other large, heavy pan.

Remove the steaks from the refrigerator and let them sit at room temperature for about 30 minutes.

Fire up the grill for a two-level fire capable of cooking first on high heat (1 to 2 seconds with the hand test) and then on medium heat (4 to 5 seconds with the hand test).

Grill the steaks uncovered over high heat for 2½ to 3 minutes per side. Move the steaks to medium heat, turning them again, and continue grilling for 2½ to 3 minutes per side for medium-rare doneness. The steaks should be turned a minimum of three times, more often if juice begins to form on the surface. If grilling covered, sear both sides of the meat first on high heat uncovered for 2½ to 3 minutes; finish cooking with the cover on over medium heat for 5 to 6 minutes, turning the steaks once midway.

Meanwhile, heat the oil for the onion rings to 375° F. Drain the onions and dredge them in the seasoned flour. Fry the onions, in batches, for 2 to 3 minutes or until crisp. Serve them immediately, piled high on the hot Pyles's steaks.

At Star Canyon, Stephan accompanies his steak with a complexly wonderful wild mushroom–pinto bean ragu. At home, we go simpler, marinating some portobello slices in extra steak rub and cooking them alongside the meat on medium heat. Then we serve wellspiced pintos to round out the feast.

TECHNIQUE TIP: Pyles says one of his secrets with steaks is searing them

quickly over leaping flames from a log fire and then finishing them over less intense embers in another area of the grill. He takes the fiery approach only with meat that can stand up to flame, such as beef and game, and never with anything as delicate as fish.

ACTING THEIR AGE

After USDA grading (see page 185), aging is the second major factor to consider in shopping for steaks. Like good red wine, Parmesan cheese, and outdoor cooks, beef improves with age, gaining in flavor and tenderness over a few weeks as enzymes in the meat break down the muscle tissue. Sometimes butchers apply the technique to average beef to bump up the quality and price a notch, but generally it's reserved for superior cuts.

The most common method is wet aging, accomplished with the steak vacuum-packed in plastic. The process results in little shrinkage and produces soft, tender meat with a mild flavor. Dry aging in cold air, almost a disappearing art, dehydrates beef, reducing its size and increasing its cost. A steak comes out firmer and more concentrated in flavor. Some people consider the less familiar taste too gamy, but most meat mavens agree with William Rice, the authoritative author of *Steak Lover's Cookbook* (Workman, 1997), who calls dry-aged beef robust and nutty.

Rice identifies other factors, apart from grade and aging, that affect steak flavor, but they are often beyond consumer knowledge and control. A label like "corn-fed" means little without the details; a year in an open grass pasture can also advance quality. Some steers are bred for tenderness, particularly Aberdeen Angus, and others for beefy gusto, like Charolais. Young cattle under thirty months old produce better steaks than their elders, who get tougher with time, again emulating the aging of outdoor cooks.

SWANK DELMONICO STEAK

Long before Texans were eating rib eyes in restaurants, America's first fancy dining establishment, Delmonico's in New York, gave its name to the steak. The Swiss owners knew the dish originally as *entrecôte* and they always served it with a rich French sauce, but their family name became more famous in the city than their preparation and it stuck on the steak to this day. In a nod to the Delmonico's tradition of refinement, we developed our own swank rib eye, dusted and then crusted with the intense resonance of wild mushrooms.

SERVES 4 OR MORE

DRIED MUSHROOM DRY RUB
⅔ cup very dry dried wild mushrooms
1 teaspoon kosher salt or other coarse salt
½ teaspoon fresh-ground black pepper

Four 1-pound boneless rib eye steaks, approximately 1
to 1¼ inches thick, at least choice grade

At least 2½ hours and up to 12 hours before you plan to grill the steaks, prepare the dry rub. In a blender on a high setting, grind the mushrooms to fine dust. Let the dust settle a bit before opening the blender. In a small bowl, mix the mushroom dust with the salt and pepper, and coat the steaks lightly with the mixture. Wrap the steaks in plastic and refrigerate.

Remove the steaks from the refrigerator and let them sit at room temperature for about 30 minutes.

Fire up the grill for a two-level fire capable of cooking first on high heat (1 to 2 seconds with the hand test) and then on medium heat (4 to 5 seconds with the hand test).

Grill the steaks uncovered over high heat for 2½ to 3 minutes per side. Move the steaks to medium heat, turning them again, and continue grilling for 2½ to 3 minutes per side for medium-rare doneness. The steaks should be turned a minimum of three times, more often if juice begins to form on the surface. If grilling covered, sear both sides of the meat first on high heat uncovered for 2½ to 3 minutes; finish cooking with the cover on over medium heat for 5 to 6 minutes, turning the steaks once midway.

Serve the steaks hot, maybe with a side of Rich Mix of Mushrooms with Polenta to play up the mushroom flavoring.

RIB EYE WITH ROCKY MOUNTAIN CHIMICHURRI

For being bullish on beef, the United States and Argentina have a lot in common. Spanish colonists introduced cattle in both the Southwest and the grassy pampas of South America, and each area developed a legendary cowboy culture. Gauchos in Argentina flavor their steaks with chimichurri sauce, a fragrant mélange of fresh herbs, and in recent years the idea has caught on big in the Southwest as well. The inspiration for this raspberry-laced version of the sauce comes from the high country of northern New Mexico, where the proprietors of the historic Plaza Hotel in Las Vegas, New Mexico, Kak and Wid Slick, celebrate the local berry harvest annually. Chimichurri brings out the savor in a rib eye, a juicy, beefy steak.

SERVES 4 OR MORE

RASPBERRY MARINADE
1 cup raspberry vinegar
2 garlic cloves, minced
1 teaspoon kosher salt or other coarse salt

Four 1-pound boneless rib eye steaks, approximately 1
    to 1¼ inches thick, at least choice grade

RASPBERRY CHIMICHURRI SAUCE
1 cup minced fresh parsley, preferably Italian flat-leaf
½ cup minced fresh mint
3 tablespoons minced onion

3 garlic cloves, minced
2 to 3 tablespoons raspberry vinegar
1 teaspoon kosher salt or other coarse salt
¼ teaspoon cayenne pepper
¾ cup extra-virgin olive oil

Kosher salt or other coarse salt and fresh-ground black pepper

• • • • • • • • • • • • • • • • • • •

At least 2½ hours and up to 6 hours before you plan to grill the steaks, prepare the marinade, combining the ingredients in a medium bowl. Place the steaks in a plastic bag or shallow dish, pour the marinade over them, and refrigerate. Turn occasionally if needed to marinate evenly.

Prepare the sauce, stirring together the ingredients in a small bowl. Cover and refrigerate the sauce until needed.

Remove the steaks from the refrigerator and drain them, blotting moisture from the surface. Salt and pepper the steaks liberally and let them sit uncovered at room temperature for about 30 minutes.

Fire up the grill for a two-level fire capable of cooking first on high heat (1 to 2 seconds with the hand test) and then on medium heat (4 to 5 seconds with the hand test).

Grill the steaks uncovered over high heat for 2½ to 3 minutes per side. Move the steaks to medium heat, turning them again, and continue grilling for 2½ to 3 minutes per side for medium-rare doneness. The steaks should be turned a minimum of three times, more often if juice begins to form on the surface. If grilling covered, sear both sides of the meat first on high heat uncovered for 2½ to 3 minutes; finish cooking with the cover on over medium heat for 5 to 6 minutes, turning the steaks once midway.

Serve the hot steaks accompanied by the chilled chimichurri sauce, passed separately.

TECHNIQUE TIP: Avoid marinating good steaks too long in vinegar-based marinades. A few hours in this raspberry marinade or the following balsamic version definitely enhances the flavor, but after a while the marinade starts to overshadow the star.

BALSAMIC-GLAZED STRIP STEAK

Nothing is more overused today than balsamic vinegar, dribbled into hundreds of dishes that don't need its potency. On the other hand, nothing can match the magnificence in the right situations, such as this glazed steak. We apply the simple, robust touch to the strip steak, also known as a Kansas City steak (in that city and elsewhere) and a New York strip (except in New York). Whatever you call it where you are, the cut comes from the short loin and is basically a porterhouse or T-bone without the bone and the tenderloin section.

SERVES 4

. . . .

BALSAMIC MARINADE AND GLAZE
¾ cup balsamic vinegar
⅛ cup olive oil
3 plump garlic cloves, chopped

Four 14- to 16-ounce strip steaks, about 1 to 1¼ inches
    thick, at least choice grade

Kosher salt or other coarse salt
Fresh-ground black pepper
Fresh herb sprigs, such as rosemary, sage, thyme, or
    parsley, for garnish

. . . .

At least 2½ hours and up to 6 hours before you plan to grill the steaks, prepare the marinade, combining the ingredients in a medium bowl. Place the steaks in a plastic bag or shallow dish, pour the marinade over them, and refrigerate. Turn occasionally if needed to marinate evenly.

Fire up the grill for a two-level fire

capable of cooking first on high heat (1 to 2 seconds with the hand test) and then on medium heat (4 to 5 seconds with the hand test).

Remove the steaks from the refrigerator and drain them, straining the marinade into a small, nonreactive saucepan. Let the steaks sit uncovered at room temperature for about 30

minutes. Bring the marinade to a boil over medium-high heat and boil vigorously until reduced to about ½ cup of syrupy liquid glaze. Blot the steaks of any moisture on the surface and sprinkle both sides of the steaks with salt and pepper to taste.

Grill the steaks uncovered over high heat for 2½ to 3 minutes per side. Move the steaks to medium heat, turning them again, and continue grilling for 2½ to 3 minutes per side for medium-rare doneness. The steaks should be turned a minimum of three times, more often if juice begins to form on the surface. Brush the steaks with the reduced glaze in the last few minutes of cooking on each side. If grilling covered, sear both sides of the meat first on high heat uncovered for 2½ to

3 minutes; finish cooking with the cover on over medium heat for 5 to 6 minutes, turning the steaks once midway. Brush the steaks with glaze when you turn them and again when they come off the grill.

Serve the steaks hot, garnished with herbs. Soak up the meaty juices with a starch such as San Francisco 'Roni with Rice.

TECHNIQUE TIP: Letting a thick beef steak sit a brief few minutes before cutting allows the heat to spread from the surface inward, cooking the meat a bit more. If you fear that the meat may already be slightly more done than you planned, slicing it immediately will help stop the cooking.

RED-HOT BAYOU-BLACKENED STRIP STEAK

A fine line separates a crisply seared surface from burned food. No one understands that better than legendary New Orleans chef Paul Prudhomme, who developed the wonderful blackening technique and then had to watch imitators turn it into sacrificial charring. In the original version, a combination of very high heat and dry spices produce the crusty blackening without incinerating the food. Prudhomme does it at K-Paul's restaurant in a blazing-hot pan, but the approach works best at home on an outdoor grill.

SERVES 4 OR MORE

Four 14- to 16-ounce strip steaks, about 1 to 1¼ inches
    thick, at least choice grade
2 tablespoons Tabasco sauce or other Louisiana-style
    hot sauce

BAYOU RUB
1 tablespoon Zesty Lemon Pepper (page 31) or other
    lemon pepper
2 teaspoons kosher salt or other coarse salt
2 teaspoons paprika
1 teaspoon ground white pepper
1 teaspoon dry mustard

· · · · · · · · · · · · · · · · · ·

At least 1½ hours and up to 8 hours before you plan to grill the steaks, coat them with the Tabasco sauce. (The longer the steaks sit, the more firepower they acquire, but even the maximum amount of time won't overwhelm good meat.) Use a spatula or the back of a large spoon to spread the Tabasco, or place the steaks in a plastic bag and rub the sauce around on them through the plastic. Wrap the steaks in plastic (if they're not already in it) and refrigerate.

About 30 minutes before you plan to grill the steaks, remove them from the refrigerator and drain them. Combine the dry rub ingredients in a small bowl and coat the steaks with the mixture. Let the steaks sit uncovered at room temperature for about 30 minutes.

Fire up the grill for a two-level fire capable of cooking first on high heat (1 to 2 seconds with the hand test) and then on medium heat (4 to 5 seconds with the hand test).

Grill the steaks uncovered over high heat for 2½ to 3 minutes per side. Move the steaks to medium heat, turning them again, and continue grilling for 2½ to 3 minutes per side for medium-rare doneness. The steaks should be turned a minimum of three times, more often if juice begins to form on the surface. If grilling covered, sear both sides of the meat first on high heat uncovered for 2½ to 3 minutes; finish cooking with the cover on over medium heat for 5 to 6 minutes, turning the steaks once midway.

Serve these sizzlers hot, paired perhaps with Bourbon and Black Walnut Sweet Potato Gratin or red beans and rice.

STRIP STEAK
WITH
ROSEMARY-BOURBON SAUCE

Belgian and French immigrants probably introduced rosemary as a steak seasoning in the United States. We pair the herb here with bourbon, a purely American spice discovered in the Appalachian hills in 1789 by the Reverend Elijah Craig, a Baptist minister.

SERVES 4

Four 14- to 16-ounce strip steaks, about 1 to 1¼ inches
    thick, at least choice grade
2 tablespoons brown mustard
Kosher salt or other coarse salt
Fresh-ground black pepper

ROSEMARY-BOURBON SAUCE
5 tablespoons unsalted butter
2 tablespoons packed chopped fresh rosemary or
    1 tablespoon crumbled dried rosemary
2 tablespoons minced onion
¼ cup bourbon or other similar American whiskey
1 tablespoon Super Wooster Sauce (page 39) or other
    Worcestershire sauce
1 teaspoon brown mustard
½ teaspoon packed brown sugar
1 teaspoon fresh lemon juice

Fresh rosemary sprigs, for garnish

At least 2½ hours and up to 12 hours before you plan to grill the steaks, rub them with the mustard and sprinkle with salt and pepper. Wrap the steaks in plastic and refrigerate.

Prepare the sauce, first melting the butter in a small skillet over medium heat. Stir in the rosemary and

onion and cook until the onions are translucent, about 5 minutes. Stir in the bourbon, remove the skillet from the heat, and let the mixture cool for 10 minutes. Strain the mixture into a small bowl and return it to the skillet. Discard the solids. Add the remaining sauce ingredients to the skillet and cook over medium-low heat for an additional 5 minutes. Keep the sauce warm. (The sauce can be prepared several days in advance and refrigerated. Reheat it before proceeding.)

Remove the steaks from the refrigerator and let them sit at room temperature for about 30 minutes.

Fire up the grill for a two-level fire capable of cooking first on high heat (1 to 2 seconds with the hand test) and then on medium heat (4 to 5 seconds with the hand test).

Grill the steaks uncovered over high heat for 2½ to 3 minutes per side. Move the steaks to medium heat, turning them again, and continue grilling for 2½ to 3 minutes per side for medium-rare doneness. The steaks should be turned a minimum of three times, more often if juice begins to form on the surface. If grilling covered, sear both sides of the meat first on high heat uncovered for 2½ to 3 minutes; finish cooking with the cover on over medium heat for 5 to 6 minutes, turning the steaks once midway.

Serve the steaks hot, garnished with the rosemary. If you have a flair for the dramatic, light the rosemary sprigs just before serving, which looks romantically primal and smells wonderful.

TO DRESS A BEEF-STAKE, SUFFICIENT FOR TWO GENTLEMEN, WITH A FIRE MADE OF TWO NEWSPAPERS

Under that long recipe title, Amelia Simmons gave us the secret to a Colonial American steak. In the first cookbook written in the country, her 1796 *American Cookery*, Simmons instructed readers to put slices of beef in a pewter platter, cover the meat with water, add salt and pepper, and place another platter on top. Then, she said, sit "your dish upon a stool bottom upwards, the legs of such length as to raise the platter three inches from the board; cut your newspaper into small strips, light with a candle and apply them gradually, so as to keep a live fire under the whole dish." When you've burned two newspapers, the steak is done and "butter may then be applied, so as to render it grateful." And grateful we are as well for the modern grill.

A few decades later, Mary Randolph provided a more straightforward recipe for "Beef Steaks" in *The Virginia Housewife Or, Methodical Cook*, one of the premier American cookbooks of the nineteenth century. She broiled half-inch-thick steaks quickly over "fine clear coals," turning the meat frequently. When the steaks were ready, she placed them on top of onion slices in a hot plate, sprinkled on salt, poured on a spoonful each of boiling water and mushroom ketchup, and garnished the dish with gratings of fresh horseradish. Randolph emphasized that "Everything must be in readiness, for the great excellence of a beef steak lies in having it immediately from the gridiron."

Up north in New York in the same era, popular cookbook author Mrs. T. J. Crowen broiled her steaks in a similar way, though turning them only once. In *The American System of Cookery* she suggested starting with a fine sirloin or porterhouse "weighing about two pounds and a half" and flavoring it with salt, pepper, and "a pound of sweet butter." Mrs. Crowen specified leaving the meat slightly red in the center and liked to serve it with tomato ketchup.

MUSTARD-RUBBED TENDERLOIN WITH HORSERADISH CREAM

True to its name, tenderloin is the most tender cut of beef. It's also a little bland in flavor compared to other portions of the short loin and sirloin, so filets or medallions from the section are frequently enlivened with a hearty sauce. Classic French and New Orleans chefs would use a béarnaise or bordelaise, but we prefer the assertive taste of horseradish on a mustard background.

SERVES 6

Six 7- to 8-ounce beef tenderloin medallions, about 1¼ inches thick, at least choice grade
¼ cup Mixed Mustard Plaster (page 28) or ¼ cup Dijon mustard

HORSERADISH CREAM
½ cup sour cream
1 tablespoon prepared horseradish
2 teaspoons grated mild onion or onion juice
¼ teaspoon kosher salt or other coarse salt

At least 1½ hours and up to 8 hours before you plan to grill the medallions, coat them with the mustard paste. Wrap the steaks in plastic and refrigerate.

Prepare the horseradish sauce, combining the ingredients in a small serving bowl. Cover and refrigerate the sauce.

Fire up the grill for a two-level fire capable of cooking first on high heat (1 to 2 seconds with the hand test) and then on medium heat (4 to 5 seconds with the hand test).

Remove the medallions from the refrigerator and let them sit covered at room temperature for 20 to 30 minutes.

Grill the medallions uncovered over high heat for 1 to 1½ minutes per side. Move the steaks to medium heat, turning them again, and continue grilling for 3½ to 4 minutes per side for

medium-rare doneness. The medallions should be turned a minimum of three times, more often if juice begins to form on the surface. If grilling covered, sear both sides of the meat first on high heat uncovered for 1 to 1½ minutes; finish cooking with the cover on over medium heat for 6 to 7 minutes, turning the medallions once midway.

Serve the steaks hot, accompanied by the horseradish sauce. Leftovers make terrific sandwiches, spread with more of the horseradish sauce or a parsley vinaigrette.

GREEN BACKS

We wrap these tenderloin filets in bacon, an old trick for adding tang, and rub them with dried green chile, a newer notion in spicing. The combination brings out the best in both flavors and gives the steak a robust resonance. We serve chopped green chile on the side, or something like our Enchilada Casserole that features the pod, but that's not mandatory east of the Mississippi.

SERVES 6

GREEN BACK RUB
3 tablespoons ground dried green chile (see Technique Tip)
1½ teaspoons paprika
1½ teaspoons ground cumin
1 teaspoon sugar
1 teaspoon kosher salt or other coarse salt

Six 7- to 8-ounce beef tenderloin medallions, about 1¼ inches thick, at least choice grade
6 thin slices uncooked bacon

At least 1½ hours and up to 8 hours before you plan to grill the medallions, prepare the dry rub, combining the ingredients in a small bowl.

Coat the medallions evenly with the rub. Wrap the edge of each steak with a slice of bacon, trimmed to fit if necessary and secured with a toothpick. Cover the medallions and refrigerate.

Fire up the grill for a two-level fire capable of cooking first on high heat (1 to 2 seconds with the hand test) and then on medium heat (4 to 5 seconds with the hand test).

Remove the steaks from the refrigerator and let them sit at room temperature for 20 to 30 minutes.

Grill the medallions uncovered over high heat for 1 to 1½ minutes per side. Move the steaks to medium heat, turning them again, and continue grilling for 3½ to 4 minutes per side for medium-rare doneness. The bacon wrapping will cause more flare-ups than usual; we don't try to tame a little flame when cooking steak, but be prepared to move the meat away from any raging fire. The steaks should be turned a minimum of three times, more often if juice begins to form on the surface. If grilling covered, sear both sides of the meat first on high heat uncovered for 1 to 1½ minutes; finish cooking with the cover on over medium heat for 6 to 7 minutes, turning the medallions once midway.

Serve the steaks hot, with the toothpicks removed. If green chile and enchiladas don't appeal as side dishes, mate the steaks with Bastille Day Beans and slices of sautéed or grilled zucchini and yellow squash.

TECHNIQUE TIP: Ground dried green chile, generally from the New Mexican or Anaheim pod, is just moderately hot and very flavorful. It's becoming more common nationwide, like all spices, but if you can't find it locally, the Santa Fe School of Cooking (800-982-4688 or 505-983-4511) is a good mail-order source.

SAVORY STUFFED TENDERLOIN

When you want to impress the boss or just one-up a colleague, a large, long chunk of tenderloin sends a major message. Here we cut a pocket in the meat and add a spinach and fennel filling for enhanced juiciness, texture, and pure pomp.

SERVES 6 TO 8

FENNEL RUB
4 plump garlic cloves
1½ teaspoons fennel seed
1½ teaspoons kosher salt or other coarse salt
1 teaspoon whole black peppercorns
1 teaspoon crushed dried red chile

2½-pound center-cut beef tenderloin section, at least
    choice grade, with a pocket cut by your butcher or
    following the instructions in the accompanying
    Technique Tip

SPINACH-FENNEL FILLING
1 tablespoon olive oil
1 small fennel bulb, cut into thin matchsticks
3 tablespoons minced red bell pepper
3 tablespoons minced onion
¼ pound fresh spinach, chopped

At least 2½ hours and up to 12 hours before you plan to grill the meat, prepare the spice rub. With a mortar and pestle or small food processor, combine the rub ingredients and purée the mixture. It will be grainy in texture. Coat the tenderloin thoroughly with the rub, massaging it inside and out. Wrap the meat in plastic and refrigerate.

Prepare the filling, first warming the oil in a medium skillet over medium heat. Add the fennel, bell pepper, and onion, and cook until softened, about 5 to 7 minutes. Stir in the spinach, cover

the skillet, and reduce the heat. Cook for an additional 5 minutes or until the vegetables are very tender. If any liquid remains, cook the filling for another 1 to 2 minutes uncovered. The mixture should be moist but not wet. Set it aside to cool.

About 30 minutes before you plan to grill the tenderloin, remove it from the refrigerator and stuff it with the filling. Let it sit covered at room temperature.

Fire up the grill for a two-level fire capable of cooking first on high heat (1 to 2 seconds with the hand test) and then on medium heat (4 to 5 seconds with the hand test).

Grill the tenderloin uncovered over high heat for 4 to 5 minutes, rolling it frequently to sear all sides. Move the tenderloin to medium heat and continue grilling for 9 to 11 minutes for medium-rare doneness, again rolling on all sides. If grilling covered, sear the meat first on high heat uncovered for 4 to 5 minutes, rolling it frequently to sear all sides; finish cooking with the cover on over medium heat for 7 to 10 minutes, turning the tenderloin once midway.

Serve the tenderloin hot, sliced into thick medallions. For a special summer meal, we'd add Colby Cheese and Cornbread Pudding, Fancy Three-Bean Salad, and pull out the stops on dessert with a Grilled Banana Split with Chocolate-Toffee Melt.

TECHNIQUE TIP: For this recipe you want a pocket sliced in the tenderloin, as opposed to a butterfly cut, which would open it like a book. A butcher can do this, though it's easy enough to manage at home too. You want a relatively small slit (about 2 inches) on the surface of the meat, but a large inside cavity for the stuffing. With a sharp medium-size knife, make a small horizontal cut in the center of one of the long sides. Slice deeply into but not through the tender meat. Turn the knife point toward one of the ends and carefully work the blade toward it, again avoiding going all the way through the meat. Repeat the cut in the other direction.

GINGER SIRLOIN WITH TORCHED BANANAS

In the teriyaki heyday of the 1950s and '60s, it wasn't unusual to soak steaks in a ginger and soy marinade for up to a week. That's not a good idea since it turns the meat to mush, but it illustrates the enthusiasm generated by the seasoning combo. Here we go for the same tasty results with a fresh ginger paste. It gives a full-bodied snap to sirloin and also adds gusto to the grilled bananas, which provide a fine, fire-touched foil for the meat.

SERVES 4 OR MORE

FRESH GINGER PASTE
2½ tablespoons minced fresh ginger
2 tablespoons mirin (syrupy sweetened rice wine)
1½ tablespoons soy sauce
1½ teaspoons Asian-style sesame oil
1½ teaspoons ground white pepper
1 plump garlic clove, minced
¼ teaspoon crushed dried hot red chile

Four 1- to 1¼-pound top sirloin steaks, about 1 to 1¼
    inches thick, at least choice grade
4 medium to large bananas, unpeeled

At least 2½ hours and up to 12 hours before you plan to grill the steaks, prepare the paste, combining the ingredients in a small bowl. Set aside 1½ tablespoons of the paste and reserve it. Coat the steaks with the remaining paste, wrap them in plastic, and refrigerate.

Remove the steaks from the refrigerator and let them sit covered at room temperature for about 30 min-utes. Slice the bananas, still in their skins, lengthwise down the middle, and rub the cut surfaces with the reserved paste.

Fire up the grill for a two-level fire capable of cooking at the same time on both high heat (1 to 2 seconds with the hand test) and medium heat (4 to 5 seconds with the hand test).

Grill the steaks uncovered over high heat for 2½ to 3 minutes per

side. Move the steaks to medium heat, turning them again, and continue grilling for 2½ to 3 minutes per side for medium-rare doneness. The steaks should be turned a minimum of three times, more often if juice begins to form on the surface. While the steaks are cooking, grill the bananas uncovered over medium heat, starting them cut-side down for 3 to 4 minutes. Turn the bananas skin-side down and continue grilling for 2 to 3 more minutes, until soft and lightly colored. (The skins will begin to sag around the edges.)

If grilling covered, sear both sides of the meat first on high heat uncov-ered for 2½ to 3 minutes; finish cooking with the cover on over medium heat for 5 to 6 minutes, turning the steaks once midway. While the steaks are cooking, grill the bananas covered, starting them cut-side down for 3 to 4 minutes. Turn the bananas skin-side down and continue grilling for 2 to 3 more min-utes, until soft and lightly colored.

Remove the bananas from their skins and cut them into bite-size chunks. Serve the steaks hot with the bananas on the side. We like to add the crisp contrast of Grant Street Pickled Vegetables to the plate and follow up with a berry-laced shortcake for dessert.

CALIFORNIA CHEESE STEAK

The famous Philadelphia cheese steak wraps thinly sliced, sautéed beef, processed cheese, and optional onions in an Italian roll. Our not-yet-famous California version substitutes grilled meat and Monterey jack cheese, and embellishes the luscious sandwich with peppers, green olives, and meaty portobellos.

SERVES 6

SUNSHINE RUB
1 tablespoon All-'Round Rub (page 23) or 2 teaspoons paprika mixed with 1 teaspoon kosher salt or other coarse salt
1 teaspoon dry mustard

Two 1- to 1¼-pound top sirloin steaks, about 1 to 1¼
   inches thick, at least choice grade

2 fresh mild green chiles, preferably Anaheim or New
   Mexican
1 large portobello mushroom
1 medium red bell pepper
1 medium onion, sliced into ⅛-inch rings
Olive oil
12 thin slices pepper jack cheese, or Monterey jack
   cheese, at room temperature

6 large Italian rolls or oversize bakery-made hot dog
   buns
Sliced green olives

• • • • • • • • • • • • • • • • • •

At least 2½ hours and up to 12 hours before you plan to grill the steaks, prepare the dry rub, combining the ingredients in a small bowl. Coat the steaks lightly with the rub, wrap them in plastic, and refrigerate.

Remove the steaks from the refrigerator and let them sit covered at room temperature for about 30 minutes. Coat the green chiles, mushroom, bell pepper, and onion slices with oil.

Fire up the grill for a two-level fire capable of cooking at the same time on both high heat (1 to 2 seconds with the hand test) and medium heat (4 to 5 seconds with the hand test).

Plan on grilling times of 8 to 10 minutes for the chiles and mushroom, 10 to 12 minutes for the steaks, 14 to 16 minutes for the bell pepper, and 16 to 18 minutes for the onion slices. Grill the steaks uncovered over high heat for 2½ to 3 minutes per side. Move the steaks to medium heat, turning them

again, and continue grilling for 2½ to 3 minutes per side for medium-rare doneness. The steaks should be turned a minimum of three times, more often if juice begins to form on the surface. Grill the vegetables uncovered over medium heat, turning them at least once. Remove each vegetable from the grill as it is done.

If grilling covered, sear both sides of the steak first on high heat uncovered for 2½ to 3 minutes; finish the cooking with the cover on over medium heat for 5 to 6 minutes, turning the steaks once midway. Cook the vegetables covered over medium heat, about 7 to 9 minutes for the chiles and mushroom, 12 to 14 minutes for the bell pepper, and 14 to 16 minutes for the onion slices.

Slice the meat as thin as possible across the grain and place it in a bowl. Pull any loose charred skin from the chiles and pepper and slice them and

the mushroom into thin ribbons. Add all of the vegetables to the meat and combine. Arrange two slices of cheese on each roll and cover with the meat and vegetable mixture. Top the sandwich with the olives and serve.

TECHNIQUE TIP: A good basic dry rub, like our All-'Round, can form the basis for other blends. Here we simply add dry mustard for another dimension of flavor, one that we think particularly enhances this combination of steak and veggies.

KINSEY'S TRI-TIP SANDWICH

Our favorite fictional detective, Sue Grafton's Kinsey Millhone, eats steak out on her stakeouts, usually in the form of a tri-tip sandwich from her favorite neighborhood restaurant. Hardly a mystery meat, though unfamiliar to many people, the tri-tip is a savory section of the sirloin. It makes a bang-up meal in this rendition, one that Kinsey wouldn't kill for but sure would chase down.

SERVES 6

1 tri-tip steak, approximately 2 pounds and 1¼ to 1½ inches thick

BARBECUE SALSA MARINADE
¾ cup Fired-Up Tomato Salsa (page 88) or other tomato-based salsa
¼ cup Classic Kansas City Sauce (page 35) or other tomato-based barbecue sauce (avoid a super-sweet variety)
¼ cup pickling liquid from a jar of pickled jalapeños, or ¼ cup cider vinegar
2 teaspoons dry mustard
½ teaspoon salt

BARBECUE SALSA
3 tablespoons Fired-Up Tomato Salsa (page 88) or other
    tomato-based salsa
3 tablespoons Classic Kansas City Sauce (page 35)
    or other tomato-based barbecue sauce (avoid a
    super-sweet variety)
3 tablespoons Super Wooster Sauce (page 39) or other
    Worcestershire sauce

6 kaiser rolls or other large crusty rolls, split
Thin-sliced onions, for garnish

· · · · · · · · · · · · · · · · ·

The night before you plan to grill the steak, marinate it. With a sharp knife, cut slashes at 1-inch intervals through the thin fat layer that covers one side of the steak, cutting to the meat but not into it. Combine the marinade ingredients in a small bowl. Place the steak in a plastic bag, pour the marinade over it, and refrigerate overnight.

Remove the steak from the refrigerator and drain it, blotting excess marinade from the surface. Let the steak sit covered at room temperature for 30 to 45 minutes. In a small bowl, mix up the Barbecue Salsa and reserve it.

Fire up the grill for a two-level fire capable of cooking first on high heat (1 to 2 seconds with the hand test) and then on medium heat (4 to 5 seconds with the hand test).

Grill the steak uncovered over high heat for 3 minutes per side. Move the steak to medium heat, turning it again, and continue grilling for 12 to 15 minutes for medium-rare doneness, turning at least two more times. Turn more often if juice begins to form on the surface, and also watch for flare-ups, more common with this steak than most because of the fat layer flavoring and protecting one side of the meat. When done, the steak will be darkly crusty on the outside. If grilling covered, sear both sides first on high heat uncovered for 3 minutes; finish the cooking with the cover on over medium heat for 10 to 12 minutes, turning the steak once midway.

When the steak is cooked, slice off its layer of fat. Cut the meat across the grain (across the smaller side) and diagonally, as thinly as possible. Pile the meat on the buns and top it with salsa and onions. If you wish, serve the sandwiches with a side of beans, either the pink *pinquitos* favored in Kinsey country or their close cousins, the more familiar pintos.

TECHNIQUE TIP: The first tri-tip we bought was almost our last, hardly more tender and tasty than a pine knot. We consulted with our meat market, which urged us to try it again with another cut that came out wonderful.

Make sure you get a steak that's well marbled throughout, with an even, thin layer of fat over one side. Marinate the tri-tip for at least 8 hours and up to 24 hours. Don't overcook the steak, and when it's done, carve the thinnest slices your knife will allow, cutting both across the grain and diagonally.

SANTA MARIA BARBECUE

In the northwest corner of Santa Barbara County in California, not far from the home of Sue Grafton's fictional heroine, the Santa Maria Valley Historical Museum's Barbecue Hall of Fame pays tribute to a great local cooking tradition. For several generations, Santa Maria fraternal organizations have staged regular community cookouts. Meat masters spear slabs of sirloin, often tri-tip, on giant metal rods and turn the beef slowly for two to three hours over an open log fire. They're spit-roasting the meat in a technique that's a cross between slow smoking and grilling, but the cooks call it "barbecuing," and a number of knowledgeable fans consider the result the best 'Q in the country.

Sunset cites the Santa Maria legacy to explain why the magazine refers to grilling as barbecuing. A reader complained once that the term *barbecue* should be reserved for the historic method of slow smoking that still thrives in the South and Midwest. The editors responded that "the Western barbecue tradition of grilling" is "equally venerable," going back a century in Santa Maria. We don't want to be disputatious, but the slow-smoked style is considerably older than that and even existed in California before then, in the *barbacoa* enjoyed by the early Spanish settlers. Whatever the merits of the case, the editors were certainly right in their finishing flourish: "Barbecue is like that other American classic, Walt Whitman: it is large, it contains multitudes."

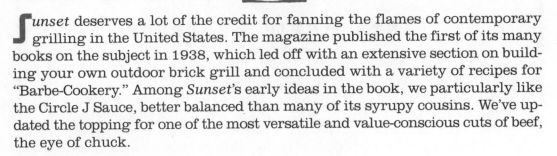

CHUCK STEAK WITH CIRCLE J SAUCE

Sunset deserves a lot of the credit for fanning the flames of contemporary grilling in the United States. The magazine published the first of its many books on the subject in 1938, which led off with an extensive section on building your own outdoor brick grill and concluded with a variety of recipes for "Barbe-Cookery." Among *Sunset*'s early ideas in the book, we particularly like the Circle J Sauce, better balanced than many of its syrupy cousins. We've updated the topping for one of the most versatile and value-conscious cuts of beef, the eye of chuck.

SERVES 4 TO 6

CHILE RUB ROJO
2 tablespoons paprika
1 tablespoon kosher salt or other coarse salt
1 tablespoon ground chipotle chile
1 tablespoon ground mild to medium-hot dried red
    chile, such as New Mexican, ancho, or pasilla, or a
    combination of these chiles
1 teaspoon ground cumin
¾ teaspoon sugar

1½ pounds eye of chuck, cut into long ½-inch-thick
    strips

CIRCLE J SAUCE
¼ cup butter
1 small onion, chopped
1 cup water
¾ cup ketchup
2 tablespoons Super Wooster Sauce (page 39) or other
    Worcestershire sauce
2 tablespoons steak sauce, such as A-1 Original
2 tablespoons minced mixed fresh herbs, such as
    parsley, marjoram, or thyme

1 tablespoon vinegar from a bottle of marinated
   Tabasco peppers, pepper vinegar, or 1 tablespoon
   cider or distilled vinegar with a dash of cayenne
   pepper
2 tablespoons prepared horseradish
1 tablespoon packed brown sugar
2 teaspoons yellow ballpark mustard
¾ teaspoon chili powder
½ teaspoon salt

Thin-sliced green onion rings, for garnish

• • • • • • • • • • • • • • • • • •

At least 1½ hours and up to 12 hours before you plan to grill the steak, prepare the dry rub, combining the ingredients in a medium bowl. Toss the chuck strips with the dry rub. Coat them well, cover, and refrigerate.

Make the sauce, warming the butter in a medium saucepan over medium heat. Add the onion and cook until translucent, about 5 minutes. Stir in the rest of the ingredients and bring the mixture to a boil. Reduce the heat to low, and cook down for 20 to 25 minutes, until the sauce is the consistency of thin ketchup. (The sauce can be made several days ahead. Cool it and refrigerate it, reheating it before serving. Mix in a little additional water if it becomes thick.)

Fire up the grill, bringing the temperature to high (1 to 2 seconds with the hand test).

Remove the meat from the refrigerator and let it sit covered at room temperature for about 15 minutes.

Grill the chuck strips uncovered over high heat for 3 to 4 minutes per side for medium doneness, until just a hint of pink remains at their centers. If grilling covered, cook for 5 to 7 minutes, turning once midway. When the meat is just cool enough to handle, shred it coarsely.

Serve the beef warm with spoonfuls of sauce and a sprinkling of green onions for color. The shredded chuck makes good sandwiches too, stuffed into onion rolls or flour tortillas.

'PEPPA FLANK STEAK

One of the earliest exotic condiments used in American grilling, Jamaican Pickapeppa sauce gets its punch from tangy tamarind, a key ingredient in Worcestershire and several commercial steak sauces today. In this preparation we rub the sweet-sour elixir inside and outside a flank steak and then stuff the meat with bitter greens, a combo almost as splendid as Caribbean sun and sand.

SERVES 4

1¼-pound flank steak

'PEPPA PASTE
3 tablespoons Pickapeppa sauce or mild jerk sauce
1 teaspoon kosher salt or other coarse salt
¾ teaspoon ground dried ginger
¾ teaspoon ground allspice

BITTER GREENS FILLING
1 tablespoon vegetable oil
1 garlic clove, cut into thin slices
6 ounces mustard greens, kale, chard, or spinach, with
    the water that clings to them after washing,
    chopped
3 ounces cream cheese
1½ tablespoons Pickapeppa sauce

At least 2½ hours and up to 12 hours before you plan to grill the steak, place it in the freezer for about 30 minutes to firm it. Using a sharp knife, cut a broad horizontal pocket starting from a small cut, as explained in detail in the Technique Tip on page 205. Carefully cut as wide an opening as you can manage without cutting through the steak.

Prepare the paste, combining the ingredients in a small bowl, and coat the steak with the paste, rubbing it thoroughly inside and out. Wrap the steak in plastic and refrigerate.

Prepare the filling, warming the oil in a medium skillet over medium heat. Stir in the garlic and cook it 1 minute, then add the greens. Reduce

the heat to medium-low, cover, and cook for about 10 minutes, stirring a couple of times to cook the greens evenly. Stir in the cream cheese and Pickapeppa sauce. When the cheese has melted evenly, remove the filling from the heat and let it cool briefly.

About 30 minutes before you plan to grill the steak, remove it from the refrigerator and stuff it with the filling. Let it sit covered at room temperature for about 30 minutes.

Fire up the grill for a two-level fire capable of cooking first on high heat (1 to 2 seconds with the hand test) and then on medium heat (4 to 5 seconds with the hand test).

Grill the steak uncovered over high heat for 2½ to 3 minutes per side. Move the steak to medium heat, turning it again, and continue grilling for 2½ to 3 minutes per side for medium-rare doneness. The steaks should be turned a minimum of three times, more often if juice begins to form on the surface. If grilling covered, sear both sides of the meat first on high heat uncovered for 2½ to 3 minutes; finish the cooking with the cover on over medium heat for 5 to 6 minutes, turning once midway.

Serve the steak hot, slicing it carefully across the grain. For an island dinner, start with rum punches and serve the steak with rice and mango chutney.

TECHNIQUE TIP: The wide surfaces of flank steak make it great for grilling, absorbing flavors readily and providing an optimum proportion of seared surface to juicy interior. It's tasty grilled in the simplest ways, with just a coating of any of our dry spice rubs or a paste such as Mixed Mustard Plaster.

FAJITAS BORRACHAS

To make "fajitas" with sirloin or flank steak, as many people do, is akin to making apple pie with pears. For authenticity and taste alike, start with skirt steak, which Mexican-American cowboys in south Texas named *fajita* for its resemblance to a small sash or girdle (*faja* in Spanish). Decades ago, the *vaqueros* cooked the meat on the range over an open fire and ate it in tortillas for a hearty meal on the go. At home you can amplify the robust beef flavor with rubs and marinades. In this drunken (*borracha*) steak, we soak the meat in a beer-and-citrus mixture and then massage the surface with chili powder and brown sugar.

BORRACHAS MARINADE
12 ounces beer
Juice of 1 orange
Juice of 3 limes
2 tablespoons Super Wooster Sauce (page 39) or other
    Worcestershire sauce

2 skirt steaks, 1 to 1¼ pounds each, trimmed of
    membrane and fat

FAJITAS DRY RUB
1 tablespoon chili powder
1 tablespoon kosher salt or other coarse salt
1 tablespoon packed brown sugar
1½ teaspoons ground cumin

Flour tortillas, warmed
Fired-Up Tomato Salsa (page 88) or other favorite salsa
Avocado slices

At least 2½ hours and up to the night before you plan to grill the fajitas, prepare the marinade, combining the ingredients in a medium bowl. Place the skirt steaks in a plastic bag, pour the marinade over them, and refrigerate.

Remove the meat from the refrigerator and drain it, blotting the surface of moisture. Combine the dry rub ingredients in a small bowl and coat the steaks with the rub. Let the steaks sit covered at room temperature for about 30 minutes.

Fire up the grill, bringing the temperature to high (1 to 2 seconds with the hand test).

Grill the meat uncovered over high heat for 4 to 5 minutes per side, until rare to medium-rare. The steaks should be turned a minimum of three times, more often if juice begins to form on the surface. If grilling covered, cook for 7 to 9 minutes, turning once midway.

Cut the steaks across the grain and diagonally into thin finger-length strips. To serve, pile a platter high with the hot meat and accompany with the tortillas, salsa, and avocado slices. Let everyone help themselves by filling the tortillas with some of the meat and portions of the garnishes.

THREE-PEPPER ROUND STEAK

I n steak au poivre and many a humbler dish, freshly ground or cracked pepper shines as a steak seasoning. It even works wonders on round steak, the basic supermarket favorite. For the most tender results, use top round, avoid overcooking, and slice the meat as thin as possible against the grain.

SERVES 6

TRIPLE-PLAY PEPPER RUB
1 tablespoon whole black peppercorns
1½ teaspoons whole white peppercorns
1½ teaspoons whole pink peppercorns
1½ teaspoons kosher salt or other coarse salt
Scant ½ teaspoon yellow mustard seeds
1½ teaspoons dried onion flakes, optional

1¾- to 2-pound top round steak, about 1 inch thick

At least 2½ hours and up to 12 hours before you plan to grill the steak, prepare the dry rub, coarsely grinding the ingredients in a blender or spice mill. Coat the meat with the spice mixture, wrap the steak in plastic, and refrigerate.

Remove the steak from the refrigerator and let it sit covered at room temperature for about 30 minutes.

Fire up the grill, bringing the temperature to high (1 to 2 seconds with the hand test). Grill the meat uncovered over high heat for 4 to 6 minutes per side, until rare to medium-rare. The steak should be turned a minimum of three times, more often if juice begins to form on the surface. If grilling cov-

ered, cook for about 8 to 10 minutes, turning once midway.

Slice the steak as thin as possible across the grain and serve hot. For a family supper, we suggest adding Sprightly Potato Salad atop some sturdy greens and Mixed Berry Cornbread.

LOVE ME TENDER

Cattle came to the nascent United States from two directions. Spanish explorers and settlers, beginning with Francisco Vásquez de Coronado in 1540, brought rugged Andalusian cattle to the Southwest, where many wandered off and formed wild herds that developed into the famed Texas longhorns. British colonists on the eastern seaboard, within a few years of their arrival, imported stock from England, mainly as beasts of burden to plow fields and pull wagons. The beef from both breeds, tough and stringy, wouldn't fetch much more than a penny a pound at a modern meat market.

Well into the nineteenth century, most American steaks had to be slain a second time before they became edible. Even when steers were bred for meat, they usually had to be driven substantial distances on hoof to a city slaughterhouse, arriving lean and hardened. Inventive cooks developed many ways to tenderize the meat, though few seem very appetizing today. Most people pounded beef into submission, leaving a masticated taste, while others drilled holes and filled them with suet or salt pork, and some relied on a long soak in vinegar.

Cookbook authors of the time generally advised frying steaks until well-done. That's certainly how chuck-wagon cooks prepared their trail-toughened longhorn beef and how the cowhands wanted it. In one oft-told tale, a cowboy ordered a steak at a fancy city restaurant, found some pink in the center, and sent it back to the kitchen with the comment, "I've seen cows git well that was hurt wors'n that."

Railroad transportation, refrigeration, and new breeds of cattle ultimately produced the juicy, well-marbled steaks Americans relish today, usually best when cooked fairly rare. The long quest for tenderness left a legacy, though, on our taste buds. We value that quality so highly, many of us have lost touch with the real beef flavor of old, preferring mushy, bland steaks over chewy, robust meat. As the balladeers say about love, a great steak needs a balance between the tender and the true.

HIGH PLAINS BUFFALO STEAK

You may not have a home where the buffalo roam, but the American bison is making a big comeback in many corners of the country, particularly the western Plains, where they once grazed in great numbers. After dwindling down to hundreds because of senseless slaughter, they now number in the hundreds of thousands, nearly doubling in population in the last ten years alone. The lean and beefy meat—not at all gamy—makes a splendid change from the usual steak, and it's an easy switch since the cuts are close to identical. We don't like most tomato sauces on fine steaks, but this zippy grilled-tomato vinaigrette brings out the best in both the meat and the fruit. Substitute a comparable beef steak here if you wish.

SERVES 4 OR MORE

Four 8- to 10-ounce strip, rib eye, or sirloin buffalo
    steaks, about 1 inch thick
Kosher salt or other coarse salt
Fresh-ground black pepper

GRILLED TOMATO VINAIGRETTE
1 pound small tomatoes, preferably Italian plum
½ cup olive oil
2 tablespoons red wine vinegar
2 teaspoons unsulphured molasses
1 plump garlic clove
1 teaspoon ground cumin
1 teaspoon kosher salt or other coarse salt
½ teaspoon fresh-ground black pepper

Fire up the grill for a two-level fire capable of cooking first on high heat (1 to 2 seconds with the hand test) and then on medium heat (4 to 5 seconds with the hand test).

Salt and pepper the buffalo steaks, cover them, and let them sit at room temperature for 20 to 30 minutes.

Grill the tomatoes uncovered over high heat, turning occasionally until

they are soft with brown, splitting skins and some black spots, about 10 to 12 minutes. If grilling covered, cook for about 8 to 10 minutes, turning once midway.

In a blender, combine the whole tomatoes—skins, cores, and all—with the remaining vinaigrette ingredients. Purée, adjust the seasoning if necessary, and reserve the warm vinaigrette.

Grill the steaks uncovered over high heat for 2 to 2½ minutes per side. Move the steaks to medium heat, turning them again, and continue grilling for 2 to 2½ minutes per side for medium-rare doneness, when the lean meat tastes the best. The steaks should be turned a minimum of three times, more often if juice begins to form on the surface. If grilling covered, sear both sides of the meat first on high heat uncovered for 2 to 2½ minutes; finish the cooking with the cover on over medium heat for 4 to 5 minutes, turning once midway.

Serve the buffalo steaks hot, on pools of the glistening vinaigrette. Kathi Long's Stupendous Baked Beans make a worthy side dish. Any leftover vinaigrette can top romaine, simple grilled veggies, or slices of fresh mozzarella cheese.

TECHNIQUE TIP: Buffalo steaks of 12 ounces or larger, like prime beef, tend to go mostly to restaurants because of limited availability. Cuts like strip, rib eye, or sirloin available to consumers are generally 8 to 10 ounces. Because the meat is denser than beef, people tend to be satisfied with a smaller portion, too. The Denver Buffalo Company, approaching a decade in age, was the first to aggressively and consistently supply buffalo to restaurants and individuals, and it remains an excellent source. The company's meat, raised naturally, finished on grain, and USDA-inspected, can be found frozen in a growing number of supermarkets nationwide or can be ordered by mail (800-289-2833).

Party-Perfect Pork, Lamb, Veal, and Venison

PARTY-PERFECT PORK, LAMB, VEAL, AND VENISON

CHURCH-PICNIC PORK CHOPS

Bill grew up in Texas, where they put dry rubs on the baby food, but Cheryl didn't experience the seasoning technique in Illinois until she was a teenager attending an annual church picnic. One of the local cooks dressed his pork chops with a basic but stalwart blend of dry spices, rubbing in the mixture while a crowd gathered and stared. In an era of plain foods and commercialized condiments, the intensity of the taste and the crispness of the coating brought Cheryl a joy never forgotten. We recapture that early rapture in these simple chops, though our rub today is a little more devilish than the original.

SERVES 6

CHILE RUB ROJO
2 tablespoons paprika
1 tablespoon kosher salt or other coarse salt
1 tablespoon ground chipotle chile
1 tablespoon ground mild to medium-hot dried red
    chile, such as New Mexican, ancho, or pasilla, or a
    combination of these chiles
1 teaspoon ground cumin
¾ teaspoon sugar

Six 10-ounce to 11-ounce bone-in center-cut pork
    chops, about ¾ inch thick
Vegetable oil spray

Classic Kansas City Sauce (page 35), Georgia Grilling
    Sauce (page 36), or other tomato- or mustard-based
    barbecue sauce, optional

At least 1 hour and up to 8 hours before you plan to grill the pork chops, prepare the dry rub, combining the ingredients in a small bowl. Coat the chops with the spice mixture, place them in a plastic bag, and refrigerate.

Fire up the grill, bringing the temperature to medium (4 to 5 seconds with the hand test).

Remove the chops from the refrig-

erator and let them sit covered at room temperature for about 20 minutes.

Spritz the chops with oil and transfer them to the grill. Grill uncovered over medium heat for 20 to 23 minutes, turning several times while cooking. If grilling covered, cook for 17 to 20 minutes, turning once midway. The chops are done when barely white at the center with clear juices. (Don't confuse the colors of the dry rub and the juices.)

Serve the chops hot, with barbecue sauce if you wish. Simply Superb Corn on the Cob makes a worthy accompaniment.

UP-TO-DATE PORK CHOPS

When you're eating "high on the hog," as enlisted men in the military used to say about officers, you're eating tender cuts from the loin, like the chop. This one lives up to the term in all ways, featuring a juicy and tangy filling laden with dates.

SERVES 4

GARLIC PASTE
3 plump garlic cloves, minced
1 tablespoon kosher salt or other coarse salt
1 teaspoon vegetable oil

Four 10-ounce to 12-ounce double-cut boneless pork
  chops, about 1 to 1¼ inches thick, cut with a pocket

DATE FILLING
½ small onion, chopped
¼ pound dates, chopped
¼ cup red wine
2 tablespoons red wine vinegar
1 tablespoon brandy
¼ teaspoon salt, or more to taste
1 tablespoon butter
2 tablespoons chopped walnuts

At least 1 hour and up to 8 hours before you plan to grill the chops, prepare the paste, combining the ingredients in a small bowl. Coat the chops with the paste, wrap them in plastic, and refrigerate.

Make the filling. In a small, heavy saucepan, combine the onion, dates, wine, vinegar, brandy, and salt and simmer the mixture over medium heat for 10 to 15 minutes, until jam-like in consistency. Stir in the butter and walnuts, remove the filling from the heat, and let it cool for at least 20 minutes. (The filling can be made a day ahead and refrigerated. Bring it back to room temperature before proceeding.)

Remove the chops from the refrigerator. Spoon the filling equally into the pocket of each chop, securing with toothpicks if needed. Let the chops sit covered at room temperature for about 30 minutes.

Fire up the grill, bringing the temperature to medium (4 to 5 seconds with the hand test).

Grill the chops uncovered over medium heat for 25 to 28 minutes, turning several times while cooking. If grilling covered, cook for 21 to 24 minutes, turning once midway. The chops are done when barely white at the center with clear juices.

Serve the chops hot, perhaps with Buttermilk Potato Casserole.

BANANA-GLAZED BUTTERFLIED PORK CHOPS

Butterflying pork chops, or cutting them open like a book, doubles their surface area, increasing the flavor impact of a fruity glaze.

SERVES 6

ALL-'ROUND RUB
3 tablespoons paprika
1 tablespoon coarse-ground black pepper
1 tablespoon kosher salt or other coarse salt
1½ teaspoons chili powder
1 teaspoon packed brown sugar
Pinch of cayenne, optional

Six 10-ounce to 12-ounce double-cut boneless pork
   chops, about 1¼ to 1½ inches thick, butterflied by
   your butcher

BANANA GLAZE
1 tablespoon butter
2 large shallots, minced
1 large ripe banana, mashed
½ cup chicken stock
¼ cup orange juice
2 teaspoons Super Wooster Sauce (page 39) or other
   Worcestershire sauce
Kosher salt or other coarse salt
1 teaspoon brown sugar, optional

Vegetable oil spray

• • • • • • • • • • • • • • • • •

At least 1 hour and up to 8 hours before you plan to grill the pork chops, combine the dry rub ingredients in a small bowl. If the chops don't already lie flat, pound them lightly along their "seam." Coat the chops with the spice mixture, place them in a plastic bag, and refrigerate.

Make the glaze. In a small, heavy saucepan, melt the butter over medium heat. Add the shallots and sauté them briefly until translucent. Add the remaining glaze ingredients, reduce the heat to medium-low, and cook for about 10 minutes, stirring frequently. The finished glaze should be thickened but quite pourable.

Fire up the grill, bringing the temperature to medium (4 to 5 seconds with the hand test).

Remove the chops from the refrigerator and let them sit covered at room temperature for about 20 minutes.

Spritz the chops with oil and transfer them to the grill. Grill uncovered over medium heat for 20 to 23 minutes, turning several times and brushing the glaze on the chops in the last 3 to 5 minutes of cooking. If grilling covered, cook the chops for 17 to 20 minutes, turning once midway; glaze the top side during the last 3 to 5 minutes of cooking. The chops are done when barely white at the center with clear juices. (Don't confuse the colors of the dry rub and the juices.) Brush again with glaze as the chops come off the grill.

Serve the chops hot with additional glaze on the side if you wish. We like Bourbon and Black Walnut Sweet Potato Gratin and Southern-style collard greens or mustard greens with the chops.

HOG-WILD ABOUT PORK

One of the oldest domesticated animals on earth—right after dogs—hogs have provided many centuries of great eating. The bounty doesn't always reach the grill, however. Outside the Midwest at least, pork often takes a back seat to beef and chicken on American backyard menus. A griller will slap on a steak one evening for a quick fix of meaty tenderness and then switch to a skinless breast the next night to feel virtuous about saturated fat—without ever stopping to think that a juicy chop could satisfy both yearnings at once. It's time to dig deeper into the country's brimming pork barrel.

Now a much leaner meat than in the past, but still a hearty partner for a broad range of spices and other seasonings, pork presents a wealth of potentials. A number of different cuts grill easily and well, affording variety in tastes and textures, and even the tough, fire-resistant ribs make a magnificent meal with a little extra effort. The advertising jingle says pork is "what's next," but on our patio table it's often what's now.

Our only caution is to watch the heat so you don't scorch the meat. In general, pork grills best on a medium fire, which crusts the surface slowly to allow thorough cooking of the interior. You want a just-white center with clear juices, measuring 155° F to 160° F on an instant-read meat thermometer. We usually check for doneness by cutting into the meat and peeking inside, in the same way we describe for steaks, but we use a thermometer more regularly for pork than beef, particularly with a thick tenderloin. Along with pre-cooked ham steaks, tenderloin is an exception to the rule about heat; it thrives on a two-level fire, searing quickly on high before finishing on medium. It's also exceptional in flavor compared to many foods, but only one of several pork cuts that make us want to pig out grandly on the grill.

MOJO-MARINATED PORK TENDERLOIN

A lively herb- and citrus-perfumed cross between a sauce and a relish, Cuban-inspired *mojo* makes a potent marinade and sauce for tenderloin. We picked up the idea in south Florida, but the Caribbean sparkle seems even finer in a cooler clime.

SERVES 6

MOJO MARINADE AND SAUCE
Juice of 3 large oranges (approximately 1½ cups)
Juice of 2 large limes
6 tablespoons olive oil
⅓ cup minced fresh parsley
2 tablespoons minced fresh oregano
1 teaspoon salt
2 plump garlic cloves, minced

Two 12-ounce to 14-ounce sections of pork tenderloin
Avocado slices and red-ripe tomato slices, for garnish

At least 2½ hours and up to the night before you plan to grill the pork tenderloins, mix the *mojo* ingredients in a small bowl. Place the tenderloins in a plastic bag and pour about two-thirds of the *mojo* over them; cover the remaining *mojo*. Refrigerate the pork and the remaining *mojo*, which will become a sauce.

Remove the pork from the refrigerator, drain it, and blot any excess moisture from it. Let the pork sit covered at room temperature for 20 to 30 minutes.

Fire up the grill for a two-level fire capable of cooking first on high heat (1 to 2 seconds with the hand test) and then on medium heat (4 to 5 seconds with the hand test).

Transfer the tenderloins to the grill, arranging them so that the thin end is angled away from the hottest part of the fire. Grill the tenderloins uncovered on high heat for 3 minutes, rolling them on all sides. Move the tenderloins to medium heat and estimate the rest of the cooking time according to the thickness of the meat.

Thin tenderloins (about 1½ inches in diameter) need an additional 10 to 12 minutes on medium, and fat ones (about 2½ inches in diameter) require up to 25 minutes. Continue rolling the meat on all sides for even cooking. The pork is done when its internal temperature reaches 155° F to 160° F.

If grilling covered, sear the tenderloins first on high heat uncovered for 3 minutes, rolling them on all sides. Finish the cooking with the cover on over medium heat for at least 8 to 10 minutes (for 1½-inch-diameter meat) or up to 20 minutes (for 2½-inch-diameter meat).

Carve the pork into thin slices, garnish with avocado and tomato, and serve hot accompanied by the reserved *mojo*. For a fiesta, serve a salad of black beans, rice, corn, and red bell peppers followed by Piña Colada Pineapple Spears.

TECHNIQUE TIP: Consider turning this tenderloin into a sandwich, the way most *mojo*-flavored pork is served in Florida. On toasted Cuban bread or a split crusty roll, pile the meat, a slice of ham, black beans, and sharp cheese, all topped with more *mojo*. Immensely sloppy and intensely good, the sandwich demands lots of napkins.

CRUSTY PORK TENDERLOIN WITH WINTER BERRY SAUCE AND CUCUMBER-MINT SALAD

Cooks often use a marinade or wet paste rub on pork tenderloin, as we did in the previous recipe, to help keep the lean meat juicy. Dry rubs work equally well as long as you avoid overcooking at too high a temperature, and they also yield a crustier surface. We enhance the effect here with a tartly sweet sauce based on garnet-red lingonberries—long a staple in Swedish settlements in the upper Midwest and now widely available—and a light, refreshing salad to offset the richness of everything else.

SERVES 6

SUGAR AND SPICE
2 heaping teaspoons ground allspice
1½ teaspoons turbinado sugar or ¾ teaspoon sugar
1 heaping teaspoon kosher salt or other coarse salt
¾ teaspoon ground dried mild red chile, such as
    New Mexican
¾ teaspoon ground cinnamon
½ teaspoon ground white pepper

Two 12-ounce to 14-ounce sections of pork tenderloin

CUCUMBER-MINT SALAD
1 cup white vinegar
⅔ cup sugar
¼ cup minced fresh mint, or more to taste
½ teaspoon kosher salt or other coarse salt
⅛ teaspoon ground white pepper
2 cucumbers, peeled, seeded, and chopped
½ cup diced green bell pepper

BERRY SAUCE
3 tablespoons butter
2 large shallots, minced
½ teaspoon Sugar and Spice (dry rub)
1 cup lingonberries, fresh, bottled, or frozen, or fresh
    or canned whole-berry cranberry sauce

• • • • • • • • • • • • • • • • • •

At least 2 hours and up to 12 hours before you plan to grill the pork tenderloins, prepare the Sugar and Spice dry rub, combining the ingredients in a small bowl. Set aside ½ teaspoon of the rub, then coat the tenderloins with the remaining rub. Place the tenderloins in a plastic bag and refrigerate.

Prepare the salad, first combining in a large bowl the vinegar, sugar, mint, salt, and white pepper. Stir until the sugar dissolves. Mix in the cucumbers and bell pepper and refrigerate the salad for at least an hour. (The salad can be made a day ahead, covered, and refrigerated, but leave out the mint until just before serving.)

Prepare the sauce, first warming the butter in a small skillet. Stir in the shallots and the reserved dry rub and sauté briefly until the shallots are translucent. Add the berries and warm the mixture through. (The sauce can be made a day ahead, covered, and refrigerated. Reheat before serving.)

Remove the pork from the refrigerator and let it sit covered at room temperature for 20 to 30 minutes.

Fire up the grill for a two-level fire capable of cooking first on high heat (1 to 2 seconds with the hand test) and then on medium heat (4 to 5 seconds with the hand test).

Transfer the tenderloins to the grill, arranging them so that the thin end is angled away from the hottest part of the fire. Grill the tenderloins uncovered on high heat for 3 minutes, rolling them on all sides. Move the tenderloins to medium heat and estimate the rest of the cooking time according to the thickness of the meat. Thin tenderloins (about 1½ inches in diameter) need an additional 10 to 12 minutes on medium, and fat ones (about 2½ inches in diameter) require up to 25 minutes. Continue rolling the meat on all sides for even cooking. The pork is done when its internal temperature reaches 155° F to 160° F.

If grilling covered, sear the tenderloins first on high heat uncovered for 3 minutes, rolling them on all sides. Finish the cooking with the cover on over medium heat for at least 8 to 10 minutes (for 1½-inch-diameter meat) or up to 20 minutes (for 2½-inch-diameter meat).

Carve the pork in thin slices and arrange them on individual plates atop small pools of the berry sauce. Spoon the cucumber-mint salad on the side and serve immediately.

TECHNIQUE TIP: Most meats sear best when they first go on the grill, but pork is a partial exception. The usual method works fine, but you can also start chops, tenderloin, and other cuts on a lower heat to cook through and then crisp them over higher heat at the end. We often take this alternative approach on a gas grill, where it's easy to jack up the temperature quickly, but we don't recommend it in the recipes because it's difficult to do on a charcoal grill and we try to keep the instructions applicable to all kinds of equipment.

PEPPERED PORK WITH BRANDIED MUSTARD CREAM

A wonderful steak au poivre one evening got us thinking about the possibility of a similar approach with pork. The result tastes much different, but shares the succulence.

SERVES 6

TRIPLE-PLAY PEPPER RUB
2 tablespoons whole black peppercorns
1 tablespoon whole white peppercorns
1 tablespoon whole pink peppercorns
1 tablespoon kosher salt or other coarse salt
¾ teaspoon yellow mustard seeds
1½ teaspoons dried onion flakes, optional

Two 12-ounce to 14-ounce sections of pork tenderloin

BRANDIED MUSTARD CREAM
1 tablespoon butter
2 medium shallots, chopped
¼ cup brandy
½ cup whipping cream
1 tablespoon Dijon mustard
Kosher salt or other coarse salt

At least 2 hours and up to 12 hours before you plan to grill the tenderloins, prepare the dry rub, coarsely grinding the ingredients in a blender or spice mill. Coat the tenderloins with the spices, place them in a plastic bag, and refrigerate.

Prepare the sauce, first melting the butter in a medium skillet over medium heat. Stir in the shallots and sauté briefly until softened. Add the brandy and continue cooking several additional minutes until it reduces by half. Add the cream and the mustard and heat through. Taste and add salt as you wish. Keep the sauce warm.

Remove the tenderloins from the refrigerator and let them sit covered at

room temperature for 20 to 30 minutes.

Fire up the grill for a two-level fire capable of cooking first on high heat (1 to 2 seconds with the hand test) and then on medium heat (4 to 5 seconds with the hand test).

Transfer the tenderloins to the grill, arranging them so that the thin end is angled away from the hottest part of the fire. Grill the tenderloins uncovered on high heat for 3 minutes, rolling them on all sides. Move the tenderloins to medium heat and estimate the rest of the cooking time according to the thickness of the meat. Thin tenderloins (about 1½ inches in diameter) need an additional 10 to 12 minutes on medium, and fat ones (about 2½ inches

in diameter) require up to 25 minutes. Continue rolling the meat on all sides for even cooking. The pork is done when its internal temperature reaches 155° F to 160° F.

If grilling covered, sear the tenderloins on high heat uncovered for 3 minutes, rolling them on all sides. Finish cooking with the cover on over medium heat for at least 8 to 10 minutes (for 1½-inch-diameter meat) or up to 20 minutes (for 2½-inch-diameter meat).

Carve the pork in thin slices and arrange them on individual plates atop small pools of the sauce. A spring dinner might include asparagus spears, San Francisco 'Roni with Rice, and strawberry-rhubarb cobbler or crisp.

CHILEHEAD PORK AND CORN SKEWERS

No one makes better dry spice mixtures than North of the Border in Santa Fe, probably because founders Gayther and Susie Gonzales rank among the most headstrong chileheads on earth. This dish emulates their union, combining pork and corn from Susie's native Iowa with ground red chile from Gayther's New Mexico homeland. We use a home version of their dried chipotle chile rub for the kebobs, but you can mail-order the original or many other dynamite blends from 505-982-0681.

SERVES 6

1¾ to 2 pounds pork tenderloin, cut into 1-inch cubes
2 ears of corn, fresh or frozen, husked and cut into 12
    rounds about ¾ inch thick
12 ounces beer

GONZO CHIPOTLE RUB
1 tablespoon paprika
1½ teaspoons ground chipotle chile
1½ teaspoons ground mild to medium-hot dried red
    chile, such as New Mexican, ancho, or pasilla, or a
    combination of these chiles
1½ teaspoons granulated garlic
1 teaspoon salt
1 teaspoon turbinado sugar or ½ teaspoon sugar

Metal skewers, preferably 2 per kebob
1 large onion, cut into chunks
½ medium red bell pepper, cut into 1-inch squares
½ medium yellow or orange bell pepper, cut into 1-inch
    squares
½ medium mild fresh green chile, such as poblano, or
    ½ green bell pepper, cut into 1-inch squares

Vegetable oil spray

• • • • • • • • • • • • • • • • • •

At least 1½ hours and up to 4 hours before you plan to grill the kebobs, place the pork and corn in a bowl or plastic bag, pour the beer over them, and refrigerate. Prepare the dry rub, combining the ingredients in a small bowl, and reserve.

Remove the pork and corn from the refrigerator and drain them, discarding the marinade. Separate the corn from the pork cubes, cover the corn, and reserve it. Coat the pork with the dry rub, using at least half and up to all of it, depending on your chile-head credentials. Let the pork sit covered at room temperature for about 20 minutes.

Fire up the grill, bringing the temperature to medium (4 to 5 seconds with the hand test).

Divide the pork cubes, corn, and the onion, bell pepper, and green chile chunks in 6 portions and thread them on the skewers, preferably using 2 skewers per kebob to hold the ingredients securely while cooking. Arrange several pepper and chile pieces together on the skewers, preferably in alternating colors, and push them together tightly so that they don't dry out before the other ingredients are cooked through. Spritz the kebobs with the oil.

Grill the kebobs uncovered over medium heat for 14 to 16 minutes, until the meat is barely white at its center with clear juices. (Don't confuse the colors of the dry rub and the juices.) Turn the kebobs every few minutes to cook the food evenly on all sides. If grilling covered, cook for 11 to 13

minutes, turning once midway.

Serve the kebobs immediately. A Gonzales feast would begin with margaritas and tortilla chips served with several salsas made from North of the Border mixes. We would add Smokin' Chipotle Coleslaw, Mixed Berry Cornbread, and a citrus sorbet to finish off the meal.

TECHNIQUE TIP: While we recommend bamboo skewers for the finger foods featured in "Happy-Hour Skewers and Spreads," we usually switch to metal versions for main-course kebobs. Even after soaking, bamboo skewers can burn over the time needed to cook big cubes of meat, and they also sometimes lack the piercing power for such dense ingredients. With metal skewers, look for square-sided or twisted shafts so that the food itself doesn't twist in the wind. Double-shafted metal skewers, now popular, or a pair of side-by-side skewers, anchor the food even more securely.

RED-EYE TENDERLOIN SANDWICH

Southern cooks taught the country the glories of coffee flavor in red-eye gravy, traditionally served at breakfast over ham, biscuits, and grits. We experimented with the pork and coffee combo in creating this sandwich, which swaggers with an eye-opening marinade and rub.

SERVES 6

RED-EYE MARINADE
¾ cup brewed coffee
3 tablespoons cider vinegar
1 tablespoon unsulphured molasses

Two 12-ounce to 14-ounce sections of pork tenderloin

CALICO PEPPER RELISH (Optional)
6 tablespoons finely diced red bell pepper
6 tablespoons finely diced yellow bell pepper
¼ cup finely diced red onion
2 teaspoons minced pickled jalapeño plus 1 tablespoon
    juice from the jar or can
2 teaspoons cider vinegar
2 teaspoons coarse-ground yellow mustard seeds
1 teaspoon unsulphured molasses

RED-EYE RUB
2 tablespoons coarse-ground coffee beans
1 tablespoon coarse-ground black pepper
1 teaspoon kosher salt or other coarse salt

1 cup Classic Kansas City Sauce (page 35) or other
    tomato-based barbecue sauce
6 large kaiser rolls or large bakery-made buns, split

• • • • • • • • • • • • • • • • • •

At least 2 hours and up to 12 hours before you plan to grill the pork, prepare the marinade, combining the ingredients in a small bowl. Place the tenderloins in a plastic bag, pour the marinade over them, and refrigerate.

Prepare the relish, if you wish, mixing together all the ingredients in a small bowl. Refrigerate the relish for at least 30 minutes to allow the mustard seeds to soften and mellow.

Remove the tenderloins from the refrigerator and drain half of the marinade into a small saucepan, discarding the rest. Blot the tenderloins of excess moisture.

Prepare the dry rub, combining the ingredients in a small bowl, and coat the tenderloins with the spice mixture. Let them sit covered at room temperature for 30 minutes.

Bring the marinade to a boil over high heat and boil vigorously for several minutes, until reduced by one-half. Stir the barbecue sauce into the boiled marinade and reserve as the sauce.

Fire up the grill for a two-level fire capable of cooking first on high heat (1 to 2 seconds with the hand test) and then on medium heat (4 to 5 seconds with the hand test).

Transfer the tenderloins to the grill, arranging them so that the thin end is angled away from the hottest part of the fire. Grill the tenderloins uncovered on high heat for 3 minutes, rolling them on all sides. Move the tenderloins to medium heat and estimate the rest of the cooking time according to the thickness of the meat. Thin tenderloins (about 1½ inches in diameter) need an additional 10 to 12 minutes on

medium, and fat ones (about 2½ inches in diameter) require up to 25 minutes. Continue rolling the meat on all sides for even cooking. The pork is done when its internal temperature reaches 155° F to 160° F. Toast the rolls on the edge of the grill.

If grilling covered, sear the tenderloins first on high heat uncovered for 3 minutes, rolling them on all sides. Finish the cooking with the cover on over medium heat for at least 8 to 10 minutes (for 1½-inch-diameter meat) or up to 20 minutes (for 2½-inch-diameter meat).

Carve the pork in thin slices. Brush the toasted rolls lightly with sauce and pile them high with pork. Top with generous dollops of pepper relish, if using it, then squish the rolls lightly so the juices mingle, and serve. Hoppin' John Salad with Tabasco Dressing makes a jazzy side dish.

Spice Rack Pork Loin with Persimmon Chutney

Because of its thickness, pork loin benefits from butterflying when you're grilling the meat. It also benefits in this case from a spice rack of seasonings and a tangy chutney garnish. Apricots or peaches can replace persimmons out of season.

Serves 4

1½ pound section of pork loin, butterflied by your
    butcher

Spice Rack Dry Rub
2 garlic cloves
2 teaspoons fennel seed
1½ teaspoons ground cardamom
1½ teaspoons kosher salt or other coarse salt
1½ teaspoons ground coriander
1½ teaspoons dried ginger
1½ teaspoons packed brown sugar
⅛ teaspoon cayenne pepper

PERSIMMON CHUTNEY
⅓ cup chopped onion
⅓ cup golden raisins
Zest and juice of ½ lemon
¼ cup cider vinegar
3 tablespoons packed brown sugar
¼ teaspoon ground coriander
¼ teaspoon dried ginger
1½ cups persimmon pulp, from about 4 medium
    persimmons (see Technique Tip)

Minced green onion tops, optional, for garnish

. . . .

At least 2 hours and up to 12 hours before you plan to grill, prepare the pork. Pound it lightly along the butterfly seam, enough to flatten the meat laid open, but not so much that the pork separates into two pieces. Continue pounding if needed for an even thickness, about 1½ inches for an average loin section.

Prepare the dry rub, first mashing together the garlic and fennel seeds into a paste with a mortar and pestle. Add the other rub ingredients, or if your mortar is small, mix the garlic-fennel mixture into the other rub ingredients in a bowl. Coat the pork with the rub, wrap it in plastic, and refrigerate it for at least 2 hours and preferably at least twice that long.

For the chutney, combine all the ingredients except the persimmon pulp in a heavy, nonreactive saucepan and simmer over medium heat until the mixture reduces to a syrupy consistency, about 10 to 15 minutes. Add the persimmon pulp and reduce the heat to low. Cook an additional 5 minutes or until thick, stirring frequently. The chutney can be served warm, at room temperature, or chilled. (The chutney can be made several days in advance, covered, and refrigerated.)

Remove the pork from the refrigerator and let it sit at room temperature for about 30 minutes.

Fire up the grill, bringing the temperature to medium (4 to 5 seconds with the hand test).

Grill the pork uncovered over medium heat for 50 to 55 minutes, turning at least 3 times or more often if juice begins to form on the surface. If grilling covered, cook for 35 to 40 minutes, turning once midway. The pork is done when its internal temperature reaches 155° F to 160° F on an instant-read thermometer.

Serve the pork sliced, with spoonfuls of chutney on the side and, if you wish, a scattering of minced green onion over the meat. Try pairing the pork with green beans topped with chopped pine nuts.

TECHNIQUE TIP: Most persimmons arrive at supermarkets as hard as a horseshoe and as puckery as an unwanted kiss. Treat them like avocados, letting them ripen at room temperature until soft, when the mellow flavor peaks.

THE MANLY ART

A recent Barbecue Industry Association survey showed that men grill more often than women, by a margin approaching two to one. It wasn't always that way. Not many years ago, men did all the grilling.

At least that's what both sexes claimed to want. James Beard spoke up on the subject early, as he often did, saying in 1941 that "outdoor cooking is man's work and man-sized menus and portions should be the rule." *Sunset* backed that point of view a few years later, adding the explanation that "two good whiffs" of sizzling meat "make a man want to try his own hand at barbecue cookery. And once he dons cap and apron, he is on his way to becoming a master chef."

Esquire didn't see chefdom as much of a motivation for men, but did find a lot of deeper drives at work. The magazine's 1949 *Handbook for Hosts* (Grosset & Dunlap) states that every adult male retains "some of the qualities of a small boy. He is secretly plagued by a spirit of pyromania and he delights in playing with fires." Wives encourage the impulse, the editors maintain, because they are sick of cooking and would never be expected to do any outdoors. "A woman presiding over a barbecue grill looks as incongruous as a man engaged in doing a trifle of lacy tatting." Bachelors have even more reason than husbands to pursue the craft, according to the theory, because it attracts the opposite sex. *Esquire* supports this claim with a story about a single man grilling a steak for breakfast and arousing the interest of his sunbathing neighbor, "a most delectable young lady, unchastely clad in the briefest possible sun suit."

Even great women grillers preferred to put men behind the grate. The best of them all perhaps in the early years, Helen Evans Brown, took that position on numerous occasions, including in her 1951 *Patio Cook Book* (Ward Ritchie Press). "Let there be but one, at least but one at the grill. Whenever possible let it be a man. No smart woman ever officiates at a broiler in male company. If she knows the subject well she'd best keep her knowledge to herself—the only thing a man resents more than being told by another man how best to cook a steak is to be directed by a woman."

PORK STEAK WITH MRS. DULL'S LIVELY SAUCE

The food editor of the Atlanta *Journal*, Mrs. S. R. Dull presented the original version of the delightful sauce in this dish in her seminal 1928 *Southern Cooking*. We apply our adaptation of the vinegar-based sauce to pork steaks, but it invigorates any straightforward pork preparation.

SERVES 6

ALL-'ROUND DRY RUB
1½ tablespoons paprika
1½ teaspoons coarse-ground black pepper
1½ teaspoons kosher salt or other coarse salt
¾ teaspoon chili powder
½ teaspoon packed brown sugar
Pinch of cayenne, optional

Six ¾- to 1-inch-thick pork steaks, cut from the sirloin,
    about 10 to 12 ounces each

MRS. DULL'S LIVELY SAUCE
3 tablespoons butter
½ small onion, minced
1 garlic clove, minced
¾ cup cider vinegar
¾ cup water
5 tablespoons ketchup (see Technique Tip)
¼ cup chili sauce (the ketchup-style sauce)
1½ tablespoons Super Wooster Sauce (page 39) or other
    Worcestershire sauce
Zest and juice of ½ lemon
½ teaspoon dry mustard
¼ teaspoon kosher salt or other coarse salt

At least 1½ hours and up to 6 hours before you plan to grill, prepare the dry rub, combining the ingredients in a small bowl. Coat the pork with the dry rub, wrap it in plastic, and refrigerate.

Prepare the sauce, first warming the bacon drippings in a heavy, nonreactive saucepan over medium heat. Add the onion and sauté until very soft, about 5 to 7 minutes. Stir in the garlic and cook another minute. Add the rest of the ingredients and bring the mixture to a boil. Reduce the heat to medium-low and cook for 30 to 35 minutes. The sauce will remain thin. (The sauce can be made several days in advance, covered, and refrigerated. Reheat it before serving.)

Fire up the grill, bringing the temperature to medium (4 to 5 seconds with the hand test).

Remove the pork from the refrigerator and let it sit covered at room temperature for about 20 minutes.

Grill the pork uncovered over medium heat for 20 to 25 minutes, turning at least three times while cooking. Turn the steaks more frequently if juice begins to form on the surface. If grilling covered, cook for 17 to 20 minutes, turning once midway. The steaks are done when barely white at the center with clear juices. (Don't confuse the colors of the dry rub and the juices.)

Serve the steaks hot, drizzled with sauce, along with Buttermilk Potato Casserole or mashed sweet potatoes. Leftover sauce will keep for weeks and isn't likely to go wasting.

TECHNIQUE TIP: In most recipes that call for ketchup we state a preference for the homemade Quintessential Ketchup in the chapter "An American Grill Pantry." Mrs. Dull's sauce is a case where we actually prefer the sweeter, less complex taste of store-bought brands. The blander base of the commercial product keeps it in the background while still providing enough strength to balance the vinegar's assertiveness.

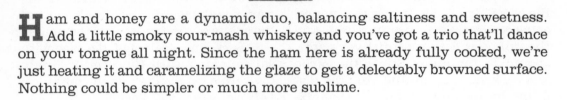

HONEY-BOURBON HAM STEAK

Ham and honey are a dynamic duo, balancing saltiness and sweetness. Add a little smoky sour-mash whiskey and you've got a trio that'll dance on your tongue all night. Since the ham here is already fully cooked, we're just heating it and caramelizing the glaze to get a delectably browned surface. Nothing could be simpler or much more sublime.

SERVES 4

HONEY-BOURBON HAM GLAZE
3 tablespoons honey
2 tablespoons bourbon or other similar American
    whiskey
1 tablespoon soy sauce
2 garlic cloves, roasted and mashed
½ teaspoon dry mustard

Two 1-pound fully cooked bone-in ham steaks, about
    ½ inch thick

Prepare the glaze, combining the ingredients in a food processor.

Fire up the grill, bringing the temperature to high (1 to 2 seconds with the hand test).

Grill the steaks uncovered over high heat for 7 to 9 minutes, turning once midway and brushing with the glaze, and glazing again in the last couple of minutes of cooking. If grilling covered, cook for 6 to 8 minutes, glazing and turning in a similar manner. If you wish, pour any remaining glaze over the ham steaks after taking them from the grill. Serve hot.

MEZCAL MAGIC
BABY BACK RIBS

Like bourbon, good Mexican mezcal has an underlying tone of smooth smokiness that's absent in its more refined cousin, tequila. We take advantage of that quality in these ribs, pairing its resonance with the smoldering warmth of chipotle chiles, dried over wood fires. Most big liquor stores today carry mezcal, and any of the imported brands is worthy of this dish, but you can substitute tequila without losing all of the magic.

SERVES 4
. . . .

¼ cup mezcal or tequila
Four 1¼-pound slabs pork baby back ribs, the thin
        membrane on the ribs' lower side stripped off

CHILE RUB ROJO
¼ cup paprika
2 tablespoons kosher salt or other coarse salt
2 tablespoons ground chipotle powder
2 tablespoons ground mild to medium-hot dried red
        chile, such as New Mexican, ancho, or pasilla, or a
        combination
2 teaspoons ground cumin
1½ teaspoons sugar

MEZCAL-CHIPOTLE BARBECUE SAUCE
2 tablespoons bacon drippings or butter
1 medium onion, chopped
2 cups Quintessential Ketchup (page 32) or other
        ketchup
1 cup plus 2 tablespoons mezcal or tequila
1 cup water
¼ cup canned chipotle chiles in adobo sauce, any whole
        chiles minced
¼ cup orange juice

3 tablespoons unsulphured molasses
2 teaspoons dry mustard
2 teaspoons chili powder
½ teaspoon kosher salt or other coarse salt

• • • • • • • • • • • • • • • • • • • •

At least 6 hours and up to 24 hours before you plan to grill, bake the ribs. Preheat the oven to 300° F. Drizzle the mezcal over the ribs and rub it in thoroughly. Combine the dry rub ingredients in a small bowl and coat the ribs liberally with the spice mixture.

Wrap the ribs tightly in two layers of foil and bake for 1 hour. Cool the ribs, opening the foil to speed the process. Re-wrap the ribs in the foil and refrigerate them for at least 4½ hours.

Prepare the sauce, first melting the bacon drippings in a large, heavy saucepan over medium heat. Add the onion and sauté it until soft, about 5 minutes. Add the ketchup and 1 cup of the mezcal, reserving the remaining 2 tablespoons. Stir in the rest of the sauce ingredients and bring the mixture to a boil. Reduce the heat and simmer it for 20 to 25 minutes, stirring occasionally, until reduced to the consistency of thin ketchup. Just before removing the sauce from the heat, stir in the remaining 2 tablespoons of the mezcal.

Reserve the sauce at room temperature if you plan to grill the ribs within the hour, or refrigerate it. (The sauce can be made several days in advance, covered, and refrigerated. Thin with a little water if it is too thick to brush easily.)

Fire up the grill, bringing the temperature to medium (4 to 5 seconds with the hand test).

Remove the ribs from the refrigerator and let them sit at room temperature for about 30 minutes.

Grill the ribs uncovered over medium heat for 25 to 30 minutes, turning every 8 to 10 minutes. Baste the ribs with sauce in the last 5 minutes of cooking. The ribs are done when very tender with a surface that's crisp in some spots and gooey with sauce in others.

Serve the ribs hot with more sauce and perhaps Colby Cheese and Cornbread Pudding, Tucson Tortillas, coleslaw, and icy beer.

ALL RIBBING ASIDE

Pork ribs bring out the best of our atavistic instincts, luring us to grab up a messy slab of bones with our hands and gnaw with unmannered abandonment. It's mainly the magnificent taste, of course, but the pleasure of the pursuit—as we deftly nab that last morsel of meat—certainly adds something to the pleasure of the palate. In our least circumspect moments we do it indoors, particularly in restaurants, but all unabashed rib eaters prefer the great outdoors, where our primitive ids are in closer communion with our ancestors.

Ribs resist going outside, however, at least for quick grilling. The people who cook them that way, as some do, must have the incisors of saber-tooth tigers. Even baby backs, the smallest cut, take substantial cooking time at low to moderate temperatures to break down their tough muscle fibers. Slow smoking in the old barbecue fashion accomplishes the job with lip-smacking success, but similar low-heat strategies in a covered grill often yield wimpy results and can be frustrating to control in charcoal models.

After testing a range of approaches to grilling ribs, we finally settled on baking them first in an oven or covered gas grill—easily accomplished the night before or the morning of a rib-out—and then finishing them over an open outdoor fire. Don't do the pre-cooking by boiling or microwaving, as some people suggest, because you'll leave much of the flavor in the kitchen in a pool of grease. As the recipes indicate, we generally wrap the ribs and appropriate seasonings in foil before baking, a method that allows the meat to absorb spice while rendering some of the fat, and then we glaze the rack at the end for a crisply gooey exterior.

Baby backs are usually the ribs of choice for grilling, simply for size and time considerations. They don't come from little piggies and they aren't more tender than other cuts, just more manageable. Demand, rather than quality, drives the price above the larger spareribs, which take longer to cook and can be clumsy in size for grilling. Either provides ageless joy when you pick them apart with your hands and teeth.

Coco-Glazed Baby Backs

We're nuts for coconut, even more so in savory dishes like these crispy and gooey baby backs than in desserts.

SERVES 4

3 tablespoons rice vinegar

3 tablespoons Dijon mustard

1 teaspoon Chinese chile paste or chile-garlic paste, or
   ¼ teaspoon cayenne pepper

Four 1¼-pound slabs pork baby back ribs, the thin
   membrane on the ribs' lower side stripped off

COCO GLAZE

14- to 15-ounce can unsweetened coconut milk

3 tablespoons hoisin sauce

2 tablespoons honey

2 tablespoons Dijon mustard

1 teaspoon Chinese chile paste or chile-garlic paste or
   ¼ teaspoon cayenne pepper

All-Star Pickled Starfruit (page 45), optional, for
   garnish

At least 6 hours and up to 24 hours before you plan to grill, bake the ribs. Preheat the oven to 300° F. Combine in a small bowl the vinegar, mustard, and chile paste. Rub the ribs liberally with the mixture.

Wrap the ribs tightly in two layers of foil and bake for 1 hour. Cool the ribs, opening the foil to speed the process. Re-wrap the ribs in the foil and refrigerate them for at least 4½ hours.

Make the glaze. In a large, heavy saucepan, combine the ingredients and bring to a boil over high heat. Reduce the heat and simmer the glaze for 20 to 25 minutes, until reduced to the consistency of thin syrup. Reserve the glaze at room temperature if you plan to grill the ribs within the hour, or refrigerate it. (The glaze can be made

several days in advance, covered, and refrigerated. Thin with a little water if it is too thick to brush easily.)

Fire up the grill, bringing the temperature to medium (4 to 5 seconds with the hand test).

Remove the ribs from the refrigerator and let them sit at room temperature for about 30 minutes.

Grill the ribs uncovered over medium heat for 25 to 30 minutes, turning every 8 to 10 minutes. Brush the ribs with glaze in the last 5 minutes of cooking. The ribs are done when very tender with a surface that's crisp in some spots and gooey with glaze in others.

Serve the ribs hot. They look impressive piled on a platter garnished with the pickled starfruit.

JAVA BONES

These spareribs jump with a double jolt of java, provided by a combination of a coffee marinade and a rub of ground coffee beans and spices. The mix juices up baby backs too, cooked according to the instructions in the previous recipes, or you can convert any of those baby-back preparations to spareribs following the approach described here.

SERVES 4 TO 6

1 cup brewed coffee
Four slabs pork spareribs, "St. Louis cut" (trimmed of the chine bone and brisket flap), each 3 pounds or less

JAVA RUB
6 tablespoons ground coffee beans
2 tablespoons paprika
2 tablespoons turbinado sugar or 1 tablespoon sugar
2 tablespoons kosher salt or other coarse salt
1 tablespoon ground cinnamon
1 tablespoon ground allspice
2 teaspoons dried ginger

Classic Kansas City Sauce (page 35) or other tomato-based barbecue sauce

. . . .

At least 8 hours and up to 24 hours before you plan to grill, bake the ribs. Preheat the oven to 300° F. Drizzle the coffee over the ribs and rub it in thoroughly. Combine the dry rub ingredients in a small bowl and coat the ribs liberally with the spice mixture.

Wrap the ribs tightly in two layers of foil and bake for 1½ hours. Cool the ribs, opening the foil to speed the process. Re-wrap the ribs in the foil and refrigerate them for at least 6 hours.

Fire up the grill, bringing the temperature to medium (4 to 5 seconds with the hand test).

Remove the ribs from the refrigerator and let them sit at room temperature for about 30 minutes.

Grill the ribs uncovered over medium heat for 30 to 35 minutes, turning every 8 to 10 minutes. Brush the ribs with sauce in the last 5 minutes of cooking. The ribs are done when very tender with a surface that's crisp in some spots and gooey with glaze in others.

Serve hot in a ribfest with Potluck Macaroni and Cheese Salad, St. Louis Italian Salad, and Campfire Classic S'mores.

STOUT COUNTRY RIBS

Stout in flavor even before a soak in stout, country ribs feature a few mouthfuls of hearty pork loin, usually reserved for roasting. One meaty rib satisfies an average indoor appetite, but twice that many usually disappear outside.

SERVES 4

. . . .

8 individual pork country ribs, each about 7 to 8
    ounces

STOUT MARINADE
12 ounces stout or other hearty beer
¼ cup cider vinegar
4 garlic cloves, chopped

COUNTRY RIB RUB
1½ tablespoons chili powder
1½ teaspoons fresh-ground black pepper
1 teaspoon ground cinnamon
1 teaspoon kosher salt or other coarse salt

Georgia Grilling Sauce (page 36) or other mustard-
    based barbecue sauce, optional

About 1 hour before you plan to grill the ribs, begin their preparation. Preheat the oven to 325° F. Place the ribs, meatier-side down, in a shallow 9-by-12-inch baking dish. Combine the marinade ingredients in a medium bowl and pour the mixture over the ribs.

Cover the dish tightly and bake for 45 to 50 minutes.

Fire up the grill, bringing the temperature to medium (4 to 5 seconds with the hand test).

Remove the ribs from the liquid, discarding it. Combine the rub ingredients, and when the ribs are cool enough to handle, coat them with the rub.

Grill the ribs uncovered over medium heat for 12 to 15 minutes, turning several times. The ribs are done when very tender with a crisp surface.

The ribs are tasty as they are, hot and "dry," but if you want to serve a sauce on the side, we suggest a mustard-based one.

HELLENIC SHISH KEBOBS

Americans will put anything on a skewer and call it a shish kebob, but the Greek and other Mediterranean immigrants who first popularized the idea and the name of the dish never used any meat except lamb. It's still an Olympian way to string together a merry meal.

SERVES 6

2 pounds lamb leg or sirloin, cut into 1¼-inch cubes
1 medium onion, minced
2 cups dry red wine
3 tablespoons olive oil

SHISH KEBOB RUB

1 tablespoon crumbled dried marjoram or oregano
1 tablespoon lemon zest
1½ teaspoons kosher salt or other coarse salt
1 teaspoon ground cumin
½ teaspoon fresh-ground black pepper

Metal skewers
12 small onions, such as "boiling" onions, par-cooked
    until nearly tender
1 large green bell pepper, cut into 1-inch squares
1 large yellow, orange, or red bell pepper, cut into
    1-inch squares

Fresh marjoram or oregano sprigs, optional, for
    garnish

· · · · · · · · · · · · · · · · · ·

At least 2½ hours and up to 12 hours before you plan to grill, place the lamb cubes in a plastic bag. Cover them with the onion, wine, and oil and refrigerate.

Fire up the grill, bringing the temperature to medium-high (3 seconds with the hand test).

Remove the lamb cubes from the refrigerator and drain them, discarding the liquid. Prepare the dry rub, combining the ingredients in a small bowl. Toss the lamb with the rub, cover, and let sit at room temperature for about 20 minutes.

Avoiding crowding, thread the lamb cubes on skewers, adding 1 or 2 onions and a few pepper pieces per skewer.

Grill the kebobs uncovered over medium-high heat for 6 to 9 minutes for medium-rare doneness. Turn often to cook on all sides. If grilling covered, cook for 5 to 7 minutes, turning once midway.

Serve the kebobs hot, on a bed of brown rice pilaf if you wish.

TECHNIQUE TIP: For variety, substitute chunks of lamb sausage for some of the loin cubes. The sausage can be marinated, dry-rubbed, or both along with the rest of the meat, but if it's already highly seasoned, we'd skip the extra flavoring. The cooking time and temperature remain the same.

SHASHLIK WITH POMEGRANATE MARINADE

Today you don't hear much about shashlik, the old Russian version of shish kebob, but it used to be a favorite in outdoor cooking circles until around the time that Senator Joe McCarthy started skewering alien influences instead of food. With the Cold War on ice now, the dish deserves revival.

SERVES 6

SHASHLIK MARINADE
2 cups fresh-squeezed or bottled pomegranate juice, preferably, or cranberry juice
½ cup minced fresh mint
3 tablespoons olive oil
4 plump garlic cloves, minced
1½ teaspoons dried ginger

2 pounds lamb leg or sirloin, cut into 1½-inch cubes
12 button mushrooms
Olive oil
Metal skewers
1 large orange or 2 medium oranges, skins on, cut into 12 chunks
Kosher salt or other coarse salt

Minced fresh mint, for garnish
Pomegranate seeds, optional, for garnish

At least 4 hours and up to 12 hours before you plan to grill, prepare the marinade, combining all the ingredients in a small bowl. Place the lamb cubes in a plastic bag, pour the marinade over the lamb, and refrigerate.

Fire up the grill, bringing the temperature to medium-high (3 seconds with the hand test).

Remove the lamb cubes from the refrigerator and drain them, discarding the marinade. Let the lamb sit at room temperature for about 20 minutes. Coat the mushrooms with oil.

Avoiding crowding, thread the lamb cubes on skewers, mixing in the mushrooms and orange chunks equally. Salt the kebobs lightly.

Grill the kebobs uncovered over medium-high heat for 6 to 9 minutes for medium-rare doneness. Turn often to cook on all sides. If grilling covered, cook for 5 to 7 minutes, turning once midway.

Sprinkle mint over the kebobs and maybe pomegranate seeds as well in the fall when the fresh fruit is available. Serve hot, perhaps on Russian kasha, hulled buckwheat kernels cooked like rice and sold in whole-food stores.

ELKO LEG OF LAMB

Around the turn of the twentieth century, Basque immigrants from the Pyrenees brought their sheepherding skills and food customs to the high country of Idaho, Nevada, and California. The shepherds are usually with their flocks, but occasionally come into towns like Elko for a few days of frolic and feasting. Local boarding houses cater to their tastes with bounteous preparations such as this leg of lamb. Most people roast lamb leg, but it's also wonderful grilled if you butterfly the meat to reduce its thickness.

SERVES 8

ELKO MARINADE
½ cup olive oil
½ cup dry sherry
½ medium onion, minced
6 plump garlic cloves, minced
3 bay leaves, crumbled
¼ cup minced fresh tarragon or 2 tablespoons dried
    tarragon
1 teaspoon kosher salt or other coarse salt

4½-pound to 5-pound leg of lamb, boned, butterflied,
    and pounded to uniform thickness, about 1½ inches
Sprigs of fresh tarragon, optional, for garnish

At least 4 hours and up to the night before you plan to grill, prepare the marinade, combining the ingredients in a small bowl. Coat the lamb with the marinade, wrap it in plastic, and refrigerate.

Remove the lamb from the refrigerator, drain the marinade, and discard it. Blot the lamb of excess moisture and let it sit covered at room temperature for about 45 minutes.

Fire up the grill for a two-level fire capable of cooking first on high heat (1 to 2 seconds with the hand test) and then on medium heat (4 to 5 seconds with the hand test).

Grill the lamb uncovered over high heat for 2½ to 3 minutes per side. Move the lamb to medium heat, turning it again. Continue grilling for 12 to 16 minutes for rare to medium-rare doneness, turning at least two more times. Turn more often if juice begins to form on the surface. If grilling covered, sear both sides first on high heat uncovered for 2½ to 3 minutes; finish cooking with the cover on over medium heat for 10 to 13 minutes, turning once midway.

Serve the lamb hot, maybe with Buttermilk Potato Casserole, green beans cooked with more garlic, and crusty bread. Leftovers can go into Lamb and Pine-Nut Salad on Grape Leaves.

MINT JULEP LAMB CHOPS

Residents of western Kentucky like mutton barbecued in the old slow-smoked way. For young, tender lamb, they would enjoy this approach, which toasts the Bluegrass State with its signature drink. Don't cook the chops beyond medium-rare or they lose flavor.

SERVES 4

MINT JULEP MARINADE
1 cup bourbon or other similar American whiskey
½ cup minced fresh mint
2 teaspoons vegetable oil
1 teaspoon kosher salt or other coarse salt

8 loin lamb chops, about ¾ to 1 inch thick

BLUEGRASS STATE SAUCE
1 cup Super Wooster Sauce (page 39) or other
    Worcestershire sauce
½ cup bourbon or other similar American whiskey
½ cup white vinegar
2 tablespoons packed brown sugar
2 teaspoons fresh-ground black pepper
2 garlic cloves, minced
Kosher salt or other coarse salt

Mint sprigs, optional, for garnish

At least 1½ hours and up to 4 hours before you plan to grill the lamb, prepare the marinade, combining the ingredients in a small bowl. Place the lamb chops in a plastic bag, pour the marinade over them, and refrigerate, turning occasionally if needed to submerge all of the chops.

Prepare the sauce, combining the ingredients in a small, nonreactive saucepan. Simmer the mixture over medium-low heat for 10 to 15 minutes and reserve. (The sauce can be made several days in advance, covered, and refrigerated. Reheat before serving.)

Fire up the grill for a two-level fire capable of cooking first on high heat (1 to 2 seconds with the hand test) and then on medium (4 to 5 seconds with the hand test).

Remove the chops from the refrig-erator and drain them, discarding the marinade but leaving as much mint as possible clinging to the chops. Let the chops sit uncovered at room temperature for about 15 minutes.

Grill the chops uncovered over high heat for 1 to 1½ minutes per side. Move the chops to medium heat, turning them again, and continue grilling for 2 to 2½ minutes per side for medium-rare doneness. If grilling covered, sear both sides of the meat first on high heat uncovered for 1 to 1½ minutes; finish the cooking with the cover on over medium heat for 4 to 5 minutes, turning once midway.

Serve the chops hot with a drizzle of the sauce. Steamed new potatoes, greens with a lemony vinaigrette, and Honeyed Rainbow Fruit Kebobs complement the lamb nicely.

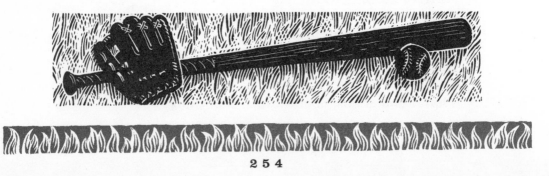

DIJON-DEVILED LAMB CHOPS

Mustard may not seem demonic as a seasoning by today's standards, but it has long been one of the main ways to flavor a "deviled" dish. These tender rib chops, identifiable by their long, slender bones, start on the grill under a mustard wrap and then get coated with bread crumbs for their last few minutes of cooking, producing a crunchy, golden-brown crust.

SERVES 4

¼ cup Dijon mustard
3 garlic cloves, minced
8 frenched lamb rib chops, ¾ to 1 inch thick
   (see Technique Tip)

DEVILED CRUMB COATING
¾ cup dry bread crumbs
1 teaspoon kosher salt or other coarse salt
¼ teaspoon cayenne pepper

Vegetable oil spray

At least 1 hour and up to 4 hours before you plan to grill the lamb, combine the mustard and garlic. Rub the mustard mixture over the lamb chops to coat them heavily, wrap the chops in plastic, and refrigerate.

Prepare the crumb coating, combining the ingredients on a plate.

Fire up the grill for a two-level fire capable of cooking first on high heat (1 to 2 seconds with the hand test) and then on medium (4 to 5 seconds with the hand test).

Remove the chops from the refrigerator and let them sit at room temperature for about 15 minutes.

Transfer the chops to a well-oiled grate. Grill the chops uncovered over high heat for 1 to 1½ minutes per side. With tongs, dunk each side of the chops in the bread crumb mixture. Spritz the chops with oil. Return the chops to the grill, turning them again, and continue grilling for 2 to 2½ minutes per side at medium heat for medium-rare doneness. If grilling covered, sear both sides of the meat first on high heat uncovered for 1 to 1½ minutes; then dip the chops in the crumb coating, spritz with oil, and finish the cooking with the

cover on over medium heat for 4 to 5 minutes, turning once midway.

Serve hot, perhaps with roasted garlic mashers and Broccoli Salad.

TECHNIQUE TIP: If your supermarket says it doesn't sell individual lamb rib chops, ask instead for a frenched eight-rib rack of lamb and have it cut into eight individual chops. Frenching is the technique for stripping the fat off the top several inches of a rib bone, leaving a nugget of meat and a soaring bone.

PECAN AND WILD MUSHROOM VEAL CHOPS

Rich in all respects, a veal chop demands an elegant preparation and presentation. This dish fits the bill, both the one from the butcher and the one you owe your friends.

SERVES 4

VEAL CHOP MARINADE
⅓ cup inexpensive brandy
2 tablespoons cider vinegar
2 tablespoons walnut oil or other nut oil

Four 1-inch-thick veal chops, each about 12 ounces

PECAN AND WILD MUSHROOM COMPOTE
3 tablespoons butter
3 tablespoons walnut oil or other nut oil
3 tablespoons minced shallots
1½ cups chopped fresh wild mushrooms, such as portobello or porcini
1½ teaspoons finely crumbled dried tarragon leaves
3 tablespoons inexpensive brandy
3 tablespoons toasted pecan pieces
Kosher salt or other coarse salt and fresh-ground black pepper

PECAN AND WILD MUSHROOM DRY RUB
¼ cup dried wild mushrooms
¼ cup pecan pieces
1½ tablespoons finely crumbled dried tarragon leaves
¾ teaspoon kosher salt or other coarse salt
¾ teaspoon fresh-ground black pepper

· · · · · · · · · · · · · · · · · ·

At least 1½ hours and up to 8 hours before you plan to grill the veal chops, prepare the marinade, combining the ingredients in a small bowl. Place the chops in a plastic bag, pour the marinade over them, and refrigerate.

Prepare the compote, first melting the butter with the walnut oil in a small saucepan over medium heat. Sauté the shallots briefly until soft, then add the mushrooms and tarragon, and continue cooking for 8 to 10 minutes until the mushrooms are very tender. Pour in the brandy and cook for 5 more minutes to reduce it. Stir in the pecans and add salt and pepper to taste. Keep the compote warm.

Prepare the dry rub. In a blender on a high setting, grind the mushrooms to fine dust. Let the dust settle a bit before opening the blender. Add the remaining ingredients to the blender and combine briefly, just long enough to make a coarse meal out of the pecans.

Remove the veal chops from the refrigerator and drain them, discarding the marinade. Coat the chops with the dry rub and let them sit covered at room temperature for about 20 minutes.

Fire up the grill, bringing the temperature to medium to medium-low (5 to 6 seconds with the hand test).

Transfer the chops to a well-oiled grate. Grill the chops uncovered over medium to medium-low heat for 20 to 24 minutes, turning at least three times, more often if juice begins to form on the surface. Don't cook the chops beyond medium-rare or an internal temperature of 150° F. If grilling covered, cook over medium to medium-low heat for 17 to 21 minutes, turning once midway.

Serve hot with a simple risotto or Land of the Lakes Wild Rice–Pecan Salad.

SAGE-RUBBED VEAL CHOPS WITH JERKY SAUCE

Italians like to pair sautéed veal with their luscious air-dried prosciutto. To hit some of those same chords in grilling in a more American fashion, we replace the ham with hearty beef jerky, strong enough to stand up to the intensity of the crusted meat.

SERVES 4

SAGE PASTE
¾ cup packed fresh sage leaves
2 garlic cloves
¾ teaspoon kosher salt or other coarse salt
2 tablespoons extra-virgin olive oil

Four 1-inch-thick veal chops, each about 12 ounces

JERKY SAUCE
2 tablespoons extra-virgin olive oil
1 medium onion, chopped
1 medium carrot, chopped
2 garlic cloves, minced
3 cups veal or chicken stock
2 ounces beef jerky, pulled or cut into fine pieces
1 teaspoon Super Wooster Sauce (page 39) or other
    Worcestershire sauce
4 sage leaves
Kosher salt or other coarse salt

At least 2 hours and up to 8 hours before you plan to grill the veal chops, make the sage paste. Combine the sage, garlic, and salt in a food processor and process until the sage is minced. With the processor still running, add the oil in a thin stream until a thick paste forms. Coat the chops with the paste, wrap them in plastic, and refrigerate.

Prepare the sauce, first warming the oil in a heavy saucepan over medium heat. Add the onion and carrot

and sauté until the onion is translucent, about 5 minutes. Stir in the garlic and cook for 1 minute longer. Pour in the stock and add the jerky, Worcestershire sauce, and sage. Reduce the heat to low and cook the sauce for 45 to 55 minutes, until the jerky is very soft. Purée the sauce in a blender, taste, and add salt as you wish. Return the sauce to the pan to keep warm. (The sauce can be made a day ahead and refrigerated. Reheat before serving.)

Fire up the grill, bringing the temperature to medium to medium-low (5 to 6 seconds with the hand test).

Remove the chops from the refrigerator and let them sit covered at room temperature for about 20 minutes.

Grill the veal uncovered over medium to medium-low heat for 20 to 24 minutes, turning at least three times, more often if juice begins to form on the surface. Don't cook the chops beyond medium-rare or an internal temperature of 150° F. If grilling covered, cook over medium to medium-low heat for 17 to 21 minutes, turning once midway.

Serve immediately, topped with spoonfuls of the jerky sauce. San Francisco 'Roni with Rice makes a good foil for the sauce.

WESTERN TURF AND SURF

The usual restaurant surf-'n'-turf slaps lobster and steak on the same plate, suggesting a marriage that has no bond beyond butter and expense. For a more harmonious union, try this equally simple mating of venison and oysters.

SERVES 4 TO 6

8 venison backstrap medallions, each 4 to 5 ounces, cut
    1 to 1¼ inches thick
4 tablespoons Chinese oyster sauce
Fresh-ground black pepper
12 shucked medium to large briny oysters, liquor reserved

Dried Fruit Chutney (page 46) or other chutney

At least 1½ hours and up to 8 hours before you plan to grill the oysters and venison, coat the venison with 3 tablespoons of the oyster sauce. Immediately wrap the medallions tightly in plastic (venison dries out very quickly) and refrigerate.

Remove the venison from the refrigerator, drain the medallions of any accumulated liquid, coat them generously with pepper, and let them sit covered at room temperature for 20 to 30 minutes. Place the oysters and their liquor in a bowl or plastic bag and mix with the remaining oyster sauce. Let them sit covered at room temperature along with the venison.

Fire up the grill for a two-level fire capable of cooking first on high heat (1 to 2 seconds with the hand test) and then on medium heat (4 to 5 seconds with the hand test).

Grill the venison uncovered over high heat for 1 to 1¼ minutes per side.

Move the steaks to medium heat, turning them again, and continue grilling for 3½ to 5 minutes per side, turning once, for rare to medium-rare doneness. If grilling covered, sear both sides first on high heat uncovered for 1 to 1¼ minutes; finish the cooking with the cover on over medium heat for 6 to 8 minutes, turning once midway.

When you move the venison to medium heat, drain the oysters and place them (preferably on a well-oiled small-mesh grill rack) over high heat. Grill the oysters uncovered just until the edges curl, about 1½ to 2 minutes per side. If grilling with a cover, cook for the same amount of time, turning once midway.

Serve the venison and oysters together on a platter accompanied by a bowl of chutney. We like to offer the duo with a grilled vegetable or two, perhaps Simply Superb Corn on the Cob or Honeyed Baby Onions.

MIXING IT UP ON THE GRILL

The surf-'n'-turf concept probably derives from the older restaurant tradition of the mixed grill, which offers various combinations of beef, chicken, lamb, pork, sausage, and other meats. With or without seafood, the idea works for outdoor meals as well as for dining out. You usually have to do some juggling at the grill, but you're amply rewarded with an impressive party meal.

Think in trios, mixing three preparations of meat, seafood, or poultry with three grilled accompaniments, such as green onions, thick mushroom slices, and small whole tomatoes. We sometimes serve several types of kebobs together, perhaps the Chilehead Pork and Corn Skewers, Hellenic Shish Kebobs, and Venison and Red Onion Skewers. An afloat-on-the-flame banquet might feature swordfish steak, seafood sausage, and shrimp. Shrimp also go well with andouille sausage and quail, or mix the quail with Italian sausage and Canadian bacon, as friends did at a recent feast. The possibilities are as boundless as the kudos you can expect.

VENISON STEAK WITH BERRY-WINE SAUCE

Today's commercially available venison tastes great, with a robust but mild flavor that lacks gamy overtones. Here we use meltingly tender backstrap medallions, the venison equivalent of beef filets, and we bring out the natural savor with an intense berry sauce. For proper appreciation, avoid cooking the steaks beyond rare to medium-rare. When we can't find venison locally, we mail-order from Broken Arrow Ranch in Ingram, Texas (800-962-4263 or 210-367-5875), which also sells its meat through some supermarkets.

SERVES 4

VENISON DRY RUB

1 tablespoon paprika
1 teaspoon fresh-ground black pepper
1 teaspoon kosher salt or other coarse salt
1 teaspoon packed brown sugar
1 teaspoon minced dried orange zest
¼ teaspoon cayenne pepper
¼ teaspoon ground cloves
¼ teaspoon crushed juniper berries
8 venison backstrap medallions, each 4 to 5 ounces, cut
    1 to 1¼ inches thick

BERRY-WINE SAUCE

1 pound blueberries, blackberries, or wild
    huckleberries
1½ cups pinot noir or other dry red wine
1½ cups beef stock
1 large onion, chopped
1 teaspoon crushed juniper berries
1 teaspoon kosher salt or other coarse salt
½ teaspoon dry mustard
1 tablespoon honey
1 tablespoon butter

• • • • • • • • • • • • • • • • • •

At least 1½ hours and up to 8 hours before you plan to grill the venison, prepare the dry rub. Combine all the ingredients in a medium bowl. Coat the venison thickly with the spice mixture, immediately wrap it tightly with plastic (venison dries out very quickly), and refrigerate.

In a heavy saucepan, combine the blueberries, wine, stock, onion, juniper berries, salt, and dry mustard. Simmer the mixture over medium-low heat for 30 minutes, until the berries have disintegrated and the sauce has reduced by about one-third. Strain the liquid, extracting as much of the liquid as possible from the solids, and return it to the saucepan. Continue cooking the sauce until it has reduced to about 1½ cups. Taste the sauce and add up to 1 tablespoon of honey to offset the tartness of the berries without masking their tang. Whisk the butter into the sauce and keep it warm. (The sauce can be made several days in advance and refrigerated. Reheat it before proceeding.)

Fire up the grill for a two-level fire capable of cooking first on high heat (1 to 2 seconds with the hand test) and then on medium heat (4 to 5 seconds with the hand test).

Let the venison sit covered at room temperature for 20 to 30 minutes.

Grill the venison uncovered over high heat for 1 to 1½ minutes per side. Move the steaks to medium heat, turning them again, and continue grilling for 3½ to 5 minutes per side, turning once, for rare to medium-rare doneness. If grilling covered, sear both sides of the meat first on high heat uncovered for 1 to 1½ minutes; finish the cooking with the cover on over medium heat for 6 to 9 minutes, turning once midway.

Spoon the sauce onto a platter or individual plates, top with the venison, and serve immediately. An elegant game dinner could also include smoked trout appetizers, Land of the Lakes Wild Rice–Pecan Salad, sautéed broccoli rabe, and baked vanilla-scented pears.

Fowl Play

FOWL PLAY

SUNNY SUNDAY CHICKEN BREASTS

Sunday used to be synonymous with chicken in many American homes, the course of choice for the special family meal of the week. When we yearn for a return to that tradition, or have another occasion to celebrate, we like to grill bone-in, skin-on breasts. They take longer to cook than the convenient boneless variety, and can be trickier, but they boast more true poultry flavor. We also try to find premium chicken, tastier than the common commercial product, and then season it lightly but spryly, as we do here with a golden sunshine sauce.

SERVES 6

Two 6½-ounce jars marinated artichoke hearts, undrained
Juice of 1½ lemons
4 garlic cloves, minced
6 bone-in, skin-on chicken breasts, preferably from premium chicken (see "Flying the Coop")
2 tablespoons extra-virgin olive oil
2 tablespoons butter
2 tablespoons white wine
½ teaspoon dried oregano
Salt

Chopped fresh basil or parsley and lemon zest, for garnish

At least 3 hours and up to the night before you plan to grill, drain the oil from the artichokes into a small bowl. To prepare the marinade, stir the juice of 1 lemon and 3 of the garlic cloves into the oil. Place the chicken breasts in a plastic bag and pour the marinade over them, rubbing some of the liquid under the skin without tearing the skin. Refrigerate the chicken.

Remove the chicken from the refrigerator and drain it, discarding the marinade. Let the chicken sit uncovered at room temperature for 20 to 30 minutes. Blot any excess liquid from the surface.

Fire up the grill, bringing the temperature to medium (4 to 5 seconds with the hand test).

While the grill preheats, purée the artichoke hearts in a blender with the olive oil. Warm the butter in a small, nonreactive saucepan over medium heat and add the remaining garlic. Sauté the garlic briefly until just soft and then stir in the wine, oregano, and puréed artichoke-and-oil mixture. Cook

the sauce for several minutes, bringing it to a good simmer. Stir in the remaining lemon juice, taste, and add salt to taste. Remove the sauce from the heat, but keep it warm. (The sauce can be made a day ahead, kept refrigerated, and then reheated.)

Transfer the chicken to the grill skin-side down. Grill the chicken uncovered over medium heat for 30 to 35 minutes, turning four times. Watch for flare-ups, shifting the breasts away from the flame if necessary. If grilling

FLYING THE COOP

When you find chicken on the menu at an up-to-date upscale restaurant, it's likely to be labeled "free-range" this or that. New York chef Larry Forgione is usually credited with coining the term, which to him meant the kind of flavorful bird that used to forage freely in American barnyards. Government inspectors don't expect as much, requiring merely that such chickens get slightly more range than their factory-cooped cousins.

Most mass-produced chickens see little or no sunlight in their short two-month life and never claw any real earth. Computers feed them a scientifically designed diet that plumps the flesh efficiently and brings them to the market quickly at a uniform size, color, and blandness.

Some free-range chickens are fully emancipated from this system, and allowed to develop a richer, natural quality, but to merit the official label breeders only have to crack the dungeon doors enough to allow a little movement.

Ask questions when you're shopping for premium chicken. Any good meat market knows how its birds were raised. The term "field-grazed" is gaining currency to represent what Forgione originally intended, but it's as subject to interpretation as "free-range." You pay more, of course, for chickens that have roamed the great outdoors, but you don't need to dump the entire spice rack into a dish just to get some flavor.

covered, cook for 24 to 28 minutes, turning twice. End the grilling in either case with the chicken skin-side down to give it a final crisping. The chicken breasts are done when opaque down to the bone but still juicy.

Stir the sauce to reblend and spoon it onto a platter. Top the sauce with the chicken breasts, and scatter the basil or parsley and the lemon zest over the chicken. Given the voluptuousness of the sauce, we pair the chicken with a simple spinach and mushroom salad along with roast potatoes or rice. We particularly like California-grown wehani rice as a side because of its burnished color and chewy texture.

TECHNIQUE TIP: The dietitians tell us not to eat chicken skin because of its fat, but that doesn't mean you can't cook it. The skin helps keep chicken juicy when you're grilling and can be removed easily at the table. Flare-ups are more likely, but they can be managed most of the time in the ways we describe on page 9. When we're grilling skin-on breasts, we start and finish them skin-down, rendering much of the fat and crisping the skin at the end just in case we want a nibble of the forbidden fruit.

VINAIGRETTE CHICKEN

A mustard-tomato vinaigrette brightens both the taste and the appearance of pale breast meat. The dressing also gives you the option of turning the chicken into a salad, by cutting it into strips and serving it hot or chilled on top of your favorite greens tossed with the vinaigrette.

SERVES 4 TO 6

DIJON MUSTARD PASTE
1 tablespoon Dijon mustard
2 teaspoons olive oil
½ teaspoon kosher salt or other coarse salt

6 bone-in, skin-on chicken breasts, preferably from
   premium chicken

MUSTARD-TOMATO VINAIGRETTE
6 tablespoons extra-virgin olive oil
2 tablespoons red wine vinegar
2 teaspoons Dijon mustard
1 small red-ripe tomato, preferably Italian plum, diced
   fine
¼ cup sliced black olives, preferably Kalamata
2 medium shallots, minced
1 tablespoon small capers plus 1 teaspoon of the brine
   from the jar
Fresh-ground black pepper

Watercress or arugula, for garnish

At least 3 hours and up to the night before you plan to grill, prepare the mustard paste, combining the ingredients in a small bowl. Coat the chicken breasts with the paste, rubbing it both over and under the skin without tearing the skin. Place the chicken in a plastic bag and refrigerate.

Remove the chicken from the refrigerator and let it sit uncovered at room temperature for 20 to 30 minutes.

Fire up the grill, bringing the temperature to medium (4 to 5 seconds with the hand test).

While the grill preheats, prepare the dressing. Whisk together the oil, vinegar, and mustard in a medium bowl. Add the tomato, olives, shallots, capers, and a good grinding of pepper and combine again. Refrigerate the dressing until needed.

Transfer the chicken to the grill skin-side down. Grill the chicken un-covered over medium heat for 30 to 35 minutes, turning four times. Watch for flare-ups, shifting the breasts away from the flame if necessary. If grilling covered, cook for 24 to 28 minutes, turning twice. End either type of grilling with the chicken skin-side down to give it a final crisping. The chicken breasts are done when opaque down to the bone but still juicy.

Arrange the watercress on a platter, and top it with the chicken breasts. Spoon about half the vinaigrette over the chicken and greens, pour the rest into a small bowl to pass at the table, and serve.

CINNAMON CHICKEN WITH CRUNCHY CASHEW RELISH

A recent survey showed that chicken came right after hamburgers—and before steaks, hot dogs, and seafood—as the favorite food for grilling in the United States. Among the various parts of the bird, nothing rivals the popularity of the boneless, skinless breast, and nothing in the whole repertory of outdoor cooking gets tortured so often over fire. The delicate meat demands moderate rather than high heat, and even then remains a blank canvas in need of a proper palette of seasoning. In this case we dust the breasts with a fragrant cinnamon and curry powder and top them with a zesty relish.

SERVES 6

CINNAMON DRY RUB
1 tablespoon ground cinnamon
1½ teaspoons curry powder
1 teaspoon kosher salt or other coarse salt
1 teaspoon fresh-ground black pepper
½ teaspoon sugar

6 large boneless, skinless individual chicken breasts,
    pounded ½ to ¾ inch thick

CRUNCHY CASHEW RELISH
¼ cup chopped onion, soaked in hot water for at least
    15 minutes and drained
¼ cup diced red bell pepper
2 teaspoons sherry vinegar
½ teaspoon sugar
¼ teaspoon curry powder
1 cup coarsely chopped salted cashews
3 to 4 tablespoons minced fresh mint

Vegetable oil spray

At least 1 hour and up to 8 hours before you plan to grill, prepare the dry rub, combining the ingredients in a small bowl. Coat the chicken breasts evenly with the rub, place them in a plastic bag, and refrigerate.

Remove the chicken from the refrigerator and let it sit covered at room temperature for about 20 minutes.

Fire up the grill, bringing the temperature to medium (4 to 5 seconds with the hand test). While the grill preheats, begin the relish. Combine the onion, pepper, vinegar, sugar, and curry powder in a medium bowl.

Just before grilling, spritz the breasts with the oil. Grill the chicken uncovered over medium heat for 5 to 6 minutes per side, until opaque but still juicy. If grilling covered, cook the chicken for about 10 minutes, turning once midway.

Place the breasts on a colorful platter. Stir the cashews and mint into the relish, adjust the seasoning if needed, and top each breast with a big spoonful of the crunchy relish. Serve hot.

TECHNIQUE TIP: One of the common complaints about cans or bottles of spray oil is a slightly "off" flavor, particularly in the olive oil varieties. You can avoid the problem by spritzing your own oil. The niftiest solution we've found is the Eco-Pump, a bottle that works with vacuum pressure rather than propellants. You fill it with your choice of oil, giving you more flavor options, saving you money, and cutting waste. One mail-order source is the Santa Fe School of Cooking (800-982-4688 or 505-983-4511).

MAPLE-GLAZED CHICKEN BREASTS

After a good shake of pepper, this bird bounds through the northern woods. The maple glaze works well with duck breasts too, following the cooking technique outlined in Sherry-Marinated Duck Breasts (page 297).

SERVES 4 TO 6

6 large boneless, skinless individual chicken breasts, pounded ½ to ¾ inch thick
2 teaspoons fresh-ground black pepper
Kosher salt or other coarse salt

MAPLE GLAZE
1 tablespoon vegetable oil
2 uncooked bacon slices, chopped
1 plump garlic clove, minced
3 tablespoons maple syrup
1 teaspoon Super Wooster Sauce (page 39) or other
    Worcestershire sauce

Vegetable oil spray

Coat the chicken breasts with the pepper and salt to taste. Cover them and refrigerate.

Prepare the glaze, first warming the oil with the bacon over medium heat. Fry until the bacon is brown and crisp. With a slotted spoon, remove the bacon, drain it, and reserve it. Stir the garlic into the pan drippings and sauté a quick minute. Remove the skillet from the heat, stir in the maple syrup and Worcestershire sauce, and reserve the glaze.

Fire up the grill, bringing the temperature to medium (4 to 5 seconds with the hand test).

Remove the chicken from the refrigerator and let it sit covered at room temperature for about 20 minutes. Just before grilling, spritz the breasts with the oil.

Grill the chicken uncovered over medium heat for 5 to 6 minutes per side, until opaque but still juicy. Brush with the glaze when you turn the cooked side of the chicken up, and coat the second side when it comes off the grill. If grilling covered, cook the chicken for about 10 minutes, turning once midway and glazing in a similar manner.

The breasts can be served whole, but we prefer to slice and fan them and then sprinkle the chopped bacon over the top. The presentation works particularly well when you place the chicken slices over a bed of wilted greens. Serve with butternut or acorn squash, too, if you like.

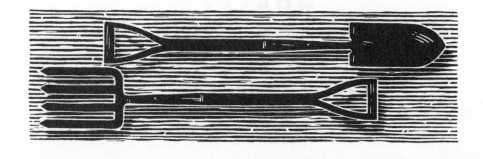

A Breast on Every Grill

Campaigning for president in 1928, just before the Great Depression, Herbert Hoover promised voters a chicken in every pot. A politician today would have to update the rhetoric. Hardly anyone remembers now what a whole chicken looks like, much less how to cook it in a pot. All we want is a plump, tender breast, separated from the homely parts of the bird, and preferably boned and skinned so that it's ready to plop on the grill.

As passions go, it's a simple one to understand. A flat skinless breast cooks quickly and evenly, and the health authorities hype it as a great alternative to burgers, dogs, and steaks. The problem is flavor, or rather the lack of it. It's easier to find good white bread today than good supermarket chicken.

We deal with the dilemma in two ways. If we're grilling breasts for a special occasion, we shop for premium, naturally raised or kosher chicken, gradually becoming more widely available, and we usually cook it bone-in, in the manner described for the Sunny Sunday Chicken Breasts and Vinaigrette Chicken. For everyday meals, we accept the trade-off between the taste limitations of ordinary boneless breasts and their convenience for grilling. In that case, as illustrated in most of the breast recipes, we treat the chicken as a foil for other flavors, a juicy but neutral medium for a bounty of seasonings.

Calypso Chicken Breasts

A splash of Caribbean hot sauce and a little rum add punch to peaches, and together the trio makes chicken chirp a fruity, tropical tune.

Serves 4 to 6

CALYPSO MARINADE
⅔ cup light rum
½ medium onion, minced
Juice of 2 limes
1 tablespoon vegetable oil

6 large boneless, skinless individual chicken breasts,
    pounded ½ to ¾ inch thick

BURNIN' PEACH RELISH
1½ cups chopped peaches, fresh or frozen
2 tablespoons rum
Zest and juice of 1 lime
Splash or 2 of Caribbean hot sauce (see Technique Tip)
Pinch of salt

Salt
Lime wedges, for garnish

• • • • • • • • • • • • • • • • • •

At least 1½ hours and up to 8 hours before you plan to grill, prepare the marinade, combining the ingredients in a small bowl. Place the chicken breasts in a plastic bag, pour the marinade over them, and refrigerate.

Prepare the relish, combining the ingredients in a small bowl. Refrigerate until needed.

Remove the chicken from the refrigerator, drain it, and discard the marinade. Salt the chicken lightly and let it sit at room temperature for about 20 minutes.

Fire up the grill, bringing the temperature to medium (4 to 5 seconds with the hand test).

Grill the chicken uncovered at medium heat for 5 to 6 minutes per side, until opaque but still juicy. If grilling covered, cook for 9 to 10 minutes, turning once midway.

Serve the chicken hot, with spoonfuls of relish on the side, and limes for squeezing over the top. All-Star Pickled Starfruit can add another festive note to the plates.

TECHNIQUE TIP: Caribbean hot sauces generally share a foundation built on fragrant, super-hot habanero or Scotch bonnet chiles, often with a hint of mustard in the background. The sauces vary in the amount of chile, but generally have enough firepower to use by the drop or splash rather than the tablespoon. Many good brands can be found throughout the United States today.

APPLE CHICKEN SAUSAGE KEBOBS

These kebobs do a duet with chicken and apples, mixing cubes of each with a sausage made from both. The Aidells Sausage Company first popularized chicken-apple links, but now many regional meat companies have joined the bandwagon. Look for the nationally distributed Aidells, find a version from closer to home, or substitute another mildly seasoned poultry sausage.

SERVES 4 TO 6

APPLE MARINADE AND SAUCE
1 cup apple cider or juice
½ medium onion, chopped
¼ cup olive oil
2 tablespoons cider vinegar
2 tablespoons brown mustard
4 teaspoons minced fresh sage or 2 teaspoons crumbled
    dried sage
1 tablespoon minced fresh thyme or 1½ teaspoons dried
    thyme
1 tablespoon Dijon mustard
½ teaspoon salt

1 pound plump boneless, skinless chicken breasts, cut
    in ¾- to 1-inch cubes

Metal skewers
8 ounces fully cooked chicken-apple sausage, or other
    mildly seasoned fully cooked poultry sausage, sliced
    into 1-inch chunks
4 green onions, limp green portions discarded, cut into
    1-inch pieces
1 red delicious apple, cut into bite-size chunks so that
    each has some skin on it

At least 1½ hours and up to 8 hours before you plan to grill, prepare the marinade, combining the ingredients in a small bowl. Place the chicken chunks in a plastic bag, pour the marinade over them, and refrigerate.

Remove the chicken from the refrigerator, draining the marinade into a small saucepan and reserving it.

Avoiding crowding, thread the chicken, sausage, green onions, and apple chunks onto skewers, beginning and ending with the apple and using just occasional green onion pieces. Let the kebobs sit covered at room temperature for about 15 minutes.

Fire up the grill, bringing the temperature to medium (4 to 5 seconds with the hand test).

Bring the marinade to a vigorous boil over high heat, cooking for several minutes, until reduced by one-fourth.

Remove the reduced marinade sauce from the heat and adjust the seasoning.

Grill the kebobs uncovered over medium heat for 8 to 10 minutes, turning to cook on all sides, until the chicken is opaque but still juicy. Brush the kebobs with the sauce in the last few minutes of cooking. If grilling covered, cook for 7 to 9 minutes, turning once midway and brushing with the sauce.

Serve the kebobs hot. Try them with Simply Superb Corn on the Cob and steamed fresh broccoli spears.

TECHNIQUE TIP: For this recipe, look for plump chicken breasts, about 1 inch at their thickest. The fatter breasts will stay juicier when cut into the chunks needed for kebobs. If less-endowed breasts are all you can find, reduce the cooking time by a minute or two.

WHIMSICAL CHICKEN CLUB

We first relished the lively sauce on this sandwich at The Sugar Mill, a splendid inn on Tortola in the British Virgin Islands. Local cook Pete Whims created the blend for a burger, but we've modified it for a triple-decker chicken club. You need to toss together the hot sauce at least a day before you plan to grill, to spark the combustion, but it'll keep blazing for a long week afterward.

SERVES 4

WHIMSICAL HOT SAUCE
¼ cup chopped black olives, preferably Kalamata
¼ cup chopped green pimiento-stuffed olives
3 large red-ripe tomatoes, peeled, seeded, and chopped
3 green onions, green and white portions, sliced into
    thin rings
3 tablespoons olive oil
2 garlic cloves, minced
½ habanero or Scotch bonnet chile, or 2 large fresh
    jalapeños, minced, or several splashes Caribbean hot
    sauce

4 medium boneless, skinless individual chicken
    breasts, pounded ½ inch thick
Olive oil
Kosher salt or other coarse salt
4 large, thin slices Monterey jack or fontina cheese, at
    cool room temperature, optional
12 thin slices good bread, such as sourdough, whole
    wheat, or a country loaf
¼ cup Enriched Mayonnaise (page 38) or other
    mayonnaise
2 tablespoons Dijon mustard
Leaf lettuce leaves
2 medium red-ripe tomatoes, sliced
1 small Hass avocado, sliced thin
8 crisp cooked bacon slices

. . . .

At least 1 day and up to several days before you plan to grill, prepare the hot sauce, combining the ingredients in a medium bowl. Wear rubber gloves if handling the fiery habanero and avoid taking any direct deep breaths of its powerful aroma. Cover the sauce and refrigerate.

Rub the chicken breasts with just enough oil to coat them, and sprinkle them lightly with salt. Cover the chicken and let it sit at room temperature for 20 to 30 minutes.

Fire up the grill, bringing the temperature to medium (4 to 5 seconds with the hand test).

Grill the chicken uncovered over medium heat for 4 to 5 minutes per side, until opaque but still juicy. If grilling covered, cook the chicken for 7 to 9 minutes, turning once midway. If you are using cheese, arrange a slice

on top of each chicken breast in the last couple of minutes of cooking, so it can begin to melt. Toast the bread on the edge of the grill, as many slices at a time as the grate will accommodate.

Combine the mayonnaise and mustard in a small bowl and coat one side of 8 slices of bread generously with the spread. Place a lettuce leaf and a chicken breast on 4 of those bread slices. Spoon on as much hot sauce as you wish and then add a piece of dry toast to each sandwich. Continue building upward, with equal portions of tomatoes, avocado, and bacon, topped with another lettuce leaf. Finish with the remaining toast. Slice each sandwich into halves or quarters, skewering each together with toothpicks if you wish.

Serve the sandwiches immediately, perhaps with sweet potato chips or shoestring potatoes. Pass more of the hot sauce on the side. Any remaining sauce revs up burgers or grilled cheese sandwiches, or becomes a piquant accompaniment to simply grilled fish fillets or pork chops.

CHOCK-FULL CHICKEN ROLL-UPS

We refuse to call this a "wrap," a trendy food term for an idea as old as eating, but some would say it's so. Whatever name you use, an assertive marinade allows the tortilla-rolled chicken to keep center stage in the midst of an effusive supporting cast of condiments. We pound a boneless breast very thin in this case to increase its grilled surface, so the chicken cooks quite quickly and should be watched carefully.

SERVES 6

SPICY LIME MARINADE
½ cup fresh lime juice
1½ tablespoons honey
2 to 3 canned chipotle chiles, plus adobo sauce from the
     can to taste
1 tablespoon vegetable oil
3 garlic cloves

4 large boneless, skinless chicken breasts, pounded ¼ to
   ½ inch thick

6 thin flour tortillas, approximately 8 inches in
   diameter, either Tucson Tortillas (page 113) or
   store-bought
6 tablespoons Fired-Up Tomato Salsa (page 88) or other
   tomato-based salsa
Leaf lettuce leaves
1 medium cucumber, peeled, seeded, and cut into thin
   strips
4 ounces grated mild cheddar cheese
1 Hass avocado, sliced thin
Minced red onion
Cilantro leaves, optional

Additional Fired-Up Tomato Salsa (page 88) or other
   tomato-based salsa

At least 1 hour and up to 8 hours before you plan to grill, prepare the marinade, combining all the ingredients in a blender. Place the chicken breasts in a plastic bag, pour the marinade over them, and refrigerate.

Remove the chicken from the refrigerator, drain it, and discard the marinade. Let the chicken sit covered at room temperature for about 20 minutes.

Fire up the grill, bringing the temperature to medium (4 to 5 seconds with the hand test).

Grill the chicken uncovered over medium heat for 3½ to 5 minutes per side, until opaque but still juicy. If grilling covered, cook the chicken for 6 to 8 minutes, turning once midway. Warm the tortillas briefly on the grill and, if needed, wrap them in foil to keep warm.

To serve, slice the chicken into thin strips. Lay out the tortillas side by side on a work surface and brush each with equal portions of the salsa. Add the lettuce, followed by the chicken, cucumber, cheese, avocado, onion, and optional cilantro. Each of the ingredients should be strewn across the whole surface of the tortillas to within about ½ inch of the edges. Ingredients cut in strips should be scattered in the same direction. Carefully roll up each tortilla, pressing it lightly to wrap compactly but without squeezing the fillings. Cut each roll on a slanted diagonal with a sharp knife into two or more sections. (Cutting them into smaller 1½-inch sections makes a hearty party appetizer.) If you have difficulty getting the tortilla to cling tightly to the roll, use toothpicks to keep them in place.

Serve the rolls warm with cut sides up to show off the bands of color, and accompany with more salsa. Citrus-Onion Salad makes a good complement.

CHICKEN THIGHS WITH GREEN OLIVE PASTE

We're always leering at the legs. The darker meat of thighs and drumsticks starts out with a deeper flavor than breasts and stays moister during grilling. Here we massage the thighs in advance with a savory paste, adding another layer of delectability.

SERVES 3 TO 4

GREEN OLIVE PASTE
½ small onion, chunked
¼ cup pitted green olives
3 tablespoons beer or chicken stock
1 tablespoon olive oil
1 tablespoon All-'Round Rub (page 23), or
    1 tablespoon paprika plus 1 teaspoon kosher salt
    or other coarse salt

8 bone-in, skin-on chicken thighs

Diced tomato, green olive slices, and lime wedges, for
    garnish

At least 2 hours and up to the night before you plan to grill the thighs, prepare the paste, combining the ingredients in a food processor or blender. Coat the thighs thoroughly with the paste, rubbing it over and

under the skin, working it as far as possible under the skin without tearing the skin. Place the chicken in a plastic bag and refrigerate.

Remove the chicken from the refrigerator and let it sit covered at room temperature for 20 to 30 minutes.

Fire up the grill for a two-level fire capable of cooking first on high heat (1 to 2 seconds with the hand test) and then on medium-low heat (6 seconds with the hand test).

Grill the thighs uncovered over high heat for 3 to 4 minutes, turning to sear all sides. Move the chicken to medium-low heat and continue grilling for an additional 12 to 15 minutes, turning every 3 minutes or so. Watch for flare-ups, shifting the thighs away from the flame if necessary. The thighs are done when the skin is brown and crisp and the juices run clear. If grilling covered, sear all sides of the thighs first on high heat uncovered for 3 to 4 minutes; finish the cooking with the cover on over medium-low heat for 10 to 12 minutes, turning the chicken once midway.

Arrange the thighs on a platter, scatter tomatoes and olive slices over the top, and accompany with lime wedges. Serve immediately.

TECHNIQUE TIP: Unlike white breast meat, the richer dark meat of thighs and drumsticks benefits from a two-level fire. The time on a hot fire should be brief, however, and the heat used for finishing should be medium-low, which is lower than usual in a two-level fire. Turn the parts regularly to render and crisp all the skin, watching for possible flare-ups.

SO MISO DRUMSTICKS

The soybean paste known as miso migrated into American grilling circles about the same time as the hibachi. An old favorite by now, it offers perfect consistency for a paste to spread over and under chicken skin. We apply the potion to drumsticks here, but it works equally well on thighs or whole legs.

SERVES 4

MISO PASTE
3 tablespoons miso, preferably yellow miso
1 tablespoon soy sauce (preferably a reduced-salt variety)
1 tablespoon grated fresh ginger
½ teaspoon crushed dried hot red chile, optional

8 chicken drumsticks
Thin green onion rings, for garnish

At least 2 hours and up to the night before you plan to grill, prepare the paste, combining the ingredients in a small bowl. Loosen the skin on the drumsticks. Coat the drumsticks thoroughly with the paste, rubbing over and under the skin, working it as far as possible under the skin without tearing the skin. Place the chicken in a plastic bag and refrigerate.

Remove the chicken from the refrigerator and let it sit at room temperature for 20 to 30 minutes.

Fire up the grill for a two-level fire capable of cooking first on high heat (1 to 2 seconds with the hand test) and then on medium-low heat (6 seconds with the hand test).

Grill the drumsticks uncovered over high heat for 3 to 4 minutes, turning to sear all sides. Move the chicken to medium-low heat and continue grilling for an additional 12 to 15 minutes, turning every 3 minutes or so. Watch for flare-ups, shifting the drumsticks away from the flame if necessary. The drumsticks are done when the skin is brown and crisp and the juices run clear. If grilling covered, sear all sides of the drumsticks first on high heat uncovered for 3 to 4 minutes; finish the cooking with the cover on over medium-low heat for 10 to 12 minutes, turning the chicken once midway.

Arrange the drumsticks on a platter, scatter green onions over them, and

serve immediately. We like to accompany them with Grant Street Pickled Vegetables and pickled ginger, the kind you find in jars or refrigerated tubs to accompany sushi.

TECHNIQUE TIP: We frequently prefer pastes as the seasoning technique for bone-in, skin-on chicken parts and halves. The flavoring power is more intense than a liquid marinade, the mixture easily stays under the poultry skin for added taste, and the moisture in the paste helps keep the food from drying out during the relatively longer cooking time for bone-in chicken.

LEMON-ROSEMARY CHICKEN HALVES

You can roast a full chicken in a covered grill, but for open grilling you can't cook more than half a bird. After a long soak in lemon juice and rosemary, these halves add up to more than a whole.

SERVES 4 HEARTY EATERS

LEMON-ROSEMARY PASTE
¼ cup packed fresh rosemary sprigs
⅓ cup olive oil
Zest and juice of 1 lemon
1½ tablespoons chopped onion
2 garlic cloves
1½ teaspoons kosher salt or other coarse salt

Two 3-pound to 3¼-pound whole chickens, halved
1 lemon, cut in wedges
Fresh rosemary sprigs and lemon slices, optional, for
    garnish

At least 3 hours and up to the night before you plan to grill the chicken, prepare the paste. Purée the rosemary with the oil in a blender, preferably, or a food processor. Let the rosemary steep in the oil for 5 to 10 minutes. Strain the mixture to remove the tough little leaves. Return the oil to the blender, add the remaining ingredients, and purée. The paste will be somewhat soupy.

Coat each chicken half thoroughly with the paste, rubbing it inside and out and working it as far as possible under the skin without tearing the skin. Place the chicken in a plastic bag and refrigerate.

Fire up the grill, bringing the temperature to medium (4 to 5 seconds with the hand test).

Remove the chicken from the refrigerator and let it sit covered at room temperature for about 30 minutes. Drain the chicken and blot any excess moisture from the surface.

Transfer the halves to the grill and arrange them skin-side up. Grill uncovered over medium heat for about 20 minutes, without turning, then cook an additional 30 to 40 minutes, turning every 5 to 10 minutes, ending with the chicken skin-side down for a final crisping. (You want the chicken skin to face the grill enough to render its fat and brown, but not burn.) Watch for flare-ups, shifting the halves away from the flame if necessary. Squeeze the lemon wedges over the chicken's cavity about halfway through the cooking. If grilling covered, cook the chicken starting skin-side up over medium heat for about 15 minutes, without turning, then cook an additional 25 to 30 minutes total, turning three times and squeezing the lemon wedges over the chicken's cavity about halfway through the cooking.

Arrange the chicken on a platter. Garnish with rosemary and lemon slices, if you wish, and serve immediately. We would offer the dish with Amazing Aspic or A+ Baked Pasta on the side.

TECHNIQUE TIP: While the flavor of this paste is intense, like other surface seasonings it leaves a lighter kiss on food than you might expect. For additional gusto, inject some of the seasonings into the chicken with a kitchen syringe, an oversized needle that looks like something a visiting vet left behind. You'll need to modify the paste's preparation a little, first combining just the strained rosemary-scented oil with the lemon juice. Push down the plunger of the syringe to expel air and then dip the needle into the liquid. Draw the plunger back slowly until the syringe fills and then inject the liquid deep into the chicken breasts and thighs, using up about three-quarters of the liquid. Mix the remaining liquid with the other paste ingredients and rub it both over and under the skin. Be sure to clean the syringe after each use with hot, soapy water.

HEARTY RANCH CHICKEN HALVES

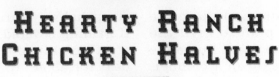

Down on the ranch, the cowhands like to beef up their chicken, as we do here with a punchy paste.

SERVES 4 HEARTY EATERS

RANCH PASTE
2 tablespoons butter
2 tablespoons Super Wooster Sauce (page 39) or other
    Worcestershire sauce
1 tablespoon paprika
1 tablespoon minced canned chipotle chiles and 1½
    teaspoons adobo sauce from the can
1 teaspoon Tabasco sauce or other hot pepper sauce
1 teaspoon kosher salt or other coarse salt
½ teaspoon dry mustard

Two 3-pound to 3¼-pound whole chickens, halved

RANCH BASTE
2 tablespoons Super Wooster Sauce (page 39) or other
    Worcestershire sauce
1 tablespoon water

At least 3 hours and up to the night before you plan to grill the chicken, prepare the paste, first combining the ingredients in a small saucepan. Warm over medium heat just until the butter melts and the mixture can be blended evenly. Refrigerate the mixture for a few minutes until it becomes the consistency of room temperature butter. Massage the chicken halves thoroughly with the paste, rubbing it inside and out and working it as far as possible under the skin without tearing the skin. Place the halves in a plastic bag and refrigerate.

Fire up the grill, bringing the temperature to medium (4 to 5 seconds with the hand test).

Remove the chicken from the refrigerator and let it sit covered at room

temperature for about 30 minutes. Mix together the baste, combining the Worcestershire sauce and water.

Transfer the halves to the grill and arrange them skin-side up. Grill uncovered over medium heat for about 20 minutes, without turning, then cook an additional 30 to 40 minutes, turning every 5 to 10 minutes and ending with the chicken skin-side down for a final crisping. (You want the chicken skin to face the grill enough to render its fat and brown, but not burn.) Watch for flare-ups, shifting the halves away from the flame if necessary. Brush or spritz the baste over the chicken's cavity about halfway through the cooking. If grilling covered, cook the chicken starting skin-side up over medium heat for about 15 minutes, without turning, then cook an additional 25 to 30 minutes total, turning three times and brushing or spritzing the baste over the chicken's cavity about halfway through the cooking.

Arrange the chicken halves on a platter and serve immediately.

TECHNIQUE TIP: Because of their relatively long grilling time, we add a little flavorful liquid to the cavity of chicken halves about halfway through the cooking to help keep the meat moist. We don't baste the skin side, though, because we want to render the fat and crisp the skin.

APRICOT-GLAZED GAME HENS

Not in the least gamy or ever wild, little Cornish hens are simply an American cross-breed of two domestic chickens. They don't taste like much without some serious seasoning, like this mustard rub and cardamom-scented apricot glaze.

SERVES 4

1 tablespoon Mixed Mustard Plaster (page 28) or Dijon
    mustard
1 tablespoon butter, at room temperature
½ teaspoon kosher salt or other coarse salt
4 Cornish game hens, or poussins (young chickens),
    about 1 to 1¼ pounds each, halved

APRICOT GLAZE
2 tablespoons butter
½ cup apricot jam or preserves
1½ tablespoons Mixed Mustard Plaster (page 28) or
    Dijon mustard
1½ teaspoons ground cardamom
¼ teaspoon kosher salt or other coarse salt
2 tablespoons water

. . . .

At least 3 hours and up to the night before you plan to grill the game hens, combine the mustard paste or mustard with the butter and salt. Coat the hens thoroughly with the mixture, rubbing them both over and under the skin, working the paste as far as possible under the skin without tearing the skin. Place the hens in a plastic bag and refrigerate.

Prepare the glaze, first melting the butter in a medium saucepan over medium heat. Add the remaining ingredients and bring the mixture just to a boil. Reduce the heat to low and simmer 5 minutes until the glaze is thickened but still brushable. (The glaze can be made a day ahead if you wish. Warm it again before proceeding, adding a little water if the glaze is too stiff to brush easily.)

Remove the hens from the refrigerator and let them sit covered at room temperature for 20 to 30 minutes.

Fire up the grill, bringing the temperature to medium (4 to 5 seconds with the hand test).

Transfer the hens to the grill skin-side down. Grill the hens uncovered over medium heat for 30 to 35 minutes, turning them four times. Watch for flare-ups, shifting the hens away from the flame if necessary. If grilling covered, cook for 24 to 29 minutes, turning twice. With either type of grilling, brush the hens with the glaze in the last 2 to 3 minutes of cooking. The hens are done when opaque down to the bone but still juicy.

Arrange the hens on a platter and serve immediately, perhaps with Mixed Herb Tabbouleh.

THE BIRTH OF THE GRILL

Perhaps the country's first book on grilling, *Sunset's Barbecue Book* from 1938, dealt with food and cooking only as a secondary interest. Most of the slender volume concerned how to build your own outdoor fireplace grill, using brick, rock, and mortar. It seemed a natural, woodsy fixture in a suburban backyard, particularly in sunny regions of the West, where grilling gained its initial foothold in the nation.

Other early outdoor cookbooks followed the *Sunset* lead, providing detailed plans for permanent installations as late as the 1950s, when Lucy and Ricky Ricardo illustrated some of the possible pitfalls of do-it-yourself construction in an "I Love Lucy" episode. The TV show didn't turn the tide against the brick behemoths, but it marked the ebb of the trend. Portable metal grills had already become the wave of the future.

By 1942, one cookbook noted—after a lengthy review of wood-burning fireplace grills—that "the growing popularity of charcoal for outdoor cooking has acted as a real incentive for what you might call 'mass production' of various appliances designed for the use of this fuel. Almost every hardware store carries them and there seem to be more models and makes of charcoal stoves than automobiles." The book pictured two styles, neither very recognizable as an ancestor of the modern metal grill.

Simple charcoal braziers and hibachis hit the market within a few years, and the first covered grills didn't lag far behind. Tulsa pioneer Grant Hastings brought out his innovative Hasty-Bake in 1948, though he had a hard time selling it in the early days because of the hood, widely viewed as an unnecessary frill. George Stephen had more success with the covered Weber kettle, introduced in 1951, which established a design and a company that still dominate the industry. At the time total grill sales barely topped 250,000 a year, but they shot up 2,000 percent in the next fifteen years, to over five million annually by 1965.

PERFUMED GAME HENS

The quintessential "Cosmo Girl" and author of the blockbuster *Sex and The Single Girl*, Helen Gurley Brown told aspiring women (i.e., "girls") how to win their man in *The Single Girl's Cookbook*. The unsinkable Mrs. Brown said to forget about Jell-O molded in his initials and pimiento happy faces on food. The ticket to marital bliss, she suggested, was the Cornish game hen, as simple as chicken but much more impressive. She would approve of this come-hither version, scented coquettishly with herbs.

SERVES 4

PERFUMED PASTE
⅓ cup chopped onion
6 tablespoons chopped summer savory (see Technique Tip)
2 tablespoons minced fresh thyme
2 tablespoons chopped fresh parsley, preferably Italian flat-leaf
1½ teaspoons kosher salt or other coarse salt
Zest and juice of 1 lemon
2 tablespoons olive oil

4 Cornish game hens, or poussins (young chickens), about 1 to 1¼ pounds each, halved

Summer savory or thyme sprigs, for garnish

At least 3 hours and up to the night before you plan to grill the game hens, prepare the paste, puréeing the ingredients in a food processor or blender. Coat the hens thoroughly with the paste, rubbing them both over and under the skin, working the paste as far as possible under the skin without tearing the skin. Place the hens in a plastic bag and refrigerate.

Remove the hens from the refrigerator and let them sit covered at room temperature for 20 to 30 minutes.

Fire up the grill, bringing the temperature to medium (4 to 5 seconds with the hand test).

Transfer the hens to the grill skin-side down. Grill the hens uncovered

over medium heat for 30 to 35 minutes, turning them four times. Watch for flare-ups, shifting the hens away from the flame if necessary. If grilling covered, cook for 24 to 28 minutes, turning twice. End either type of grilling with the hens skin-side down for a final crisping. The hens are done when opaque down to the bone but still juicy.

Arrange the hens on a platter, garnish with herbs, and serve immediately. We like to accompany them with kasha or couscous and Citrus-Onion Slaw.

TECHNIQUE TIP: Found in both summer and winter varieties, savory tastes a bit like a cross between thyme and mint. Even the milder summer form used here is slightly assertive, though tamed somewhat in the paste mixture. Rather than substitute dried savory or thyme in this recipe, go for other fresh herbs, such as marjoram or oregano in place of the savory and perhaps rosemary or additional parsley for the thyme. The freshness of the flavor is more important to the success of the dish than the specific herbs.

BOURBON TURKEY BREAST FILLETS

You may have heard that Ben Franklin preferred the turkey to the bald eagle as a symbol for the fledgling United States, but do you know why? Ben reckoned that the eagle "is a bird of bad moral character, like those among men who live by sharpening and robbing," and the turkey is "much more respectable." He might resist the idea of taking the noble fowl for a swim in bourbon, as we do here, but we think it elevates the bird's virtues.

SERVES 6

BOURBON MARINADE
¾ cup bourbon or other similar American whiskey
2 tablespoons white wine Worcestershire sauce
½ teaspoon fresh-ground black pepper

6 turkey breast fillet sections, 5 to 6 ounces each,
  pounded to ⅛- to ¾-inch thickness
1 tablespoon honey
1 tablespoon butter

• • • • • • • • • • • • • • • • • •

At least 2 hours and up to 8 hours before you plan to grill, prepare the marinade, combining the ingredients in a small bowl. Place the turkey breast fillets in a plastic bag, pour the marinade over them, and refrigerate.

Remove the turkey from the refrigerator and drain the marinade from it into a small saucepan. Blot any excess liquid from the surface. Let the turkey sit covered at room temperature for 20 to 30 minutes.

Fire up the grill, bringing the temperature to medium (4 to 5 seconds with the hand test).

While the grill preheats, bring the marinade to a vigorous boil, boiling for several minutes. Remove the marinade from the heat and immediately add the honey and butter, stirring to melt both into the hot liquid, which will become the sauce.

Grill the breast fillets uncovered over medium heat for 5 to 6 minutes per side, until opaque but still juicy. Brush the turkey with the sauce in the last couple of minutes of cooking and again after it comes off the grill. If grilling covered, cook for 9 to 10 minutes, turning once midway and brushing with the sauce at the end.

Serve the breast fillets sliced thin, then fanned on plates, perhaps with cheese- and garlic-laced grits and sautéed mustard greens.

THYME-RUBBED TURKEY KEBOBS WITH CRANBERRY GLAZE

Easy enough for a weekend supper, but tasty enough for a special meal, these kebobs shine with a ruby cranberry glaze. For maximum color, use green-skinned apple chunks and a combination of red and white pearl onions. Meaty chicken breasts can fill in for the turkey if you wish.

SERVES 4 TO 6

THYME DRY RUB
1 tablespoon dried thyme
1 teaspoon dried sage
1 teaspoon kosher salt or other coarse salt
½ teaspoon fresh-ground black pepper
½ teaspoon ground white pepper

1¼ pounds plump turkey breast fillet sections, or chicken breasts, pounded to ¾- to 1-inch thickness and cut into ¾- to 1-inch cubes

CRANBERRY GLAZE
1 cup cranberries, fresh or frozen
6 tablespoons red wine
¼ cup sugar
¼ cup turkey or chicken stock
¼ teaspoon minced garlic

1 large Granny Smith or other green-skinned apple
Metal skewers
16 to 18 pearl onions, parboiled and peeled, with root ends trimmed
3 thin bacon slices, uncooked, cut into 6 to 8 pieces each

At least 1 hour and up to 8 hours before you plan to grill, prepare the dry rub, combining the ingredients in a medium bowl. Add the turkey cubes to the bowl and toss them until coated with the spice mixture. Cover and refrigerate the turkey.

Prepare the glaze, combining the ingredients in a small saucepan. Cook over medium-high heat for 5 to 10 minutes, just until the cranberries pop and the sauce thickens but is still brushable.

Fire up the grill, bringing the temperature to medium (4 to 5 seconds with the hand test).

Cut the apple into chunks just slightly smaller than the turkey cubes, making sure each one has some of the peel attached. Avoiding crowding, thread the turkey cubes on skewers interspersed as you wish with apple chunks, onions, and bacon.

Grill the kebobs uncovered over medium heat for 8 to 10 minutes, turn-ing on all sides, until the turkey cubes are opaque but still juicy. Brush the kebobs with glaze in the last several minutes of cooking and again when they come off the grill. If grilling covered, cook the kebobs for 7 to 9 minutes, turning once midway and glazing them at the end.

Serve the kebobs hot. We like them with Land of the Lakes Wild Rice–Pecan Salad and Bourbon and Black Walnut Sweet Potato Gratin.

TECHNIQUE TIP: Be vigilant about the possible contamination of grilled poultry or meats by their raw counterparts. Always use clean utensils, brushes, and plates after the food is cooked. One way to cut down on the dishwashing is to carry raw food to the grill on a platter lined with plastic wrap or foil. Place the chow on the grill, throw away the plastic or foil, and use the clean platter for the grilled food when it's done.

GRILLED TURKEY TAQUITOS WITH TOMATILLO-MINT SALSA

Taquitos are deep-fried corn-tortilla flutes, stuffed in this case with grilled turkey breast. They require an extra step after grilling, but one that produces a tasty and colorful Southwestern treat. The multiple steps allow you to prepare the turkey one day, perhaps while grilling other food, and the taquitos the next day. Substitute chicken breasts for the turkey if you like.

MAKES 2 DOZEN TAQUITOS

TOMATILLO-MINT SALSA
1 pound tomatillos, husked and rinsed
2 fresh jalapeño or serrano chiles
½ cup packed fresh mint leaves
½ small onion, chopped
2 tablespoons water
½ teaspoon salt

3 turkey breast fillet sections, or chicken breasts, 5 to 6
     ounces each, pounded to ½- to ¾-inch thickness
2 green onion tops, minced
Salt
1 small Hass avocado, optional
Vegetable oil for deep-frying
24 Corn Tortillas Rojo (page 119) or other thin corn tortillas

● ● ● ● ● ● ● ● ● ● ● ● ● ● ● ● ● ●

At least 1½ hours and up to 8 hours before you plan to grill, prepare the salsa. If your grill is easy and quick to fire up, grill the whole tomatillos over medium-high to high heat just long enough to brown the skins. While not necessary, it adds a more robust note to their tangy citrus-like flavor. Whether grilled or not, chop the tomatillos roughly. Transfer them to a blender or food processor with the remaining salsa ingredients and purée. Spoon half the salsa into a serving bowl and refrigerate. Place the turkey in a plastic bag, pour the remaining salsa over it, and refrigerate.

Remove the turkey from the refrigerator, drain the marinade, and discard it. Let the turkey sit covered at room temperature for 20 to 30 minutes.

Fire up the grill, bringing the temperature to medium (4 to 5 seconds with the hand test).

Grill the turkey uncovered over medium heat for 5 to 6 minutes per side, until opaque but still juicy. Brush the turkey with the salsa in the last couple of minutes of cooking and again after it comes off the grill. If grilling covered, cook for 9 to 10 minutes, turning once midway and brushing with the salsa at the end.

When the turkey is cool enough to handle, shred it finely. In a medium bowl, mix the turkey with any accumulated juices, the green onion, and salt to taste. (The turkey can be used immediately or refrigerated for a couple of days.)

Shortly before you plan to serve the taquitos, cut the avocado in small dice, if using it, and stir it into the salsa. Pour about 2 inches of oil into a deep skillet or heavy saucepan. Heat the oil until it ripples. With tongs, dunk a tortilla into the hot oil long enough for it to go limp, a matter of seconds. Don't let the tortilla turn crisp. Repeat with

the remaining tortillas and drain them.

Spoon 1½ to 2 tablespoons of the shredded turkey on a tortilla and roll it up tight. Secure the taquito with a toothpick. Repeat with the remaining filling and tortillas.

Heat the oil to 375° F. Add several taquitos to the oil and fry for about 2 minutes, turning as needed to cook until crisp. Repeat with the remaining taquitos.

Remove the toothpicks and serve immediately, accompanied with the tomatillo salsa.

HOT-TO-TROT TURKEY LEGS

As George W. Martin said in one of the country's first grill cookbooks, turkey is "especially welcomed at the outdoor fireplace where Emily Post's table manners will not encumber you from holding a drumstick in the natural manner." These hearty drumsticks, slathered with a mustard coat, may also make you grab impolitely.

SERVES 6

. . . .

HONEY BEER PASTE
¼ cup Honey-Beer Mustard (page 37) or other sweet hot
   mustard
2 tablespoons Super Wooster Sauce (page 39) or other
   Worcestershire sauce
2 teaspoons vegetable oil
1½ teaspoons kosher salt or other coarse salt

6 small turkey drumsticks, no larger than ¾ pound
   each
Georgia Grilling Sauce (page 36) or other mustard-
   based barbecue sauce, optional

. . . .

At least 2 hours and up to the night before you plan to grill, prepare the paste, combining the ingredients in a small bowl. Loosen the skin on the turkey legs, running your fingers under it as far as possible without tearing the skin. Coat the turkey with the mixture, massaging over and under the

skin. Place the drumsticks in a plastic bag and refrigerate.

Remove the turkey legs from the refrigerator, blot excess moisture from the surface, and let them sit covered at room temperature for about 30 minutes.

Fire up the grill, bringing the temperature to medium (4 to 5 seconds with the hand test).

Arrange the drumsticks on the grill with their thinner ends toward a cooler edge of the grill. Grill the drumsticks uncovered over medium heat for 45 to 55 minutes, turning on all sides, until opaque but still juicy, with clear juices. The skin will become very deep brown but should not burn. If grilling covered, cook the turkey for 35 to 45 minutes, turning once midway.

Serve the turkey legs hot, to be eaten with your fingers, with Georgia Grilling Sauce on the side if you wish.

SHERRY-MARINATED DUCK BREASTS

When Americans raised their own poultry, they had a number of tricks for flavoring and tenderizing the birds in the last few days before the butchering. One method was force-feeding glasses of sherry, a technique that works just as well and meets less resistance after the wings stop flapping.

SERVES 4

4 individual boneless, skin-on duck breasts, each about 6 to 7 ounces

SHERRY MARINADE
½ cup dry sherry
2 whole star anise, crushed
⅛ teaspoon cayenne pepper

At least 2 hours and up to the night before you plan to grill, prepare the duck breasts. If the skin is any thicker than ¼ inch, trim it to that thickness with a sharp knife, shearing off portions as needed. Also slice off any portions of

skin or fat that hang beyond the top of the breasts. (Save the skin and fat trimmings to render the fat and make crisp cracklings, if you wish, in the manner described in the Technique Tip.) Make crisscross cuts down through the remaining skin on the breasts. Make the cuts about ½ inch apart, through the skin but not into the flesh. This will help the marinade absorb initially, and during cooking, it promotes gradual and easy rendering of fat.

Prepare the marinade, combining the ingredients in a small bowl. Place the duck breasts in a plastic bag, pour the marinade over them, and refrigerate.

Fire up the grill, bringing the temperature to medium (4 to 5 seconds with the hand test).

Remove the duck from the refrigerator, drain the marinade, and discard it. Let the duck sit uncovered at room temperature for 20 to 30 minutes.

Transfer the duck breasts to the grill skin-side down. Grill the duck uncovered over medium heat for 4 to 6 minutes, rotating once, or until the skin is deep golden brown and crisp. Watch for flare-ups, moving the breasts away from the flame if necessary. Turn the breasts over and grill skin-side up for an additional 2 to 3 minutes for medium-rare. If grilling covered, cook for the same amount of time, starting skin-side down and turning once after 4 to 6 minutes.

Slice the duck thinly, so that each piece has a bit of the crisp skin, and fan the slices on plates. Serve the duck hot with Grant Street Pickled Vegetables or other ginger- or soy-flavored accompaniments.

TECHNIQUE TIP: Rendered duck fat and cracklings are wonderful bonuses from duck skin, a little excessive for everyday eating but a delight now and then. Place any skin or fat trimmings in a heavy skillet and warm over medium-low heat. Cook for about 20 minutes, turning occasionally, until the pieces of skin are deep brown and crisp. Drain the fat for use in other savory dishes in place of butter or a flavored oil. It keeps indefinitely in the refrigerator in a covered jar. Even a teaspoon or two adds intense flavor to sauces, as demonstrated in the following pheasant recipe, and it makes a superlative secret ingredient in rice pilaf, fried or mashed potatoes, or our Buttermilk Potato Casserole.

Pheasant with Rhubarb Sauce

Once common on American tables, pheasant is coming back due to new supplies made available by farm raising. It tastes heartier than the average chicken, more like a premium, field-grazed bird, though not always as naturally tender. The game birds go great with fruit flavors such as this tangy marinade and rhubarb sauce. We've only found pheasant whole, so for grilling we ask the butcher to halve the bird and then at home we quarter it into breast and leg sections, which require different cooking times. We don't recommend covered grilling for this recipe, because of the need for frequent access to the grate, but you could roast the whole pheasant covered as an alternative approach if you wished.

Serves 4

Two small farm-raised pheasants, about 2 to 2½ pounds
 each, halved

Fruity Pheasant Marinade
1 cup raspberry vinegar
2 teaspoons dried ginger
2 teaspoons vegetable oil
1 teaspoon salt
½ teaspoon fresh-ground black pepper

Rhubarb Sauce
2 cups chopped rhubarb, fresh or frozen
½ cup fruity but dry red wine, such as Zinfandel
6 tablespoons chicken stock
6 tablespoons sugar
⅛ teaspoon dried ginger
Pinch of salt
Generous grinding of black pepper
1 tablespoon butter

1 tablespoon rendered duck fat (see Technique Tip,
    page 298) or additional butter

Vegetable oil spray

. . . .

At least 2 hours and up to 8 hours before you plan to grill, prepare the pheasants. With a large, sharp knife, cut away the back and wings, saving them for stock. Slice the breasts apart from the leg-thigh sections, ending with four of each from the two pheasants.

Prepare the marinade, combining the ingredients in a small bowl. Place the pheasant pieces in a plastic bag, pour the marinade over them, and refrigerate.

Prepare the sauce, combining all of the ingredients except the butter and duck fat in a heavy saucepan. Bring the sauce to a boil over medium heat, then reduce the heat to medium-low and simmer the sauce for 20 to 25 minutes, stirring occasionally, until thick but still spoonable, with the rhubarb dissolved into the sauce. Whisk the butter and duck fat into the sauce just before removing from the heat. (The sauce can be made a day ahead and refrigerated. Reheat before continuing, adding a tablespoon or two of water if it seems too thick.)

Fire up the grill, bringing the temperature to medium (4 to 5 seconds with the hand test).

Remove the pheasant from the refrigerator, drain the marinade, and discard it. Let the pieces sit covered at room temperature for about 20 minutes. Spray the breast pieces generously with oil.

Transfer the leg-thigh pieces to the grill first, skin-side down. Grill them uncovered over medium heat for a total of 12 to 16 minutes, turning twice so that the majority of the cooking is done with the skin down. Add the breast pieces to the grill, skin-side down, about the time you first turn the leg-thigh pieces. Grill the breasts uncovered over medium heat for 8 to 12 minutes, again turning twice. This should result in all the pieces being done about the same time, but take them off as each is ready. The pheasant is done when opaque but still juicy. Expect the cooked pheasant to be pinker than chicken, with pink juices.

Spoon several tablespoons of sauce on each plate, and arrange a breast and thigh-leg piece over each pool of sauce. Serve hot with additional sauce on the side.

SIMPLY ZESTY QUAIL

We enjoy fried quail, but the bantam birds are never better than when they're grilled. Each one yields just a few morsels of meat, in this case fragrant with lemon zest.

SERVES 4

ZESTY LEMON PASTE
1½ tablespoons minced lemon zest
2 plump garlic cloves, minced
1 tablespoon olive oil
2 teaspoons minced fresh thyme or 1 teaspoon dried
    thyme
1 teaspoon kosher salt or other coarse salt

8 quail, halved
Thyme sprigs, for garnish

At least 2½ hours and up to 8 hours before you plan to grill, prepare the paste, combining the ingredients in a small bowl. Coat the quail with the paste, rubbing it over and under the skin without tearing the skin. Place the quail in a plastic bag and refrigerate.

Fire up the grill, bringing the temperature to medium-high (3 seconds with the hand test).

Remove the quail from the refrigerator, drain them, and let them sit covered at room temperature for about 20 minutes.

Grill the quail uncovered over medium-high heat for 4 to 6 minutes per side, until opaque but still juicy. Expect the cooked quail to be a little pinker than chicken. If grilling covered, cook the quail for 7 to 10 minutes, turning once midway.

Serve the quail hot with warm wilted greens and maybe our grilled Minted Figs for dessert.

COFFEE-RUBBED QUAIL

A versatile bird, quail shines with light, simple flavors, as in the previous recipe, but it can also take stout seasonings such as this ground coffee bean and black pepper rub.

SERVES 4

RED-EYE RUB WITH SAGE
2 tablespoons coarse-ground coffee beans
1 tablespoon coarse-ground black pepper
1 heaping teaspoon kosher salt or other coarse salt
½ teaspoon dried sage

8 quail, halved

At least 2½ hours and up to 8 hours before you plan to grill, prepare the dry rub, combining the ingredients in a small bowl. Coat the quail with the rub, massaging it over and under the skin without tearing the skin. Place the quail in a plastic bag and refrigerate.

Fire up the grill, bringing the temperature to medium-high (3 seconds with the hand test).

Remove the quail from the refrigerator and let them sit covered at room temperature for about 20 minutes.

Grill the quail uncovered over medium-high heat for 4 to 6 minutes per side, until opaque but still juicy. Expect the cooked quail to be a little pinker than chicken. If grilling covered, cook the quail for 7 to 10 minutes, turning once midway.

Serve the quail hot, possibly with a side of black-eyed peas.

SIZZLING FISH
AND
SHELLFISH

Sizzling Fish and Shellfish

Peppered Tuna Steak with Horseradish Cream

Grill tuna as you would a fine beef steak and it'll make you wonder what you ever saw in meat. Start with a thick, premium cut of scarlet yellowfin tuna—the even better bluefin is rarer in this country than a blue moon because of the prices paid for it in Japan—and cook it like a prime porterhouse over a two-level fire until it's just warmed through and still red or pink in the center. Coat it with a pepper crust and add a dollop of creamy horseradish sauce, as you might with beef, and you've got a seafaring steak that'll cause a stampede to the table on any ranch.

Serves 4

LEMON-PEPPER PASTE
1 tablespoon fresh lemon juice
1½ teaspoons vegetable oil
1½ teaspoons coarse-ground black pepper
½ teaspoon kosher salt or other coarse salt

Two 1-inch-thick tuna steaks, preferably yellowfin,
    approximately 1 pound each

HORSERADISH CREAM
½ cup sour cream
1 tablespoon prepared horseradish
2 teaspoons grated mild onion or onion juice
¼ teaspoon kosher salt or other coarse salt

At least 1 hour and up to 4 hours before you plan to grill the tuna steaks, prepare the paste, combining the ingredients in a small bowl. The mixture will be very wet. Coat the steaks with the paste, cover them, and refrigerate.

Make the horseradish cream, mixing the ingredients together in a small serving bowl. Refrigerate until needed.

Remove the tuna from the refrig-

erator and let it sit covered at room temperature for about 30 minutes. Blot any accumulated liquid from the surface of the steaks.

Fire up the grill for a two-level fire capable of cooking first on high heat (1 to 2 seconds with the hand test) and then on medium heat (4 to 5 seconds with the hand test).

Transfer the steaks to a well-oiled grate and grill uncovered over high heat for 2 minutes per side. Move the tuna to medium heat and continue cooking for an additional 2 to 3 minutes per side, leaving a distinctly pink center. If there is any resistance when you turn the fish, re-oil the grate. If grilling covered, sear both sides of the fish first on high heat uncovered for 2 minutes; finish the cooking with the cover on over medium heat for 4 to 5 minutes, turning once midway.

Serve the steaks immediately, halved for four diners, with dollops of the horseradish cream. For a summer supper, pair the tuna with new potatoes and string beans, dressed with vinaigrette, and served warm or chilled. Georgia Peaches with Praline Crunch make a mighty fine finale.

TECHNIQUE TIP: When we're serving 8-ounce fish steaks, as we suggest in many of these recipes, we grill thick 1-pound cuts and then halve them at the table. If you ask a seafood market for half-pound portions, they're likely to slice the fish too thin. With something as meaty as tuna, we want steaks, not bologna.

FENNEL-CRUSTED TUNA

A dry rub of fennel seeds and lemon zest provides a simple but savory coat for tuna, dressing up steaks for any occasion.

SERVES 4

ZESTY FENNEL DRY RUB
1 tablespoon plus 1 teaspoon crushed fennel seed
1 tablespoon plus 1 teaspoon minced lemon zest
1 teaspoon kosher salt or other coarse salt

Two 1-inch-thick tuna steaks, approximately 1 pound each
Olive oil spray, preferably, or vegetable oil spray
Lemon wedges for garnish
Fresh feathery fennel tops, optional, for garnish

At least 1 hour and up to 4 hours before you plan to grill the tuna steaks, prepare the dry rub, combining the ingredients in a small bowl. Rub the steaks with the dry rub, wrap them in plastic, and refrigerate.

Remove the steaks from the refrigerator and let them sit covered at room temperature for about 30 minutes.

Fire up the grill for a two-level fire capable of cooking first on high heat (1 to 2 seconds with the hand test) and then on medium heat (4 to 5 seconds with the hand test).

Just before grilling, spritz the steaks thoroughly with oil. Transfer the steaks to a well-oiled grate and grill uncovered over high heat for 2 minutes per side. Move the tuna to medium heat and continue cooking the steaks for an additional 2 to 3 minutes per side, leaving a distinctly pink center. If there is any resistance when you turn the fish, re-oil the grate. If grilling covered, sear both sides of the fish first on high heat uncovered for 2 minutes each; finish the cooking with the cover on over medium heat for 4 to 5 minutes, turning once midway.

Serve the steaks immediately, halved for four diners and garnished with lemons and, if you wish, fennel tops. For weeknight family fare, add St. Louis Italian Salad; for a special event, perhaps Garlic Bread Salad and True-Guilt Creamed Spinach.

FISHING FOR COMPLIMENTS

Grilling is a superb way to cook steaks, burgers, chops, and chicken, but other methods also work well and sometimes even a bit better. That's not the case with fish and shellfish, the only general food category in which grilling consistently excels as the best cooking process. You wouldn't try to grill a whole octopus or a number of other sea and freshwater denizens, but most of the common creatures and cuts sold in American fish markets thrive on the flame.

They aren't the easiest items to grill, however, and many of the standard backyard techniques fail to bring out the full flavor potential. Because of the delicacy of the flesh compared to meat, a lot of cooks assume fish and shellfish need a gentle medium fire. Some go so far as wrapping the food in foil, which steams the meal instead of grilling it, and others suggest that you shouldn't ever put flaky fish on the grate, ignoring the fact that fragile petrale sole holds an old and honorable place in the American grill tradition.

You do have to take proper precautions in applying fire to anything from the water, but when you do and you cook as quickly as possible, usually over high or medium-high heat, you end up with a freshness of flavor that'll shame a sushi chef. Before you start grilling, always make sure the cooking grate is spanking clean, well oiled but not dripping, and warmed with the cover on until it's hot. Oil again when you turn fish if there's the slightest hint of sticking. In most cases, turn only once but also rotate fillets and steaks 180° during the cooking to prevent burning the flesh that's in direct contact with the metal. For particularly delicate or small items, invest in a small-mesh grill rack to provide extra support for the food, keeping it as clean and oiled as the grate.

The general rule about cooking time for fish is 8 to 10 minutes per inch, but exceptions abound. Tuna and salmon overcook in that period, at least if you want them in the pink, but a dense monkfish will still be ready for a swim. Unless otherwise noted in the recipes, cook fish and shellfish until just opaque, being vigilant about taking them off the fire at that point to preserve freshness and tenderness. To test for doneness, cut into a steak and peek, as we advise for a similar cut of beef, and flake into a fillet with a fork. Don't be hesitant to look inside after a reasonable cooking time because it's important to reel in your catch with a swift and sure hand.

SWORDFISH STEAK WITH TART TOMATILLO VINAIGRETTE

Meaty, thick steaks other than tuna, such as cuts of swordfish and halibut, grill best on a medium-high fire, which simultaneously sears the surface and cooks the flesh through. Try the temp on these coriander-rubbed steaks, graced at the table with a tangy vinaigrette.

SERVES 4

CORIANDER DRY RUB
2 tablespoons ground coriander
2 tablespoons paprika
2 teaspoons kosher salt or other coarse salt
1 teaspoon ground cumin

Four 1-inch-thick swordfish steaks, approximately
    ¾ pound each

TOMATILLO VINAIGRETTE
¼ pound tomatillos (about 4 medium), husked and
    rinsed, preferably, or an equivalent amount of
    canned tomatillos
¼ cup vegetable oil
1 tablespoon minced onion
1 tablespoon fresh lime juice
½ fresh jalapeño, minced
1 garlic clove, minced
⅛ teaspoon salt

Vegetable oil spray
Diced red-ripe tomato, for garnish

At least 1 hour and up to 4 hours before you plan to grill the swordfish steaks, prepare the dry rub, combining the ingredients in a small bowl. Rub the steaks with the mixture, wrap them in plastic, and refrigerate.

Prepare the vinaigrette, combining the ingredients in a food processor.

Remove the steaks from the refrigerator and let them sit covered at room temperature for about 30 minutes.

Fire up the grill, bringing the temperature to medium-high (3 seconds with the hand test).

Transfer the steaks to a well-oiled grate and grill uncovered over medium-high heat for 4 to 5 minutes per side, until opaque throughout. Rotate the fish 180° once on each side. If there is any resistance when you turn or rotate the fish, re-oil the grate. If grilling covered, cook for the same amount of time, turning and rotating in a similar manner.

Serve the steaks hot, drizzled with the vinaigrette. Swordfish doesn't make good leftovers, so eat up. If you're looking for a different kind of side dish, the tangy steaks can hold their own with a red chile Enchilada Casserole.

Two-Fisted Swordfish Sandwich

When we tested this one on friends, they grimaced at the idea of pairing Tabasco-laced swordfish and country ham. After a few bites, they were grinning as big as Huck Finn on a Mississippi River hustle.

SERVES 4

Two 1-inch-thick swordfish steaks, cut horizontally in half to create 4 thin steaks
Juice of 2 lemons
½ teaspoon Tabasco sauce or other hot pepper sauce

QUICK SWORDFISH RUB
1 teaspoon kosher salt or other coarse salt
1 teaspoon fresh-ground black pepper
1 teaspoon paprika

Vegetable oil spray
8 thin slices country bread
Enriched Mayonnaise (page 38) or other mayonnaise
Watercress sprigs
8 paper-thin slices country ham or other smoky ham
Red-ripe tomato slices

• • • • • • • • • • • • • • • • • •

Place the swordfish steaks in a shallow dish or plastic bag. Pour the lemon juice and Tabasco over the steaks. Cover and refrigerate the swordfish for 20 to 30 minutes, turning to coat evenly.

Fire up the grill, bringing the temperature to medium-high (3 seconds with the hand test).

Remove the steaks from the refrigerator and drain them, discarding the liquid.

Prepare the dry rub, combining the ingredients in a small bowl. Coat the steaks with the rub, cover them, and let them sit at room temperature for about 15 minutes. Just before grilling, spritz the steaks with oil.

Transfer the swordfish to a well-oiled grate and grill uncovered over medium-high heat for about 3 minutes per side, until opaque throughout. Rotate the steaks 180° once on each side. If there is any resistance when you turn or rotate the fish, re-oil the grate. If grilling covered, cook for the same amount of time, turning and rotating in a similar manner. Toast the bread on the edge of the grill.

Spread mayonnaise generously on the toast. Pile the four sandwiches high, starting with watercress, a slice of ham, a fish steak, another slice of ham, tomatoes, and the remaining bread. Serve immediately with something crunchy, like sweet potato chips, on the side.

HALIBUT "WHALE" STEAK

The biggest halibuts stand taller than Michael Jordan and weigh in at more than a sumo wrestler, earning them their nickname of "whales." Their steaks or fillets are grand in taste as well, somewhat similar to swordfish but with a deeper flavor. They need little seasoning to shine, no more here than a smoked salmon butter and caper garnish.

SERVES 4

SMOKED SALMON BUTTER
6 tablespoons unsalted butter
3 ounces smoked salmon, minced
Zest and juice of 1 small lemon

1½-pound to 1¾-pound halibut steak or skinned fillet,
    approximately 1 inch thick
Olive oil
Kosher salt or other coarse salt

Minced fresh parsley
Large capers or larger caper berries

In a small skillet, melt the butter over medium-low heat. Stir in the salmon and, with the back of a fork, mash it until nearly dissolved into the butter. Remove the butter from the heat and stir in the lemon zest and juice. (The butter can be made a day or two ahead and refrigerated or frozen for several weeks. Reheat it before proceeding.) This makes a moderate amount of butter for four portions. Those who want bigger servings can easily increase the size of the batch proportionately.

If you purchased a single large halibut steak, cut around its center bone to make 4 medallions. If working with a fillet, slice it into 4 equal portions. Coat the fish lightly with the oil and sprinkle it with salt. Let it sit covered at room temperature for about 20 minutes.

Fire up the grill, bringing the heat to medium-high (3 seconds with the hand test).

Transfer the halibut to a well-oiled grate and grill uncovered over medium-high heat for 8 to 10 minutes per inch

of thickness, turning once, until opaque throughout. Rotate the fish 180° once on each side. If there is any resistance when you turn or rotate the fish, re-oil the grate. If grilling covered, cook for the same amount of time, turning and rotating in a similar manner.

Serve the halibut hot with spoonfuls of the smoked salmon butter and a garnish of parsley and capers.

FORTY-NINE-STAR HALIBUT WITH SWEET MUSTARD

Until recently most Alaskan halibut reached the rest of the country frozen, but today it's widely available fresh. Moister than its North Atlantic cousins, it stands up well to high-heat cooking. This recipe calls for steaks or fillets, but also try the seasonings with the small, tender halibut cheeks, long a delicacy to native Alaskans and now being sold in the lower Forty-Eight (see Technique Tip).

SERVES 4

1½-pound to 1¾-pound halibut steak or skinned fillet, approximately 1 inch thick

MUSTARD-TARRAGON PASTE
2 tablespoons Honey-Beer Mustard (page 37) or other sweet hot mustard
1 tablespoon minced fresh tarragon
1 teaspoon vegetable oil
½ teaspoon kosher salt or other coarse salt

If you purchased a single large halibut steak, cut around its center bone to make 4 medallions. If working with a fillet, slice it into 4 equal portions.

Prepare the paste, combining the ingredients in a small bowl, and rub the mixture over the steaks. Wrap the halibut in plastic and let it sit covered

at room temperature for 20 to 30 minutes.

Fire up the grill, bringing the heat to medium-high (3 seconds with the hand test).

Transfer the halibut to a well-oiled grate. Grill the halibut uncovered over medium-high heat for 8 to 10 minutes per inch of thickness, turning once, until opaque throughout. Rotate the fish 180° once on each side. If there is any resistance when you turn or rotate the

---

THE CATCH OF THE DAY

Living in the land-locked mountain West, the only thing we get direct out of the water is grains of silt from the bottom of the well. It's taken a lot of learning over the years to ferret out fresh seafood. That's been an advantage in some ways, at least in contrast to the unquestioning smugness of friends who live on the coast and simply assume they always enjoy the best of Neptune's bounty.

Today, dedication to quality by the fish market and the shopper count for more in securing fresh seafood than proximity to a harbor. Location can matter, but only when the other factors are equal. Some inland purveyors go to great lengths to carry the finest catch of the day—flying it from the dock to their door with more care than airlines give human passengers on the same planes—while some of their counterparts on the waterfront can be complacent. Wherever you live, look for a local market that specializes in seafood and demonstrates a true pas-

sion for freshness. The place should smell pleasantly briny but not "fishy," and the employees should know the intimate life story of every creature in the case, including when it left the water and arrived on shore and how it was handled and transported.

Keep up your end of the commitment by asking questions—even when you have no idea of the right answer—and by staring down potential purchases. Whole fish should have shiny skin and bright gills, and most should have clear eyes. Steaks and fillets should be cut to order, or at least earlier that day and kept since in a cold, closed case. Try to avoid anything pre-wrapped in plastic, which can disguise flaws. On hot days, take along a cooler for storing seafood for the trip home or have it packed in ice. For an important party, or when you want something different, call a few days in advance and see about placing a special order, usually possible at a good market and an easy way to establish yourself as an important customer.

fish, re-oil the grate. If grilling covered, cook for the same amount of time, turning and rotating in a similar manner.

Serve the halibut immediately, perhaps with Bastille Day Beans.

TECHNIQUE TIP: Halibut cheeks are meaty little nuggets, vaguely oval-shaped and weighing several ounces. More pronounced in taste than halibut steaks or fillets, and a little denser, they pull apart in shreds, something like what you'd expect with crab. Season or grill them as you would other cuts of halibut, but remember to reduce the cooking time depending on their size.

HILO FISH MARKET FEAST

Any visitor to Hawaii should take a break from the beach at least once to see the amazing, century-old Suisan Fish Auction in Hilo. Every morning except Sunday, the large, multiethnic fishing fleet sells its catch in rapid-fire pidgin English. The fish always include dense-textured deep-sea varieties such as ono, known in Florida waters as wahoo. If you miss a bid on the ono, substitute any similar fish from the same depths, including mahi-mahi or halibut. The accompanying pineapple sauce is fruity but without the cloying sweetness of some blends.

SERVES 6

PINEAPPLE SAUCE
3 tablespoons butter
3 tablespoons chopped sweet onion, such as Maui or Vidalia, or shallots
2 tablespoons minced fresh ginger
1 pound fresh pineapple, chopped, with any accumulated juice
1 cup orange juice
1 teaspoon curry powder
½ teaspoon crushed dried hot red pepper
¼ cup chopped fresh mint
Salt

6 skinned 6-ounce to 7-ounce ono (wahoo), mahi-mahi,
   or halibut fillet sections
Vegetable oil spray
Salt and fresh-ground black pepper
6 banana leaves, optional, for garnish

• • • • • • • • • • • • • • • • • •

Prepare the sauce, first warming the butter in a medium saucepan over medium heat. Add the onion and the ginger and sauté for about 5 minutes, until the onion is translucent. Stir in the pineapple and its juice, the orange juice, curry powder, and red pepper. Continue cooking 8 to 10 more minutes, until the mixture is reduced and thick. Stir in the mint while the sauce is hot and add salt to taste. Keep the sauce warm. (The sauce can be made a day ahead, covered, and refrigerated. Reheat it before serving, adding a little water if it becomes too thick to spoon easily.)

Fire up the grill, bringing the heat to medium-high (3 seconds with the hand test).

Spritz the fillets with oil and salt and pepper them lightly. Let them sit covered at room temperature for about 20 minutes.

Transfer the fillets to a well-oiled grate. Grill uncovered over medium-high heat for 8 to 10 minutes per inch of thickness, turning once, until opaque throughout. Rotate the fillets 180° once on each side. If there is any resistance when you turn or rotate the fish, re-oil the grate. If grilling covered, cook for the same amount of time, turning and rotating in a similar manner.

Serve the fillets hot. For an exotic touch, arrange them on banana leaves, often available fresh or frozen in Asian groceries. Spoon a dollop or two of the pineapple sauce over each fillet and pass the remaining sauce at the table.

ORANGE AND OREGANO SHARK STEAK

A bland fish, shark favors strong flavors, especially acids like vinegar or the citrus juice we use here. The marinade's sprightly mix of orange and lime juices emulates the tang of sour oranges, relatively rare in this country still but deservedly popular south of the border. If your fishmonger is short of shark, substitute swordfish steaks.

SERVES 4

Four 8-ounce mako or other shark steaks, skin
    removed, or swordfish steaks, about 1 inch thick

SOUR ORANGE MARINADE
1½ cups orange juice
¼ cup fresh lime juice
1 tablespoon dried oregano
1 tablespoon Mexican hot sauce, such as Cholula, or 1½
    teaspoons Tabasco sauce

Salt
Fresh oregano sprigs, optional, for garnish

At least 1 hour and up to 4 hours before you plan to grill, prepare the shark steaks. Score both sides of the flesh about ¼ inch deep at ½-inch intervals to allow the dense meat to absorb more flavoring. Prepare the marinade, mixing together the ingredients in a small bowl. Place the steaks in a plastic bag, pour the marinade over them, and refrigerate.

Remove the steaks from the refrigerator and drain them, discarding the marinade. Let them sit covered at room temperature for about 30 minutes. Blot any excess moisture from the surface and salt the steaks lightly.

Fire up the grill, bringing the temperature to high (1 to 2 seconds with the hand test).

Transfer the steaks to a well-oiled grate. Grill them uncovered over high heat for 8 to 10 minutes per inch of thickness, turning once, until opaque throughout. Rotate the steaks 180°

once on each side. If there is any resistance when you turn or rotate the fish, re-oil the grate. If grilling covered, cook for the same amount of time, turning and rotating them in a similar manner.

Serve the steaks hot, garnished with oregano if you wish. The shark tastes great paired in a fish-and-chips style with Crispy Cumin Fries.

TAPENADE-TOPPED FISH

The briny bite of a green olive tapenade, combined with a cracked-pepper coating, tames mackerel, bluefish, and other assertively flavored oily fish, but doesn't overrun other meaty but milder fish like marlin.

SERVES 4

GREEN OLIVE TAPENADE
½ cup packed drained briny green olives
2 teaspoons capers
1 medium anchovy fillet
1½ teaspoons fresh lemon juice
⅓ cup olive oil

Two 1-inch-thick meaty fish steaks, ¾ to 1 pound each
1 tablespoon coarse-ground black pepper

Prepare the tapenade. In a food processor, combine the olives, capers, anchovy, and lemon juice. With the processor running, pour in the oil in a steady stream to make a thick purée. Spoon out ¼ cup of the tapenade and reserve it. Rub the rest of the tapenade over the fish steaks, pat them with the pepper, and wrap them in plastic. Let the fish marinate at room temperature for about 30 minutes.

Fire up the grill, bringing the temperature to high (1 to 2 seconds with the hand test).

Transfer the steaks to a well-oiled grate. Grill them uncovered over high heat for 4 to 5 minutes per side, until opaque throughout. Rotate the steaks 180° once on each side. If there is any resistance when you turn or rotate the fish, re-oil the grate. If grilling covered, cook for the same amount of time,

turning and rotating them in a similar manner.

Serve the steaks immediately, halved for four diners, topping each portion with a dollop of the reserved tapenade.

TECHNIQUE TIP: In his impressive tome *Fish* (Macmillan, 1994)—a great reference work for any seafood lover—Mark Bittman makes the good point that marinating fish before grilling "is not a bad idea; it is just one that has been overplayed." While we enjoy lively seasonings that complement food, it's important to match their strength and character with what you're cooking. Even a fish as robust as mackerel can be washed away with too much of a good thing.

SAGE AND BACON MONKFISH KEBOBS

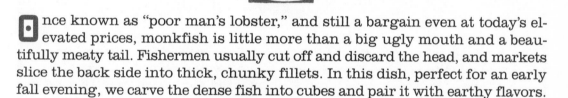

Once known as "poor man's lobster," and still a bargain even at today's elevated prices, monkfish is little more than a big ugly mouth and a beautifully meaty tail. Fishermen usually cut off and discard the head, and markets slice the back side into thick, chunky fillets. In this dish, perfect for an early fall evening, we carve the dense fish into cubes and pair it with earthy flavors.

SERVES 4 TO 6

SIMPLE SAGE PASTE
1½ tablespoons Sage Oil (page 40), or 1 tablespoon
    extra-virgin olive oil plus 1 tablespoon minced fresh
    sage
3 garlic cloves, minced
2 teaspoons paprika

2 pounds monkfish, cut into 2-inch chunks
Metal skewers, preferably 2 per kebob
1 large red onion, cut into thin 1-inch chunks
Sage leaves, for garnish

Prepare the paste, combining the ingredients in a shallow dish. Toss the monkfish cubes with the mixture, coating them well. Cover and let the fish sit at room temperature for about 30 minutes.

Fire up the grill, bringing the temperature to high (1 to 2 seconds with the hand test.)

Thread the kebobs, preferably using 2 skewers per kebob to hold the ingredients securely while cooking. Thread the monkfish alternately with the onions. Push the onions right up against the fish so that they don't burn before the fish is done.

Transfer the kebobs to a well-oiled grate. Grill them uncovered over high heat for 12 to 14 minutes, turning on all sides. The monkfish is ready when quite firm and easily pierced with a fork (it doesn't flake). If grilling covered, cook the kebobs for 10 to 12 minutes, turning once midway.

Serve the kebobs immediately. We like them on a bed of sautéed red cabbage, followed by Bourbon Caramel Apples.

NOT TRULY TRASHY

Just a decade ago, monkfish was considered a "trash fish," a label applied to many sea creatures that have little market value because of their unsightly appearance, bony body, or other daunting characteristics. Like Cinderella before the ball, not all deserve their reputation. Some actually taste great when properly prepared and may even be favorites in other parts of the world.

Our recipes call for types of fish and shellfish that are widely available, but they can be adapted to these trashier subjects when you find them on sale for pennies a pound. All of us are likely to be making such adjustments anyway in the years ahead as we continue to chow down the supply of our most popular seafoods.

The first problem in many cases is just getting beyond the name. Do you really want to tell your friends—much less your kids—that you're cooking up some fine dogfish, croakers, or pouts? So call them something else. Then you have to square the looks with the taste. Once you've tried them, though, you'll find that parrot fish won't send you psychedelic, despite their tie-dyed appearance, the snaggle-toothed wolffish won't bite back, and the tiny transparent eels known as elvers slide down as easy as oysters. If you're eating luscious monkfish, after all, you've already mastered ugly.

BOSTON STRIPER

Found mainly on the middle and upper East Coast, striped bass has been a regional favorite since Colonial days, so tasty that anglers depleted the population dangerously by the 1980s and forced a fishing ban. They're back now in the wild and also available in a milder, farm-raised form, actually a hybrid. We grill them whole in a simple preparation that makes an impressive presentation.

SERVES 6

3 small whole striped bass, hybrid striped bass, other
    small bass, or other mild-flavored fish, about 2
    pounds each, gutted and cleaned
2 tablespoons olive oil
1 medium onion, sliced thin
Zest and juice of 1 lemon
½ teaspoon ground fennel seed
Kosher salt or other coarse salt
¼ cup minced feathery fennel tops

Additional olive oil, optional
Fennel tops and lemon wedges, for garnish

At least 1 hour and up to 4 hours before you plan to cook the bass, prepare them for grilling. To promote even cooking and flavor absorption, cut 3 deep diagonal slashes into the sides of each fish. In a small skillet, warm the oil over medium heat. Add the onion and cook for 2 to 3 minutes until it begins to soften. Drain the oil off into a small bowl and add to it the lemon zest and juice and fennel seed. Rub this mixture over the fish and into the slashes, coating the bass inside and out. Salt the

fish lightly, then fill the cavity of each loosely with the par-cooked onion slices and chopped fennel tops. Wrap the fish in plastic and refrigerate.

Fire up the grill, bringing the temperature to medium-high (3 seconds with the hand test).

Remove the bass from the refrigerator and let them sit covered at room temperature about 20 minutes.

Transfer the fish to a well-oiled grate with their tails arranged away from the hottest part of the fire. Grill

the fish uncovered over medium-high heat for 9 to 10 minutes per inch of thickness, turning once, until opaque throughout. To turn the fish, roll each of them over gently rather than lifting them up and flipping them. If there is any resistance when you turn the fish, re-oil the grate. If grilling covered, cook the fish for 8 to 9 minutes per inch of thickness, turning once midway.

Brush the top side of each fish with oil for a shinier appearance. Transfer the fish to a platter, garnish generously with more fennel tops and lemon wedges, and serve hot.

TECHNIQUE TIP: When grilling whole fish, look for ones that are no thicker than about 1¼ inches at their most portly point and are just large enough for one or two full servings. They are relatively easy to handle at that size and provide an optimum proportion of grilled surface to moist interior. Using medium-high heat gets a good surface sear but allows the center to cook through before the skin burns. A gentle rolling over is preferable to lifting up and flipping the somewhat fragile whole fish.

MERMAID'S TREASURE

When you cut into this small whole fish at the table, you find a fortune of flavors, with a robust Louisiana-style hash nestled in the creamy flesh. If you can't locate the andouille sausage for the stuffing, use another hearty-flavored sausage and add a healthy pinch of cayenne. The hash can be prepared a day in advance, but refrigerate the andouille-bacon mixture separately from everything else, stirring it in shortly before reheating the filling.

SERVES 6

2 small whole snapper, grouper, redfish, or other mild white fish, about 2 pounds each, gutted and cleaned, preferably boned

CREOLE SLATHER
1 tablespoon Creole mustard
Juice of 1 lemon
1 teaspoon kosher salt or other coarse salt
¼ teaspoon fresh-ground black pepper

ANDOUILLE HASH

3 tablespoons butter

8 ounces andouille sausage links, quartered lengthwise and chopped fine

4 ounces uncooked bacon, chopped

1½ pounds red waxy potatoes, peeled or unpeeled, and cut into ⅛-inch chunks

2 cups chopped onion

2 cups chopped celery

1 medium red bell pepper, chopped

2 garlic cloves, minced

¼ cup water

2 teaspoons Creole mustard

1½ teaspoons dried thyme or 1 teaspoon crumbled dried sage

1 teaspoon kosher salt or other coarse salt, or more to taste

Pinch of cayenne, optional

1 egg, slightly beaten

Vegetable oil, optional

Lemon slices, for garnish

• • • • • • • • • • • • • • • • • •

At least 1 hour and up to 4 hours before you plan to cook the fish, prepare them for grilling. To promote even cooking and flavor absorption, cut 3 deep diagonal slashes into the sides of each fish. Prepare the slather, combining the ingredients in a small bowl. Rub the mixture over the fish and into the slashes, coating the fish inside and out. Wrap the fish in plastic and refrigerate.

Prepare the hash. In a large, heavy skillet, melt the butter over medium heat. Add the andouille and bacon and sauté until both are brown and crisp, about 10 minutes. Remove the andouille and bacon with a slotted spoon, drain them, and reserve. Stir the potatoes into the pan drippings and sauté over medium heat until the potatoes have softened and begun to crust, 15 to 20 minutes. Pour off and discard the excess pan drippings from the potatoes, leaving just a thin glisten of oil in the skillet and on the potatoes. Add the onion, celery, bell pepper, and garlic and continue cooking until the vegetables are soft and cooked through. Stir in the water, mustard, thyme, salt, and optional cayenne and cook just until the liquid is absorbed. (The hash can be made to this point a day ahead, cooled, and then refrigerated. Reheat before proceeding.) Stir in the reserved

andouille and bacon and taste for seasoning. Mix in the egg and remove from the heat. You will have more hash than will fit inside the two fish.

Preheat the oven to 350° F.

Fire up the grill, bringing the temperature to medium-high (3 seconds with the hand test).

Fill the fish loosely with as much hash as they will easily hold. Spoon the rest of the hash into an oiled loaf pan or small shallow baking dish, cover it, and bake it for about 20 minutes at 350° F.

Transfer the fish to a well-oiled grate with their tails arranged away from the hottest part of the fire. Grill the fish uncovered over medium-high heat for 9 to 10 minutes per inch of thickness, turning once, until opaque throughout. To turn the fish, roll each of them over gently rather than lifting them up and flipping them. If there is any resistance when you turn the fish, re-oil the grate. If grilling covered, cook the fish for 8 to 9 minutes per inch of thickness, turning once midway.

Brush the top side of each fish with oil for a shinier appearance. Transfer the fish to a serving platter, spoon the oven-baked hash around them, top them with the lemon slices, and serve hot. If the fish weren't boned before cooking, slice the flesh portions off the top of their sides, from over the bones, scoop hash from inside the cavities, and discard the bones. If boned, you can slice down through the fish and just scoop up each portion of fish and hash together.

TECHNIQUE TIP: We suggest baking the hash in the oven indoors because it works for everyone. If you have a gas grill, however, you can avoid heating up the house by baking the hash on the grill instead. Use the grill, covered, as an oven with the heat at medium, cooking for the same amount of time as called for. When done, crank up the heat a notch for grilling the fish uncovered and keep the hash warm until you're ready to serve.

CIDER AND BROWN SUGAR SALMON FILLET

We prefer to grill salmon fillets rather than steaks because of a trick we learned from chef Mark Miller. If you start a fillet skin-side down, you can cook the fish partially on high heat without drying it out. After grilling the flesh side to complete the cooking, remove the skin and serve the salmon with the other, seared side up on the plate. We always re-oil the grate, and wait for any flames to subside, before turning the fillet, to keep the flesh from sticking to the metal. Prepared in this way, salmon remains moist while developing a deliciously crusty surface, and it takes readily to fruity or savory seasonings, combined in this preparation.

SERVES 6

· · · · · · · · · · · · · · · · · · · ·

CIDER AND BROWN SUGAR MARINADE
6-ounce can frozen apple cider or juice concentrate,
    thawed
2 tablespoons vegetable oil
1 tablespoon brown sugar
1 tablespoon salt

2-pound skin-on salmon fillet, about 1 inch thick

MIXED SPICE RUB
1 tablespoon cracked black pepper
1 tablespoon cracked mustard seeds
1 teaspoon crushed dried hot red chile
1 teaspoon paprika
1 teaspoon ground coriander

Vegetable oil spray

· · · · · · · · · · · · · · · · · · ·

At least 1 hour and up to 4 hours before you plan to grill, prepare the marinade, combining the ingredients in a small bowl. Place the salmon in a plastic bag or shallow dish and pour the marinade over it. Cover and refrigerate.

Remove the salmon from the refrigerator. Drain it, discarding the marinade. Combine the dry rub ingredients in a small bowl and coat the flesh side of the salmon with the mixture. Cover the salmon again and let it sit at room temperature for about 30 minutes.

Fire up the grill, bringing the temperature to high (1 to 2 seconds with the hand test).

Just before you grill the salmon, spritz it with the oil. Transfer the salmon to a well-oiled grate and grill it skin-side down over high heat for 5 to 6 minutes, until the skin chars nearly black. Turn the salmon and cook for an additional 3 to 3½ minutes, rotating the fillets 180° once. If there is any resistance when you turn or rotate the fish, re-oil the grate. The salmon is done when just barely opaque pink at the center with a touch of translucence remaining. If grilling covered, cook the salmon for the same amount of time, turning and rotating in a similar manner.

Carefully strip the skin off the bottom of the salmon fillet and serve hot. We like to start with Amazing Aspic or a chilled cucumber soup, toss in a toss-up of seasonal greens, and end with blackberries and buttery shortbread.

TECHNIQUE TIP: Most salmon are great for grilling because of their high fat content, which keeps them juicy over a hot fire and provides wonderful flavor. The only kinds we avoid are pink and chum salmon, both relatively lean fish that tend to dry out in high-heat cooking. All the other American varieties—king, sockeye, coho, and Atlantic—work fine, even when frozen out of season. Some markets skin their salmon fillets, trying to make them more attractive to a prospective customer. If that's all you see in the case, ask for assistance. There may be plenty of unskinned fish behind the scene.

SALMON WITH MAC NUTS AND MANGOS

The Hawaiian love of salmon inspired this combo, featuring the fish with luscious mangos and sumptuous macadamia nuts.

SERVES 4

MANGO MARINADE
6 tablespoons mango vinegar, such as Consorzio, or other fruit vinegar, such as Peach Vinegar (page 41)
2 tablespoons macadamia nut oil, or other nut oil
2 tablespoons minced chives or green onions
½ teaspoon kosher salt or other coarse salt

Four 5-ounce to 6-ounce sections skin-on salmon fillet, each preferably ¾ to 1 inch thick

2 medium mangos, peeled and diced
1 tablespoon mango vinegar, such as Consorzio, or other fruit vinegar, such as Peach Vinegar (page 41)
4 tablespoons toasted macadamia nuts, chopped
Minced chives, for garnish

Prepare the marinade, combining the ingredients in a small bowl. Place the salmon fillets in a shallow dish or plate, skin-side down. Drizzle the flesh of each fillet with the marinade, covering the entire surface. Cover the salmon and let sit at room temperature for 20 to 30 minutes.

Fire up the grill, bringing the temperature to high (1 to 2 seconds with the hand test).

Drain the salmon, discarding the marinade.

Transfer the salmon to a well-oiled grate and grill it skin-side down over high heat for 5 to 6 minutes, until the skin chars nearly black. Turn the salmon and cook for an additional 3 to 3½ minutes, rotating the fillets 180° once. If there is any resistance when

you turn or rotate the salmon, re-oil the grate. The salmon is done when just barely opaque pink at the center with a touch of translucence remaining. If grilling covered, cook the salmon for the same amount of time, turning and rotating in a similar manner.

Carefully strip the skin off the bottom of each salmon fillet. Serve the salmon hot on a platter or individual plates. In a small bowl, combine the mangos with the mango vinegar and macadamia nuts. Top the fillets with equal portions of the mango-nut mixture and sprinkle chives over each. We like to accompany the salmon with a spinach salad dressed with a mango vinegar vinaigrette.

TECHNIQUE TIP: If you ever have the misfortune to find your macadamia nuts still in the shell, forget that little hand-held cracker. In the days before commercial production, Hawaiians extracted the meat by placing the tough nuts between thick boards and driving a car over their woodsy version of a Big Mac sandwich. Once the nut is out of the shell, store macadamias in the refrigerator or freezer or they will go rancid quickly because of their high oil content. Pine nuts make the best substitute.

GRILLED GRAVLAX

A brined salmon fillet firms up while curing, making it a breeze to grill on a hot fire. For the vodka cure, use only fresh dill, not dried, and soak the fish in the mixture for at least 12 hours. The unconventional gravlax works as either an entrée or an appetizer.

SERVES 6 AS A MAIN DISH OR 8 AS AN APPETIZER

2-pound skin-on salmon fillet, ¾ to 1 inch thick

VODKA CURE
2 tablespoons vodka
2 tablespoons minced fresh dill
2 tablespoons kosher salt or other coarse salt
2 tablespoons sugar
1 tablespoon coarse-ground black pepper

MUSTARD-DILL SAUCE
½ cup sour cream or plain yogurt
2 tablespoons minced fresh dill or 1 tablespoon dried
   dill
1 tablespoon Dijon mustard
¼ teaspoon white pepper
Pinch of sugar

Vegetable oil spray
Fresh dill, optional, for garnish

• • • • • • • • • • • • • • • • • • •

At least 12 hours and preferably up to 24 hours before you plan to grill the salmon, place it in a shallow dish, flesh side up. Pour the vodka evenly over the salmon. Combine the remaining cure ingredients in a small bowl and rub them evenly over the top and sides of the salmon. Cover the dish tightly and refrigerate.

Fire up the grill, bringing the temperature to high (1 to 2 seconds with the hand test).

Remove the salmon from the refrigerator, drain it of accumulated liquid, and let it sit at room temperature for 20 to 30 minutes.

Prepare the sauce, combining the ingredients in a small bowl.

Just before you grill the salmon, spritz it with the oil. Transfer the salmon to a well-oiled grate and grill it skin-side down over high heat for 5 to 6 minutes, until the skin chars nearly black. Turn the salmon and cook for an additional 3 to 3½ minutes, rotating the fillet 180° once. If there is any resistance when you turn or rotate the fish, re-oil the grate. The salmon is done when just barely opaque pink at the center with a touch of translucence remaining. If grilling covered, cook the salmon for the same amount of time, turning and rotating in a similar manner.

Remove the skin and serve the fillet whole on a platter. Unlike regular gravlax, which is sliced thin, this version can be cut into individual fillet portions with the sauce spooned on the side for a main course or, for an appetizer, can be flaked in small chunks and served on bread or cucumber slices with dollops of sauce. Chilled leftovers will be tasty too.

THE KING OF AMERICAN WATERS

The traditional New England Fourth of July menu features salmon, bathed in a creamy hard-boiled egg sauce and accompanied by pickled green peas. Across the continent on the farthest Pacific shore, Hawaiians call the fish "the pig in the sea" and make their *lomi lomi* version a highlight of luaus, alongside the pork from the *imu*. From coast to coast—salted, smoked, canned, and fresh—nothing from our waters has ever rivaled the eminence of salmon.

Bountiful in the North Atlantic before the twentieth century, salmon thrived even more in the Northwest, to such an extent that spawning schools almost halted the country's "Manifest Destiny," temporarily blocking the progress of Lewis and Clark down the Columbia River. Natives of the region revered the fish, shrouding its spirit in rituals and myths. According to Dale Brown in *American Cooking: The Northwest* (Time-Life Books, 1970), the Chinook Indians went so far as to bury the terminally ill alive because they believed that "anyone involved in preparing a corpse for burial could drive the fish away." They also burned salmon hearts to prevent them from being devoured by dogs, a sacrilege, and prohibited menstruating women from eating the fish, for fear of tainting the catch.

Today, the vast majority of wild salmon comes from Alaska and is shipped from there across the country, fresh in the summer and frozen the rest of the year. The prized king salmon (also called chinook) goes mainly to restaurants, but fish markets usually get a good supply of the equally delectable sockeye or red variety. Rich and fatty, both types taste untamed, unlike farm-raised, year-round-fresh Atlantic salmon, also laden with fat and preferred by some for its milder moistness. Hot off the grill, any of these salmon makes a majestic meal.

DILLED SALMON STEAK

When you're in a pickle about what to grill, think about this salmon steak, rubbed with dill and served with a cucumber-dill relish. The herb mates well with salmon in both this and the previous recipe, but the results are entirely different.

SERVES 4

DILL RUB
2 tablespoons minced fresh dill
1 teaspoon kosher salt or other coarse salt
½ teaspoon ground white pepper

Four 1-inch-thick salmon steaks

CUCUMBER-DILL RELISH
1 medium cucumber, peeled, seeded, and diced
⅛ cup fresh asparagus tips, chopped if larger than
    bite-size, optional
3 tablespoons minced onion
6 tablespoons white vinegar
¼ cup sugar
¼ teaspoon kosher salt or other coarse salt, or more to
    taste
Pinch of white pepper
1 to 2 tablespoons water

Vegetable oil spray

At least 1 hour and up to 4 hours before you plan to grill the salmon steaks, prepare the rub, combining the ingredients is a small bowl. Coat the steaks with the rub, cover them, and refrigerate.

Prepare the relish, combining the ingredients in a medium bowl. Add as much of the water as necessary to keep the relish moist. Refrigerate covered until serving time.

Fire up the grill, bringing the temperature to high (1 to 2 seconds with the hand test).

Remove the steaks from the refrigerator and let them sit covered at room temperature for about 20 minutes. Just before you are ready to grill the steaks, spritz them heavily with oil.

Transfer the steaks to a well-oiled grate. Grill them uncovered over high heat for 4 to 4½ minutes per side, rotating them 180° once on each side. If there is any resistance when you turn or rotate the fish, re-oil the grate. The salmon is done when just barely opaque pink at the center with a touch of translucence remaining. If grilling covered, cook the salmon for the same amount of time, turning and rotating in a similar manner.

Arrange the steaks on individual plates, spooning equal portions of the relish over each and in the V of the "tails." Serve immediately.

TECHNIQUE TIP: When selecting salmon steaks or other fish steaks for the grill, try to pick ones with thick "tails," for more even cooking. If you have no other choice than skinny tails, they can be curled inward and secured with toothpicks.

LEAPING SALMON CLUB

Salmon takes its name from the Latin word that means "to leap," which the fish does with gravity-defying strength as it swims upstream to spawn. We're way out of that league, but we've done a little leaping of our own over this summery, single-decker club sandwich.

SERVES 4

BASIL PASTE
¼ cup minced fresh basil
2 teaspoons vegetable oil
1 teaspoon kosher salt or other coarse salt
1 teaspoon fresh-cracked black pepper

Four 5-ounce to 6-ounce sections skin-on salmon fillet,
    each preferably ½ to ¾ inch thick
3 slices uncooked bacon, chopped
1 small red onion, slivered

BASIL MAYONNAISE
¼ cup Enriched Mayonnaise (page 38) or other
   mayonnaise
1½ tablespoons minced fresh basil

8 thin slices sturdy sourdough or semolina bread
Red-ripe tomato slices
Lettuce leaves

• • • • • • • • • • • • • • • • • • •

At least 1 hour and up to 4 hours before you plan to grill the salmon fillets, prepare the paste, combining the ingredients in a small bowl. Rub the paste over the salmon, wrap it in plastic, and refrigerate.

In a small skillet, fry the bacon until brown and crisp. With a slotted spoon, remove the bacon and drain it, reserving the drippings. Sauté the onion briefly in the bacon drippings until soft. Drain the onion and reserve it.

Prepare the basil mayonnaise, combining both ingredients, and reserve it.

Fire up the grill, bringing the temperature to high (1 to 2 seconds with the hand test).

Remove the salmon from the refrigerator and let it sit covered for about 20 minutes.

Transfer the salmon to a well-oiled grate and grill it skin-side down over high heat for 5 to 6 minutes, until the skin chars nearly black. Turn the salmon and cook for an additional 3 to 3½ minutes, rotating the fillets 180° once. If there is any resistance when you turn or rotate the fish, re-oil the grate. The salmon is done when just barely opaque pink at the center with a touch of translucence remaining. If grilling covered, cook the salmon for the same amount of time, turning and rotating in a similar manner. Toast the bread on the edge of the grill.

Carefully strip the skin off the bottom of each salmon fillet. Slather the basil mayonnaise over one side of each slice of toasted bread. Place a salmon fillet section on each of 4 slices of bread. Spoon equal portions of sautéed onion over the fish and then layer on equal portions of bacon, tomato slices, and lettuce over the fish. Top each sandwich with one of the remaining slices of bread. Serve immediately, with potato chips and Green Onion Dip, if you like.

Sage Trout with Apple-Pecan Crunch

A kissing cousin to the salmon, trout can be equally rich, but it doesn't take as well to farm cultivation. You have to be a fisherman, or owed a major favor by one, to get full-flavored wild trout today. If you can manage it, you'll be homesteading cloud nine. The rest of us have to make do with blander farm-raised trout, which needs a little help, provided here by sandwiching sage leaves between fillets and topping the fish with a crunchy relish.

Serves 4

4 small trout, about 12 ounces each, cleaned and gutted
Salt
Fresh or dried sage leaves

Apple-Pecan Crunch
¼ cup butter
1 cup large pecan pieces
¾ teaspoon Super Wooster Sauce (page 39) or other
    Worcestershire sauce
Pinch of cayenne
1 small tart apple, such as Granny Smith, peeled,
    cored, and diced
Salt

Vegetable oil spray

With a sharp knife, slice off the head and tail of each fish. On the lower side of each trout, continue the cut made from gutting the fish, slicing from front to back. Use the knife to pry the backbone out, taking care to avoid cutting through the fish. (This is simpler than it may sound.) At this point you will have two connected skin-on fillets. Lightly salt the fish. Scatter a small handful of sage leaves on one fillet and fold the other side over like a closed book. Repeat with the remaining fish. Cover and let the trout sit at room temperature for about 30 minutes.

Fire up the grill, bringing the temperature to medium-high (3 seconds with the hand test).

While the grill preheats, prepare the apple-pecan mixture. Warm the butter in a small, heavy skillet over medium heat. Add the pecans, Worcestershire sauce, and cayenne, stirring and toasting for a couple of minutes. Stir in the apples and heat another couple of minutes until they are warmed through but still crunchy. Add salt to taste. Keep the mixture warm.

Spritz the fish with oil and transfer them to a well-oiled grate, still folded over like closed books. Grill uncovered over medium-high heat for 3 to 4 minutes per half-inch of thickness, turning the fish over on their other skin-side about halfway through. Then open each fish so that you see the side-by-side fillets, quickly oil the grate again, and turn the fish flesh-side down. Some of the sage will fall into the fire and other bits will cling to the fish, both creating a delicious aroma. Grill for 1 to 2 minutes, until the fish is opaque and flaky with light grill marks. If grilling covered, cook for the same amount of time in a similar manner.

Serve the trout immediately skin-side down, each topped by a portion of the apple-pecan mixture.

SAN FRANCISCO SOLE

The 1849 gold rush brought more than prospectors to the booming bay city called San Francisco. Italian fishermen and Croatian cooks, among others, helped feed the hordes, probing the waters for local seafood and preparing the catch in Old World ways. Pacific flatfish became one of the specialties of the area, sold around the harbor and simply pan-seared in nearby restaurants under such names as petrale sole, rex sole, and sand dabs. All more closely related to flounder than true European sole, the flaky white fish are sometimes too fragile for grilling, but petrale in particular can take a high heat, especially when cloaked in a protective wrap of moist seasonings.

SERVES 4

PETRALE MARINADE
Juice of 1½ lemons
3 tablespoons vegetable oil
½ teaspoon salt

......

1½ to 2 pounds petrale sole fillets, preferably 4 or 8
 fillets, or flounder fillets
¼ cup butter
Juice of ½ lemon
1½ teaspoons minced fresh thyme or ¾ teaspoon dried
 thyme
Splash of Tabasco sauce or other hot pepper sauce

Thin lemon slices and small thyme sprigs, for garnish

. . . .

Prepare the marinade, combining the ingredients in a shallow dish. Dunk the fillets in the marinade, coating them lightly on both sides. Cover the fillets and let them sit at room temperature while you heat the grill.

Fire up the grill, bringing the heat to medium-high to high heat (2 to 3 seconds with the hand test).

While the grill heats, warm the butter in a small saucepan over medium heat. When the butter has melted, add the lemon juice, thyme, and Tabasco sauce and remove the pan from the heat.

Transfer the fillets to a well-oiled grate or, preferably in this case, to a well-oiled small-mesh grill rack or hinged grill basket. Grill the fillets uncovered over medium-high to high heat for 2 to 2½ minutes per side per half-inch of thickness. Rotate the fillets 180° once on each side. The fish is done when opaque throughout and flaky. If grilling covered, cook for the same amount of time, rotating and turning in a similar manner.

Arrange the fillets on a decorative platter, drizzle with the butter mixture, and scatter a few lemon slices and thyme sprigs over them. Serve immediately, perhaps with Amazing Aspic as a starter or a side. We also like to add crusty hash browns or roast new potatoes.

TECHNIQUE TIP: A small-mesh grill rack or hinged grill basket helps in cooking flaky white fish such as petrale sole, flounder, snapper, and catfish. The baskets get more hype, but we prefer the racks, which also provide support for small items like shrimp and scallops. If you're grilling directly on the grate, use a heavy-duty metal spatula with a thin, relatively sharp edge that's large enough to slide all the way under whole fish or fillets. When you turn flaky fish or remove them from the fire, push the front edge of the spatula down, applying pressure toward the grate and scraping it instead of the underside of the fish.

THE ORIGINAL COLD DAY RESTAURANT

Few restaurants in the country boast such a colorful history as San Francisco's Tadich Grill, stubbornly non-trendy in its devotion to great local seafood. Three Croatian immigrants began the business in 1849 as a coffee bar in a tent on the old Yerba Buena harbor. The New World Coffee Stand grew steadily as a restaurant and saloon over the next few decades before John Tadich, a fellow Croatian, joined the operation and eventually bought out the founders.

The regular customers at the time included the infamous county assessor, Alexander Badlam, Jr., and his high-rolling cronies. Badlam ran for re-election in 1882, campaigning on the arrogant slogan "It's a Cold Day When I Get Left." Infuriated at the conceit, voters drove him from office and into refuge at The New World. Even after the defeat, newspaper cartoonists continued to lambaste the demagogue and began referring to his hangout as "The Cold Day." Tadich and his partners, refusing to be intimidated, officially adopted the tag as the restaurant's new name.

A century later, the current Buich family owners (Croatian-American, of course) still flaunt the motto "The Original Cold Day Restaurant," even though the sign above the door has said "Tadich Grill" since 1912. Michael Buich, the third generation of his clan in the business, talked to us about old and new meanings of "grill" in the restaurant trade. When Tadich and other San Francisco dining pioneers first used the term, they meant pan-frying or griddle cooking, which is known as grilling in many parts of the world. The fire may have come from wood or charcoal in the days when few other fuels existed, but the heat wasn't direct.

Louie Buich, Mike's grandfather, introduced contemporary grilling at Tadich's in 1925. He brought the technique directly from his Dalmatian coast homeland and applied it most successfully in the early years to petrale sole and other local fish. The menu—then and now—calls this style of cooking "charcoal broiling," to distinguish it from the pan-grilling that's always been featured. Mike thinks those are still the proper terms for the two methods and wishes the rest of us would wise up. Under his roof, at least, we're happy to oblige, particularly since it's the only way to place an order at the Tadich Grill, one of the warmest places in a city where every day is cold.

CRISPY CATFISH WITH HOT SHOT TARTAR SAUCE

Most people deep-fry catfish and serve it with a commercial tartar sauce. The rub in this recipe allows you to achieve some of the same crusty surface through grilling, and our homemade sauce adds a riverful of flavor compared to the bottled brands.

SERVES 4

HOT SHOT TARTAR SAUCE
1 cup Enriched Mayonnaise (page 38) or other
    mayonnaise
1 tablespoon minced pickled jalapeño
2 teaspoons small capers or minced large capers
2 teaspoons minced fresh dill or 1 teaspoon dried dill
1 teaspoon fresh lemon juice
¼ teaspoon Dijon mustard

CELERY DRY RUB
1½ tablespoons celery salt
1½ teaspoons ground black pepper
1½ teaspoons paprika
⅛ teaspoon cayenne pepper

Four 8-ounce to 10-ounce catfish fillets, about ¾ inch
    thick
Vegetable oil spray

Prepare the tartar sauce, combining the ingredients in a small bowl. Refrigerate the mixture for at least 30 minutes. (It can be made up to several days in advance and kept covered in the refrigerator.)

Prepare the dry rub, combining the ingredients in a small bowl. Coat the catfish with the rub. Wrap them in plastic and let them sit at room temperature for 20 to 30 minutes.

Fire up the grill, bringing the temperature to medium-high to high (2 to 3 seconds with the hand test).

Just before grilling, spritz the fillets with oil. Transfer the fillets to a well-oiled grate or, preferably in this case, to a well-oiled small-mesh grill rack or hinged grill basket. Grill the fillets uncovered over medium-high to high heat for 7 to 9 minutes, carefully turning twice so that one side crisps a bit more than the other. (This is one of the few exceptions to our "turn fish only once" rule.) Rotate the fillets 180° when they are turned back onto the side that was grilled previously. The fish is done when flaky and opaque. If grilling covered, cook for the same amount of time, rotating and turning in a similar manner.

Serve immediately with the crisper side up, accompanied by the tartar sauce. For Southern succor we'd opt for sides such as golden hominy, vinegar-based coleslaw, and piping-hot Mixed Berry Cornbread or biscuits.

TECHNIQUE TIP: Spray oil is an easy and efficient way to coat fish for grilling. Just don't squirt the same stuff onto a grate that's above a live fire unless singed hair is fashionable in your neighborhood. It's better to heat the grate and then carefully brush it with oil, allowing any flare-ups to recede before you proceed. If you re-oil the grate during the cooking, be cautious again to avoid drips into the fire.

OLVERA STREET FISH TACOS

Flaky white fish works great in tacos since you crumble it into chunks after cooking anyway. We cover the fish first with a paste based on achiote (also known as annatto), which turns a burnished brown-red on the grill. The kicker is a hot habanero salsa, tamed a bit with cooling, creamy slices of avocado. We named this dish for the street that runs through the heart of Latino Los Angeles, as vibrant as the tacos themselves.

SERVES 6 OR MORE

BRICK-RED PASTE
1 tablespoon achiote paste (see Technique Tip, page 425)
Juice of ½ lime
1 teaspoon olive oil

1 plump garlic clove, minced
1 teaspoon ground cumin
1 teaspoon kosher salt or other coarse salt

Three 8-ounce to 10-ounce catfish, snapper, or flounder
    fillets

HABANERO SALSA
4 small red-ripe tomatoes, chopped
¼ cup minced onion
¼ cup minced fresh cilantro
1 plump garlic clove, minced
¾ teaspoon ground cumin
1 to 3 teaspoons Mexican- or Caribbean-style habanero
    hot sauce
2 to 3 teaspoons fresh lime juice
Salt

Small flour tortillas, preferably no larger than 6 inches
    in diameter, or Corn Tortillas Rojo (page 119) or
    other corn tortillas, warmed
Shredded lettuce
Avocado slices

. . . .

At least 1 hour and up to 4 hours before you plan to grill the fish, prepare the paste, combining the ingredients in a small bowl. Rub the paste over the fish fillets, wrap them in plastic, and refrigerate.

Prepare the salsa, combining the tomatoes, onion, cilantro, garlic, and cumin. Add splashes of hot sauce, the quantity depending on its level of firepower and your level of heat tolerance. Add enough lime juice to give it a noticeable but not pronounced tang and salt to taste. Refrigerate the salsa until needed.

Fire up the grill, bringing the temperature to medium-high to high (2 to 3 seconds with the hand test).

Remove the fillets from the refrigerator and let them sit covered at room temperature for about 20 minutes.

Transfer the fillets to a well-oiled grate or, preferably in this case, to a well-oiled small-mesh grill rack or hinged grill basket. Grill uncovered over medium-high to high heat for 8 to 10 minutes per inch of thickness, turning once. Rotate the fillets 180° on each side. The fish is done when flaky and opaque. If grilling covered, cook for the same amount of time, turning and rotating in a similar manner.

Break the fish into bite-size pieces. Serve immediately along with the tortillas, lettuce, avocado slices, and salsa so that your guests can assemble the soft tacos for themselves. The ingredients should be piled on the flat tortillas and then folded over in the familiar taco shape for eating by hand.

A Fine Mess of "Barbecue" Shrimp

In the shellfish family, we favor crustaceans such as shrimp, lobster, and soft-shell crab for the grill. It's easy to cook mollusks like oysters and clams on the grill too, but the common method—in the shell—tends to roast or stew them in their juices, resulting in little or no true grill flavor. The same thing happens with shrimp cooked in their shell, an approach often recommended as a means to keep the meat moist. We peel shrimp first, so the flame can kiss and sear the surface, and get the desired succulence by grilling them in a flash on high heat. Their sweet natural taste responds well to assertive seasonings, such as the robust barbecue sauce that gives this dish its name.

SERVES 4 OR MORE

CREOLE BARBECUE SAUCE
¼ cup butter
2 tablespoons Creole mustard
Juice of 1 medium lemon
5 plump garlic cloves, minced
1 tablespoon plus 1 teaspoon Super Wooster Sauce
    (page 39) or other Worcestershire sauce
1½ teaspoons fresh-ground black pepper
1 teaspoon Tabasco sauce or other hot pepper sauce, or
    more to taste
½ teaspoon salt
¼ teaspoon cayenne pepper

2 pounds medium shrimp, peeled but with tails left on
and, if you wish, deveined
Super Wooster Sauce (page 39) or other Worcestershire
sauce, or Tabasco sauce or other hot pepper sauce,
or both

. . . .

Melt the butter in a saucepan over medium heat. Add the remaining sauce ingredients and stir to heat through. Place the shrimp in a plastic bag or shallow dish, pour the sauce over them, and refrigerate for about 30 minutes.

Fire up the grill, bringing the temperature to high (1 to 2 seconds with the hand test).

Remove the shrimp from the refrigerator and let them sit at room temperature for about 20 minutes.

Transfer the shrimp to a well-oiled grate or, preferably in this case, to a well-oiled small-mesh grill rack. Grill the shrimp uncovered over high heat for 1½ to 2 minutes per side, until just opaque with lightly browned edges. If grilling covered, cook the shrimp for the same amount of time, turning once midway.

Serve the shrimp hot, with Worcestershire sauce and Tabasco sauce on the side for customizing the flavor. We'd start with bowls of gumbo, add a hearty green salad on the side, and end with bread pudding.

TECHNIQUE TIP: Fresh shrimp is hard to find anymore. It deteriorates so quickly, most modern shrimpers flash-freeze their catch right out of the water. The freshness question with shrimp concerns when and how it's thawed. If you're buying the little crustaceans already thawed, make sure the market did it the day you plan to grill. It's often best to buy a still-frozen block of shrimp, which keeps well for several weeks, and thaw the shrimp yourself in cold water or the refrigerator. We don't bother to devein medium shrimp, the size we usually choose for grilling. The tiny intestinal tract isn't particularly visible or unpleasant in texture. We're more likely to remove the larger vein in jumbo shrimp, where it can look unsightly and sometimes taste gritty.

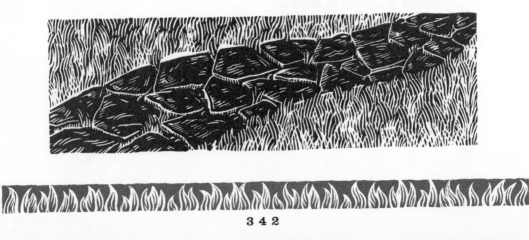

ORANGE-SAUCED COCKTAIL SHRIMP

Here's an easy grilled and chilled shrimp entrée or starter to make ahead, equally fine for a crisp winter evening or a sultry summer night. Standard cocktail sauces can be tasty, but too often their tomato bases mask rather than boost the shrimp flavor. We prefer this pair of sauces, both beholden to oranges and horseradish.

SERVES 4 AS A MAIN DISH OR 6 AS AN APPETIZER

CRANBERRY-ORANGE SAUCE
¾ cup cranberries, fresh or frozen
Zest and juice of ½ medium orange
1½ to 2 tablespoons sugar
1 tablespoon raspberry vinegar or other fruity vinegar
¾ teaspoon prepared horseradish, or more to taste
Pinch of cayenne

MUSTARD-ORANGE SAUCE
¼ cup Honey-Beer Mustard (page 37) or other sweet hot
    mustard
¾ teaspoon prepared horseradish, or more to taste
Zest and juice of ½ medium orange

2 pounds medium shrimp, peeled but with tails left on
    and, if you wish, deveined
2 tablespoons melted butter
Juice of ½ medium orange
1 garlic clove, minced
½ teaspoon salt

Prepare the two sauces. For the cranberry-orange sauce, combine the ingredients in a food processor until puréed. Pour the sauce into a small bowl. For the mustard-orange sauce, stir the ingredients in a small bowl. Cover both and refrigerate.

Fire up the grill, bringing the

temperature to high (1 to 2 seconds with the hand test).

In a large bowl, combine the shrimp with the remaining ingredients. Cover and let sit at room temperature for about 20 minutes. Drain the shrimp and blot them of any remaining moisture.

Transfer the shrimp to a well-oiled grate or, preferably in this case, to a well-oiled small-mesh grill rack. Grill the shrimp uncovered over high heat for 1½ to 2 minutes per side, until opaque with lightly browned edges. If grilling covered, cook the shrimp for the same amount of time, turning once midway.

To chill the shrimp, transfer them to a shallow dish and place in the freezer for 10 to 15 minutes. Remove the shrimp from the freezer, cover them, and refrigerate for at least 30 minutes and up to several hours.

Arrange the shrimp on a platter and serve with the sauces. For a grand summer seafood feast, start with the shrimp and sauces and Piquant Snapper Spread. Offer two entrées, perhaps Sage and Bacon Monkfish Kebobs and Boston Stripers along with sides such as boiled corn on the cob, new potatoes, and whole small onions. Finish off the day with Gingered Pineapple Sundaes.

TECHNIQUE TIP: A lot of good shrimp comes from warm American waters, especially the Gulf of Mexico. For the grill, though, we favor the Alaska spot shrimp for their firmer texture and almost nutty flavor. To mail-order spot shrimp fished off the coast of Sitka in southeast Alaska, call Alaskan Harvest at 800-824-6389. The shrimp come frozen, often with their roe still attached.

MEMPHIS SHRIMP SALAD SANDWICH

We can't get enough of seafood sandwiches. This one is spiked with a mustard-laced cabbage slaw, similar to the topping you often find on a barbecued pork sandwich in the mid-South.

SERVES 4

MUSTARD SLAW
½ medium red or green cabbage head, grated
½ cup chopped onion
2½ tablespoons yellow ballpark mustard

2½ tablespoons Enriched Mayonnaise (page 38) or
    other mayonnaise
2 tablespoons white vinegar
1½ teaspoons sugar
½ teaspoon salt

1½ pounds medium shrimp, peeled and, if you wish,
    deveined
Juice of 1 lemon
1 teaspoon yellow ballpark mustard
¼ teaspoon salt, or more to taste
3 celery stalks, minced
3 tablespoons minced fresh parsley
2 tablespoons Enriched Mayonnaise (page 38) or other
    mayonnaise
Salt

8 large slices sturdy bread, preferably a cornmeal or
    semolina wheat bread, or sourdough bread

• • • • • • • • • • • • • • • • • •

Prepare the slaw, combining the cabbage in a medium bowl with the remaining ingredients. The slaw will look a little dry. Chill the slaw until ready to serve. (The slaw can be made a day ahead if you wish.)

Fire up the grill, bringing the temperature to high (1 to 2 seconds with the hand test).

Mix the shrimp together with the lemon juice, mustard, and salt in a medium bowl and let them sit at room temperature for about 20 minutes.

Transfer the shrimp to a well-oiled grate or, preferably in this case, to a well-oiled small-mesh grill rack. Grill the shrimp uncovered over high heat for 1½ to 2 minutes per side, until opaque with lightly browned edges. If grilling covered, cook for the same amount of time, turning once midway.

Chop the shrimp coarsely and place in a bowl with any accumulated juices. Mix in the celery, parsley, mayonnaise, and more salt to taste. Again, the mixture won't be overly moist. Serve the shrimp salad warm or refrigerate it, covered, for up to several hours and serve chilled. Pile the shrimp salad and slaw on half the bread, then top with the remaining slices, and serve. Hoppin' John Salad with Tabasco Dressing would be a fine choice on the side.

The sandwich filling makes a tasty shrimp salad unadorned, too. For a more attractive presentation in that case, slice each of the grilled shrimp lengthwise rather than chopping them as described for the sandwich. Add a sprinkling of green onions over the top.

TECHNIQUE TIP: We call for peeled shrimp in our recipes, but we never buy them pre-peeled at a supermarket. You lose more in flavor and texture than what you gain in convenience. Shelling them yourself isn't much of a chore and you get the added advantage of having the discards to make stock.

LOBSTER MIMOSA

We don't grill real lobsters, the great cold-water *homarus* from Maine and other northeastern waters that tastes best boiled or steamed. For grilling, we use split tails from the warm-water, clawless spiny or rock lobster, which lacks the richness of its more expensive cousin but has a similar flavor otherwise. Usually found frozen, the tails provide the meat that benefits most from grilling and they are easier to manage than a whole or halved lobster. In this preparation we compensate for the diminished richness with an extravagant touch, a champagne-and-butter bath. More of the same bubbly makes a perfect beverage for the feast.

SERVES 4

Two 1-pound rock lobster tails, fresh or frozen
Vegetable oil

MIMOSA DRIZZLE
3 tablespoons butter
Juice of 1 orange
Pinch of salt
1 split of champagne or sparkling wine, at room
    temperature or chilled

Watercress and orange wedges, for garnish

Fire up the grill, bringing the temperature to medium-high (3 seconds with the hand test).

Place the lobster tails on a clean

towel over a cutting board. The towel will help keep the lobsters from sliding as you cut them, but be careful to avoid slicing your towel too. Split the lobster tails in half vertically with a cleaver or other heavy knife. Watch your fingers because the shells tend to be slick. Oil the shell and meat of each tail section well.

Prepare the Mimosa Drizzle, first melting the butter in a small saucepan over medium heat. Stir in the orange juice and salt and remove from the heat.

Just before taking the lobsters to the grill, pop open the champagne, stir it into the butter mixture, and heat through.

Transfer the lobsters to the grill, cut-side down. Grill the lobsters uncovered over medium-high heat for 3 minutes. Turn them shell-side down and baste the meat of each lobster thickly with the butter-champagne drizzle. Grill for 8 to 9 additional minutes, until cooked through and opaque but still juicy. If grilling covered, cook in the same manner but reduce the final, shell-down time to 7 to 8 minutes, basting when you turn.

Transfer the lobsters to a serving platter, shell-side down, and spoon additional drizzle over them. Garnish with watercress and orange wedges and serve immediately.

THE COMPANY BLLT

You won't find this seafood version of a BLT on any diner menu. Full of comforting tastes but jazzed up with the luxury of lobster, the sandwich makes a fine supper for friends. As in the preceding recipe, we start with rock lobster tails and grill on medium-high, searing the exposed meat first and then finishing it shell-down to retain succulence. Cut the sandwich bread from the center of a large round or oval loaf of hearty bread.

SERVES 4

Two ¾-pound rock lobster tails, fresh or frozen
Extra-virgin olive oil

BLLT Baste

3 tablespoons extra-virgin olive oil
Minced zest and juice from 1½ lemons
1 teaspoon minced fresh thyme or ½ teaspoon dried
    thyme
½ teaspoon kosher salt or other coarse salt

⅔ cup Enriched Mayonnaise (page 38) or other
    mayonnaise
1 teaspoon lemon zest
Tabasco sauce or other hot pepper sauce
6 thin but large slices of country or sourdough bread
Lettuce leaves
1 red-ripe medium tomato, sliced thin
6 slices crisp cooked bacon

• • • • • • • • • • • • • • • • • •

Fire up the grill, bringing the temperature to medium-high (3 seconds with the hand test).

Place the lobster tails on a clean towel over a cutting board. This will help keep them from sliding as you cut them, but be careful to avoid slicing your towel too. Split the lobster tails in half vertically with a cleaver or other heavy knife. Watch your fingers because the shells tend to be slick. Oil the shell and meat of each tail section well.

Prepare the baste, combining the ingredients in a small bowl, and reserve. In another small bowl, mix together the mayonnaise, lemon zest, and a generous splash of the Tabasco sauce.

Transfer the lobsters to the grill, cut-side down. Grill the lobsters uncovered over medium-high heat for 2½ minutes. Turn them shell-side down and baste the meat of each lobster

thickly. Grill for 6 to 8 additional minutes, until cooked through and opaque but still juicy. Baste again right before removing the lobster from the grill. If grilling covered, cook in the same manner but reduce the final, shell-down time to 5 to 7 minutes, basting when you turn and at the end.

Transfer the lobsters to a work surface, wait a couple of minutes until the shells become cool enough to handle, and remove the meat from each tail (using a fork works best for us). Chop the meat coarsely.

Spread the bread slices with the mayonnaise mixture. Cover two with half of the lettuce and tomatoes and arrange the bacon equally over them. Add another bread slice to each and divide the remaining tomatoes, the lobster, and remaining lettuce between the two sandwiches. Top with the last two bread slices, and skewer with

toothpicks if you wish. Press down on the sandwiches lightly to mingle the juices and slice the two sandwiches into four. Serve warm.

CHINATOWN CRAB

Even if you crack the shell of a regular crab, grilling it in its usual suit of armor doesn't gain you any flavor advantage over other methods of cooking. For live fire, we favor soft-shell blue crabs snapped up from Atlantic or Gulf coast waters during their short molting season. Nothing more than skinny-dippers who have shed their shells temporarily, these tasty crustaceans appreciate a blanket of moist Chinese condiments. The crabs are highly perishable and pricey too, so protect your investment by grilling them on the day of purchase.

SERVES 4

CHINATOWN PASTE
2 tablespoons hoisin sauce
1 tablespoon soy sauce
2 teaspoons Asian-style sesame oil
½ teaspoon Asian-style chile paste or chile-garlic paste

8 soft-shell crabs, 3 to 3½ ounces each, cleaned

16 whole chives, with blossoms if possible

Fire up the grill, bringing the temperature to high (1 to 2 seconds with the hand test).

Prepare the paste, mixing together the ingredients in a small bowl. Gently massage the paste over the delicate crabs, getting it in and around all of their nooks and crannies. Place the crabs on a platter, cover them with plastic, and let them sit at room temperature for about 15 minutes.

Transfer the crabs to a well-oiled

grate, bottoms down. Grill the crabs uncovered over high heat for 1½ to 2 minutes, until the bodies and legs turn a burnished red and opaque white. The crab bodies are full of moisture, so watch out for a little popping while they cook. Carefully flip the crabs over, brushing a bit more oil on the grate if you get any sticking at all. Grill the crabs for an additional 1½ to 2 minutes, keeping a close watch on them. The legs should get dark and crunchy but not burned black, and the bodies should have a crispy burnished red surface but still be very moist. If grilling covered, cook the crabs for the same amount of time, turning once midway.

Serve the crabs hot, garnished with crisscrossed chives. Every bit of the succulent soft shell is edible. Add Grant Street Pickled Vegetables and rice-like orzo pasta on the side, and grill Lychee Magic Wands to serve for dessert along with ginger ice cream. Then call us for dinner.

Sea Scallops on Confetti Goat Cheese Sauce

On a hot fire, seafood goes quickly from succulent to stiff. Scallops in particular can overcook in seconds. Try to get them off the grill while the centers are still slightly translucent and let them finish cooking through on their way to the table. Serve this version on brightly colored plates to emphasize the festive sauce, which makes the dish as elegant as it is easy.

Serves 6 as a light main dish or 4 hearty eaters

CONFETTI GOAT CHEESE SAUCE
1 uncooked bacon slice, chopped
2 medium to large shallots, minced
¼ cup white wine
1 cup cream
4 ounces creamy fresh goat cheese, crumbled

PAPRIKA RUB
3 tablespoons paprika
1 teaspoon chili powder
¾ teaspoon kosher salt or other coarse salt
½ teaspoon sugar

24 sea scallops, rinsed and dried on paper towels
Vegetable oil spray
1 small red-ripe tomato, such as Italian plum, diced fine
⅛ to ½ cup finely slivered fresh spinach

• • • • • • • • • • • • • • • • • •

Fire up the grill, bringing the temperature to high (1 to 2 seconds with the hand test).

While the grill preheats, prepare the sauce. In a heavy medium saucepan, fry the bacon over medium heat until crisp. Remove the bacon with a slotted spoon and reserve. Add the shallots and sauté them 1 minute. Add the wine, which will cause the mixture to hiss and steam. Cook briefly until the wine reduces by half. Stir in the cream and heat it through. Remove the mixture from the heat and immediately add the cheese, stirring until smooth. Keep the sauce warm.

In a small bowl, mix together the rub ingredients. Dunk each side of the scallops into the rub, place them on a plate or platter large enough to hold them in a single layer (they give off less juice this way), and let them sit at room temperature for about 15 minutes. Spritz the scallops lightly with oil on both sides.

Transfer the scallops to a well-oiled grate or, preferably in this case, to a well-oiled small-mesh grill rack. Grill the scallops uncovered over high heat for 2 to 2½ minutes per side, until just opaque with lightly browned edges. If grilling covered, cook for the same amount of time, turning once midway.

Spoon equal portions of sauce onto individual plates and arrange the scallops on the pools of sauce. Scatter the bacon, tomato bits, and spinach over and around the scallops and serve immediately. If you have leftover sauce, pair it with grilled zucchini or toss it with pasta.

TECHNIQUE TIP: Scallops are often treated with a phosphate-type preservative to keep them moist. You may prefer to avoid such stuff in your diet anyway, but it has other disadvantages as well, disguising true freshness and making the scallops retain water that gets expelled during cooking. The wetness presents problems in grilling, making it difficult to crisp the surface. Many seafood purveyors today can provide the unpreserved or "dry" scallops, but in most markets you have to ask for them and you may need to order a day or two ahead.

LIGHTNING-QUICK CALAMARI

Squid is one of the rare seafoods that cook well at both ends of the heat spectrum, from low and slow to high and quick. On a grill, go for the fast blast, but be careful not to overcook or you'll end up with a texture Goodyear would envy.

SERVES 4 TO 6

2 pounds small squid bodies, preferably about 3 inches in length, with tentacles separated, cleaned, or 2 pounds squid steaks
3 plump garlic cloves, minced
Olive oil
Salt

Lemon wedges and crushed dried hot red chile, for garnish
Minced fresh parsley, optional, for garnish

Fire up the grill, bringing the temperature to high (1 to 2 seconds with the hand test).

Mix the squid in a medium bowl with the garlic. Drizzle in olive oil by the teaspoon, adding just enough to barely coat the bodies, and add a good sprinkling of salt. Rub the bodies and tentacles to distribute the seasonings.

Transfer the squid to a well-oiled grate or, preferably in this case, to a well-oiled small-mesh grill rack. The squid bodies will take about 1 more minute to cook than the tentacles, so place the bodies on the grill first. Cook the bodies uncovered over high heat for 3 to 4 minutes, rolling them to cook all sides. After 1 minute, add the tentacles and cook them for 2 to 3 minutes, again rolling on all sides. For squid steaks, cook them uncovered for 3 to 4 minutes, turning once midway. The squid should feel firm but tender. If grilling covered, cook for the same amount of time, turning once midway.

Slice the squid bodies into thin rings, or the steaks into thin strips, and serve heaped together on a platter with the tentacles. Squeeze lemon wedges over the squid, and tuck more into the edges of the platter. Dust with a bit of red chile and scatter parsley over the top if you wish. Serve immediately.

Getting Fresh in the Garden

GETTING FRESH IN THE GARDEN

SIMPLY SUPERB
CORN ON THE COB

Nothing goes with grilled meat like corn on the cob, America's first vegetable in both historic and culinary senses. We used to grill the old favorite in the way that's generally recommended, soaking the ear in water and cooking it with the husk on. We realized finally that the traditional method actually steams and roasts the corn, instead of grilling it, producing a good result but little true grill taste. Now we remove the husk and silk before cooking, exposing the kernels directly to the heat, which sizzles surface juices and concentrates the corn flavor. To keep it classic and elemental, we add no seasoning except salt and butter, preferably a premium version of the latter.

SERVES 6

6 ears of corn, husked and silk removed
Butter, preferably an unsalted premium butter such as
    Plugra (see Technique Tip, page 180), melted
Salt or All-'Round Rub (page 23)
Finely minced fresh parsley or cilantro, optional, for
    garnish

Fire up the grill, bringing the temperature to medium (4 to 5 seconds with the hand test).

Brush the corn lightly with butter. Grill the corn uncovered on medium heat for 20 to 25 minutes, turning on all sides to cook evenly and brushing with more butter after about 10 minutes. If grilling covered, cook for 18 to 22 minutes, turning once midway and brushing with butter. The cooking time is longer than technically necessary to cook the corn, but helps concentrate the juices a bit, giving the corn a more intense taste and crisper texture.

Brush the corn again with butter, sprinkle it with salt or dry rub, and serve hot. If you can't resist the urge to add a little something extra, scatter on a bit of parsley or cilantro for color.

TECHNIQUE TIP: While we no longer soak corn in the husks before grilling, we occasionally soak husked ears if the corn is more than a day or two old. We bathe the ears in water for 10 minutes, to help keep the kernels from parching on the grill. Drain the corn before putting it on the grate.

VEGGING OUT

Vegetables on the grill used to be as rare as wildflowers in winter. Adventuresome outdoor cooks might roast an ear of corn alongside their steaks, or stick a whole potato in the coals to bake while they charbroiled their burgers, but hardly anyone went beyond that in the early years of American grilling.

The first tentative steps toward more came with kebobs and foil. By the 1950s a growing number of grillers had discovered skewered cooking and began slipping a few lonely onion wedges and button mushrooms between hefty cubes of lamb and beef. It was only a nibble of garden goodness, but at least the veggies got a kiss of the flame, unlike when they were covered in aluminum foil, the other popular option in the same era. Suburban chefs wrapped and baked anything green, red, or white, even icy blocks of frozen beans and peas.

As American tastes broadened in the following decades, so did the grilling repertory. We learned to love a wide range of vegetables, from artichokes to zucchini, and found that many cooked well directly over the fire, without need of a meat convoy or a foil blanket. In the enthusiasm over the new flavors, grilled cauliflower was an inevitable accident but at least not fatal. Outdoor cooks are beginning to understand the limitations now as well as the possibilities, mastering the secrets that make vegetables as much a treat to grill as meat.

Two keys to success—neither a rule in all cases—are moderate heat and a wet flavoring method such as a marinade, paste, or simple oil coating. Some vegetables (juicy tomato slices, for example) prefer a hotter fire, and others (onion rings for one) like it lower, but most grill best on medium. Even when the seasoning is no more than oil, match the flavor with the food, taking full advantage of all the vegetable, nut, and infused oils on the market today. Experiment with these principles on anything from the garden and you're bound to find a bounty of new delights.

GRILLED FRIES

Most people who cook potatoes on the grill like to roast them whole, a dish Americans used to call a "mickey" when vendors sold them as fast food on city streets years ago. We take our cue from another fast-food favorite, the French fry, cutting potatoes in similar-size slices, rubbing them with spices to promote crusting, and grilling the spears in a light coat of oil. Crisp on the outside, dry and fluffy inside, they disappear as quickly as the country ham at a Southern boarding house.

SERVES 4 TO 6

ALL-'ROUND RUB
1 tablespoon paprika
1 teaspoon coarse-ground black pepper
1 teaspoon kosher salt or other coarse salt
½ teaspoon chili powder
Scant ¼ teaspoon packed brown sugar
Pinch of cayenne, optional

4 medium to large russet or other baking potatoes,
     scrubbed but unpeeled
Olive oil
Grated mild cheese, such as cheddar or Monterey jack,
     at room temperature, optional
Quintessential Ketchup (page 32), Classic Kansas City
     Sauce (page 35), or other ketchup- or tomato-based
     barbecue sauce

Fire up the grill, bringing the temperature to medium-low (6 seconds with the hand test).

Prepare the dry rub, combining the ingredients in a small bowl. Cut the potatoes lengthwise in half and then slice each half into long wedges ½ inch thick at their widest side. Coat the potato spears with oil and then sprinkle them generously with the dry rub.

Grill the potatoes uncovered over medium-low heat for 30 to 35 minutes, turning them every 5 to 10 minutes and dabbing them lightly with additional oil once or twice. The potatoes are ready when the exteriors are brown

and crisp and the interiors soft and tender. If grilling covered, cook for 18 to 22 minutes, turning once midway.

To gild the lily, top the potato slices with cheese as soon as they come off the grill. Serve hot with ketchup or barbecue sauce.

TECHNIQUE TIP: For spicy fries, substitute Chile Rub Rojo for the milder All-'Round Rub. We might even skip the ketchup in that case.

POTATO SLICES WITH MUSTARD-TOMATO VINAIGRETTE

To get moist potato slices, our goal here in contrast to the previous recipe, we parboil whole potatoes to tenderness before cutting them into pieces for the grill. A basic marinade takes on additional flavors to become a robust and colorful dressing. Save any leftover vinaigrette to top salads, pasta, or toasted bread.

SERVES 6

2½ pounds russet or other baking potatoes (about 3 medium to large potatoes), scrubbed but unpeeled
⅓ cup extra-virgin olive oil
1 tablespoon red wine vinegar
1 teaspoon Dijon mustard

MUSTARD-TOMATO VINAIGRETTE
⅔ cup extra-virgin olive oil
2 tablespoons red wine vinegar
2 teaspoons Dijon mustard
1 small red-ripe tomato, preferably Italian plum, diced fine

¼ cup sliced black olives, preferably Kalamata
2 medium shallots, minced
1 tablespoon small capers plus 1 teaspoon of the brine
from the jar
Generous grinding of black pepper

Leaf lettuce, cut into thin ribbons, for garnish

• • • • • • • • • • • • • • • • • •

Parboil the whole potatoes for 15 to 20 minutes, until fork-tender but short of mushy. Drain the potatoes. When cool enough to handle, cut the potatoes into ⅓-inch slices on the diagonal. (The potatoes can be prepared to this point a day in advance. Wrap them tightly and refrigerate, bringing them back to room temperature before proceeding.)

Arrange the potato slices in a single layer on a baking sheet with a lip or in a large, shallow dish or platter. In a lidded jar, shake together the oil, vinegar, and mustard and pour over the potatoes, turning them to coat evenly. Let the potatoes sit covered for 30 to 45 minutes.

Fire up the grill, bringing the temperature to medium (4 to 5 seconds with the hand test).

In the same lidded jar, prepare the vinaigrette. Shake together the oil, vinegar, and mustard. When combined, add the remaining ingredients. (The dressing can be made several days ahead and kept covered and refrigerated.)

Drain the potatoes, discarding the marinade, which takes on a pasty taste.

Grill the potatoes uncovered over medium heat for 4 to 5 minutes per side, until the potatoes are very tender, light brown, and slightly crisp. If grilling covered, cook for 8 to 9 minutes, turning once midway.

Arrange the potatoes on a platter. (The potatoes can be prepared to this point several hours in advance and left covered at room temperature.) Edge the platter with the lettuce and drizzle the vegetables with the vinaigrette. Serve with lots of crusty bread to soak up the dressing.

CRISPY SPUD SKINS

Typically deep-fried and drowned in mounds of sour cream, bacon, and cheese, potato skins are usually vehicles for other flavors. We like the original taste ourselves, preserved here by grilling the skins to crispness and topping them with a complementary lemon-and-herb dressing.

SERVES 4

4 medium to large russet or other potatoes, scrubbed
    but unpeeled

LEMON-CHIVE DRESSING
¾ cup extra-virgin olive oil
3 tablespoons fresh lemon juice
1 plump garlic clove, minced
2 teaspoons fresh-grated Parmesan cheese
1 teaspoon Super Wooster Sauce (page 39) or other
    Worcestershire sauce
2 tablespoons minced chives
Salt and fresh-ground black pepper

Minced chives, for garnish
Crumbled crisp cooked bacon, optional, for garnish

Preheat the oven to 375° F.

Prick each potato in several places with a fork to let steam escape. Bake the potatoes directly on the oven rack for about 1 hour, until tender. Remove the potatoes from the oven and let them sit until cool enough to handle. Slice them in half lengthwise and scoop out the cooked potato, leaving a shell about ¼ inch thick. Halve each potato shell lengthwise again. Reserve the scooped-out potato for another use. (The skins can be made to this point a day ahead, cooled, and kept covered and refrigerated. Bring them back to room temperature before proceeding.)

Prepare the dressing, whisking together the ingredients in a small bowl. (The dressing can be made a day ahead and kept covered and refrigerated.)

Fire up the grill, bringing the temperature to medium (4 to 5 seconds with the hand test).

Brush the skins lightly with the dressing and grill them uncovered over medium heat for 3 to 4½ minutes per side, until crisp. If grilling covered, cook for the same amount of time, turning once midway.

Arrange the skins on a platter and sprinkle them with chives and, if you wish, a little bit of bacon. Serve immediately with the dressing for drizzling or dunking. Use any extra dressing on your favorite greens.

RED AND WHITE ONION RINGS

Savory with a hint of deep sweetness, the marinade on these onion rings brings out their caramelized flavor. A grill basket makes the cooking easy, by keeping the onions together when you flip them, and the big payoff on the plate with the rings warrants the small investment.

SERVES 4 TO 6

BALSAMIC SOY MARINADE
4 tablespoons balsamic vinegar
1½ tablespoons soy sauce
1½ tablespoons vegetable oil

1 large red onion, sliced into ⅛-inch rings
1 large white onion, preferably a sweet onion such as Vidalia, Maui, or Texas 1015, sliced into ⅛-inch rings

Minced chives, for garnish

Prepare the marinade, combining the ingredients in a small bowl. Place the onion rings in a large plastic bag or shallow bowl, pour the marinade over them, and let them sit at room temper-ature for about 30 minutes, turning occasionally.

Fire up the grill, bringing the temperature to medium-low (6 seconds with the hand test).

You can grill the onion rings directly on the grate or in a grill basket. Grill them uncovered for 18 to 20 minutes, turning every few minutes to cook each side twice. The onions are ready when they are very soft with browned edges. If grilling covered, cook for about 15 minutes, turning once midway.

Arrange the onion rings on a platter, sprinkle with chives for a bit of color, and serve hot or at room temperature.

HONEYED BABY ONIONS

We developed the honey-mustard marinade in this recipe to flavor young bulbous onions on the stem. In the market, they look like steroid-charged versions of thin green onions or scallions, which also work in the dish if you reduce the cooking time substantially.

SERVES 4 TO 6

HONEY-MUSTARD MARINADE
½ cup vegetable oil
2 tablespoons white vinegar
1 tablespoon sweet mustard
1 tablespoon honey
¼ teaspoon salt

16 baby onions on the stem

Prepare the marinade, combining the ingredients in a small bowl. Place the onions in a plastic bag or shallow dish, pour the marinade over them, and let them sit at room temperature for about 30 minutes.

Fire up the grill, bringing the temperature to medium (4 to 5 seconds with the hand test).

Drain the onions, discarding the marinade.

Transfer the onions to the grill, with their tops positioned away from the hottest part of the fire. Grill them

uncovered over medium heat for 8 to 12 minutes, depending on size, turning regularly until tender with some brown spots. If grilling covered, cook the onions for 6 to 10 minutes, turning once midway.

Serve the onions hot or at room temperature.

TECHNIQUE TIP: Honeyed Baby Onions are outstanding with burgers. Start the onions on the cooler section of a two-level fire a few minutes before you begin to grill the burgers, or just cook them ahead and serve warm or at room temperature.

CALICO PEPPERS WITH FRESH SPINACH SAUCE

With three shades of peppers crowned in an emerald cape, this colorful medley will let your friends know you're no shrinking violet. They'll think you labored all day on their behalf; but everything is actually relatively quick and easy to prepare.

SERVES 4 TO 6

YELLOW PEPPER SAUCE
2 tablespoons extra-virgin olive oil
2 yellow bell peppers, chopped
¼ cup chopped onion, preferably yellow onion
1 teaspoon minced lemon zest
½ teaspoon salt

FRESH SPINACH SAUCE
2 cups packed stemmed fresh spinach leaves
¼ cup pine nuts
¼ cup minced fresh parsley
2 garlic cloves
2 teaspoons capers
1 teaspoon minced lemon zest
¼ teaspoon salt
¾ cup extra-virgin olive oil

2 large green bell peppers
2 large red bell peppers
Extra-virgin olive oil

Prepare the yellow pepper sauce, first warming the oil in a skillet over medium heat. Stir in the bell peppers and onion and sauté 8 to 10 minutes, until soft and golden. Add the lemon zest and salt and spoon the warm mixture into a blender. Purée the sauce and keep it warm. (The sauce can be made a few hours ahead and kept covered and refrigerated. Reheat the sauce and stir it well before proceeding.)

Prepare the spinach sauce. In a food processor, combine the spinach, pine nuts, parsley, garlic, capers, lemon zest, and salt. With the processor running, pour in the oil in a slow, steady stream and process until incorporated. Reserve the sauce. (The sauce can be made a few hours ahead too. Cover and refrigerate it.)

Fire up the grill, bringing the temperature to medium (4 to 5 seconds with the hand test).

Coat the green and red peppers with oil. Grill the peppers uncovered over medium heat for 12 to 15 minutes, turning on all sides, until tender. If grilling covered, cook the peppers for 10 to 12 minutes, turning once midway.

Transfer the peppers to a plastic bag and close it to let them steam, loosening the skin. When cool enough to handle, pull off any loose, charred pieces of skin. Remove the peppers' stems and seeds, slice them into thin strips, and stir them together.

Pool the yellow pepper sauce on a platter of contrasting color. Top with the mixed pepper strips, leaving at least a 1-inch border at the platter's edge. Serve hot or at room temperature, with the spinach sauce spooned over the top at the end. Leftover spinach sauce can top garlic toast, plain bread, or baked potatoes.

GRILLING THE GARDEN

We've been known to fire up the grill to cook vegetables as a side dish for a non-grilled main course, particularly with a pasta, but many people think that's too much trouble for a simple accompaniment. They won't grill garden goodies unless the veggies themselves are the main course or they have the grill going anyway for a meat entrée. We've tried to keep this constraint in mind in developing recipes for the chapter.

Some of the choices make fine centerpieces for a light meal. Especially during the peak of the growing season, we're always happy with a dinner featuring one of the mixed vegetable platters, garden sandwiches, or hearty preparations such as Layered Eggplant with Fresh Tomato Relish. If your grate space is adequate, you can also grill any of our dishes alongside an entrée that cooks at the same temperature. Since most vegetables grill best over a medium fire, they nestle cozily with chicken and pork, which usually like the same heat, and also cook well on the lower end of the two-level fires we use for burgers, steaks, and tuna.

If the grate space is too limited for that approach, grill the veggies first and then follow up with the meat. Most of our dishes, as noted in the serving instructions, lose little by sitting at room temperature for an hour before eating. Cooking two courses in sequence is a breeze on a gas grill and hardly any hassle on a charcoal model, requiring at the most the addition of some extra preheated coals. Even when it takes more time and effort, a grilled vegetable side makes any outdoor meal a harvest feast.

LAYERED EGGPLANT WITH FRESH TOMATO RELISH

One of the most delightful and versatile vegetables to grill, eggplant goes great with other summer produce. We like to serve it with a lusty red-and-white relish of good, ripe tomatoes and silky mozzarella cheese.

SERVES 6

Two 1-pound globe eggplants, peeled and cut
    lengthwise into ⅛- to ½-inch-thick slices
Kosher salt or other coarse salt

LAYERED EGGPLANT MARINADE AND BASTE
½ cup extra-virgin olive oil
2 tablespoons minced fresh thyme sprigs or 1
    tablespoon dried thyme
1 teaspoon crushed dried hot red chile, optional

FRESH TOMATO RELISH
2 cups halved tiny tomatoes, such as pear, Sweet 100s,
    or cherry, preferably red and yellow
3 ounces fresh mozzarella cheese, preferably
    water-packed, cut into small cubes
1 tablespoon extra-virgin olive oil
Scant ¾ to 1 teaspoon balsamic vinegar
⅛ teaspoon salt, or more to taste
Generous grinding of black pepper

Place the eggplants in a colander and sprinkle heavily with salt. Arrange the colander in a sink or over a plate and let it sit for 30 minutes to draw out bitter juices. Rinse the eggplant well and pat dry.

Prepare the marinade, combining the ingredients in a small bowl. Place the eggplant in a plastic bag, pour the marinade over it, and let it sit covered at room temperature for 15 to 30 minutes.

Prepare the relish, combining the ingredients. Cover and refrigerate it

until needed. (The relish can be made several hours in advance if you wish. Let it sit at room temperature for a few minutes before serving.)

Fire up the grill, bringing the temperature to medium (4 to 5 seconds with the hand test).

Drain the eggplant, reserving any marinade not absorbed by the thirsty vegetable.

Grill the eggplant uncovered over medium heat for 10 to 12 minutes,

until soft and juicy. Turn once or twice and baste with the reserved marinade. If grilling covered, cook for 8 to 10 minutes, turning once midway.

Arrange the eggplant slices on a round platter in a spoke-like pattern, overlapping them at the center. Serve hot or at room temperature, with the relish spooned on top at the end. The eggplant makes a fine meal accompanied by Mixed Herb Tabbouleh.

GINGERED EGGPLANT

In the late summer months, farmers' markets and prime produce stores feature small, sweet eggplants such as the Japanese variety. They don't require the salting, rinsing, and draining of the large, mature eggplants— which can be substituted here by following the preparation instructions in the previous recipe—and they need little seasoning, nothing more in this case than a ginger-and-butter bath.

SERVES 4 TO 6

1½ pounds small eggplants

BUTTER-SOY BASTE
5 tablespoons butter
2 tablespoons soy sauce
1 tablespoon minced fresh ginger
1 tablespoon syrup from a bottle of candied "stem ginger," preferably, or 1 tablespoon ginger jam or preserves

Peel the eggplants, but leave strips of the skin on at intervals to provide a little color contrast. Cut lengthwise into ⅓-inch slices. Place the eggplant slices on a baking sheet. Prepare the baste, melting the butter with the soy sauce and ginger in a small saucepan. Brush both sides of the eggplant slices with the mixture, using about half of it. Cover the eggplants and let them sit at room temperature for 15 to 30 minutes. Mix the ginger syrup into the remaining butter mixture and keep it warm.

Fire up the grill, bringing the temperature to medium (4 to 5 seconds with the hand test).

Grill the eggplant slices uncovered over medium heat for 9 to 11 minutes, turning them after 4 to 5 minutes and basting with the remaining butter mixture. If grilling covered, cook for 7 to 10 minutes, turning and basting midway.

Serve the eggplant hot or at room temperature. We especially enjoy it accompanying So Miso Drumsticks or as a lunch entrée with Grant Street Pickled Vegetables.

Asparagus with Warm Bacon Vinaigrette

Fresh asparagus grills wonderfully. We sometimes make a light meal of it accompanied by warm goat cheese or grilled mushrooms, but we like it best of all with this vinaigrette, a slightly refined version of an old American standard.

Serves 4

Warm Bacon Vinaigrette
2 slices uncooked bacon, chopped
3 tablespoons extra-virgin olive oil
1 to 1½ tablespoons white vinegar
¼ teaspoon sugar
Pinch of salt

1 pound to 1¼ pounds asparagus spears, preferably thin, trimmed of tough ends

Prepare the vinaigrette, first frying the bacon in a skillet over medium heat until crisp. Drain the bacon with a slotted spoon and crumble it, reserving both the bacon and the drippings. Reduce the heat under the skillet to low and add the oil, 1 tablespoon of vinegar, sugar, and salt to the bacon drippings. Taste and add the remaining vinegar if needed to balance the tang of the dressing. Keep the vinaigrette warm. (The dressing can be made a day ahead, covered, and refrigerated. Reheat before serving.)

Spoon out 2 to 3 teaspoons of the dressing and rub it evenly over the asparagus.

Fire up the grill, bringing the temperature to medium (4 to 5 seconds with the hand test) if using pencil-thin asparagus, or to medium-low (6 seconds with the hand test) if working with thicker spears.

Transfer the asparagus to the grill, placing the stem ends over the hottest part of the fire and the tips out toward a cooler edge. Grill thin asparagus uncovered over medium heat for 5 to 6 minutes, rolling it frequently to cook on all sides. Fatter asparagus requires 6 to 8 minutes of cooking time, again rolled on all sides. If grilling covered, cook for the same amount of time, turning once midway.

Serve the asparagus hot or chilled on a long platter, with the dressing drizzled over the stems and the crumbled bacon scattered over all.

FIRE-FLAVORED CHILE RELLENO

A Southwestern favorite, the cheese-stuffed chiles known as rellenos are usually fried in a heavy batter. We prefer to grill them, which brings out the fruity flavor of the chiles better. It's a two-step process, blistering and peeling the skins first and then cooking the chiles through to melt the cheese inside. We serve them with a sprightly cilantro sauce, as either a main course or a side dish.

SERVES 6

CILANTRO SAUCE
¾ cup chopped fresh cilantro
½ fresh jalapeño or serrano chile
¾ cup crème fraîche or Mexican *crema* (see Technique
    Tip, page 118), preferably, or sour cream
⅛ teaspoon salt

CHEESE FILLING
6 ounces Chihuahua or Muenster cheese, grated
6 ounces creamy fresh goat cheese or cream cheese, at
    cool room temperature
3 tablespoons pine nuts, toasted in a dry skillet
2 tablespoons minced red onion
½ teaspoon minced fresh epazote or ¼ teaspoon dried
    epazote, optional

6 meaty medium poblano chiles or other fresh, fat mild
    green chiles such as New Mexican or Anaheim
Vegetable oil spray

Pine nuts, toasted in a dry skillet, for garnish
Chopped tomato, optional, for garnish

Prepare the cilantro sauce. In a food processor, mince the cilantro and the jalapeño very fine. Spoon in the crème fraîche and salt and process again until well blended. Refrigerate until needed. (The sauce can be made 1 to 2 hours ahead, but the cilantro's sparkle and vibrancy begin to fade after that point.)

Prepare the filling, mixing together the ingredients in a medium bowl. Cover and chill until needed. (The filling can be combined 1 day in advance and kept covered and refrigerated.)

Fire up the grill, bringing the temperature to medium (4 to 5 seconds with the hand test).

Grill the chiles uncovered over medium heat for 8 to 10 minutes, turning occasionally so that the skin blackens and blisters all over. Place the chiles in a plastic bag briefly to steam as they cool.

When the chiles are cool enough to handle, peel them, wearing rubber gloves if your skin is sensitive. Slit each chile from end to end and remove any loose seeds. Don't remove the seed pod or it will weaken the walls of the chile. (The chiles can be prepared to this point a day ahead, covered, and refrigerated. Bring them back to room temperature before proceeding.)

Stuff the cheese mixture into the chiles, bringing the slit edges of each chile back together tightly. Spritz the chiles with oil. Return the chiles to the grill, slit side down. Grill uncovered for 5 to 7 minutes, turning once, until the cheese is quite soft. If grilling covered, cook for the same amount of time, turning once midway.

Serve the chiles hot with a drizzle of the sauce. Cut the chile heat and richness with Citrus-Onion Slaw if you like.

ORANGE-SCENTED FENNEL

The increasing popularity of Mediterranean cooking has brought new and deserved attention to fennel, a plant previously known in the United States primarily for its seeds. During grilling, the orange-flavored marinade in this preparation caramelizes on the surface of the fennel slices while the center of the vegetable becomes tenderly creamy.

SERVES 4 TO 6

ORANGE MARINADE
Juice of 2 large oranges
1½ tablespoons extra-virgin olive oil
½ teaspoon packed brown sugar
½ teaspoon salt

3 medium fennel bulbs, each cut into 4 thick slices
through the stem end

Prepare the marinade, combining the ingredients in a small bowl. Place the fennel slices in a plastic bag, pour the marinade over them, and let them sit at room temperature for about 30 minutes.

Fire up the grill, bringing the temperature to medium (4 to 5 seconds with the hand test).

Drain the marinade from the fennel and reserve.

Grill the fennel uncovered over medium heat for 12 to 15 minutes. Turn the fennel several times, brushing it with the reserved marinade halfway through cooking and at the end. If grilling covered, cook for 10 to 12 minutes, turning and basting in a similar manner. The fennel is done when the slices are softened and singed lightly on a few edges.

The fennel can be eaten immediately, at room temperature, or chilled. Try it with compatibly seasoned pork or beef. We also relish it accompanying a simple spaghetti dressed with approximately equal portions of lemon juice, olive oil, Parmigiano-Reggiano cheese, and Pecorino Romano cheese.

WILTED FANCY LETTUCES

Small heads of endive and radicchio make simple but fancy flourishes for a grilled meal. Each is splendid on its own, but in combination the color contrast of pale green and deep burgundy lights up a serving platter. Taste the lettuces raw for bitterness before deciding whether to add the optional sugar to the marinade.

SERVES 4 TO 6

VINAIGRETTE MARINADE
3 tablespoons extra-virgin olive oil
1 tablespoon red wine vinegar
1 plump garlic clove, minced
¼ teaspoon sugar, optional

4 small to medium heads of endive, halved vertically
2 small to medium heads of radicchio, quartered
   through the stem end

Prepare the vinaigrette, whisking together the ingredients in a small bowl. Place the endive and radicchio in a plastic bag or bowl and pour the marinade over them. Let the lettuces sit at room temperature for 15 to 30 minutes, turning occasionally.

Fire up the grill, bringing the temperature to medium (4 to 5 seconds with the hand test).

Drain the endive and radicchio, discarding the marinade.

Grill the lettuces uncovered over medium heat for 8 to 12 minutes, depending on size, turning once, until soft with a few browned edges. If grilling covered, cook for 7 to 10 minutes, turning once midway.

Serve the lettuces hot or at room temperature. The endive and radicchio pair well with a hearty steak like Pale Ale Porterhouse and can be cooked at the same time on the medium heat of the two-level fire.

PRINCELY PORTOBELLOS

Wild mushrooms, portobellos in particular, grill as well as any food on earth. This dish doubles the pleasure with a dollop of mushroom ketchup. If you don't have time to make the condiment, substitute the faster alternative suggested. You sacrifice the double play but certainly won't strike out.

SERVES 4

1 pound portobello mushrooms, sliced ⅛ inch thick
Porcini-flavored oil, other mushroom-flavored oil,
   roasted garlic oil, or olive oil

½ teaspoon salt
½ cup Spicy Mushroom Ketchup (page 34) or ¼ cup
    Super Wooster Sauce (page 39) or other Worcester-
    shire sauce mixed with ¼ cup bottled steak sauce
2 small red-ripe tomatoes, diced, for garnish

Fire up the grill, bringing the temperature to medium (4 to 5 seconds with the hand test).

Place the mushrooms in a shallow bowl or dish. Drizzle them with just enough oil to coat and toss them gently with the salt.

If the mushroom ketchup is refrigerated, take it out now to take the chill off of it.

THE GRILLER'S KRAFT

Few food companies in the country have done more than Kraft to promote grilling. The corporation always cared mostly about its profits, of course, rather than the glory of the craft, but the marketing department never reached the bottom of the bottle in finding ways to sauce up outdoor cooking.

Americans once called vinaigrette "French" dressing, but Kraft changed that by the 1950s, popularizing a new commercial style under that name that contained a strong suggestion of ketchup. When the company released a purer vinaigrette a few years later, the topping had hopped the Alps to become Italian. Both dressings, according to the ad campaigns, were meant for much more than lettuce. The French version, among many possibilities, made a bragging-rights baste for "New Way Steaks," "Tasty Grilled Spareribs, " and "Company Hamburgers," while the Italian variation gave the "gourmet touch" to a range of chicken dishes.

Kraft introduced the first nationally distributed bottled barbecue sauce in 1960 and it's still the top seller in its field across the country today. The new product offered outdoor cooks the chance to stake their "claim to barbecue fame" with "the zip of real Western cooking." The secret, said a newspaper promotion, was that "Kraft Barbecue Sauce penetrates the meat and gives a richer, more appetizing color because it's made with a special Kraft ingredient." The bottom line for the ad, for the company, and for the cook, was "Make it *your* brand, partner."

Grill the mushrooms uncovered for 2 to 3 minutes per side, until tender. If grilling covered, cook the mushrooms for 4 to 5 minutes, turning once midway.

Serve the warm mushrooms hot or at room temperature, topped at the end by spoonfuls of the ketchup and a scattering of tomato to add a little color.

RICH MIX OF MUSHROOMS AND POLENTA

This is comfort food at its classiest, a mating of several varieties of wild mushrooms with creamy polenta, which is just grits gone elegant. Extravagant and easy.

SERVES 4 AS A MAIN DISH OR 6 AS A SIDE DISH

CREAMY POLENTA
1½ cups chicken stock
1½ cups water
½ teaspoon salt
¾ cup stone-ground polenta (coarse) cornmeal
½ cup mascarpone cheese, preferably, or cream cheese
3 tablespoons porcini-flavored oil, other mushroom-flavored oil, roasted garlic oil, or olive oil
1 tablespoon butter

1½ pounds mixed wild mushrooms, preferably a combination of portobellos, porcini, cremini, oyster, or shiitakes, sliced ⅛ inch thick
Porcini-flavored oil, other mushroom-flavored oil, roasted garlic oil, or olive oil
1 tablespoon minced fresh thyme or 1½ teaspoons dried thyme
¾ teaspoon salt
1 tablespoon butter

Fire up the grill, bringing the temperature to medium (4 to 5 seconds with the hand test).

In a large, heavy saucepan, bring the chicken stock and water to a boil over high heat. Add the salt and sprinkle in the polenta gradually, stirring continually. Reduce the heat to medium-low and simmer the polenta until thick and soft, about 20 to 25 minutes. Stir occasionally and more frequently as the spoon meets resistance. When cooked through, stir in the cheese, oil, and butter. Cover and keep warm.

Place the mushrooms in a shallow bowl or dish. Drizzle them with just enough oil to coat and toss them gently with the thyme and salt.

Grill the mushrooms uncovered over medium heat for 2 to 3 minutes per side, until tender. If grilling covered, cook for 4 to 5 minutes, turning once midway.

As the mushrooms come off the grill, toss them in a bowl with the remaining tablespoon of butter. Spoon the warm polenta into the center of a platter, top with the mushrooms, and serve immediately.

Nopales with Tijuana Dressing

L ong a favorite food in Mexico, and gaining now in popularity north of the border, the broad, thin pads of the prickly pear cactus taste something like green beans. Grilling intensifies the natural flavor, enhanced further here with a dressing inspired by the classic Caesar, formulated first decades ago just south of San Diego in Tijuana.

Serves 6

TIJUANA DRESSING
2 tablespoons white wine vinegar
1 tablespoon Enriched Mayonnaise (page 38) or other
    mayonnaise

1 teaspoon Dijon mustard
1 teaspoon Super Wooster Sauce (page 39) or other
  Worcestershire sauce
1 anchovy fillet
2 garlic cloves
½ teaspoon ground cumin
½ teaspoon ground dried red chile
¾ cup extra-virgin olive oil

2 pounds *nopales* (cactus pads), stickers removed

Prepare the dressing, combining all the ingredients in a food processor or blender. (The dressing can be prepared several days ahead and kept covered and refrigerated.) Rub several tablespoons of the dressing over the *nopales*, enough to coat them well.

Fire up the grill, bringing the temperature to medium (4 to 5 seconds with the hand test).

Grill the *nopales* uncovered over medium heat for 3 to 4 minutes per side, until well softened and dark green with brown grill marks. If grilling covered, cook for 6 to 8 minutes, turning once midway.

For maximum visual impact, serve the *nopales* whole, piled on a colorful platter and drizzled with dressing, before cutting them into strips at the table. Sliced, they look like oversize bronzed green beans. Serve the *nopales* hot or at room temperature alongside Riata Ranch Cowboy Quesadilla, Church-Picnic Pork Chops, or just accompanying a hearty bean dish and warm flour tortillas.

SPICE BOX PUMPKIN SLICES

When winter squash such as pumpkin and acorn start showing up in late summer, we season them for the grill with a tumbler of tangerine juice and thimblefuls of several aromatic spices.

SERVES 6

SPICE BOX MARINADE
¼ cup butter
1½ teaspoons ground cardamom
1 teaspoon turmeric
1 teaspoon ground cinnamon
½ teaspoon curry powder
½ teaspoon salt
1 cup tangerine juice or orange juice

1 small baking pumpkin or large acorn squash, halved, cleaned of seeds, and sliced into 12 or more slices about ½ inch thick

Crème fraîche, Mexican *crema*, or sour cream, for garnish

Prepare the marinade, first melting the butter in a large, heavy skillet over medium heat. Stir in the cardamom, turmeric, cinnamon, curry powder, and salt and simmer for a minute or two, until fragrant. Pour in the tangerine juice. Add the pumpkin slices and raise the heat to high. Simmer the pumpkin in the marinade for 2 minutes, moving the slices around as necessary to make sure all are submerged at least briefly. Remove the skillet from the heat and let the pumpkin mixture cool in the liquid.

Fire up the grill, bringing the heat to medium (4 to 5 seconds with the hand test).

Drain the pumpkin slices, discarding the marinade. Grill them uncovered for 10 to 12 minutes, turning once, until very tender and lightly browned. If grilling covered, cook for 9 to 10 minutes, turning once midway.

Serve the pumpkin slices hot or at room temperature, spooning a small dollop of crème fraîche on each at the end.

HOT AND SASSY SWEET POTATOES

The earliest recipe we've found for grilled sweet potatoes came from a cooking contest in the late 1950s. Called "Ham-n-Yam Volcanoes," it featured half a sweet potato, cut to look like a mountain and placed on a base of ham and pineapple slices. You scooped out a crater on top of the spud, added a brown-sugar lava sauce, wrapped everything in foil, and baked the concoction on the grill. When it was done, you spooned brandy into the crater and ignited the volcano for serving. We can't match the presentation, but our yam spears offer a little heat of their own from a jalapeño glaze.

SERVES 4 TO 6

SWEET JALAPEÑO GLAZE
2 tablespoons butter
¼ cup minced onion
⅛ teaspoon ground allspice
6 tablespoons lime, lemon, or orange marmalade
2 to 3 tablespoons minced pickled jalapeños, plus 1
    tablespoon of pickling juice from the jar

2 to 2¼ pounds sweet potatoes (about 2 large), peeled
    and halved lengthwise

Prepare the glaze, first melting the butter in a small, heavy skillet over medium heat. Stir in the onion and allspice and sauté until the onion is translucent, about 5 minutes. Add the marmalade and the jalapeños and their juice and heat through. (The glaze can be made several days ahead, covered, and refrigerated. Reheat it to lukewarm before using.)

Slice the sweet potato halves into long wedges ½ inch thick at their widest side. Steam the sweet potatoes until tender, about 10 minutes. (The sweet potatoes can be prepared to this point a day in advance, covered, and refrigerated. Bring them back to room temperature before proceeding.)

Fire up the grill, bringing the temperature to medium (4 to 5 seconds with the hand test).

Transfer the sweet potatoes to a

well-oiled grate. Grill uncovered over medium heat for 8 to 10 minutes, turning once, until very tender. Brush with the glaze in the last couple of minutes of grilling and again when the potatoes are done. If grilling covered, cook for 7 to 9 minutes, turning once midway and glazing in a similar fashion.

Serve the sweet potatoes hot.

DOUBLY GOOD TOMATO SANDWICH

The best garden tomatoes of the season taste great any way you eat them, including right off the grill on a sandwich doubled-up in flavor with sun-dried tomatoes. We grill ripe tomato slices on higher heat than most vegetables to sear their juices into the surface as quickly and thoroughly as possible without burning the delicate fruit.

SERVES 4

SUN-DRIED TOMATO PESTO
½ cup drained oil-packed sun-dried tomatoes
3 tablespoons minced fresh basil
2 tablespoons fresh-grated Parmesan cheese
1½ tablespoons minced fresh parsley, preferably Italian flat-leaf
1 medium shallot, chopped
½ teaspoon salt
¼ teaspoon Tabasco sauce or other hot pepper sauce, optional
½ cup extra-virgin olive oil or ¼ cup extra-virgin olive oil plus ¼ cup oil drained from the sun-dried tomatoes

2¼ pounds large, juicy height-of-season tomatoes, preferably a combination of red and yellow

Extra-virgin olive oil
8 slices sourdough or country bread
Salt and fresh-ground black pepper
Watercress or arugula, for garnish

Prepare the pesto, first mincing the sun-dried tomatoes in a food processor. Add the basil, Parmesan, parsley, shallot, salt, and Tabasco sauce and combine until a thick purée forms. With the processor running, pour in the oil in a slow, steady stream and process until incorporated. Reserve the pesto. (The pesto can be made ahead and kept covered and refrigerated for at least a week. Bring the mixture back to room temperature before proceeding.)

Fire up the grill, bringing the temperature to medium-high (3 seconds with the hand test).

Just before grilling, peel the tomatoes if you wish, and slice them into ½-inch slabs. Coat the slices with oil.

Immediately place the tomatoes on a well-oiled grate before they have the chance to lose additional juice. Grill the tomatoes uncovered over medium-high heat for 3 to 4 minutes, turning once, until hot and browned on a few edges. If grilling covered, cook for 6 to 7 minutes, turning once midway.

Make the sandwiches with the tomatoes hot or at room temperature. Spread a tablespoon or two of the pesto on each slice of bread. Arrange the tomatoes neatly on half of the slices, dividing out the yellow and red among the sandwiches if you used both colors. Salt and pepper the tomatoes, scatter the watercress on top, and add the remaining bread. We like Olive Oil Dills on the side. Leftover pesto can be saved for additional sandwiches, tossed with pasta, spread on a pizza, or served over fresh goat cheese or cream cheese with crackers.

GRILLED GREEN TOMATOES

L ike potatoes and onion rings, here's another vegetable that we take out of the frying pan and put onto the fire.

SERVES 4 TO 6

3 tablespoons butter, melted
¼ teaspoon Tabasco sauce or other hot pepper sauce
6 medium green tomatoes, sliced ½ inch thick
Salt and fresh-ground black pepper

Fire up the grill, bringing the temperature to medium (4 to 5 seconds with the hand test).

Combine the melted butter and Tabasco sauce in a small bowl. Brush the mixture over both sides of the tomato slices and sprinkle them with salt and pepper.

Grill the tomatoes uncovered over medium heat for 7 to 9 minutes, turning once, until tender and juicy. If grilling covered, cook the tomatoes for the same amount of time, turning once midway.

Serve the tomatoes hot, perhaps with Piedmont Porkers and Hoppin' John Salad with Tabasco Dressing. The tomatoes are also as tasty a match as their ripe cousins with slices of fresh mozzarella.

TECHNIQUE TIP: Green tomatoes typically get harvested and used in a big spurt as frost ends the growing season. You can pick and eat them earlier, however, and they're beginning to appear more frequently throughout the summer at some farmers' markets and produce stores. The tomatoes keep for several days in a refrigerator crisper.

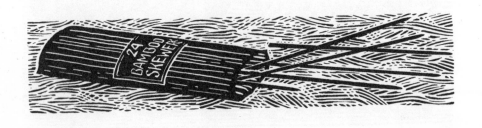

MIXED VEGGIE PLATTER WITH WALNUT DUNKING SAUCE

Grilled vegetable platters make festive meal centerpieces. Here we've selected some of our favorite finger-food veggies to dunk in a walnut sauce and munch along with savory blue cheese croutons. In this and the following two recipes, we don't recommend covered grilling because of the number of items that need watching.

SERVES 4 AS A MAIN DISH, 8 AS A SIDE DISH

WALNUT DUNKING SAUCE
½ cup walnut pieces, toasted
¼ cup chopped fresh parsley
1 garlic clove
1 tablespoon crumbled creamy blue cheese
1 teaspoon sherry vinegar
¼ teaspoon salt
Generous grinding of black pepper
½ cup extra-virgin olive oil

BLUE CHEESE BUTTER
3 tablespoons butter
3 tablespoons crumbled creamy blue cheese

8 baby artichokes, toughest exterior leaves removed
8 ounces baby yellow summer squash, in ⅛- to ½-inch-
    thick slices (ideally, find squash so small that
    you can just halve them lengthwise to get this
    thickness)
16 thin asparagus spears
1 bunch green onions, limp ends trimmed
Extra-virgin olive oil
Salt

8 baguette slices
Minced fresh parsley, for garnish

Prepare the sauce, first combining the walnuts, parsley, and garlic in a food processor. When coarsely mixed, add the blue cheese, vinegar, salt, and pepper and process again. With the motor running, add the oil in a slow, steady stream. Keep the sauce at room temperature. (The sauce can be made several days ahead, covered, and refrigerated. Bring it back to room temperature before proceeding.)

Prepare the blue cheese butter, first melting the butter in a small skillet or pan over medium heat. Mix in the blue cheese, stirring until melted. (The butter can be made several days ahead, covered, and refrigerated. Bring it back to room temperature before proceeding.)

Fire up the grill, bringing the temperature to medium (4 to 5 seconds with the hand test).

Trim any remaining tough edges from the artichoke leaves and slice them in half vertically. Using a small

spoon, remove the tiny fuzzy choke near the base of each half. Coat the artichokes and other vegetables with oil and sprinkle them with salt.

Grill the vegetables uncovered over medium heat until crisp-tender, 5 to 6 minutes for the asparagus, 8 to 10 minutes for the squash and green onions, and 15 to 18 minutes for the artichokes. Roll the asparagus on all sides and turn the other vegetables at least once, brushing with additional oil if they appear dry. Toast one side of the bread slices on the edge of the grill, then spread the toasted sides with the blue cheese butter. Return them to the edge of the grill, toasting the second side and softening the butter.

Pour the sauce into a small bowl on a platter. Arrange each vegetable on the platter, scattering the yellow squash among the green vegetables and ringing everything with the toasts. Top with parsley and serve hot to eat with your fingers or a fork.

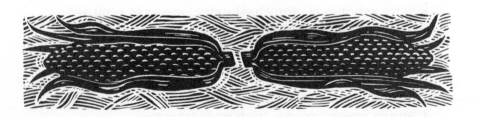

AUGUST VEGETABLE BOUNTY

This medley of late-summer vegetables, bathed in a fresh herb dressing, can be eaten hot off the grill or prepared earlier in the day and chilled. We cook and serve it with a round of goat cheese, wrapped in grape leaves to shield it from the fire.

SERVES 6 TO 8

FRESH OREGANO DRESSING
⅓ cup packed fresh oregano
1 tablespoon rinsed capers
1 garlic clove
½ cup extra-virgin olive oil
1 to 2 tablespoons red wine vinegar
¼ teaspoon salt
Fresh-ground black pepper

WRAPPED CHEESE
4-ounce to 6-ounce round of creamy fresh goat cheese
3 to 4 large grape leaves, blanched if fresh or rinsed if
    bottled
2 teaspoons extra-virgin olive oil

1½ pounds small eggplants such as the Japanese purple
    or other varieties that appear at farmers' markets,
    or small purple globe eggplants
¾ pound porcini, portobello, or cremini mushrooms, or
    large button mushrooms, sliced ⅛ inch thick
2 whole medium red, orange, or yellow bell peppers, or
    a combination
1 large red onion, sliced into ½-inch rings
4 small to medium heads of endive, halved vertically
4 small red-ripe tomatoes, preferably Italian plum,
    halved vertically

Olive oil
Salt to taste
Capers or larger caper berries
Briny green or black olives, or both

• • • • • • • • • • • • • • • • • •

Prepare the dressing. In a blender, purée the ingredients, starting with the smaller quantity of vinegar. Taste and add more vinegar if you wish. Reserve the dressing. (The dressing can be made earlier in the day, covered, and refrigerated.)

Fire up the grill, bringing the temperature to medium (4 to 5 seconds with the hand test).

Prepare the cheese, first arranging it on overlapping grape leaves. Pour 1 teaspoon of the oil over the cheese and bring the leaves up over it, covering the cheese completely. Coat the leaves with the remaining oil.

Prepare the vegetables. Peel the eggplants, but leave strips of the skin on at intervals to provide a little color contrast. Cut the eggplant in ⅛-inch slices, vertical for long slender eggplants or in rounds for rounder eggplants. Coat all the vegetables with oil, rubbing the eggplant and mushroom slices more heavily. Sprinkle all the vegetables with salt.

Transfer the vegetables to the grill, in batches if necessary. Arrange the tomatoes cut-side down. Grill the vegetables uncovered over medium heat until tender, 4 to 6 minutes for the tomatoes and the mushroom slices, 8 to 12 minutes for the eggplant and endive, 12 to 15 minutes for the peppers, and 15 to 18 minutes for the

onion. Turn the peppers on each side to cook evenly and the rest of the vegetables at least once, brushing with additional oil if any appear dry. Place the cheese on the grill about the time you take off the eggplant and endive. Grill the cheese for 7 to 10 minutes, turning once, until soft but short of oozing out of the protective wrap of semi-charred leaves.

Transfer the peppers to a plastic bag and close it to let them steam, loosening the skin. When cool enough to handle, pull off any loose charred pieces of skin. Slice the peppers into thin strips, eliminating the seeds.

If you're serving the vegetables hot, fold the grape leaves back from the top of the cheese and place it in the center of a platter. If you're serving the vegetables chilled, refrigerate the cheese as well but let it soften at room temperature for 20 to 30 minutes before placing it on the platter. Arrange the vegetables attractively around the cheese and drizzle dressing over them. Scatter the capers and olives over the platter and serve.

GARDEN'S GLORY SANDWICH

The various vegetables layered in this sandwich are available year-round, but they reach their peak of flavor at the height of the summer grilling season.

SERVES 4 TO 6

CLASSIC HERB MARINADE
½ cup plus 1 tablespoon extra-virgin olive oil
3 tablespoons red wine vinegar
½ teaspoon salt
2 tablespoons minced fresh herbs, such as thyme, oregano, basil, or rosemary

1 large eggplant, cut into ⅛-inch slices
8-ounce zucchini, cut into ⅛-inch slices
1 fresh mild green chile, such as poblano, New Mexican, or Anaheim
1 medium onion, preferably a sweet onion such as Vidalia, Maui, or Texas 1015, sliced into ⅛-inch-thick rings
6 tablespoons Enriched Mayonnaise (page 38) or other mayonnaise
3 plump garlic cloves, roasted and mashed
1½-pound to 2-pound country loaf of bread, split horizontally
2 small red-ripe tomatoes, chopped

Minced fresh herbs, such as thyme, oregano, basil, or rosemary, for garnish

Prepare the marinade, whisking together the ingredients in a small bowl. Place the eggplant, zucchini, chile, and onion in a plastic bag or shallow dish, pour the marinade over them, and let them sit at room temperature

387

for 15 to 30 minutes, turning occasionally to coat evenly.

Fire up the grill, bringing the temperature to medium (4 to 5 seconds with the hand test).

Drain the vegetables, reserving the marinade.

Grill the vegetables uncovered over medium heat until tender, 10 to 12 minutes for the eggplant and chile, 12 to 15 minutes for the zucchini, and 16 to 18 minutes for the onions. Turn the vegetables once midway, brushing again with the marinade if they appear dry.

Transfer the chiles to a plastic bag and close it to let them steam, loosening the skin. When cool enough to handle, pull off any loose charred pieces of skin. Slice the chile into thin strips,

eliminating the seeds.

Make the sandwich with the vegetables hot or at room temperature. Combine the mayonnaise with the garlic in a small bowl and spread each cut side of the bread generously with the mixture. On the bottom slice of the bread, stack the grilled vegetables in layers, sprinkle with the tomatoes, and top with a generous handful of herbs. Add the top slice of bread, place the sandwich on a cutting board or plate, and cut into fat slices or wedges at the table. We like serving the sandwich with Amazing Aspic. A friend who came to taste recipes one day liked the combo so well she now spoons the tomato aspic onto the sandwich too.

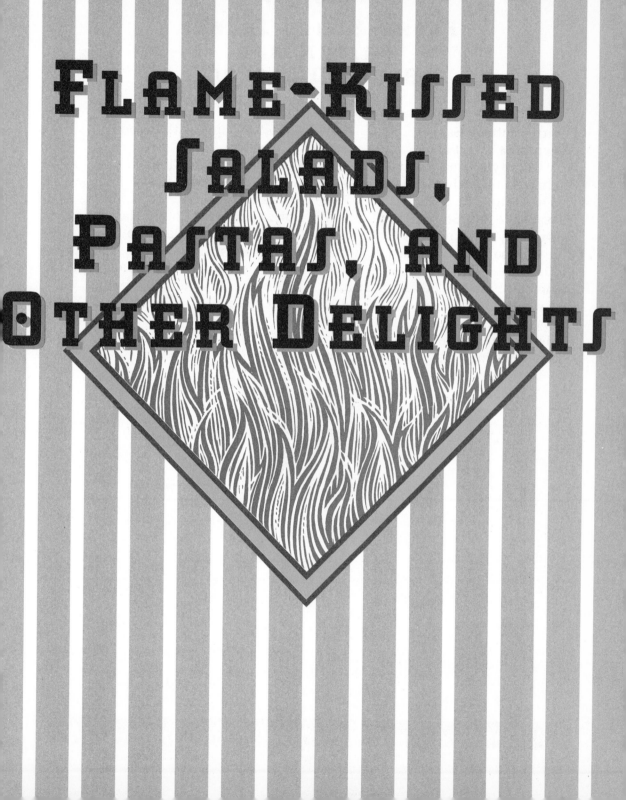

Flame-Kissed Salads, Pastas, and Other Delights

FLAME-KISSED SALADS, PASTAS, AND OTHER DELIGHTS

FRUITFUL SALMON SALAD

Juicy summer melons and grapes pair perfectly with salmon in this light and delightful main-course salad. The tang of citrus and smooth sweetness of honey accent the dressing, which helps to blend the different tastes without blurring their individuality.

SERVES 4 TO 6

HONEY-CORIANDER DRESSING
Zest and juice of 1 orange
⅓ cup vegetable oil
2 tablespoons honey
1 tablespoon cider vinegar
1 tablespoon minced onion
½ teaspoon ground coriander
¼ teaspoon dry mustard
¼ teaspoon kosher salt or other coarse salt

8-ounce to 10-ounce skin-on salmon fillet
Vegetable oil
Kosher salt or other coarse salt

1½ cups cubed cantaloupe or other orange-fleshed
    melon
1½ cups cubed honeydew or Ogan melon or other
    green-fleshed melon
½ cup halved seedless red grapes
Watercress, for garnish

Prepare the dressing, combining the ingredients in a blender. (The dressing can be made a day ahead and refrigerated, but if the honey coagulates, blend it again before serving.)

Fire up the grill, bringing the temperature to high (1 to 2 seconds with the hand test).

Coat the salmon lightly with oil and sprinkle it with salt. Let it sit covered at room temperature for 20 to 30 minutes.

Transfer the salmon to a well-oiled grate, skin-side down. Grill the salmon

uncovered over high heat for 5 to 6 minutes, until the skin chars nearly black. Turn the salmon and cook an additional 3 to 3½ minutes, rotating the fillets 180° once. If there is any resistance when you turn or rotate the fish, re-oil the grate. The salmon is done when just barely opaque pink at the center with a touch of translucence remaining. If grilling covered, cook the salmon for the same amount of time, turning and rotating in a similar manner.

Carefully strip the skin off the bottom of each salmon fillet and chill for at least 30 minutes and up to 24 hours. With a sharp knife, cut the salmon as neatly as possible into bite-size chunks.

In a bowl, toss both types of melons and the grapes together with the dressing. Spoon the fruit onto a platter or large shallow bowl. Add the chilled salmon and combine gently. Tuck watercress around the edges and serve.

DELIBERATE LEFTOVERS

Many of the recipes in this chapter evolved out of lowly leftovers, scraps of grilled food that we saved until the next day and then used to liven up salads, pastas, and other dishes. These almost-accidental creations proved so tasty, they became intentional. Now we make most of the dishes fresh as a way to stretch grilled food and to enjoy it in lighter, healthier ways.

We haven't abandoned our old leftovers mentality, though. It led us to such good meals, we made it standard procedure. Any time we're grilling, we think ahead about ways we might recycle what we're cooking. Some foods save better than others, of course, and most things don't survive well beyond a day or two, but when the ingredients and timing work, we grill extra amounts for deliberate leftovers.

Try that with the appropriate dishes in this chapter, or just use them as examples for creating your own concoctions that allow you to cook a couple of meals at once. We provide instructions for making everything here from scratch, but all the options except the Chesapeake Soft-Shells Salad, the Vietnamese Fajitas Salad, and the Paella Mixed Grill can be prepared from compatible leftovers, usually with only a small loss in flavor. Consider other possibilities as well, such as Saturday's chicken in a Sunday pot pie, vegetables or seafood for the next morning's omelet, or enough spare sirloin for a big pot of chili that'll keep you fired up for a week. With a little advance planning, grilling keeps on giving.

CHOPPED SALMON SALAD

A chopped salad—where the ingredients are finely diced, sliced, and shredded—brings together the full range of flavors in every bite. It can also make a vibrant presentation, with bold ribbons of color blazing across the plate. To change the hues or tastes, add other vegetables or legumes to the lettuce base, perhaps carrots, beets, or cooked white beans.

SERVES 4 TO 6

WARM BACON VINAIGRETTE
4 slices uncooked bacon, chopped
6 tablespoons extra-virgin olive oil
2 to 2½ tablespoons white or white wine vinegar
½ teaspoon sugar
¼ teaspoon salt

8-ounce to 10-ounce skin-on salmon fillet
Extra-virgin olive oil
Salt
Fresh-ground black pepper

4 cups shredded romaine or Bibb lettuce
1 Hass avocado, diced
2 hard-boiled eggs, grated
1 red-ripe medium tomato, chopped
2 green onions, sliced into thin rings

Prepare the dressing, first frying the bacon in a skillet over medium heat until crisp. Drain the bacon with a slotted spoon, reserving it and the drippings. Reduce the heat to low and add the oil, 2 tablespoons of vinegar, sugar, and salt to the drippings. Taste and add the remaining vinegar if needed to balance the tang of the dressing. Keep the vinaigrette warm. (The dressing can be made a day ahead, covered, and refrigerated. Reheat before serving.)

Fire up the grill, bringing the temperature to high (1 to 2 seconds with the hand test).

Coat the salmon lightly with oil and sprinkle it with salt and pepper. Let it sit covered at room temperature

for 20 to 30 minutes.

Transfer the salmon to a well-oiled grate, skin-side down. Grill the salmon uncovered over high heat for 5 to 6 minutes, until the skin chars nearly black. Turn the salmon and cook an additional 3 to 3½ minutes, rotating the fillets 180° once. Should there be any resistance when you turn or rotate the fish, re-oil the grate. The salmon is done when just barely opaque pink at the center with a touch of translucence remaining. If grilling covered, cook the salmon for the same amount of time, turning and rotating in a similar manner. Carefully strip the skin off the bottom of each salmon fillet. Use the salmon either warm or chilled for the salad.

Toss the lettuce in a bowl with several tablespoons of the dressing. Arrange the lettuce on a platter or in a large, shallow bowl. Chop the salmon and sprinkle it over the center of the lettuce in a thick wide band. To either side of the salmon, sprinkle rows of avocado, egg, bacon, and tomato, so that you have a swath of pink in the center bordered by narrower green, yellow, brown, and red stripes. Scatter the green onions over the salmon. Drizzle additional warm vinaigrette over the salad and serve.

New Old-Style Tuna Salad

A fresh variation on a canned favorite, this non-tinny tuna salad will make you ditch Charlie in an instant. The recipe suggests serving it on lettuce, but we also love it in a sandwich.

Serves 4 to 6

TUNA RUB
¼ cup finely chopped pecan pieces
1 teaspoon kosher salt or other coarse salt
1 teaspoon fresh-ground black pepper

Two 1-pound tuna steaks, approximately 1 inch thick,
    any skin removed
Vegetable oil spray
6 tablespoons Enriched Mayonnaise (page 38) or other
    mayonnaise
½ cup minced celery
2 tablespoons minced fresh parsley
Lettuce leaves

2 hard-boiled eggs, grated, optional, for garnish
Minced fresh parsley, for garnish

All-Star Pickled Starfruit (page 45) or other sweet
    pickles for garnish

Prepare the dry rub, combining the ingredients in a small bowl. Rub the tuna steaks with the mixture and let them sit covered at room temperature for about 30 minutes.

Fire up the grill for a two-level fire capable of cooking first on high (1 to 2 seconds with the hand test) and then on medium (4 to 5 seconds with the hand test).

Spritz the steaks with oil. Transfer the steaks to a well-oiled grate. Grill them uncovered over high heat for 2 minutes per side. Move the tuna to medium heat and continue cooking for an additional 2 to 3 minutes per side, leaving a distinctly pink center. If grilling covered, sear both sides of the fish first on high heat uncovered for 2 minutes; finish the cooking with the cover on over medium heat for 4 to 5 minutes, turning once midway.

Chill the tuna for at least 30 minutes and up to 24 hours. With a sharp knife, cut the tuna neatly into bite-size chunks. In a medium bowl, toss the tuna with the mayonnaise, celery, and parsley and mound it over the lettuce leaves on a platter. Sprinkle the hard-boiled eggs over the chilled tuna, if you like, and scatter parsley over the top. Add some pickles to the edge of the platter and serve the salad with crisp toast. We like to round out the meal with a bowl of Tomato and Tortilla Soup.

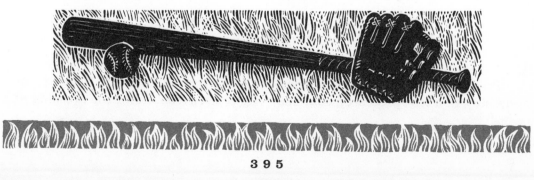

SHRIMP SALAD WITH GREEN GODDESS DRESSING

According to John Mariani in his excellent *The Dictionary of American Food and Drink* (Hearst Books, 1994), San Francisco's Palace Hotel created Green Goddess dressing in the 1920s for actor George Arliss, who was appearing in town in William Archer's play *The Green Goddess*. We made this grill variation for stars of outdoor summer theater, backyard cooks like you and us.

SERVES 6

GREEN GODDESS DRESSING
½ cup Enriched Mayonnaise (page 38) or other
    mayonnaise
½ cup sour cream
⅓ cup chopped fresh parsley
2 tablespoons chopped fresh chives
1 tablespoon chopped fresh tarragon
1 tablespoon tarragon vinegar
2 tablespoons water
1 green onion, chopped
2 medium anchovy fillets
¼ teaspoon salt, or more to taste

1¼ pounds medium shrimp, peeled and, if you wish,
    deveined
3 tablespoons tarragon vinegar
2 teaspoons olive oil
½ teaspoon salt

3 ripe Hass avocados, halved and peeled
Minced fresh chives, for garnish

Prepare the dressing. In a blender, preferably, or a food processor, combine all the ingredients until smooth and light pea green. Cover the dressing and

refrigerate for at least 30 minutes. (The dressing can be made to this point several days in advance.)

In a bowl, toss the shrimp together with the vinegar, oil, and salt. Let the shrimp sit at room temperature while you heat the grill.

Fire up the grill, bringing the temperature to high (1 to 2 seconds with the hand test).

Drain the shrimp, discarding the liquid. Blot them of any excess moisture.

Transfer the shrimp to a well-oiled grate. Grill the shrimp uncovered over high heat for 1½ to 2 minutes per side, until just opaque with lightly browned edges. If grilling covered, cook the shrimp for the same amount of time, turning once midway.

Chill the shrimp for at least 1 hour and up to 24 hours before serving. Arrange the avocados on individual plates and mound the chilled shrimp over them. Spoon the salad dressing over the shrimp, scatter the chives over the salad, and serve.

CHESAPEAKE SOFT-SHELLS SALAD

In the Washington, D.C., of old, a tumultuous public market sat on Pennsylvania Avenue in the spot now occupied by the National Archives Building. Gentlemen did much of the shopping, to shield the ladies from the hurly-burly of the place, but few took to the task with the concentration of the Olympian orator from Massachusetts, Daniel Webster. In season, he often selected the local soft-shell crabs for entertaining, still a capital idea. They tend to be pricey today, but this main-dish salad spreads the cost over more dinner plates. Since the molting crabs are highly perishable, follow Senator Webster's lead and do your marketing on the day of the party. Serve the salad as soon as the soft-shells come off the grill and forget any possibility of leftovers.

SERVES 6

SWEET MUSTARD PASTE AND DRESSING
1 cup Enriched Mayonnaise (page 38) or other
    mayonnaise
1 tablespoon packed brown sugar

2 teaspoons dry mustard

2 teaspoons Super Wooster Sauce (page 39) or other
  Worcestershire sauce

2 teaspoons steak sauce, such as A-1 Original

1 garlic clove, minced

⅛ teaspoon cayenne

3 tablespoons milk

6 soft-shell crabs, preferably at least 3 ounces each

7 cups shredded romaine

1 cup sliced red cabbage or radicchio

4 green onions, sliced into thin rings

4 bacon slices, chopped and cooked crisp

1 ripe Hass avocado, peeled and diced

· · · · · · · · · · · · · · · · · · · ·

Prepare the paste, mixing together the ingredients in a medium bowl. Spoon out about 2 tablespoons of the paste into a small bowl and reserve. Whisk the milk into the bigger bowl of paste to make the dressing and refrigerate until needed.

Fire up the grill, bringing the temperature to high (1 to 2 seconds with the hand test).

Gently massage the 2 tablespoons of remaining paste equally over the delicate crabs, getting it in and around all of their nooks and crannies. Place the crabs on a platter, cover them, and let them sit at room temperature for about 15 minutes.

Transfer the crabs to a well-oiled grate, bottoms down. Grill the crabs uncovered over high heat for 1½ to 2 minutes, until the bodies and legs turn a burnished red and opaque white. The crab bodies are full of moisture, so watch out for a little popping while they cook. Carefully flip the crabs over,

brushing a bit more oil on the grate if you get any sticking at all. Grill the crabs for an additional 1½ to 2 minutes, keeping a close watch on them. The legs should get dark and crunchy but not burned black, and the bodies should have a crispy burnished red surface but still be very moist. If grilling covered, cook the crabs for the same amount of time, turning once midway.

In a large bowl, quickly toss the romaine and the cabbage with enough dressing to coat them well. Spoon the greens onto individual plates and top each with a crab. Scatter onions, bacon, and avocado over the salad and serve immediately, passing the remaining dressing at the table. Every bit of the succulent soft-shells is edible.

The salad needs little embellishment to make a meal, maybe just some crunchy breadsticks and a fruit dessert such as Georgia Peaches with Praline Crunch or Honeyed Rainbow Fruit Kebobs.

THE PURSUIT OF HAPPINESS

You have to admire a man who can write about the freedom to pursue happiness and then go broke eating well. When Thomas Jefferson died—on July 4, 1826, exactly fifty years after the signing of the Declaration of Independence that he penned—he was deeply in debt, largely because he never restrained his appetite for fine food, wine, and hospitality. Despite the simplicity and modesty of much of his life, his Epicurean expenditures for the table often outpaced his income, even the presidential salary he earned for eight years.

Along with expensive wine and French cuisine, Jefferson loved salads and anything else fresh from the garden. Patrick Henry once claimed that his fellow Virginian had "abjured his native victuals," but that certainly wasn't true of fruits and vegetables. As the U.S. envoy to France, Jefferson carefully studied the produce in Paris and declared everything inferior to the American equivalents except apricots, pears, and turnips. During his time in the White House, he kept track of the local season for all the vegetables at the Washington market, noting the first and last dates he could count on getting them on his frequent personal shopping forays.

Jefferson devoted even more attention to his own garden, which gave him as much pride as any of his political and diplomatic accomplishments. He grew everything suitable to the soil of Charlottesville, from American corn and black-eyed peas to European endive and broccoli, and tried to raise a number of crops that weren't, including olives. He carried his passion into competition with the pea harvest, joining his neighbors in an annual contest to produce the earliest patch of the season, with the victor hosting the losers to a gala dinner featuring the championship peas. Jefferson may have died broke, but he lived well on the way there.

SALSA-SASSY CHICKEN SALAD

If you're bored with conventional chicken salad, this Southwestern twist will make the old bird fly again.

SERVES 4

SALSA MARINADE
¼ cup Fired-Up Tomato Salsa (page 88) or other favorite
    tomato- or tomatillo-based salsa
Juice of 2 limes
2 teaspoons olive oil

Four 6-ounce boneless, skinless individual chicken
    breasts, pounded to ½-inch thickness

SALSA MAYO
½ cup Enriched Mayonnaise (page 38) or other
    mayonnaise
6 tablespoons Fired-Up Tomato Salsa (page 88) or other
    tomato- or tomatillo-based salsa
Juice of ½ lime

½ cup peeled, diced jícama, or water chestnuts
¼ cup minced fresh cilantro
Romaine or other crisp lettuce, shredded
2 to 3 tablespoons shelled pumpkin seeds (*pepitas*),
    preferably, or slivered almonds

Lime wedges, for garnish

At least 2 hours and up to the day before you plan to serve the salad, prepare the marinade, combining the ingredients in a small bowl. Place the chicken breasts in a plastic bag or shallow dish, pour the marinade over them, and refrigerate.

Prepare the mayonnaise, combin-

ing the ingredients in another small bowl, and refrigerate until needed. (The mayonnaise can be made several days in advance if you wish.)

Fire up the grill, bringing the temperature to medium (4 to 5 seconds with the hand test).

Remove the chicken breasts from the refrigerator, drain them, and let them sit covered at room temperature for about 20 minutes.

Grill the chicken uncovered over medium heat for 5 to 6 minutes per side, until opaque but still juicy. If grilling covered, cook the chicken for about 10 minutes, turning once midway. When the chicken is cool enough to handle, shred it by hand into neat bite-size pieces. (The chicken can be prepared to this point a day ahead, covered, and refrigerated.)

Combine the chicken in a medium bowl with the jícama, cilantro, and mayonnaise and refrigerate for at least 30 minutes and up to several hours. Arrange a bed of shredded romaine on a platter. Spoon the salad out onto the romaine and scatter pumpkin seeds over the salad for a contrasting crunch. Tuck lime wedges on the sides and serve. Offer a basket of crisp tortilla chips along with the salad, if you like, or roll the salad up in Tucson Tortillas or other flour tortillas for an on-the-run lunch.

BLUE-CHEESE TURKEY SALAD

Spinach and blue cheese would be near the top of our wish list for elements in a last meal. Turkey might not make the cut for that occasion, but it's a mighty good way to bring together the other two in an everyday salad.

SERVES 6 TO 8

FRUITY WORCESTERSHIRE MARINADE
4 tablespoons Super Wooster Sauce (page 39) or other Worcestershire sauce
4 tablespoons Peach Vinegar (page 41) or other fruit vinegar
2 teaspoons vegetable oil

Four 5-ounce to 6-ounce turkey breast fillet sections,
pounded to ½- to ¾-inch thickness

FRUITY VINAIGRETTE
4 tablespoons vegetable oil
1 to 1½ tablespoons Peach Vinegar (page 41) or other
   fruit vinegar
2 teaspoons Dijon mustard
½ teaspoon Super Wooster Sauce (page 39) or other
   Worcestershire sauce
¼ teaspoon salt, or more to taste

10 to 12 cups fresh spinach or mixed greens
8 tablespoons pecan pieces, toasted
4 to 6 ounces creamy blue cheese, crumbled
4 to 6 slices crisp cooked bacon, crumbled
1 Hass avocado, sliced or chunked
Fresh-ground black pepper

At least 1 hour and up to 12 hours before you plan to grill the turkey, prepare the marinade, combining the ingredients in a small bowl. Place the turkey in a plastic bag or shallow dish, pour the marinade over it, and refrigerate.

In a small bowl, whisk together the vinaigrette ingredients, adjusting the seasoning if needed. (The dressing can be made a day ahead and kept covered and refrigerated.)

Fire up the grill, bringing the temperature to medium (4 to 5 seconds with the hand test).

Remove the turkey from the refrigerator, drain it, and let it sit at room temperature for 20 to 30 minutes.

Grill the turkey uncovered over medium heat for 5 to 6 minutes per side, until opaque but still juicy. If grilling covered, cook for 9 to 10 minutes, turning once midway. When the turkey is cool enough to handle, cut it into neat ¼-inch-thick slices. (The turkey can be prepared a day ahead, covered, and refrigerated.)

In a large salad bowl, toss the greens with the vinaigrette. Top the greens with the sliced turkey and sprinklings of pecans, cheese, bacon, and avocado. Add pepper to taste and serve.

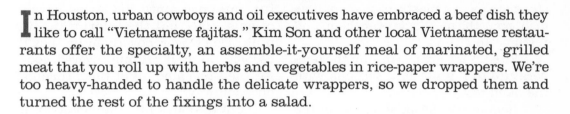

VIETNAMESE FAJITAS SALAD

In Houston, urban cowboys and oil executives have embraced a beef dish they like to call "Vietnamese fajitas." Kim Son and other local Vietnamese restaurants offer the specialty, an assemble-it-yourself meal of marinated, grilled meat that you roll up with herbs and vegetables in rice-paper wrappers. We're too heavy-handed to handle the delicate wrappers, so we dropped them and turned the rest of the fixings into a salad.

SERVES 4 OR MORE

SOY-LEMONGRASS MARINADE
3 tablespoons soy sauce
2 tablespoons minced lemongrass (from the tender
    inner stalks) or 1 tablespoon minced lemon zest
2 tablespoons sugar
1½ tablespoons peanut oil or vegetable oil
2 garlic cloves, minced

1-pound to 1¼-pound flank or skirt steak, sliced thin
    across the grain

VIETNAMESE FAJITAS TABLE SAUCE
¼ cup soy sauce
¼ cup sugar
1½ tablespoons rice vinegar or white vinegar
¾ cup water

1 head Bibb or Boston lettuce or other soft leaf lettuce,
    torn into bite-size pieces
1 large carrot, grated
½ medium cucumber, peeled, seeded, and sliced into
    thin strips
½ cup bean sprouts
⅓ cup fresh mint leaves
⅓ cup fresh cilantro leaves

At least 4 hours and up to 12 hours before you plan to grill, prepare the marinade, mixing together the ingredients in a small bowl. Place the steak strips in a plastic bag or shallow dish, pour the marinade over them, and refrigerate.

Fire up the grill, bringing the temperature to high (1 to 2 seconds with the hand test).

Remove the steak strips from the refrigerator and drain them, discarding the marinade. Let the steak strips sit covered at room temperature for about 20 minutes. Blot any accumulated liquid from the surface.

Prepare the table sauce, stirring together the ingredients until the sugar dissolves. Place the lettuce in a shallow salad bowl or on a platter and toss it with 1 to 2 tablespoons of the sauce.

Grill the steak strips uncovered over high heat for 2½ to 4 minutes, turning once, until the strips have a crisp surface but the interior is still pink. Don't overcook them or they'll become tough. If grilling covered, cook for the same amount of time, turning once midway.

Cut the steak into thinner strips if you wish. Transfer the steak to the bowl or platter. Top the steak with the remaining ingredients and toss lightly. Serve immediately, passing the remaining sauce on the side. Since the fire's blazing anyway, why not grill dessert? Mango-Marinated Mangos match up splendidly with the fajitas.

LAMB AND PINE-NUT SALAD ON GRAPE LEAVES

The Greeks stuff grape leaves with rice and pine nuts to make dolmathes. We just added a little of the country's favorite meat for a different take on a Greek salad.

SERVES 4 TO 6

LAMB SALAD RUB
1 tablespoon minced lemon zest
1 tablespoon dried oregano
2 teaspoons dried mint
2 teaspoons ground cumin
¾ teaspoon kosher salt or other coarse salt

1 to 1½ pounds lamb sirloin or leg, in one chunk
¼ cup olive oil
1 medium onion, chopped
2 garlic cloves, minced
1¼ cups uncooked rice
1 teaspoon ground cumin
2½ cups chicken stock
⅓ cup dried currants
Salt
½ cup pine nuts, toasted
⅓ cup chopped fresh mint
1 tablespoon white wine vinegar
Grape leaves, rinsed if bottled

Olive oil and mint for garnish

• • • • • • • • • • • • • • • • •

At least 1 hour and up to 12 hours before you plan to serve the salad, prepare the dry rub, combining the ingredients in a small bowl. Massage the mixture over the lamb, wrap it in plastic, and refrigerate.

In a heavy medium saucepan, warm the oil over medium heat. Add the onion and garlic and sauté until well softened, about 5 minutes. Stir in the rice and cumin and continue cooking several additional minutes until the rice is translucent. Pour in the stock, add the currants, and salt to taste. Cover and simmer until the rice is tender, about 18 to 20 minutes. Stir the

nuts, mint, and vinegar into the rice and let it cool covered.

Remove the lamb from the refrigerator and let it sit covered at room temperature for about 30 minutes.

Fire up the grill for a two-level fire capable of cooking first on high heat (1 to 2 seconds with the hand test) and then on medium heat (4 to 5 seconds with the hand test).

Grill the lamb uncovered over high heat for 2½ to 3 minutes per side. Move the lamb to medium heat, turning it again, and continue grilling for 10 to 14 minutes for rare to medium-rare, turning at least two more times. Turn

more often if juice begins to form on the surface of the meat. If grilling covered, sear both sides first on high heat uncovered for 2½ to 3 minutes; finish cooking with the cover on over medium heat for 8 to 11 minutes, turning once midway.

Arrange the grape leaves around the edge of a platter with their tips facing out. (The grape leaves can be eaten or left behind as you wish.) Pile the rice on the platter, leaving an inch or two of the grape leaf border exposed. Cut the warm lamb into thin slices and arrange the slices in a spiral over the rice. Drizzle the salad with oil to taste, scatter mint over it, and serve immediately.

For a truly Olympian meal, just add a chunk of feta cheese, some briny olives, a bunch of grapes, and a beautiful summer evening.

DRESSED-UP CORN SALAD

The dressing provides the luster on this simple, straightforward salad. Any corn oil will work in it, but the unrefined variety gives the mixture a special touch of field freshness.

SERVES 6 TO 8

CORN OIL DRESSING
¼ cup corn oil, preferably unrefined (see Technique Tip)
1½ tablespoons cider vinegar
1 teaspoon minced fresh thyme or ½ teaspoon dried thyme
¾ teaspoon salt
½ teaspoon packed brown sugar
½ teaspoon ground cumin
Splash of Tabasco sauce or other hot pepper sauce

5 ears of corn, husked and silk removed
Corn oil, preferably unrefined (see Technique Tip)
Salt

2 celery stalks, minced
1 small red bell pepper, diced fine
½ large red onion, minced

Thyme sprigs, optional, for garnish

• • • • • • • • • • • • • • • • • • •

In a lidded jar, combine the dressing ingredients and refrigerate until needed. (The dressing can be made a day ahead if you wish.)

Fire up the grill, bringing the temperature to medium (4 to 5 seconds with the hand test).

Coat the corn with oil and sprinkle it lightly with salt. Grill the corn uncovered on medium heat for 20 to 25 minutes, turning on all sides to cook evenly and brushing with more oil after about 10 minutes. If grilling covered, cook for 18 to 22 minutes, turning once midway and brushing with oil. The cooking time is longer than technically necessary to cook the corn, but helps concentrate the juices a bit, giving the corn a more intense taste and a crisper texture.

Let the corn sit covered until cool enough to handle. (The corn can be grilled a day ahead, wrapped, and refrigerated.)

With a knife, carefully remove the kernels from the ears of corn, slicing deeply enough to cut through the milky bottom portion of the kernels but avoiding the cob. Place the corn in a large bowl, and combine it with the celery, bell pepper, and onion. Pour the dressing over the salad and toss gently. Refrigerate the salad for at least 1 hour and up to overnight. Serve chilled, garnished with thyme sprigs if you like.

Consider an old-time farm feast on a summer Sunday. Make the corn salad, Sprightly Potato Salad, and Fancy Three-Bean Salad the day before the party. Then fire up the grill around serving time for Church-Picnic Pork Chops and Sunny Sunday Chicken Breasts. Have a neighbor bring peach pie or cobbler, and if you're really ambitious, churn up some ice cream. Hefty glasses of iced tea are a must.

TECHNIQUE TIP: Unrefined corn oil is great for dressings and marinades—or mixing with butter to slather on fresh corn on the cob—but it's not as good for cooking as the more refined oils, which have higher smoke points. If you don't find the unrefined version on your supermarket shelves with other oils, look for it in whole foods or health food stores.

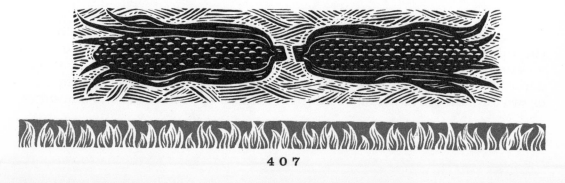

MADEIRA SCALLOPS AND SPAGHETTINI

We usually avoid cream sauces with grilled food because they tend to overwhelm the flavor of the flame. Scallops are an exception, capable of standing up to the richness, especially in a pasta.

SERVES 6

MADEIRA SAUCE
¼ cup extra-virgin olive oil
3 tablespoons chopped prosciutto (see Technique Tip)
2 plump garlic cloves, minced
¼ cup minced fresh parsley, preferably Italian flat-leaf
6 tablespoons Madeira, preferably, or brandy or grappa
1½ cups half-and-half
4 ounces mascarpone cheese or cream cheese
⅛ teaspoon ground white pepper

MADEIRA MARINADE
½ cup Madeira, preferably, or brandy or grappa
2 teaspoons olive oil
2 teaspoons sugar
½ teaspoon kosher salt or other coarse salt

1½ pounds sea scallops, halved if larger in diameter
than a 50-cent coin
1 pound spaghettini or other thin spaghetti
Minced fresh parsley, preferably Italian flat-leaf, for
garnish

Prepare the sauce, first warming the oil in a heavy saucepan over medium heat. Add the prosciutto, garlic, and parsley and cook a minute or two until the garlic softens. Pour in the Madeira and increase the heat to medium-high, reducing the Madeira by about half. Add the half-and-half and continue cooking until the liquid is reduced by half, about 5 to 8 minutes.

Strain the sauce and, while still warm, stir in the cheese until it dissolves into the sauce. If the cheese doesn't melt completely, don't worry; the hot pasta will complete the job later. Season with pepper and reserve.

Prepare the marinade, mixing together the ingredients in a small bowl. Add the scallops to the marinade and let them sit at room temperature while you heat the grill.

Fire up the grill, bringing the temperature to high (1 to 2 seconds with the hand test).

Cook the spaghettini according to the package directions. When done, toss it with the sauce in a large, shallow serving bowl and keep it warm.

Drain the scallops and blot them of any remaining moisture.

Transfer the scallops to a well-oiled grate. Grill them uncovered over high heat for 2 to 2½ minutes per side, until just opaque with lightly browned edges. If grilling covered, cook the scallops for 4 to 5 minutes, turning once midway. (The scallops can be grilled earlier in the day, covered, and refrigerated. Remove them from the refrigerator and let sit at room temperature for about 20 minutes before serving. Toss them with the pasta to warm through, rather than place them on top of it, as directed in the next step.)

Arrange the scallops over the spaghettini and scatter parsley over the top. Serve immediately. With the richness of the pasta, we opt for simple vegetable accompaniments, perhaps steamed baby carrots and shelled Sugar Snap peas.

TECHNIQUE TIP: Since you're chopping the prosciutto anyway for this sauce, you don't need to pay for beautiful thin slices. Ask whether your market has prosciutto ends, which taste as good but usually cost less.

SIZZLED SHRIMP WITH LEMON NOODLES

Shrimp never flop on a warm and fragrant bed of basil- and lemon-scented linguine.

SERVES 6

LEMON PASTE
Juice of 1 lemon
1 teaspoon olive oil
1½ teaspoons crumbled dried basil or dried marjoram
½ teaspoon kosher salt or other coarse salt
½ teaspoon crushed dried hot red chile

1¼ pounds medium shrimp, peeled and, if you wish, deveined

LEMON SAUCE
⅔ cup extra-virgin olive oil
Zest and juice of 2 medium lemons
1 cup fresh-grated Parmesan cheese, at room temperature
½ teaspoon fresh-ground black pepper

1 pound linguine
⅓ cup fresh basil, torn or sliced in shreds

Prepare the paste, mixing together the ingredients in a medium bowl. Add the shrimp to the bowl, rub them with the paste, and cover. Let them sit at room temperature for about 20 minutes.

Fire up the grill, bringing the temperature to high (1 to 2 seconds with the hand test).

Prepare the sauce, first pouring the oil in a large, shallow serving bowl. Whisk in the lemon juice, cheese, and pepper. Cook the linguine according to the package directions and, when done, toss with the sauce.

Drain the shrimp and blot them of any remaining moisture. Grill the

shrimp uncovered over high heat for 1½ to 2 minutes per side, until opaque with lightly browned edges. If grilling covered, cook the shrimp for the same amount of time, turning once midway. (The shrimp can be grilled earlier in the day, covered, and refrigerated. Remove them from the refrigerator and let sit at room temperature for about 20 minutes before serving. Toss them with the pasta to warm through, rather than place them on top of it, as directed in the next step.)

Arrange the shrimp over the linguine, scatter basil over the top, and serve immediately.

FANNIE FARMER LEARNS TO GRILL

Perhaps no one has influenced American cooking more than Fannie Merritt Farmer, who achieved national prominence with *The Boston Cooking-School Cook Book*, first published in 1896. Revised thirteen times since then, under a succession of editors and authors, the tome remains a top seller today as *The Fannie Farmer Cookbook*.

Fannie didn't grill or barbecue in the early years. She broiled a few foods—including Hamburg steaks—in the kitchen "over or in front of a clear fire," but made no mention of outdoor cooking methods or traditions. It took four decades to broach the subject at all, and then the first steps were cautious and a little confused. In an update of Fannie's cookbook released right before World War II, the erstwhile editor equated grilling with broiling and introduced two new "barbecued" dishes, both oven-broiled and basted with a sauce.

By the time Wilma Lord Perkins wrote the tenth edition in 1959—now *The All New Fannie Farmer Boston Cooking School Cookbook*—outdoor cooking had begun to get notice. Perkins tells readers that portable grills are "a practical piece of equipment for the backyard or patio." She adds only a basic selection of grilled recipes, but does suggest that cooks plan on a pound of bone-in meat per person because "out-of-door appetites are apt to be huge" and the "food tastes superb."

Fannie finally reached her stride as a grill tutor when Marion Cunningham took over the most recent revisions of the cookbook. Now outdoor cooking rates a full chapter, replete with recipes, tips, and information on equipment and fuels. The discussion of direct and indirect cooking methods is short but more to the point than many whole books on grilling. Fannie may have been a slow learner on this unfamiliar turf, but she wised up in the end.

BOW-TIED THYME CHICKEN

As the recipe script suggests, thyme, mint, spinach, white wine, and feta cheese all perform important parts in this montage of flavors. Chicken breasts set the stage and bow-tie pasta makes it a wrap.

SERVES 6

THYME-MINT PASTE
¼ cup chopped fresh thyme
¼ cup chopped fresh mint
2 plump garlic cloves, minced
½ teaspoon kosher salt or other coarse salt
3 tablespoons olive oil

Three 6-ounce boneless, skinless individual chicken
    breasts, pounded to ⅛-inch thickness

¼ cup olive oil
3 plump garlic cloves, sliced thin
¼ cup chicken stock
¼ cup dry white wine
¾ pound fresh spinach, chopped
Kosher salt or other coarse salt

1 pound bow-tie pasta (farfalle)
½ cup crumbled feta cheese, optional
Fresh thyme sprigs and chopped mint leaves, for garnish

At least 2 hours and up to the day before you plan to serve the pasta, prepare the paste, combining the ingredients in a small bowl. Rub the paste over the chicken, wrap the chicken in plastic, and refrigerate.

Fire up the grill, bringing the temperature to medium (4 to 5 seconds with the hand test).

Remove the chicken from the refrigerator and let it sit at room temperature for about 20 minutes.

Grill the chicken uncovered over medium heat for 5 to 6 minutes per side, until opaque but still juicy. If grilling covered, cook the chicken for

about 10 minutes, turning once midway. (The chicken can be prepared to this point up to two days ahead and kept covered and refrigerated. Reheat wrapped in foil in a low to medium oven.) Shred the warm chicken in pieces about the size of the pasta.

Warm the oil over medium-low heat in a large skillet. Add the garlic and cook slowly, until it just begins to color. Do not let the garlic color beyond the nutty, light-golden stage or it will become bitter in taste. Remove the garlic with a slotted spoon and reserve. To the oil, add the stock and wine, watching out for any sputtering. Turn up the heat to medium-high. Reduce the liquid by half and then add the spinach and salt to taste. Cook just until the spinach wilts, stirring as needed to cook evenly.

Cook the pasta according to the package directions and, when done, toss the pasta with the sauce, chicken, and garlic slices. Scatter the cheese over the top if you wish and garnish with thyme and mint. Serve immediately. We like to make a main dish of the pasta with a side of August Vegetable Bounty.

TECHNIQUE TIP: If you've invested in a grill with an attached side burner, you've got the tools to be an outdoor pasta pro. You can heat the water for the pasta while you're warming the grill and cook everything at once. Who said life used to be so much simpler?

GLAZED MUSHROOM PASTA

Woodsy wild mushrooms and penne pasta make a robust meal, hale enough for a linebacker but healthy enough for a cardiologist.

SERVES 6

1 pound portobellos, porcini, or other meaty wild
    mushrooms, sliced ⅛ inch thick
½ large red onion, sliced into ⅛-inch-thick rings
2 tablespoons olive oil
½ teaspoon kosher salt or other coarse salt

MUSHROOM AND ONION GLAZE
1 cup inexpensive balsamic vinegar
½ teaspoon fresh-ground black pepper

1 pound penne or other tube-shaped pasta
1 to 2 tablespoons extra-virgin olive oil
3 tablespoons minced fresh parsley

In a medium bowl, toss the mushrooms with the onion, oil, and salt. Let them sit at room temperature while you heat the grill.

Fire up the grill, bringing the temperature to medium (4 to 5 seconds with the hand test).

Prepare the glaze. In a small, heavy saucepan over high heat, boil the vinegar with the pepper until reduced by half.

Grill the mushrooms and onions uncovered over medium heat for 8 to 10 minutes, turning occasionally, until the mushrooms are juicy and tender and the onions are crisp-tender. In the last several minutes of cooking, brush the mushrooms and onions on both sides with about two-thirds of the glaze. If grilling covered, cook the mushrooms and onions for 7 to 9 minutes, turning once midway and brushing with the glaze.

Cook the pasta according to the package directions. Slice the onion rings in half and separate them. In a large serving bowl, toss the pasta with the oil and add the mushrooms and onions. Toss again, gently this time, add a little or all of the remaining glaze, and add salt to taste. Sprinkle with parsley and serve hot or at room temperature.

PAELLA MIXED GRILL

This is our favorite special-occasion grill dish, a circus of cooking and a carnival of good eats. For maximum showmanship, do as much of the cooking outside as the size and capability of your grill will allow. We give instructions for cooking the rice on a side burner or kitchen stove, but we prefer to do it on top of the grate if it's easy to vary temperatures on the grill. In either case, grill the seafood, chicken, and sausage at the same time or immediately afterward. However you manage the multiple but simple steps, you'll have the hot-doggers in the crowd salivating with gluttony and envy alike.

SERVES 8 OR MORE

PAELLA CHICKEN
2 teaspoons olive oil
1 plump garlic clove, minced
1 teaspoon paprika
1 teaspoon minced fresh thyme or ½ teaspoon dried thyme
¼ teaspoon kosher salt or other coarse salt
Two 6-ounce boneless, skinless individual chicken
    breasts, pounded to ½- to ¾-inch thickness

PAELLA SHRIMP
¾ pound medium shrimp, peeled and, if you wish, deveined
1 teaspoon Mexican hot sauce, such as Cholula, El Tapatío,
    or Búfalo
½ teaspoon olive oil
¼ teaspoon kosher salt or other coarse salt

PAELLA SQUID
½ pound small squid bodies, preferably about 3 inches
    in length, with tentacles separated, cleaned, or
    ½ pound squid steaks
Juice of ½ lemon
1 teaspoon olive oil
¼ teaspoon kosher salt or other coarse salt

Three 5-ounce to 6-ounce fresh uncooked Italian
    sausages
8 to 12 hard-shell clams, such as cherrystones or
    littlenecks, or mussels, cleaned of grit

¼ cup extra-virgin olive oil
1 medium red onion, diced
1 medium green bell pepper, diced
1 medium red bell pepper, diced
1½ tablespoons minced garlic
3 cups short-grain rice, such as arborio (Italian rice for
    risotto)
1½ teaspoons crumbled saffron threads
6 cups chicken stock, preferably homemade
Kosher salt or other coarse salt
½ cup halved briny green olives
½ cup halved briny black olives
½ cup baby peas, fresh or frozen, or slivered cooked
    artichoke hearts
½ cup minced fresh parsley

· · · · · · · · · · · · · · · · · · ·

At least 1 hour and up to 8 hours before you plan to begin cooking, marinate the chicken. In a small bowl, combine the oil, garlic, paprika, thyme, and salt. Rub the paste over the chicken breasts, place them in a plastic bag, and refrigerate. About 1 hour before you plan to begin cooking, combine the shrimp in a small bowl with the hot sauce, oil, and salt, and in another bowl, combine the squid with the lemon juice, oil, and salt. Refrigerate the shrimp and squid.

Fire up the grill for a two-level fire capable of cooking at the same time on both high heat (1 to 2 seconds with the hand test) and medium heat (4 to 5 seconds with the hand test). If you want to cook the rice over the grill fire, you'll need a capability for medium-low heat as well.

Remove the chicken, shrimp, and squid from the refrigerator and let them, the sausage, and the clams sit covered at room temperature for 20 to 30 minutes while you prepare the rice.

In a 12- to 14-inch heavy skillet or paella pan, warm the oil over medium heat. Add the onion, peppers, and garlic and sauté several minutes until softened. Stir in the rice and continue cooking until translucent but not brown, about 4 to 5 minutes. Mix the saffron into the stock and pour the stock over the rice. Add salt to taste. Cook the rice over medium-low heat uncovered, without stirring, until the liquid is absorbed, 15 to 20 minutes.

Late in the cooking, insert a spoon or spatula to the bottom of the rice in several spots, without stirring, to make sure the rice is cooking evenly. Shift the position of the pan over the heat if it is getting more done on the bottom in one area than elsewhere. When done, the perfect paella rice is moist throughout but has just a little crust on the bottom and side portions.

Remove the pan from the heat and scatter the olives, peas or artichokes, and parsley over the rice. Cover it immediately with foil and keep warm in a very low oven or on a corner of the grill.

Transfer the shrimp, squid, sausage, and clams to the grill, placing them over high heat, and add the chicken over medium heat. Grill the shrimp and squid for 3 to 4 minutes, turning once. The squid tentacles will be done about a minute sooner than the bodies. When done, the shrimp should be just opaque with lightly charred edges and the squid should feel firm yet tender. Remove them from the heat and cover with foil. Cook the clams until they pop open wide, about 8 to 10 minutes, and cover

them too. Discard any clams that don't open within a couple of minutes of the others.

Grill the sausages on high for 3 to 4 minutes, rolling them to sear evenly, and then move them to medium heat and continue cooking for an additional 15 minutes or until cooked through. Cook the chicken over medium heat for 10 to 12 minutes, turning once, until opaque throughout but still juicy.

Slice the squid and sausages into rings and the chicken into bite-size pieces. Stir all the grilled ingredients into the rice and serve immediately.

TECHNIQUE TIP: Though our paella is an Americanized amalgam of ingredients, it's true to its Spanish roots in cooking the rice over an open fire in an open pan. To maintain that spirit, and provide full attention to the multiple ingredients on the grill, we don't recommend cooking the paella (either the rice or the grilled toppings) covered. If you enjoy the dish and want to do it often, consider investing in a proper paella pan; The Spanish Table in Seattle (206-682-2827) carries an astonishing range of sizes and varieties.

PORK AND SWEET POTATO HASH

When you're grilling on a weekend night and want something great for breakfast or brunch the next day, put on an extra pork tenderloin for this hearty hash. If you're not a yam fan, substitute regular potatoes and beef steak in the same proportions.

SERVES 6

Two 12-ounce to 14-ounce sections of pork tenderloin
2 to 3 tablespoons Sugar and Spice (page 26) dry rub,
    or 1 teaspoon kosher salt or other coarse salt and
    1 teaspoon fresh-ground black pepper

2 tablespoons vegetable oil
1 tablespoon butter
2½ cups peeled, diced sweet potatoes
1½ cups diced onion
1 medium green bell pepper, diced
1 to 2 fresh or pickled jalapeños, minced
1 cup chicken stock
2 tablespoons chili sauce (the ketchup-style sauce)
1 tablespoon yellow ballpark mustard
1 teaspoon fresh-ground black pepper
Salt to taste

At least 1 hour and up to the day before you plan to serve the hash, massage the pork with the dry rub. Wrap the pork in plastic and refrigerate.

Remove the tenderloins from the refrigerator and let them sit covered at room temperature for 20 to 30 minutes.

Fire up the grill for a two-level fire capable of cooking first on high heat (1 to 2 seconds with the hand test) and then on medium heat (4 to 5 seconds with the hand test).

Transfer the tenderloins to the grill, arranging them so that the thin end is angled away from the hottest part of the fire. Grill the tenderloins uncovered on high heat for 3 minutes, rolling them on all sides. Move the

tenderloins to medium heat and estimate the rest of the cooking time according to the thickness of the meat. Thin tenderloins (about 1½ inches in diameter) need an additional 10 to 12 minutes on medium, and fat ones (about 2½ inches in diameter) require up to 25 minutes. Continue rolling the meat on all sides for even cooking. The pork is done when its internal temperature reaches 155° F to 160° F.

If grilling covered, sear the tenderloins first on high heat uncovered for 3 minutes, rolling them on all sides. Finish the cooking with the cover on over medium heat for at least 8 to 10 minutes (for 1½-inch-diameter meat) or up to 20 minutes (for 2½-inch-diameter meat).

When cool enough to handle, pull the meat into shreds or slice it fine. (The pork can be prepared to this point a day ahead and refrigerated.)

Warm the oil and butter together in a large, heavy skillet over medium heat. Add the sweet potatoes, onion, bell pepper, and jalapeño and sauté for 10 minutes. Mix in the remaining ingredients. Simmer, covered, for 10 minutes, stirring the mixture up from the bottom once about halfway through and patting it back down. Uncover the skillet and add the pork. Continue cooking uncovered until the liquid is absorbed and the mixture just begins to get crusty on the bottom, another 4 to 8 minutes.

Serve the hash hot, maybe with an egg on top and a plate of biscuits on the side.

TOMATO AND TORTILLA SOUP

Grilling the tomatoes for this soup concentrates their juices and adds a touch of outdoors, charbroiled flavor. The tortilla strips, cilantro, and cheese contribute a Southwestern tang.

SERVES 4 TO 6

3½ pounds whole small red-ripe tomatoes, preferably
    Italian plum
Vegetable oil
2 tablespoons butter
2 medium celery stalks, chopped
½ small onion, chopped
1 teaspoon ground dried red chile or chili powder
3 cups chicken stock
Salt to taste

Juice of 1 lime
2 to 3 Corn Tortillas Rojo (page 119) or other corn
    tortillas, cut into thin strips and baked or grilled
Crumbled queso fresco or feta cheese
Minced cilantro

Fire up the grill, bringing the temperature to medium-high (3 seconds with the hand test).

Cut the tomatoes in half and squeeze out their seeds and liquid. Coat the tomatoes lightly with oil.

Transfer the tomatoes skin-side up to a well-oiled grate. Grill the tomatoes uncovered over medium heat for 10 to 12 minutes, turning once, until the skins are dark and the tomatoes become firm with most of their juice evaporated. If grilling covered, cook the tomatoes for 9 to 11 minutes, turning once midway. Set the tomatoes aside until cool enough to handle.

In a skillet, warm the butter over medium heat. Sauté the celery and onion with the chile until the vegetables are softened, about 5 minutes. Pour in the stock and simmer 30 minutes.

Pull the skins off of one-half of the tomatoes and discard them. Transfer all of the tomatoes and stock mixture, in batches, to a blender. Purée the soup and add salt to taste. (The soup can be prepared to this point a day ahead and kept covered and refrigerated.)

Serve the soup hot, garnishing individual bowls with a squeeze of lime, tortilla strips, cheese, and a sprinkling of cilantro. For a hearty meal, simply add a sandwich.

TECHNIQUE TIP: To get the most out of soups made with grilled ingredients, avoid adding too many competing flavors. The edge gained from grilling is distinct but subtle, and can get lost in a complex preparation. Use the grilled ingredients within a day of cooking for the best flavor.

SAUSAGE-LENTIL STEW

Sausage says you're serious about soups and stews, dishes that don't generally get the recognition they deserve in American cooking. For this full meal in a bowl, use any robustly seasoned sausage such as a Polish or Italian variety, or a Mexican chorizo.

SERVES 6 TO 8

. . . .

1 tablespoon olive oil
3 slices uncooked peppered bacon or regular bacon
    with a good grinding of black pepper, chopped
1 large onion, chopped
4 garlic cloves, sliced thin
1 pound lentils, rinsed and picked over for remaining
    grit
1 large celery stalk, chopped
1 large carrot, grated
8 to 10 cups chicken stock
2 small tomatoes, preferably Italian plum, chopped
1½ teaspoons salt, or more to taste
3 fresh uncooked well-seasoned sausage links,
    approximately 5 to 6 ounces each

Chopped mint and crumbled feta cheese, for garnish

. . . .

Warm the oil in a Dutch oven or other large, heavy saucepan over medium heat. Add the bacon and fry until brown and crisp. Remove the bacon with a slotted spoon, drain it, and reserve it. Stir the onion into the rendered bacon drippings and sauté about 5 minutes until translucent. Add the garlic and cook for an additional minute.

Mix in the lentils, celery, carrot, and 8 cups of stock. Bring the mixture to a boil, reduce the heat to medium-low, and simmer 30 minutes, adding more stock if the mixture becomes too dry. (The final consistency should be hearty and stew-like rather than thin and soupy.) After 30 minutes of cooking, add the tomatoes and salt, being prepared to add plenty if you started with unsalted stock. Continue cooking until the lentils are very tender but still

hold their shape, approximately 15 to 30 additional minutes. Keep the stew warm while you grill the sausage. (The lentils can be prepared to this point a day ahead. Cool, cover, and refrigerate them, reheating before proceeding. Add a little water to thin them if they're too thick to spoon easily.)

Fire up the grill for a two-level fire capable of cooking first on high heat (1 to 2 seconds with the hand test) and then on medium heat (4 to 5 seconds with the hand test).

Grill the sausages uncovered for a total of 20 to 25 minutes. First cook the sausages over high heat for 8 to 10 minutes, rolling them every couple of minutes to crisp all sides. Move the sausages to medium heat and continue cooking for 12 to 15 additional min-

utes. When done, the sausages should be brown, crisp, and thoroughly cooked but still juicy. If grilling covered, sear all sides of the sausages on high heat uncovered for 3 to 4 minutes; finish the cooking with the cover on over medium heat for 13 to 15 additional minutes. (The sausage can be grilled up to two days in advance and refrigerated. It doesn't need to be reheated before being added to the stew, but make sure to heat the stew long enough to warm the sausage through.)

Slice the sausage into thin rounds and stir into the lentils just before serving in shallow soup or pasta bowls. Scatter mint and cheese over each bowl and serve piping hot. We like the stew with Mixed Berry Cornbread.

PORCINI ON POTATOES AND BEANS

When Bill suggested calling this concoction Beany Porcini, Cheryl threatened to commit suicide on the grill. By any name, it's a superb way to enjoy fresh fall mushrooms, portobellos as well as porcinis.

SERVES 4 TO 6

¾ pound fresh porcini mushrooms (cepes) or other wild
    mushrooms such as portobellos, sliced ⅜ inch thick
3 tablespoons white wine
1 tablespoon porcini-flavored oil or olive oil
Kosher salt or other coarse salt

2 tablespoons porcini-flavored oil or olive oil
6-ounce red waxy potato, diced and parboiled
4 garlic cloves, sliced thin
½ cup white wine
¾ teaspoon dried tarragon or thyme
¼ teaspoon crushed dried hot red chile
4 cups cooked cannellini, Aztec beans, or other white
    beans, drained
Kosher salt or other coarse salt and fresh-ground black
    pepper

Fresh tarragon or thyme sprigs, optional, for garnish

• • • • • • • • • • • • • • • • • •

In a medium bowl, toss the mushroom slices with the wine and oil. Salt to taste.

Fire up the grill, bringing the temperature to medium (4 to 5 seconds with the hand test).

Warm the oil in a heavy skillet over medium-high heat. Stir in the potato and cook until tender with browned edges, about 5 minutes. Reduce the heat to medium-low, add the garlic, and sauté an additional minute. Stir in the wine, tarragon, and chile and simmer 2 to 3 additional minutes. Stir in the beans and heat through, adding salt and pepper as you wish. Keep the beans warm.

Grill the mushrooms uncovered over medium heat for 5 to 7 minutes, turning once, until tender. If grilling covered, cook for the same amount of time, turning once midway. (The mushrooms can be grilled a day in advance and kept covered and refrigerated. Reheat wrapped in foil in a low to medium oven and add any accumulated juice to the beans.)

Spoon the potato-bean mixture into a large, shallow serving bowl and top with the mushrooms. Garnish with the minced herbs and serve warm.

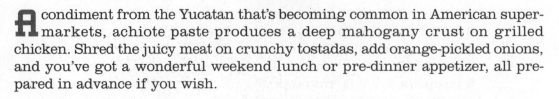

MAHOGANY CHICKEN ON CRISPY TORTILLAS

A condiment from the Yucatan that's becoming common in American super-markets, achiote paste produces a deep mahogany crust on grilled chicken. Shred the juicy meat on crunchy tostadas, add orange-pickled onions, and you've got a wonderful weekend lunch or pre-dinner appetizer, all pre-pared in advance if you wish.

SERVES 4

ORANGE-PICKLED ONIONS
1 medium red onion, sliced into thin rings
Hot water
½ cup red wine vinegar
3 ounces frozen orange juice concentrate (half a
    6-ounce can), thawed
2 garlic cloves, minced
½ teaspoon dried oregano
¼ teaspoon ground cumin

MAHOGANY MARINADE
¼ cup cider vinegar
3 ounces frozen orange juice concentrate (half a
    6-ounce can), thawed
1 tablespoon achiote paste (see Technique Tip)
3 garlic cloves, minced
2 teaspoons dried oregano
1 bay leaf, crumbled
½ teaspoon ground allspice

Two 6-ounce boneless, skinless individual chicken
    breasts, pounded to ⅛-inch thickness
Salt and fresh-ground black pepper
4 tostada shells (flat-fried taco shells)
Minced fresh cilantro, for garnish

At least a day before you plan to serve the tostadas, prepare the onions. Place the onion slices in a medium bowl. Pour enough hot water over the onions to cover them by about 1 inch. Let the onions sit for 10 minutes, then pour off the water to eliminate the strong flavor. Stir the remaining ingredients into the onions and refrigerate for at least 24 hours. (This makes enough onions for a couple of batches of chicken and tostada chips. Leftover onions keep well, refrigerated, for several weeks and are also great accompanying any grilled sandwich or quesadilla.)

At least 1 hour and up to 4 hours before you plan to grill the chicken, prepare the marinade, combining the ingredients in a small bowl. Place the chicken in a plastic bag or shallow dish, pour the marinade over it, and refrigerate.

Fire up the grill, bringing the temperature to medium (4 to 5 seconds with the hand test).

Drain the chicken, sprinkle it lightly with salt and pepper, and let it sit covered at room temperature for about 20 minutes.

Grill the chicken uncovered over medium heat for 5 to 6 minutes per side, until opaque but still juicy. If grilling covered, cook the chicken for about 10 minutes, turning once midway. (The chicken can be prepared to this point up to two days ahead and kept covered and refrigerated. Reheat wrapped in foil in a low to medium oven.)

Shred the warm chicken and toss it with 1 to 2 tablespoons of the onion pickling liquid. Pile equal portions of chicken on each tostada shell, top with a generous tangle of pickled onions and a sprinkling of cilantro, and serve immediately.

TECHNIQUE TIP: Achiote paste adds subtle background notes of flavor to chicken (or fish or pork), but color is its main contribution in cooking. If you can't locate it in your supermarket's Mexican food section or in a Mexican or Latino market, substitute the same quantity of paprika for the paste. The taste will be different but still interesting.

S'MORES AND MORE

S'MORES AND MORE

CAMPFIRE CLASSIC S'MORES

Grilling may be male turf historically in the United States, but little girls beat their daddies to dessert. The Girl Scouts began popularizing the marshmallow, chocolate candy, and graham cracker treat known as s'mores as early as 1927, when the organization published a campfire recipe in *Tramping and Trailing with the Girl Scouts*, a sophisticated manual that also talked about picking and eating elderberry flowers and the fruit from the prickly-pear cactus. The instructions for s'mores explain the name by noting that, "Though it tastes like 'some more' one is really enough." The dessert snack made the official handbook of the Girl Scouts in 1940, and became so associated with the troops over time that a logical young Cheryl couldn't understand why pubescent Scouts were called "Brownies" instead of "S'mores." The old sandwich sweet retains all of its childhood appeal, even for discriminating adults, particularly when you use your own homemade marshmallows and graham crackers.

MAKES 1 SERVING

¾ ounce milk chocolate or semi-sweet chocolate, in a
    flat square (½ the popular-size Hershey Bar) or
    chips
1 Mega-Marshmallow (page 431) or other large
    marshmallow
2 Sinful Graham Crackers (page 432) or other graham
    cracker squares

Fire up the grill, bringing the temperature to medium-low (6 seconds with the hand test).

Thread the marshmallow on a skewer, long fork, or for old times' sake, a smooth stick. Place the graham crackers on the grate over medium-low heat. Hold the marshmallow a couple of inches above the grate and toast the marshmallow on all sides for several minutes until very soft and golden. Because of the hand-toasting, an essential part of the experience, we don't recommend cooking s'mores covered.

While the marshmallow toasts, turn the graham crackers, place the chocolate on one of them, and continue heating the crackers until the marshmallow is ready. Top the chocolate with the marshmallow and the second

cracker. Grill an additional minute or two, turning again if the bottom is browning deeply. Multiply the recipe as needed, and serve with plenty of napkins and tall, frosty glasses of milk.

S'MORE OF OUR FAVORITES

The origin of s'mores is lost in a cloud of campfire smoke. No one, including the Girl Scouts, claims credit for the initial inspiration, but we do know that the three commercial components of the treat all reached the market about the same time around the turn of the twentieth century. Modern marshmallows date back to the 1880s or so, the National Biscuit Company (now Nabisco) started packaging graham crackers in 1898, and Milton S. Hershey began selling the country's first chocolate candy bars about 1905.

As soon as the anonymous creator put together the mother of all s'mores, variations began to appear. Even the Girl Scouts sanctioned a little deviation from the straight-and-narrow path, suggesting in the 1940 handbook that apple slices could substitute for graham crackers and that pineapple could be as tasty inside as chocolate. Real sweet-tooths stuffed the marshmallows with gumdrops, added jelly to the sandwich, and double-dosed on the chocolate by dumping the graham crackers in favor of chocolate-chip cookies.

We like some of the embellishments, but our own variations stay close to the original trinity of flavors. For Snow S'mores, substitute white chocolate for milk chocolate, and for Grasshopper S'mores, replace the candy bar with chocolate mints. In Peanut Butter S'mores, we opt for dark chocolate and a dollop of the namesake product. When we pull out all the stops in Turtle S'mores, we slip a pecan half into the marshmallow and add a little caramel sauce. Any way you make them, if they make you yearn for some more, you've got great s'mores.

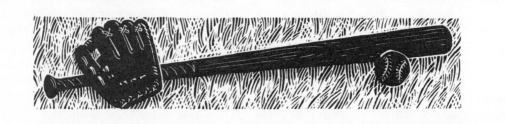

MEGA-MARSHMALLOWS

In s'mores or just alone on a stick, gooey toasted marshmallows still hold sway as the nation's favorite way to end an open-fire meal. These homemade sugar pillows—richer in flavor than store-bought brands—show you're serious about life's simple pleasures.

MAKES AN 8-INCH SQUARE PAN OF MARSHMALLOWS

. . . .

1 envelope unflavored gelatin
1¼ cups lukewarm water
Powdered sugar
1⅛ cups sugar
½ cup light corn syrup
1 teaspoon pure vanilla extract
Pinch of salt

. . . .

Sprinkle the gelatin into a small bowl and pour ½ cup water over it. Set it aside to soften. Place a square of waxed paper or baking parchment, at least 10 inches in diameter, in an 8-inch square baking pan, folding up the edges. Dust the waxed paper lightly but thoroughly with powdered sugar.

In a large, heavy saucepan, bring the sugar, corn syrup, and remaining ¾ cup water to a boil and continue boiling until a candy thermometer reaches 238° F to 240° F, the soft ball stage. Remove the mixture from the heat and immediately stir in the gelatin, watching out for steam and sputters. Add the vanilla extract and salt. At this point the mixture will be syrupy and light golden. Beat with a powerful hand mixer at high speed until the mixture is white, shiny, and thickened but stiffly spoonable, about 14 to 18 minutes. It will have expanded several times in volume.

Scrape the sticky mixture into the prepared pan, smoothing it on the top, and dust lightly but thoroughly with more powdered sugar. Set the marshmallow aside to cool and firm for several hours.

Turn the pan upside down and unmold the giant marshmallow. Cut it into smaller marshmallows, about 1 dozen of s'mores size. Roll the marshmallows in more powdered sugar and cover tightly. If not using the marshmallows within a few hours, refrigerate them for up to a week.

SINFUL GRAHAM CRACKERS

Graham crackers developed out of the country's first big food fad, an early-nineteenth-century movement that rejected the pleasures of the palate as sinful. From that Puritanical perch, our crisp, homey, honey-sweetened cookies are woefully unregenerate.

MAKES ABOUT 2 DOZEN 2¹/₂-INCH GRAHAM CRACKERS

1 cup all-purpose flour
1 cup whole-wheat flour
¼ cup sugar
1 teaspoon baking powder
½ teaspoon ground cinnamon
¼ teaspoon salt
3 tablespoons vegetable shortening, well chilled
3 tablespoons butter, well chilled
¼ cup honey
3 tablespoons ice water
1 teaspoon pure vanilla extract

Grease a 14-by-16-inch baking sheet, preferably one without sides. (You'll be rolling the dough out on the sheet later.)

In a food processor, combine the all-purpose flour, whole-wheat flour, sugar, baking powder, cinnamon, and salt. Add the shortening and butter and pulse to combine them, making a crumbly meal. Spoon in the honey, water, and vanilla extract and process again until just combined. Scrape the dough, still a little crumbly and ragged, out onto the prepared baking sheet. Roll the dough out into a ⅛-inch-thick rectangle, which should come just short of filling the entire baking sheet. Refrigerate the baking sheet and dough uncovered for 30 to 45 minutes.

Preheat the oven to 350° F, arranging one of its racks directly in its center.

With a pizza cutter or sharp knife, cut any uneven edges off of the dough, leaving a small border of the baking sheet exposed. Cutting only about halfway through the dough, slice it into squares of about 2½ inches, the size of store-bought graham crackers. Bake the crackers while the dough and cookie sheet are still cold for about 12 to 14 minutes, turning the pan around

EATING YOUR WAY TO HEAVEN

It sounds like fun, sort of praying by eating, but you might reconsider if your guide to the pearly path turns out to be the Reverend Sylvester Graham. One of a flock of crackpots and visionaries who sought to shape the American soul in the early to mid-nineteenth century, the former Presbyterian preacher crusaded around the country on behalf of a no-nonsense, ascetic approach to food and drink.

Alcohol was evil, of course, and so were any victuals "compounded and complicated by culinary processes." Graham advocated eating raw fruits and vegetables, not out of contemporary vegetarian concerns, but because God presented them whole and uncooked and we shouldn't tamper with His bounty. Meat was double trouble, carrying the stigma of the stove as well as a base tendency to excite sexual excess. According to Waverly Root and Richard de Rochemont in *Eating in America* (Ecco Press, 1981), the reverend also rejected any seasoning that improved the taste of food, since that reeked of sensuality, and believed that strong condiments like mustard could cause insanity.

In one of those inscrutable ironies of history, Graham's name survived long after his missionary efforts because of a cracker. One of his primary passions was unsifted, coarsely ground, bran-in wheat flour, which he promoted for all home baking. He knew nothing about the nutritional benefits of whole wheat, and certainly didn't care about enhanced flavor, but he believed the Creator wouldn't have put the bran in the wheat kernel unless He wanted us to eat it.

Graham railed so strongly against refined white flour that bakers mobbed him once in Boston, and eventually he gained such an association with his holy flour that it became known by his name for the rest of the nineteenth century. When the National Biscuit Company began marketing its Graham Crackers decades later, everyone instantly understood the content, even if they had no idea by that time who or what a Graham was. With his moniker now enshrined, the Girl Scouts then committed the ultimate sacrilege on his memory, turning the cracker into an indulgent morsel that made eaters cry out for "some more."

the other direction about halfway through the baking time. The crackers are ready when lightly browned. (They'll still be a little soft and flexible.)

While warm, cut the crackers apart along the previous lines and let them cool on the baking sheet for 2 or 3 minutes, until they firm up and become crisp. Transfer them carefully from the baking sheet to a rack to cool completely. The crackers can be used immediately, kept covered for up to a week, or frozen for several weeks.

TECHNIQUE TIP: When you're rolling out the graham cracker dough, if you find the baking sheet trying to scoot away from you, put a dish towel between the sheet and the counter to anchor your workstation.

A FRUITFUL FINISH

Truth be told, some of our friends look at us like hayseeds when we serve s'mores for dessert. They devour them like we're offering aphrodisiacs, but then joke about the regressive nature of our "edible complex." So usually we have to act more adult and prepare something that seems *au courant*, even if it's equally decadent.

Our choice then is generally fruit. Warming fruit over the grill caramelizes sugar on the surface, softens texture, and releases sweet juices, producing a toasty, natural wrap-up for a meal. With the addition of complementary flavors—such as brown sugar, honey, ginger, and cinnamon—you can elaborate the dimensions into a full-fledged dessert. For a total extravagance, all you're lacking is the ice cream.

We've designed our fruit desserts in this chapter so that most—and often all—of the prep work can be done prior to dinner, leaving just the final cooking until the end. If you're grilling other parts of the meal as well, think through your strategy in advance. With a gas grill, it's easy enough to shut down after the main course and then fire up again when you're ready for dessert. When you're cooking with charcoal, try to time your dinner to keep the fire hot enough for a second round of cooking. As you serve the entrée, cover the grill, shut the vents almost completely to reduce air circulation, and plan to open up again for dessert within 30 minutes, before the coals get too cool. We generally suggest warming fruit on medium heat, but since doneness isn't an issue, a lower fire works fine over a slightly longer cooking time. As long as sauces and toppings are the right temperature, it's hard to fail with a fruit dessert.

BOURBON CARAMEL APPLES

As an alternative to s'mores, Girl Scouts and other pioneering outdoor cooks liked to roast whole cored apples on a stick over a low fire, sometimes with a marshmallow or caramel candy melting inside. We prefer to start with apple slices, which take less time and are easier to baste with this high-octane, grown-up caramel sauce.

SERVES 6

BOURBON CARAMEL SAUCE
¼ cup butter
1 cup packed brown sugar
¼ teaspoon ground cinnamon
¼ cup bourbon or other American whiskey
6 tablespoons whipping cream

6 medium apples
Metal skewers, optional
6 tablespoons melted butter

Prepare the caramel sauce, first combining the butter, brown sugar, cinnamon, and bourbon in a heavy saucepan. Bring the mixture to a boil over medium heat and boil for 2 minutes, stirring frequently. Remove the syrup from the heat and stir in the cream, watching out for sputtering steam. (The sauce can be made to this point a week or more ahead. Reheat it gently before proceeding, adding a little water if it seems too stiff to drizzle after heating.)

Fire up the grill, bringing the temperature to medium (4 to 5 seconds with the hand test).

Peel and core the apples, cutting each into 1-inch thick wedges. Thread the apples onto metal skewers or lay them on a small-mesh grill rack. Brush the apples with the melted butter.

Grill the apples uncovered over medium heat for 10 to 12 minutes, turning at least once, until tender. In the last 1 to 2 minutes of cooking, baste the apples with the sauce. If grilling covered, cook for 9 to 11 minutes, turning once midway and basting in a similar manner.

Divide the apples among individual serving bowls. Drizzle additional sauce over the apples and serve immediately.

ORANGE-VANILLA PEARS

A little orange juice and vanilla heighten the fruit flavor in these pears. We serve them with tangy crème fraîche or sour cream for a cooling contrast.

SERVES 4

ORANGE-VANILLA BUTTER SAUCE
¼ cup butter
3 tablespoons frozen orange juice concentrate, thawed
½ teaspoon pure vanilla extract

4 ripe medium pears, peeled, halved, and cored (see Technique Tip)
Crème fraîche, Mexican *crema*, or sour cream
Orange zest, optional, for garnish

Prepare the butter sauce, first melting the butter in a small saucepan over medium heat. Add the orange juice concentrate and vanilla extract and warm through.

Fire up the grill, bringing the temperature to medium (4 to 5 seconds with the hand test).

Brush the pears lightly with the butter sauce. Transfer the pears to the grill cut-side down. Grill the pears uncovered over medium heat for 8 to 10 minutes, turning once. If grilling covered, cook for the same amount of time, turning once midway.

Serve the pears cut-side up, drizzling the remaining butter in the pears' cavities. Top with a small dollop of crème fraîche and, if you wish, a sprinkling of orange zest. As a variation, purée the pears after cooking with a little pear liqueur or nectar and make a sauce for gingerbread or other desserts.

TECHNIQUE TIP: A melon baller makes a perfect tool for coring pears. After halving the pears, scoop out the coarse core in one or two quick swipes, leaving a smooth, rounded cavity.

CRUNCHY WALNUT PEARS

We like to pair these pears with the previous ones, for a simple dual dessert prepared and served at the same time. In this case, we rev up the natural caramelization with brown sugar and add the crunch of toasted walnuts.

SERVES 4

. . . .

4 ripe medium pears, peeled, halved, and cored
¼ cup walnut oil
¼ cup packed brown sugar

Toasted walnut pieces, for garnish

. . . .

Fire up the grill, bringing the temperature to medium (4 to 5 seconds with the hand test).

Place the pears in a shallow dish. Pour the oil over the pears and turn them to coat evenly. Sprinkle the pears with the brown sugar and let them sit about 15 minutes. Drain the pears, reserving the oil-sugar mixture.

Transfer the pears to the grill cutside down. Grill the pears over medium heat for 8 to 10 minutes, turning once. If grilling covered, cook for the same amount of time, turning once midway.

Drizzle a little of the remaining oil-sugar mixture in the pears' cavities, sprinkle them with walnuts, and serve warm.

GRILLED BANANA SPLIT WITH CHOCOLATE-TOFFEE MELT

ave this fruit fantasy for a special party, perhaps a birthday, the Fourth of July, or just the next available Saturday. Warming the bananas on the grill mellows their taste and softens their texture, making them as meltingly luscious as the ice cream and the toffee candy sauce.

MAKES 6 GARGANTUAN SERVINGS

· · · · · · · · · · · · · · · · · · ·

1 cup sugar
⅛ cup half-and-half
6 tablespoons butter
6 medium bananas
Three 1.4-ounce Heath Bars or 4 to 5 ounces chocolate-
    covered toffee, chopped into chunks
6 large scoops each of two kinds of ice cream, such as
    vanilla, butter pecan, praline, chocolate, or banana
Whipped cream

Toasted almonds, for garnish

· · · · · · · · · · · · · · · · · · ·

Fire up the grill, bringing the temperature to medium (4 to 5 seconds with the hand test).

Combine the sugar and half-and-half in a heavy medium saucepan. Bring the mixture to a full rolling boil, stirring occasionally. Stir in the butter and remove from the heat.

Just before grilling, slice the bananas, still in their skins, lengthwise.

Transfer the bananas cut-side down to a well-oiled grate. Grill the bananas uncovered over medium heat for 3 to 4 minutes. Turn the bananas skin-side down, brush their cut surfaces with a few teaspoons of the sugar–half-and-half mixture, and grill them for 2 to 3 additional minutes, until soft and lightly colored. If grilling covered, cook for the same amount of time, turning once midway and basting then.

Remove the bananas from their skins. If you own long banana split dishes, leave the banana halves whole and place two of them in each dish. If not, cut the bananas into bite-size chunks and divide them among individual serving dishes.

Return the sugar–half-and-half mixture to medium-low heat and stir in the toffee chunks. Cook briefly until the chocolate and toffee have partially melted (leaving some chunkiness) and stir well. Top each dish of banana with one scoop of each ice cream and some of the chocolate-toffee melt. Add whipped cream, top with almonds, and serve immediately.

TECHNIQUE TIP: Banana split dishes seem to be making a retro comeback everywhere from flea markets to chic cookware stores. Williams-Sonoma (800-541-2233) sells them by mail order.

BANANA SHORTCAKE WITH CARNIVAL RUM SAUCE

Surprise strawberry shortcake fans with this variation, a brash and jazzy take on the theme.

SERVES 6

CARNIVAL RUM SAUCE
½ cup dark rum
¼ cup packed brown sugar
¼ cup crème de banane
3 tablespoons butter
2 tablespoons tangerine or orange juice
2 tablespoons brewed coffee or 2 teaspoons coffee
    crystals

5 medium bananas
6 split shortcakes or sweetened biscuits, or 12 thin
    slices of pound cake

Fresh mint sprigs, for garnish

Fire up the grill, bringing the temperature to medium (4 to 5 seconds with the hand test).

Prepare the sauce, combining the ingredients in a heavy saucepan over medium heat and bringing the mixture to a simmer. Reduce the sauce by about one-third.

Just before grilling, slice the bananas, still in their skins, lengthwise.

Transfer the bananas cut-side down to a well-oiled grate. Grill the bananas uncovered over medium heat for 3 to 4 minutes. Turn the bananas skin-side down, brush their cut surfaces with a few teaspoons of the sauce, and grill them for 2 to 3 additional minutes, until soft and lightly colored. If grilling covered, cook for the same amount of time, turning once midway and basting then.

Remove the bananas from their skins. Place one of the banana halves in a blender, pour the sauce over it, and purée.

Arrange shortcake halves on individual serving plates. Cut the remaining bananas into 1-inch-long pieces and scatter them evenly over the cakes. Top with the remaining cake halves and spoon sauce evenly over them. Garnish each with a couple of mint sprigs and serve immediately.

TECHNIQUE TIP: Bananas become very soft when cooked. Keeping the skins on when grilling helps them hold their shape until you can get them off the fire.

GINGERED PINEAPPLE SUNDAES

Think pineapple upside-down cake. Now carefully slip out the cake part, barely more than a foil anyway, substitute sherbet or ice cream, and ladle on a velvety fruit sauce. Voilà, a sensational, right-side-up sundae.

SERVES 6

1 tablespoon packed brown sugar
1 teaspoon dried ginger
¼ teaspoon ground cinnamon
20-ounce container fresh pineapple, cut into ½-inch-thick half moons, juice reserved

CREAMY PINEAPPLE SAUCE
Reserved pineapple juice
¼ cup sugar
¼ teaspoon dried ginger
5 large egg yolks
½ cup canned unsweetened coconut milk
1 teaspoon pure vanilla extract

12 large scoops pineapple sorbet or sherbet, coconut,
    ginger, or vanilla ice cream, or a combination of
    these
Chopped macadamia nuts or chopped candied
    crystallized ginger, or both
Toasted coconut, optional, for garnish

• • • • • • • • • • • • • • • • • •

In a medium bowl, stir together the sugar, ginger, and cinnamon. Add the pineapple and toss it with the dry spices. Let the pineapple sit at room temperature for 30 to 60 minutes.

Prepare the sauce, first pouring the reserved pineapple juice into a liquid measuring cup. Pour out juice if there is more than ½ cup or add water to equal ½ cup. In the top section of a double boiler, combine the juice with the remaining sauce ingredients. Heat over gently simmering water, stirring frequently, until the mixture thickens to a spoonable texture, about 15 to 20 minutes. Don't boil the sauce or otherwise rush it. Chill the sauce for at least 20 minutes before serving, covering it if you plan to refrigerate it for longer. (The sauce can be made a day ahead if you wish.)

Fire up the grill, bringing the temperature to medium (4 to 5 seconds with the hand test).

Drain the pineapple, saving any accumulated juice. Grill the pineapple uncovered over medium heat for 2 to 3 minutes per side, turning once, until soft with browned edges. If grilling covered, cook for 4 to 6 minutes, turning once midway. When done, chop the pineapple into small chunks and mix the reserved juice with it.

Arrange 2 scoops of sorbet in individual serving bowls and spoon the sauce equally over the sorbet. Top with the pineapple and nuts, ginger, or both. Sprinkle the coconut over the top, if you wish, and serve immediately.

BLAME IT ON GEORGE

The next time your neighbor the nurse scolds you for serving fat-filled ice cream, tell her you do it in enduring respect for the Father of Our Country. In 1790, during the brief period when New York was the nation's capital, President George Washington spent $200 in a single summer in the city indulging his love of ice cream. A lot more money then than it is now, those bucks bought barrels of the stuff.

If she argues that people didn't understand nutrition in those days, move on to Thomas Jefferson, who knew more about everything than a university of professors. Among his many ingenious machines at Monticello was one for making ice cream, which he used in a number of elaborate preparations. Anticipating the birth of baked Alaska by almost a century, Jefferson wrapped the cold confection in a warm pastry crust, and, in another innovative recipe, flavored his ice cream with a vanilla bean that he imported from France years before the pods became available in the United States.

Surely one of these bright presidents—or maybe Dolley Madison, who gets much of the credit for popularizing ice cream during the tenure of her husband James in the White House—thought of adding a syrup and creating a sundae. If so, the historical record leaves a void because the dish didn't surface publicly until the end of the nineteenth century. At first it was spelled with a *y* instead of an *ae*, and was associated with the day of the week, but retailers changed the ending apparently to appease preachers who objected to a frivolous sweet sharing the name of the Sabbath. Maybe the clergymen could have used a lesson on George too.

PIÑA COLADA PINEAPPLE SPEARS

Turn the classic drink into a dessert with a fresh piña brimming with colada gusto.

SERVES 4

1 medium pineapple or one 20-ounce container fresh
    unsliced pineapple

COLADA MARINADE
⅓ cup dark rum, preferably, or light rum
Juice of 1 lime
2 tablespoons canned cream of coconut
½ teaspoon ground mace, or, for a stronger flavor,
    nutmeg

Lime slices, for garnish

If you have a whole pineapple, slice off the top and reserve it for garnishing the plate. Cut off a small slice at the bottom so it rests evenly and then cut off all of the pineapple skin, slicing only as deeply as needed to remove the tiny brown eyes. Halve the pineapple lengthwise and then cut each half into long 1-inch-thick spears. Cut away the tough fibrous core side of each spear.

Place the pineapple in a plastic bag or shallow dish. Combine the marinade ingredients in a small bowl and pour the mixture over the pineapple. Let it sit at room temperature for 30 to 60 minutes.

Fire up the grill, bringing the temperature to medium (4 to 5 seconds with the hand test).

Drain the pineapple spears, discarding the marinade. Grill the pineapple spears uncovered over high heat for 5 to 6 minutes, turning on all sides, until soft with browned edges. If grilling covered, cook for the same amount of time, turning once midway.

Serve immediately.

MINTED FIGS

One of our grandmothers used to make scrumptious preserves from fresh figs. These gems offer some of the same flavor, but are much easier and quicker to prepare.

SERVES 6

MINT SYRUP
½ cup sugar
½ cup water
⅓ cup fresh mint leaves

12 fresh figs, halved vertically
Mint sprigs, for garnish

Prepare the mint syrup, bringing the sugar, water, and the mint to a boil in a small saucepan over high heat. Boil the mixture, stirring occasionally until the sugar is dissolved and the liquid is clear. Set the syrup aside to steep as it cools.

Fire up the grill, bringing the temperature to medium (4 to 5 seconds with the hand test).

Strain the syrup into a shallow bowl. Dip the cut side of each fig into the syrup.

Transfer the figs to a well-oiled grate cut-side down. Grill the figs uncovered over medium heat for 5 to 7 minutes, turning once and basting with the remaining syrup. The figs are done when soft and oozing juice. If grilling covered, cook for the same amount of time, turning and basting in a similar manner.

Serve the figs warm, garnished with mint sprigs.

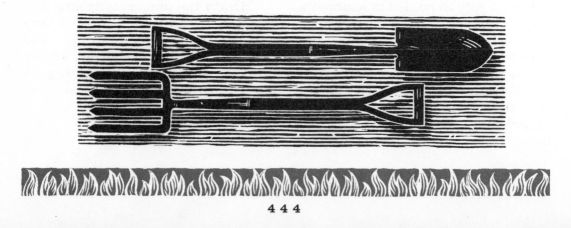

LYCHEE MAGIC WANDS

We usually stick with fresh, seasonal fruit for our desserts, but we make an exception for succulent lychees, seldom available in the United States right off the tree unless you're lucky enough to live in Hawaii. Top the lychee kebobs with a slice of starfruit (or alternatively, a fresh cherry or strawberry) to create party-perfect magic wands.

SERVES 6

¼ cup candied stem ginger or candied preserved ginger
Two 14-ounce to 15-ounce cans lychees, drained but ⅓
    cup syrup reserved
1 small starfruit (carambola), optional
Soaked bamboo skewers

FRESH PAPAYA SAUCE
¾-pound ripe papaya, peeled and cut into chunks
Reserved lychee syrup
Juice of ½ lime
1 tablespoon sugar, optional

Slice the ginger into nuggets that will fit into the cavity of the lychees and stuff one or more pieces in each fruit. If you are using the starfruit, cut off the small ends and then cut 6 star-shaped slices about ⅛ to ½ inch thick. Thread the lychees on the skewers, watching to secure the ginger inside. Top each skewer with a starfruit slice, if you wish, positioned magic-wand style.

Fire up the grill, bringing the temperature to medium (4 to 5 seconds with the hand test).

Prepare the sauce, puréeing the papaya with the lychee syrup and lime juice in a blender. Taste and add part or all the sugar if needed to round out the flavor.

Grill the wands uncovered over medium heat for 8 to 10 minutes, turning occasionally, until brown flecks appear on the lychees and the starfruit is soft but not limp. If grilling covered, cook for 7 to 9 minutes, turning once midway.

Pool the papaya sauce on a platter and arrange the wands over the sauce. Serve hot or at room temperature. Leftover sauce is good on fruit compotes or angel food cake.

GEORGIA PEACHES WITH PRALINE CRUNCH

This dessert grows out of an early American beverage called a shrub, a refreshing blend of fruit and vinegar. Here the vinegar leaves a mysteriously tasty tang, not at all harsh, that balances the sweetness of the peaches. A small-mesh grill rack or grill basket makes the cooking simpler, though it's not essential.

SERVES 6

6 large peaches, peeled, halved, and pitted
¼ cup Peach Vinegar (page 41) or other fruity vinegar
1 teaspoon walnut or macadamia nut oil or vegetable oil
1 teaspoon sugar
3 praline candies, about 2 inches in diameter, chopped into small pieces

Place the peach halves in a shallow dish or plastic bag. Pour the vinegar and oil over the peaches, sprinkle them with sugar, and let them marinate at room temperature for about 30 minutes.

Fire up the grill, bringing the temperature to medium (4 to 5 seconds with the hand test).

Drain the peaches, discarding the marinade.

Grill the peaches uncovered over medium heat for 4 to 5 minutes per side. If grilling covered, cook for 7 to 9 minutes, turning once midway.

Serve the peaches warm, with the praline pieces scattered over the top.

As a variation, create a grilled peach sorbet by puréeing the peaches after grilling and processing them in an ice cream maker.

MANGO-MARINATED MANGOS

As in the previous recipe, we're building on layers of similar flavor here, again using a vinegar of the same character as the fruit. In this case, though, the vinegar becomes the base for a sticky, sweet-savory glaze that also features Chinese hoisin sauce.

SERVES 6

3 large ripe mangos
2 tablespoons mango vinegar, such as Consorzio, or
    other fruity vinegar such as Peach Vinegar (page
    41)
1½ tablespoons hoisin sauce

With a sharp knife, halve the mangos. First, stand one mango up vertically, slicing down from the top center until you feel the wide flat seed. Cut down around the curve of the seed, staying as close to it as possible. Cut down around the seed on its other side. Repeat with the remaining mangos. In a small bowl, mix together the vinegar and the hoisin and brush it lightly over the cut surfaces of the mangos.

Fire up the grill, bringing the temperature to medium (4 to 5 seconds with the hand test).

Transfer the mangos skin-side down to a well-oiled grate. Grill the mangos uncovered over medium heat for 5 to 6 minutes per side. Brush the cut side of the mangos again with the vinegar-hoisin mixture as you take them from the grill. If grilling covered, cook the mangos for 9 to 11 minutes, turning once midway and basting in a similar manner.

When cool enough to handle, make parallel cuts ½ inch apart down into, but not through, the cut side of the mango flesh. Make a second set of similar cuts perpendicular to the first set, forming a crosshatch pattern. Push the skin side of the mangos up in the center, which will cause the cut flesh to pop up and spread open, showing off the lighter colored flesh under the caramelized surface.

Serve the mangos hot or at room temperature.

HONEYED RAINBOW FRUIT KEBOBS

In the first decades of American grilling, dessert kebobs with several ingredients usually included marshmallows, pieces of store-bought cake or packaged cookie dough, and an occasional chunk of fruit. Fresh fruit doesn't need the commercial colleagues, though we like to layer it with honey butter. Use at least three of the suggested fruits, preferably ones of different color, and perhaps a fragrant lavender honey if you have it.

SERVES 4 TO 6

2½ pounds mixed soft-textured fruit chunks, such as
 skin-on tangerine chunks, whole strawberries,
 thick kiwi slices, halved pitted plums or apricots,
 whole pitted sweet cherries, mango or pineapple
 chunks, or peach quarters
Metal skewers, preferably 2 for each kebob

HONEY BUTTER
¼ cup honey
1 tablespoon water
2 tablespoons butter

Chopped fresh mint, for garnish

Thread the fruit chunks on skewers in alternating colors (preferably using 2 skewers per kebob to hold the ingredients securely while cooking). Push the fruit together to touch but not squash the neighboring fruit.

Fire up the grill, bringing the temperature to medium (4 to 5 seconds with the hand test).

Prepare the honey butter, warm the ingredients in a small saucepan over medium heat. Stir to combine. Brush the kebobs lightly with the honey butter.

Transfer the kebobs to a well-oiled grate. Grill the kebobs uncovered over medium heat for 8 to 11 minutes, turning on all sides, until the fruits are softened and a few edges are browned. Brush the kebobs thickly with the

honey butter in the last minute of cooking. If grilling covered, cook for 7 to 10 minutes, turning once midway and basting then.

Serve the fruit hot, sprinkled with chopped mint. For a variation, replace the honey in the butter with orange or lemon marmalade and substitute a couple of good splashes of tequila and a squeeze of fresh lime for the water. Olé!

CHESTNUTS ROASTING ON AN OPEN FIRE

Yes, they're as wonderful as the song suggests. When chestnuts are roasted on a grill, they lose some of their starchy character and the flavor mellows to an earthy sweetness. Serve them with dried fruit and a hearty port.

SERVES AS MANY AS YOU WISH

Chestnuts
Salt, optional

Fire up the grill, bringing the temperature to medium-high (3 seconds with the hand test).

With a sharp knife, cut an X at the base of each chestnut. Watch your fingers, because the shells are slick.

Place the chestnuts on a small-mesh grill rack and transfer to the grill. Grill the chestnuts over medium-high heat for 3 to 6 minutes, rolling them around to cook evenly. The chestnuts are ready when the shells and bitter inner membrane gape open, and the shells turn brittle and more blackish than their usual toasty brown. The nutmeats will have turned from the color of cream to café that's very au-lait. If grilling covered, cook the chestnuts for the same amount of time, turning once midway.

Pile the chestnuts in a bowl and cool just until you can handle them. Peel the nuts and, if you wish, dip them in a bit of salt before eating.

ALL-AMERICAN ACCOMPANIMENTS

All-American Accompaniments

Sprightly Potato Salad

We read recently in a fashionable food magazine that potato salad is too boring to serve at a cookout. We thought about that awhile and decided the author must have a really lousy recipe collection. In commiseration, we threw together a spud salad studded with righteous Cajun flavors, in the same league of boring as a high-stepping zydeco tune.

Serves 8

3 pounds potatoes, preferably Yukon Gold or yellow
  Finn, halved
5 slices uncooked bacon, chopped
¼ cup olive oil
1 large sweet or mild onion, chopped
½ medium green bell pepper, diced fine
1 large celery stalk, minced
⅛ cup thin-sliced green onion tops
2 tablespoons cider vinegar
2 to 3 tablespoons Creole mustard
1 teaspoon salt, or more to taste
¼ teaspoon Tabasco sauce or other hot pepper sauce, or
  more to taste
Generous grinding of black pepper

In a large saucepan, cover the potatoes with salted water and bring them to a boil over high heat. Reduce the heat to medium and simmer the potatoes until fork-tender, about 20 to 25 minutes. Drain the potatoes and, when cool enough to handle, cut them into bite-size chunks. Transfer the potatoes to a large bowl.

In a heavy skillet, fry the bacon over medium heat until crisp. With a slotted spoon, drain the bacon and reserve it. Pour the olive oil into the bacon drippings and heat through. Stir in the onion and sauté several minutes until soft. Spoon the mixture over the potatoes. Add the remaining ingredients and toss the salad together. Let the salad sit at room temperature for 20 to 30 minutes for the potatoes to absorb the other flavors. (The salad can be made earlier in the day, covered, and refrigerated.)

Stir in the bacon and serve the

salad warm or cold. If serving cold, remove it from the refrigerator and let sit at room temperature for about 20 minutes before serving.

HOT POTATOES

No other side dish complements a grilled meal like potatoes. Whether you put them in a salad, smother them with butter and sour cream, fry them crisp, or bake them in the coals, spuds say you're serious about your eating. Grillers have cooked them every way possible—even in a pot of boiling rosin, a dangerously flammable by-product in the manufacture of turpentine.

In *The Florida Cookbook* (Alfred A. Knopf, 1993), Jeanne Voltz and Caroline Stuart conjecture that rosin potatoes originated in the old turpentine camps of north Florida, probably by accident when someone dropped a lunchtime spud in a distilling vat. The potato came out coated with the sticky cooking liquid, but as fluffy as fleece inside. The flavor eventually won acclaim from such eminent outdoor cooks as James Beard and Maggie Waldron, and the novelty of the approach produced a minor fad, big enough in the 1950s that *Look* featured a recipe in a story on the "barbecue bug." The ultimate hot potato, it had to be eaten under wraps, covered in several layers of newspaper to protect hands from the scorching, gummy rosin.

Our suggested accompaniments are much simpler and safer. We selected them first of all for their great taste alongside grilled food, but also for ease of preparation, flexibility in timing, and expandability of portions. Tried-and-true rather than trendy, the sides all pair well with many dishes in this book and most of them make great leftovers for another day of grilling. You won't burn your fingers on a single one.

St. Louis Italian Salad

We've revived this salad—in more ways than one—from Cheryl's earliest repertory of dishes in her college days. She originally discovered the idea, almost an antipasto in a bowl, in the Italian-American restaurants of St. Louis. It struck her fancy largely because the heady garlic flavor came from whole cloves rather than a powder or salt, a prodigal notion in the Midwest of that day. We still make it with the retro iceberg lettuce, necessary to support the heft of the dressing, but we no longer use canned "Parmesan" cheese and the "pure" olive oil once sold in thimble-size bottles. We usually add the optional veggies, but you won't go hungry without them.

SERVES 6 TO 8

6½-ounce jar marinated artichoke hearts
¼ cup extra-virgin olive oil
6 tablespoons fresh-grated Parmesan cheese
1 tablespoon red wine vinegar
1½ teaspoons balsamic vinegar
2 to 3 plump garlic cloves, minced
⅛ teaspoon dry mustard
½ teaspoon dried oregano
¾ teaspoon kosher salt or other coarse salt, or more to taste
¼ teaspoon fresh-ground black pepper, or more to taste
1 large head iceberg lettuce (limp leaves discarded), torn in bite-size pieces
1 large grilled or roasted red bell pepper, peeled, seeded, and sliced thin
½ large red onion, halved, sliced into paper-thin half-moons, and separated into individual pieces (if especially pungent, soak in hot water for 5 minutes and drain before using)
Hearts of palm, marinated mushrooms, halved cherry tomatoes or whole tiny tomatoes, optional
Additional fresh-grated Parmesan cheese

Drain the oil from the artichoke hearts into a large salad bowl. Cut the artichoke hearts into thin slices and reserve.

Into the oil from the artichokes, whisk the olive oil, cheese, both vinegars, garlic, mustard, oregano, salt, and pepper. (The dressing can be made to this point earlier in the day and kept covered and refrigerated in the bowl until just before you plan to eat.)

Add the lettuce to the bowl and toss the lettuce with the dressing. Scatter the artichoke hearts, bell pepper, onion, and any of the optional vegetables over the lettuce and toss it all again.

Garnish with a large handful of additional cheese, add more salt and pepper if you wish, and serve.

Smokin' Chipotle Coleslaw

A molasses-laced mélange of crisp vegetables, smoking with chipotle chile, this slaw sneaked up on us unexpectedly one night in Hartford, Connecticut, far from its natural turf. Black-Eyed Sally's, a lively barbecue and blues outpost, was cooking some dishes of ours from previous books for a local food festival. When we sat down to taste everything, we discovered with distress that we liked their imaginative slaw better than our own food. We returned home with the basics scrawled on a bar napkin and developed a home version. It keeps well for several days, though the color of the red cabbage fades slightly.

SERVES 8 OR MORE

SASSY SLAW
1 small cabbage head, grated
¼ red cabbage head, grated
2 carrots, grated
½ cup thin-sliced green onions
1 fresh poblano or other mild green chile such as New Mexican or Anaheim, grilled or roasted, peeled, and cut into thin strips
1 red bell pepper, grilled or roasted, peeled, and cut into thin strips

CHIPOTLE DRESSING
1 cup Enriched Mayonnaise (page 38) or other
    mayonnaise
½ cup sour cream
6 tablespoons cider vinegar
2½ tablespoons unsulphured molasses
1 teaspoon salt
¾ teaspoon fresh-ground black pepper
2 canned chipotle chiles, minced, plus, for more heat,
    1 to 2 teaspoons of adobo sauce from the can

• • • • • • • • • • • • • • • • •

Prepare the slaw, stirring together the ingredients in a large bowl.

Prepare the dressing, whisking together the ingredients in a medium bowl. Toss the dressing with the slaw and refrigerate for at least an hour for the flavors to develop.

Serve chilled.

STEAKHOUSE TOMATO SALAD

Our favorite steakhouse in the country, Peter Luger in Brooklyn, has a professional tomato picker, a fellow whose main responsibility is to find and secure the very best tomatoes available in the world each day of the year. That's how seriously the restaurant takes its tomato salad, one of the few accompaniments on the menu. Not all of us can shop in Argentina in the winter, but we can and should follow the Luger example during the peak growing season in our own areas, seeking out top quality at farmers' markets and produce stores. With perfectly ripe, juicy tomatoes and the sweetest onions in town, this salad will light up the summer sky. We top it with the ranch dressing given below, but it loses none of the luster under a simple vinaigrette.

SERVES 6 TO 8
• • • • • • • • • • • • • • • •

CHIVE RANCH DRESSING
½ cup buttermilk
½ cup mayonnaise
3 tablespoons chopped chives
1 tablespoon chopped fresh parsley
½ teaspoon salt
¼ teaspoon fresh-ground black pepper

1 large sweet onion, preferably a softball-size Vidalia,
   Maui, Texas 1015, or other mild onion
6 softball-size or larger red-ripe tomatoes, heavy for
   their size
Salt

. . . .

Prepare the dressing, puréeing all the ingredients in a blender. Chill the dressing for at least 30 minutes and up to a day.

Cut the onion into six thick slices. Place the slices in a bowl and pour enough very cold water over them to cover. Add a large handful of ice cubes and refrigerate the onions for at least 30 minutes. Drain the onions, which now should be a bit milder and crisper than before. Pull them into individual rings.

Slice each tomato into three or four corpulent rounds, avoiding any tough yellowish core from the top center of the tomatoes. As neatly as possible with soupy, ripe tomatoes, transfer them to individual salad plates or a platter and scatter the onions over them. Salt lightly. The salad can be chilled briefly if you wish.

Serve drizzled lightly with the dressing or pass the dressing separately at the table.

TECHNIQUE TIP: We prefer our tomatoes peeled for this and other salads, a step you can skip if you wish. Techniques abound for peeling them, but we prefer to immerse them for a couple of seconds in boiling water and then pull off the skin in strips.

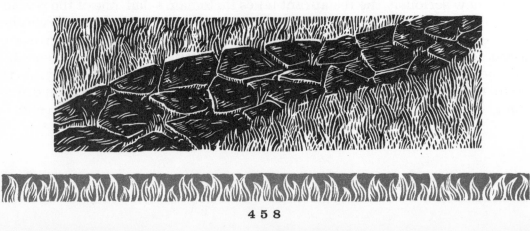

FANCY THREE-BEAN SALAD

After iceberg lettuce, the first edible green at an American cookout must have been a canned bean, probably mixed with two cousins in a simple salad. Popular even with he-men and children, the ubiquitous green-, kidney-, and wax-bean blend satisfied both the dietitians of the day and hearty outdoor appetites. Our updated version retains the original advantages, but offers tastier beans, a fresher flavor, and a zestier dressing.

SERVES 6 TO 8

8 ounces fresh *haricots verts*, or other thin young
    string beans, stemmed and halved on the diagonal
2 cups cooked garbanzo beans
2 cups cooked fresh or frozen baby lima beans
2 celery stalks, chopped fine
2 large shallots, minced

LEMON DRESSING
6 tablespoons extra-virgin olive oil
2 tablespoons minced fresh parsley
2 tablespoons minced fresh mint
1½ teaspoons Dijon mustard
½ teaspoon mashed anchovy, preferably, or anchovy
    paste
¼ teaspoon salt
⅛ teaspoon sugar
2 tablespoons fresh lemon juice

Zest of 1 lemon
Fresh mint leaves, optional, for garnish

In a steamer, cook the *haricots verts* until tender, just a few brief minutes. Run cold water over the beans, to keep their bright green hue from fading, and drain. Transfer the *haricots verts*, garbanzo beans, lima beans, celery, and shallots to a large bowl.

Prepare the dressing, whisking together the ingredients in a medium bowl. Pour the dressing over the salad,

toss until combined, and refrigerate covered for at least 1 hour for the flavors to develop.

Taste the salad, adjusting the seasoning if needed. Sprinkle the lemon zest over the salad and garnish with mint leaves if you wish. Serve the salad chilled or at room temperature.

POTLUCK MACARONI AND CHEESE SALAD

We always thank our lucky stars when we find this old standard on a buffet table today. The combination of ingredients sounds odd, but the savory result shames many contemporary pasta salads. For optimum gusto, use full-bodied cheddar and avoid nonfat mayonnaise. If you favor low-fat mayo, sweeter than the regular, start with a tablespoon less pickle relish than recommended until you taste the salad. We call for bottled roasted red bell peppers in the recipe because of their soft texture and flavorful packing liquid. Substitute a jar of blander pimientos if you can't find the bells.

SERVES 8

1 pound macaroni, preferably elbows, short tubes, or
   small shells
1 tablespoon olive oil
½ cup Enriched Mayonnaise (page 38) or other
   mayonnaise
6 tablespoons sweet pickle relish
2 tablespoons sour cream or plain yogurt
1 large sweet onion or other mild onion, diced
1½ cups uncooked shelled Sugar Snap or other peas,
   fresh or frozen
8 ounces medium cheddar cheese, diced

1 medium green bell pepper, diced
1 medium yellow bell pepper, diced
⅓ cup bottled roasted red bell peppers, chopped
Pinch of ground white pepper

. . . .

Cook the macaroni according to the package directions. It should remain a little firm when done. Drain the macaroni, pour it into a large bowl, and toss with the olive oil.

Mix the rest of the ingredients together with the macaroni. Refrigerate the salad, covered, for at least 1 hour for the flavors to develop.

Serve chilled. The salad keeps well for several days.

SWEET-SOUR CARROT AND RAISIN SALAD

Livelier and lighter in taste than most traditional versions of the salad, this rendition sparks up an old flame.

SERVES 6

. . . .

5 large carrots, sliced into very thin rounds
¾ cup raisins
½ medium green bell pepper, diced fine
3 tablespoons minced onion

SWEET-SOUR SALAD DRESSING
6 tablespoons peanut oil, preferably a roasted variety such as Loriva
2 tablespoons cider vinegar
2 teaspoons sugar
¾ teaspoon salt
½ teaspoon dry mustard

. . . .

Mix together the salad ingredients in a large bowl.

Prepare the dressing, whisking the ingredients together in a small bowl. Pour the dressing over the salad and toss it well. Refrigerate the salad, covered, for at least 1 hour or preferably overnight.

Serve chilled. The salad keeps well for several days.

CRUNCHY BROCCOLI SALAD

Vibrant in both taste and emerald effervescence, this raw salad could turn many veggie haters into broccoli lovers. It's definitely on our menu if George Bush ever comes to dinner.

SERVES 6 TO 8

4 cups fine-chopped fresh broccoli stems and florets
½ cup chopped pimiento-stuffed green olives, drained
⅛ cup thin-sliced green onions
⅛ cup plain yogurt
⅛ cup Enriched Mayonnaise (page 38) or other mayonnaise
2 teaspoons fresh lemon juice
½ teaspoon salt
¼ teaspoon fresh-ground black pepper

In a large bowl, toss together the ingredients. Refrigerate the salad for at least 1 hour and up to overnight.

Serve chilled. The salad keeps well for at least a couple of days.

GRILLING AND THE MODEL T

People have cooked with charcoal for centuries, but the familiar briquettes of today are as new as the automobile age. In the past, people made charcoal by piling logs into a pyramid, covering the mound with earth to restrict air circulation, and burning the wood down to carbon. The process resulted in irregular lumps or chunks of high-heat fuel, useful for broiling or roasting food in an outside fire pit or an indoor wood stove. This style of charcoal still exists—and works great for grilling—but the briquette replaced it as the most popular cooking fuel thanks to Henry Ford's Model T.

Ford used a number of wood appointments in his early cars, parts cut to order at a mill he operated in the northern forests of Michigan. A man who hated waste as much as he loved profits, Ford became increasingly bothered by the mushrooming stacks of wood scraps at his plant. The pieces were too small to make regular charcoal, but he realized that he could still convert them to carbon, grind the coals into a powder, add a binding agent, and compress the granulated mixture into pillow-shaped briquettes.

Ford got his friend Thomas Edison to design a production facility, which went into full operation in 1921, a few decades ahead of its time. The auto magnate initially envisioned his little packets of firepower as an industrial fuel, to be sold directly to businesses. He later marketed the charcoal to the public through Ford dealerships, but he died too soon to see how and why backyard cooks would turn his product into an industry of its own. Compact, long-burning, and uniform in heat, briquettes were destined for the grill, but they arrived there with the speed of a Model T.

GRANT STREET PICKLED VEGETABLES

As colorful and aromatic as the main street of San Francisco's Chinatown, this medley of crisp, cool vegetables sparkles with Asian seasonings.

SERVES 6 TO 8

1½ cups rice vinegar
1½ cups water
¾ cup sugar
⅔ cup dry sherry
1½ tablespoons minced fresh ginger
¾ teaspoon salt
1 to 2 small dried hot red chiles, optional

4 cups packed Napa cabbage or bok choy, cut into strips
3 large carrots, sliced on the diagonal ¼ inch thick
6 ounces snow peas, stemmed
1 medium red bell pepper, cut into matchsticks
1 medium yellow bell pepper, cut into matchsticks
3 green onions, sliced on the diagonal ¼ inch thick

In a nonreactive saucepan, combine the vinegar, water, sugar, sherry, ginger, salt, and, if you wish, chiles. Bring to a boil over high heat, then reduce the heat to a simmer and cook for 5 minutes. Cool to room temperature.

Mix together the remaining ingredients in a large bowl. Pour the vinegar mixture over the vegetables and stir to submerge all of them. Cover and refrigerate for at least 12 hours and up to a week.

Serve chilled.

AMAZING ASPIC

Don't skip over this one just because you gave up on ladies' luncheon–style tomato aspic years ago. We had, too, until a recent revelation in a Florentine restaurant named Cibrèo, where a rich tomato base and robust spices turned the quivering gel into a bold extravagance. In our home version, we start with canned tomatoes for consistency in quality and meatiness, but we insist on a premium brand such as Muir Glen, now found in a growing number of well-stocked supermarkets as well as whole foods and health stores. Small portions of the aspic go a long way.

SERVES 6 TO 8

Two 14-ounce to 15-ounce cans whole tomatoes in juice
1 package unflavored gelatin
3 tablespoons extra-virgin olive oil
2 tablespoons minced fresh basil or fresh oregano
2 tablespoons minced fresh parsley, preferably Italian
    flat-leaf
2 to 3 garlic cloves, minced
1 teaspoon salt
¼ teaspoon crushed dried hot red chile

Extra-virgin olive oil
Slivered artichoke hearts, and arugula or watercress,
    for garnish

Purée the tomatoes with their juice in a food processor or blender. Pour half of the tomatoes into a heat-proof medium bowl. Pour the other half of the tomatoes into a small saucepan.

Sprinkle the gelatin evenly over the tomatoes in the bowl and let it soften undisturbed for several minutes. Bring the saucepan of tomatoes to a boil over high heat. Mix the hot toma-toes into the bowl, stirring until the gelatin has melted into the mixture. Stir in the remaining aspic ingredients.

Oil a 5- to 6-cup mold or smooth-bottomed bowl and spoon in the aspic. Cover and refrigerate the mold for at least 4 hours and up to overnight.

Unmold the aspic just a few minutes before you plan to serve it. To unmold, run a couple of inches of hot

water into a sink and set the mold in it for 1 to 2 minutes, just long enough for it to loosen at the sides. (Don't let the aspic sit any longer in the water. Because it doesn't set as firmly as Jell-O and other similar dishes, it can go from jelled to jammy in an extra minute.) Set a plate over the mold, turn both over quickly, and give them a little sharp shake to release the aspic onto the plate.

Drizzle with just a bit of oil. Garnish with artichoke hearts and arugula and serve chilled with lots of good bread.

MIXED HERB TABBOULEH

Mixed with herbs and veggies, bulgur or cracked wheat makes a lusty base for a grill-party salad. For the best results, prepare it a few hours or even a day in advance of serving.

SERVES 8

. . . .

1 cup cracked bulgur wheat
4 cups boiling water

6 tablespoons extra-virgin olive oil
2 tablespoons fresh lemon juice
½ teaspoon hot chile paste, such as Moroccan harissa or
    Asian chile-garlic paste, or more to taste
1 plump garlic clove, minced
1 teaspoon salt
¾ cup minced fresh mint
¾ cup minced fresh parsley
¼ cup minced fresh dill
2 tablespoons minced fresh basil
1 small red onion, minced
1 small zucchini, diced

½ red bell pepper, diced
½ yellow bell pepper, diced
4 green onions, minced

**Lettuce leaves or bottled or fresh grape leaves, for
garnish**

Pour the wheat into a large, heat-proof bowl and pour the water over it. Let the wheat sit at room temperature for at least 1 hour and up to 2 hours. Drain the wheat and let it dry for another hour at room temperature for the best texture. If you need to speed the drying, squeeze out excess moisture by hand or with the wheat wrapped in cheesecloth or a clean dish towel, which leaves it slightly mushier but still good.

Return the wheat to the bowl. In a different small bowl, whisk together the oil, lemon juice, chile paste, garlic, and salt and pour over the wheat. Toss together the mixture and then stir in the herbs. Mix again and add the onion, zucchini, bell peppers, and green onions. Refrigerate the tabbouleh, covered, for at least 1 hour and up to overnight. Taste and add more lemon juice if necessary for a refreshing citrus tang.

Serve the tabbouleh chilled on top of lettuce or grape leaves.

HOPPIN' JOHN SALAD WITH TABASCO DRESSING

Hoppin' John, the Southern black-eyed pea classic, normally comes hot, but for a grilled meal we like to turn it into a chilled salad that can be made as much as a day ahead. An ample splash of Tabasco, always good on the peas, enlivens the dressing.

SERVES 8

1 pound dried black-eyed peas, preferably fresh or frozen
6 cups chicken stock
2 bay leaves
2 garlic cloves, minced
2 teaspoons minced fresh thyme or 1 teaspoon dried thyme
Salt
2 cups cooked rice
1 medium green bell pepper, diced
½ medium red onion, diced fine

TABASCO DRESSING
½ cup plus 1 tablespoon vegetable oil, preferably corn oil
3 tablespoons cider vinegar
1 teaspoon Tabasco sauce, or more to taste
⅛ teaspoon salt

In a large saucepan, combine the black-eyed peas with the stock. Add the bay leaves, garlic, thyme, and salt to taste. Simmer until the peas are cooked through and soft but short of mushy. Expect the cooking time to be at least 45 minutes for frozen peas and up to twice that long for dried peas.

Drain the peas, discarding the bay leaves and liquid (or saving it for soup), and transfer them to a large bowl. Stir in the rice, bell pepper, and onion.

Prepare the dressing, whisking the ingredients together in a small

bowl. The Tabasco flavor will be hopping out at you at this stage, but the dressing will be combined with lots of starch, which absorbs some of the zing. Pour the dressing over the salad and toss it together gently. Refrigerate the salad for at least 30 minutes and up to a day.

Before serving chilled, sample the salad and add a little more Tabasco sauce and salt to taste.

LAND OF THE LAKES WILD RICE-PECAN SALAD

Nutty wild rice from Minnesota gets even crunchier when mixed with toasted pecans. If you are among the lucky few with access to wild hickory nuts, use them in place of pecans for the most authentic regional taste. To keep the salad from being totally nutty, we add some mushrooms and dried berries.

SERVES 6 TO 8

1½ cups uncooked wild rice
6 ounces wild or button mushrooms, cut into small
    thin slices
⅛ cup dried cranberries or blueberries
3 green onions, minced
Zest of 1 orange

WILD RICE SALAD DRESSING
2 tablespoons porcini-flavored oil or vegetable oil
Juice of 1 orange
1 tablespoon Peach Vinegar (page 41) or other fruit
    vinegar
⅛ teaspoon prepared horseradish, optional
Salt

½ cup pecan pieces, or hickory nut pieces, toasted
Butter lettuce or Boston lettuce leaves

• • • • • • • • • • • • • • • • • •

Cook the wild rice according to the package directions and drain it. Transfer the rice to a large bowl and stir in the mushrooms, cranberries, green onions, and orange zest.

Prepare the dressing, whisking together the ingredients in a small bowl.

Pour the dressing over the salad and mix it well. Refrigerate, covered, for at least 30 minutes and up to a day.

Stir the pecans into the salad, ring a platter with the lettuce leaves, and mound the salad on the platter. Serve chilled or at room temperature.

THE AMBASSADOR'S NEW WALDORF SALAD

When Bill Richardson, our former New Mexico congressman, became the U.S. Ambassador to the United Nations, he and his wife, Barbara, moved to the official residence in New York's Waldorf-Astoria. To celebrate our friends' old and new residences at once, we developed this *nuevo* salad based on the hotel's most famous export and some of the state's favorite products. The salad may not be the solution to world peace, but it'll sure put a hush over a boisterous dinner table.

SERVES 6

• • • • • • • • • • • • • • •

NEW WALDORF DRESSING
½ cup Enriched Mayonnaise (page 38) or other
    mayonnaise
1 tablespoon currant liqueur, preferably, or Triple Sec
    or other orange liqueur
1 tablespoon walnut oil
½ tablespoon fresh lemon juice
½ teaspoon ground dried mild red chile
Salt

• • • • • •

2 medium apples (about 1 pound), preferably a
combination of crisp green- and red-skinned
varieties, cut into neat bite-size pieces
½ pound jícama, peeled and diced
2 medium celery stalks, sliced on the diagonal into
¼-inch-thick slices
¼ pound seedless grapes, preferably red, halved
¾ cup pecan pieces, toasted

Shredded red cabbage or watercress sprigs, for garnish

• • • • • • • • • • • • • • • • • •

Prepare the dressing, whisking the ingredients together in a small bowl.

In a large bowl, mix together the apples, jícama, celery, and grapes. Pour the dressing over the salad and mix again. Refrigerate, covered, for at least 30 minutes and up to several hours. Just before serving, stir in the pecans.

Serve the salad chilled in the bowl or on individual plates, with cabbage or watercress tucked at the edge for color.

TECHNIQUE TIP: A homely, brown-skinned root vegetable, jícama tastes something like a cross between water chestnuts and apples. Some get nearly as large as a football, but many are smaller, and markets often cut the big ones into manageable chunks. Choose firm, relatively smooth-skinned specimens, store in the refrigerator for up to two weeks, and peel before using in recipes. Substitute additional apples in the salad if you can't find jícama. Leftovers can be added to other salads or served in slices sprinkled with lime juice and ground dried red chile as a cocktail nibble.

GARLIC BREAD SALAD

Drenched in margarine, sprinkled with garlic powder, and steamed in foil on the grill, garlic bread was the only backyard bread in the country for many years. We trade the spongy bread for a crusty, chewy country loaf and toss it together with garlic and killer tomatoes for a robust summer salad. You can oven-toast the bread until just colored and use the tomatoes fresh from the garden, but grilling the bread and the tomatoes offers a subtly compelling difference in flavor. Either way you prepare it, the salad will send you sailing down memory lane on a luxury liner.

SERVES 6

- 2 pounds whole large red-ripe tomatoes, heavy for their size
- 1 pound crusty country bread, sliced 1 inch thick
- ½ cup extra-virgin olive oil
- 2 tablespoons white wine vinegar
- 3 tablespoons chopped red onion
- 2 plump garlic cloves, minced
- 1 teaspoon kosher salt or other coarse salt, or more to taste
- ¼ cup minced fresh basil
- ½ teaspoon fresh-ground black pepper

Basil leaves, optional, for garnish

If you wish to grill the tomatoes and bread, fire up the grill, bringing the temperature to medium (4 to 5 seconds with the hand test). Grill the tomatoes uncovered on a well-oiled grate, turning occasionally. The tomatoes are ready when they are soft and the splitting surfaces of each are brown with black spots, about 12 to 14 minutes. Toast the bread slices on the grill briefly, turning once, just long enough to lightly color their surfaces.

Alternatively, toast the bread on a baking sheet in a 375° F oven for several minutes.

Cut the bread into 1-inch cubes.

Place the tomatoes, whether grilled or fresh (skins, cores, and all), in a blender and purée. Pour the tomato purée into a large salad bowl and whisk

it together with the oil, vinegar, onion, garlic, and salt. (The salad can be made to this point several hours before serving. Cover and refrigerate the tomato mixture but leave the bread uncovered at room temperature.)

Just before serving, add the bread and any crumbs to the tomato mixture along with the basil and pepper and toss it well. Garnish with basil leaves, if you wish. Serve immediately, while the bread still provides contrasting textures of chewy, creamy, and crunchy.

TECHNIQUE TIP: In some of our recipes that call for tomatoes, we recommend the meaty Italian plum variety. Here though, we prefer bigger, juicier fruit because we want a high proportion of liquid for the bread to absorb.

CITRUS-ONION SLAW

Call it a slaw, call it a fruit salad, call it what you wish, but if you get hung up on the name, it'll be gone before you've had a dish.

SERVES 6

2 large pink grapefruit
2 large oranges
½ large red onion

SAVORY CITRUS DRESSING
3 tablespoons olive oil
3 tablespoons vegetable oil
¼ cup fresh orange juice (from about 1 orange)
1 tablespoon fresh lemon juice
2 teaspoons honey
½ teaspoon dry mustard
¼ teaspoon paprika
1 small garlic clove

2 to 3 cups watercress sprigs
Minced fresh mint, for garnish

Zest one of the grapefruit and one of the oranges and reserve the zest. With a sharp knife, cut off a small slice of peel from the stem ends of the whole grapefruits and oranges. Use one of these now-flat surfaces to steady each fruit on a cutting board. Following the curve of each fruit, and using downward knife strokes, slice the peel and the white pith from each fruit. Next, cut deeply down along both sides of each membrane in the fruits, to release the individual sections. Place the fruit sections in a large bowl and squeeze any juice from the remaining membranes over them. Sprinkle the onion over the fruit sections.

Prepare the dressing, combining the ingredients in a blender. Pour the dressing over the fruit-onion mixture. Refrigerate, covered, for at least 30 minutes and up to 8 hours.

Arrange the watercress on a platter and top it with the fruit-onion mixture. Sprinkle the mint over the slaw and serve chilled.

KATHI LONG'S STUPENDOUS BAKED BEANS

We think baked beans are so perfect for a cookout, we've included two completely different styles, starting with the one that's the most familiar, the easiest, and perhaps the best as an all-purpose dish. Like many home versions, it starts with store-bought baked beans in a can, but ends up priceless. We owe the recipe to cookbook author Kathi Long, who created it by adding Southwestern panache to her mother's Midwestern beans. Kathi generally writes about light foods, but as you can see, she also knows what deserves a splurge.

SERVES 8 TO 10

1 pound uncooked bacon, well chilled, cut crosswise
    into thirds and then into ¼-inch vertical strips
2 medium onions, chopped fine
2 plump garlic cloves, minced
Three 28-ounce cans B&M Original Baked Beans, or
    other canned baked beans
1½ cups chili sauce (the ketchup-style sauce)
⅓ cup Super Wooster Sauce (page 39) or other
    Worcestershire sauce
¼ cup yellow ballpark mustard
3 tablespoons crumbled dried basil or oregano
2 tablespoons crushed dried medium-hot or hot red
    chile
2 teaspoons ground cumin seeds
¼ to ½ cup packed dark brown sugar

Preheat the oven to 350° F.

In a large skillet, sauté the bacon over medium-high heat for 5 to 6 minutes, until beginning to brown though still limp. Stir in the onions and continue cooking the mixture until the onions are translucent, about 4 to 5 additional minutes. Add the garlic and cook for 2 to 3 minutes longer. Scrape the bacon-onion mixture into a large baking dish and add the rest of the ingredients, including the smaller amount of brown sugar. Taste and adjust the seasoning, adding more brown sugar if you prefer sweeter beans. Bake uncovered until bubbly throughout with a bit of browned crust at the edges, about 40 to 45 minutes.

Serve hot. If you have leftovers, the beans reheat splendidly.

BASTILLE DAY BEANS

If you don't grill on the Fourth of July, make up for the oversight ten days later on the equivalent French holiday. These twice-cooked baked beans, inspired by Gallic cassoulets, are perfect for that occasion and many others. To really impress any guests from France—and blow their stereotype of Americans as food Puritans—add a garlicky sausage or other meat to the beans, as they would at home, and substitute duck or goose fat for the olive oil.

SERVES 8 OR MORE

1 pound dried navy beans, cannellini, or other small
    white beans
6 cups chicken stock
2 cups water
1 large onion, chopped fine
6 garlic cloves, minced
1 tablespoon minced fresh thyme
2 bay leaves
1 teaspoon salt, or more to taste

3 tablespoons butter
2 cups dry bread crumbs
2 tablespoons olive oil
1 medium onion, chopped
4 garlic cloves, minced
6 to 8 ounces grilled sausage, sliced into thin rounds,
    optional

Pick through the beans carefully and rinse them, looking for any gravel or grit. Place the beans in a stockpot or large, heavy saucepan. Cover them with stock and water and add the onion, garlic, thyme, and bay leaves. Bring the beans just to a boil over high heat, then reduce the heat to low and simmer the beans, uncovered. Plan on a total cooking time of about 2 hours, possibly longer with obstinate beans.

After 1 hour, stir up the beans from the bottom and check the water level. If there is not at least 1 inch more water than beans, add enough hot water to bring it up to that level. Check the beans after another 30 minutes, repeating the process. Add the salt after the beans are well softened and continue simmering. Check every 15 minutes, keeping the level of liquid just above the beans. There should be extra liquid at the completion of the cooking time, but the beans should not be watery. (The beans can be made to this point a day in advance. Cool them, then refrigerate covered. The beans do not need to be reheated before proceeding, but add 5 to 10 minutes to the baking time.)

Preheat the oven to 350° F.

In an ovenproof skillet, preferably 10 to 12 inches in diameter, melt 2 tablespoons of the butter over medium heat. Stir in the bread crumbs and cook them until crisp and golden brown, about 5 minutes. Scrape the crumbs onto a plate and wipe out the skillet. Return the skillet to medium heat and warm the remaining tablespoon of butter and the oil. Add the onion and sauté until translucent, about 5 minutes. Stir in the garlic and cook an additional minute or two. Stir the beans and their liquid into the skillet, along with the grilled sausage if you wish. The beans should be suspended in creamy, moist liquid. If the liquid has thickened too much, add enough water to stir them easily. Spoon the bread crumbs over the beans, patting the crumbs down evenly.

Cover the skillet and bake the beans for 25 to 30 minutes. Raise the oven temperature to 425° F and uncover the beans. Bake an additional 10 to 15 minutes, or until the bread crumbs are nicely browned and the beans are thick and bubbly.

Serve the beans hot.

GATHERING AROUND THE GRILL

You have to wonder whether food flavor had much to do with the surge in popularity of grilling right after World War II. Books and magazine articles of the period often focused as much on the relaxed conviviality of the outdoor setting as on techniques and recipes. Though it was seldom stated directly, the grill became the centerpiece of a national party celebrating the end of the long, horrible war, and the return to normal family life.

No one summed up the spirit better than Helen Evans Brown in her *Patio Cook Book* (Ward Ritchie Press, 1951). In introducing her subject, she says the book is less about grilling than about the delights of outdoor dining and entertaining. "All over America the patio has become the pleasantest part of summer living. . . . That is the place where warm leisurely days begin and end, where breakfast coffee is a drink sublime, and where the simplest supper, served under the stars, becomes a memorable meal. . . . When the menu is simple, the service casual, when everyone helps and pot luck is always good luck, we need never hesitate to ask our friends to share our food. Every meal is a party meal."

Genevieve Callahan, another California cook, expressed similar sentiments in the pages of *Sunset*, and the magazine's barbecue cookbooks even included a section on types of games to play before and after a grilled feast. To keep guests from getting bored by having to stand around and talk, the editors suggested afternoon matches of croquet, horseshoes, Ping-Pong, shuffleboard, or bean bags. After dinner, they advised stringing floodlights for table games such as dominoes, or gathering everyone around the fire for guessing games, maybe "Twenty Questions," "Coffeepot," or "Geography."

A like mood prevailed on the East Coast. In *That Man in the Kitchen* (Houghton Mifflin, 1946), Malcolm LaPrade described the scene on the penthouse terraces of large New York apartment buildings. "This entire community of roof-dwellers has gone in for outdoor cookery, and on a fine summer's evening the appetizing aroma of grilled steaks and chops permeates the air, mingling with the subtle perfume of geraniums and rambler roses." On every balcony, LaPrade wrote, you could watch the men "turning well-browned pieces of meat over the flames while their wives loll at ease in deck chairs, looking most attractive in gaily colored slacks, and chatting pleasantly with groups of guests. It is a cheering spectacle which speaks well for a newly discovered appreciation of the amenities of life in a modern apartment house."

TRUE-GUILT CREAMED SPINACH

The ideal mate for a steak, this timeless creamed spinach is worth every one of its luscious calories.

SERVES 6 TO 8

3 pounds fresh spinach
2 cups whipping cream
¼ cup butter
⅓ cup minced onion
1 teaspoon salt, or more to taste
¼ teaspoon ground nutmeg
Fresh-ground black pepper

Wash the spinach leaves thoroughly in a bowl or sinkful of cold water to remove every bit of grit. Repeat the process if necessary to thoroughly clean the leaves. Place the spinach, with the water that clings to it, in a large, heavy pan. Cover the pan and wilt the spinach over medium heat, stirring it around once or twice. Wilting should take about 5 minutes. When the spinach is cool enough to handle, squeeze out any excess moisture, rinse it in ice water, and drain again. (The spinach can be prepared to this point earlier in the day, wrapped tightly, and refrigerated.)

In a blender, purée half of the spinach with about ⅓ cup of the cream, adding a little more cream if needed to combine easily. Finely chop the remaining spinach.

In a large saucepan, melt the butter over medium-low heat. Add the onion and sauté several minutes until translucent. Stir in both the puréed and chopped spinach and add the remaining cream while stirring until incorporated and heated through. Add salt, nutmeg, and a good generous grinding of pepper.

Serve hot or, if you wish, cool the spinach and refrigerate it covered. Reheat gently before serving later the same day.

CRISPY CUMIN FRIES

These pert potatoes feature a flavorful crust, extra crispy because of their double frying. The first frying can be done in advance of grilling, but save the last step until the end, right before you plan to eat.

SERVES 6

4 russets or other baking potatoes, peeled or unpeeled
Cold water
Ice cubes
3 tablespoons cumin seeds, toasted and ground (see Technique Tip)
2 teaspoons All-'Round Rub (page 23), or Chile Rub Rojo (page 24) or chili powder
2 teaspoons kosher salt or other coarse salt
Peanut oil or other vegetable oil for deep-frying

Slice the potatoes into fat matchsticks, about ⅜ inch in diameter. Toss the potatoes into a large bowl of cold water as they are cut.

Pour off the water from the potatoes, eliminating some of the starch as you do. Add more cold water to cover and put in 6 or 8 ice cubes this time. Place the bowl in the refrigerator and let the potatoes soak in the ice water for 30 minutes to 1 hour, to firm them. Drain the potatoes well on paper towels or clean dish towels. You want to eliminate all surface moisture to cut down on popping oil when frying.

In a large bowl, combine the cumin with the dry rub and salt and reserve.

Up to 1 hour before you plan to eat, fry the potatoes the first time. In a large, heavy saucepan or Dutch oven, heat 3 to 4 inches of oil to 340° F. Add the potatoes in batches and par-fry them for about 3 minutes, just until they begin to color. Drain the potatoes, which will be limp and a little sorry looking, and spread them on several layers of paper towels covering a baking sheet. Turn off the heat under the oil unless you plan to refry the potatoes immediately.

Just before serving, reheat the oil to 360° F, and fry the potatoes in batches again for 2 to 4 minutes, until they are golden brown and crisp. Drain the fries again and toss each batch, as it is drained, with the cumin spice mixture in the bowl.

Transfer the fries to a napkin-lined

platter or shallow bowl or basket. Serve piping hot.

TECHNIQUE TIP: Toasting whole spices before grinding brings the aromatic oils to the surface and deepens the taste. We always recommend it, but it's critical for the full flavor of the Crispy Cumin Fries. Toast the whole seeds in a dry skillet and then grind them with a mortar and pestle, spice mill, blender, or clean coffee grinder.

BUTTERMILK POTATO CASSEROLE

A casserole provides a convenient way to combine the texture of mashed potatoes with the taste of twice-baked spuds, each good alone and simply scrumptious together. The buttermilk adds tang and the mustard gives a background hint of horseradish, which we usually bolster with the optional amount of the real thing.

SERVES 8

3 pounds Yukon Gold or russet potatoes (about 6 medium potatoes)
½ cup butter
3 garlic cloves, minced
1¼ cups buttermilk
1 cup whipping cream or half-and-half
¾ teaspoon salt, or more to taste
1 tablespoon Creole mustard
½ to 2 teaspoons of prepared horseradish, optional
1 cup grated mild cheddar cheese
¼ cup grated dry Monterey jack, Parmesan, pecorino, or Montasio cheese
2 tablespoons minced chives or green onion tops

Preheat the oven to 375° F. Oil a shallow 8-by-14-inch baking dish.

Pierce each potato with a fork in several places to allow steam to escape while baking. You want the potatoes to be dry and fluffy to absorb the flavorings fully. Bake the potatoes directly on the oven rack for about 1 hour, or until soft in the center when poked again with a fork. Allow the potatoes to cool briefly. (The potatoes can be prepared a day ahead if you wish, then wrapped and refrigerated. Bring back to room temperature before proceeding.)

Turn the oven temperature up to 400° F.

In a heavy medium saucepan, melt the butter over medium heat. Add the garlic and sauté for about 1 minute until softened. Pour in the buttermilk and cream, add the salt, and heat through. (Just warm the mixture; boiling it will cause the buttermilk to separate.) Stir in the mustard and optional horseradish and remove from the heat.

Peel the potatoes, pulling the skin off with your fingers or using a paring knife. If you like the taste and texture of potato skins, discard only one-half of the skins and slice the rest into thin bite-size strips.

Mash or rice the potatoes (food processors tend to turn them to paste), placing them in a large bowl. Pour in the buttermilk mixture and mix it in well with a sturdy spoon. Stir in about two-thirds of each cheese and the optional potato skins. Spoon the potatoes into the baking dish, smoothing the top. Scatter the chives over the top and then sprinkle on the remaining cheeses. (The potatoes can be made to this point up to a day ahead and kept covered and refrigerated. Let them sit at room temperature for 30 to 45 minutes before proceeding.)

Bake the potatoes uncovered for 12 to 14 minutes, until heated through and beginning to brown on top.

Serve the casserole immediately.

BOURBON AND BLACK WALNUT SWEET POTATO GRATIN

Bourbon and black walnuts, which come from the same general area of the country, go together like lemonade and shade. In this gratin, they join sweet potatoes and molasses, another natural duo, for a four-fisted hit. The more common English walnuts can be successfully substituted for the native variety, but you lose a little of the vigor.

SERVES 8

2½ pounds (about 3 large) sweet potatoes, peeled and cubed
5 tablespoons whipping cream or half-and-half
¼ cup bourbon or other similar American whiskey
¼ cup butter, at room temperature
2 tablespoons unsulphured molasses
1 tablespoon walnut oil
½ teaspoon salt, or more to taste

¾ cup black walnut pieces

Preheat the oven to 375° F. Oil an 8-by-14-inch baking dish.

In a steamer, cook the sweet potatoes until very soft, about 20 to 25 minutes. Mash or rice the sweet potatoes (food processors tend to turn them to paste), placing them in a large bowl.

Stir the cream, bourbon, butter, molasses, oil, and salt into the sweet potatoes and spoon the mixture into the prepared baking dish. (The sweet potatoes can be prepared to this point up to a day ahead and kept covered and refrigerated. Let them sit at room temperature for 30 to 45 minutes before proceeding.) Sprinkle the sweet potatoes with the black walnuts and bake for 20 to 24 minutes, until heated through and a little bubbly.

Serve the gratin hot.

San Francisco 'Roni with Rice

Italian immigrant Domenico de Domenico, in addition to having a jazzy name, had the bright idea of putting rice and vermicelli together in a dish. The founder of a San Francisco pasta company, he presented the inspiration first as a recipe printed on the back of his packages. Years later, under the name Rice-A-Roni, it became a separate product, the "San Francisco Treat" that swept the nation. We return to de Domenico's original suggestion of making the carbo combo from scratch, using homemade stock to enrich the result.

Serves 6

2 tablespoons butter
1 tablespoon olive oil
1 cup uncooked rice
⅓ cup crumbled vermicelli
¼ cup minced onion
1 large celery stalk, minced
1 garlic clove, minced
2½ cups chicken stock, preferably homemade
¾ teaspoon salt, or more to taste
1 heaping tablespoon minced fresh parsley

Warm the butter and oil in a large, heavy saucepan over medium heat. Add the rice and vermicelli and sauté several minutes, until the rice is translucent and the vermicelli light brown. Add the onion, celery, and garlic and continue heating for a couple of minutes, until the vegetables begin to soften. Pour in the stock and sprinkle in the salt. Cover the pan, reduce the heat to a low simmer, and cook until the liquid is absorbed and the rice and vermicelli are tender, about 15 minutes. Sprinkle in the parsley, re-cover the pan, and let the mixture sit at room temperature for 10 to 30 minutes.

Fluff up the rice and vermicelli with a fork and serve warm.

A+ Baked Pasta

The Italian village of Amatrice specializes in a tubular pasta coated with a tomato sauce spiked with red chile and mild bacon-like pancetta. A homey, toothsome dish, at the head of its class in our book, it provided the inspiration for this baked pasta, a spicy accompaniment to grilled fare that's easy to prepare ahead. Consider making a meal out of it with grilled vegetables, or serve it alongside chicken or fish. The chile does stoke up the heat, so reduce the amount if you're shy of its sizzle.

SERVES 8

1 pound penne pasta
2 teaspoons extra-virgin olive oil

A+ PASTA SAUCE
1 tablespoon extra-virgin olive oil
3 ounces chopped uncooked bacon
3 ounces chopped prosciutto (see Technique Tip, page 409)
1 large red onion, chopped
2 tablespoons minced fresh rosemary or 1 tablespoon crushed dried rosemary
2 tablespoons minced fresh oregano or basil or 1 tablespoon crushed dried oregano or basil
½ cup dry red wine
28-ounce can whole tomatoes, with juice, tomatoes crushed a bit
8-ounce can tomato sauce
1 to 2 teaspoons crushed dried hot red chile
Salt to taste

1 cup grated Pecorino, other pecorino, or fresh-grated Parmesan cheese
1 cup grated mozzarella or fontina cheese

Cook the penne according to the package directions. It should remain a little firm when done. Drain the penne, pour it into a large baking dish, and toss it with the 2 teaspoons of oil.

Preheat the oven to 350° F.

Prepare the sauce, first warming the oil in a large skillet over medium heat. Add the bacon and fry until limp, just a couple of minutes. Stir in the prosciutto, onion, and herbs and continue cooking until the onions are soft and the mixture begins to brown and stick a bit, about 10 minutes longer. Pour in the wine, which will quickly cook down into the mixture. Stir in the tomatoes, tomato sauce, red chile, and

salt. Reduce the heat to low and let the mixture simmer for 20 minutes. It will thicken some, but should remain a bit soupy.

Mix the pecorino cheese and half of the mozzarella with the pasta. Pour the sauce over the pasta and mix again. Sprinkle the remaining cheese over the top. (The pasta can be made several hours in advance and kept covered and refrigerated. Let it sit at room temperature for 30 to 45 minutes before proceeding.) Bake the pasta 25 to 30 minutes, until heated through and bubbly with a few brown spots on the surface.

Serve the pasta hot.

ENCHILADA CASSEROLE

Most Americans think of enchiladas as a main dish, but in authentic Mexican and Southwestern cooking, they are frequently accompaniments for meat, a one-step means of adding the complementary tastes of corn, cheese, and chile to beef and pork plates. For a grill-party shortcut, we mix the hearty flavors in a casserole instead of individually rolled tortillas.

SERVES 6 TO 8

RED CHILE SAUCE
2 tablespoons vegetable oil
1 medium onion, minced

3 garlic cloves, minced
¾ cup ground dried mild red chile, such as New
    Mexican or Anaheim
4 cups water
1 teaspoon dried oregano, preferably Mexican
1 teaspoon salt

Vegetable oil for pan-frying
18 corn tortillas
¼ cup minced onion
1½ pounds mild cheddar cheese, grated

• • • • • • • • • • • • • • • • • • •

Preheat the oven to 350° F. Oil a shallow 8-by-14-inch baking dish.

Prepare the sauce, first warming the oil in a large, heavy saucepan over medium heat. Add the onion and sauté until the onion is translucent, about 5 minutes. Stir in the garlic and cook an additional minute. Stir in the chile and then the water, a cup at a time. Add the oregano and salt and bring the sauce just to a boil. Reduce the heat to a low simmer and cook for 20 to 25 minutes. When ready, the sauce should coat a spoon thickly but still drop off of it easily. (The sauce can be prepared several days ahead and kept covered and refrigerated. Reheat it before proceeding.)

Heat ½ to 1 inch of oil in a medium skillet over medium-high heat until the oil ripples. With tongs, dunk a tortilla in the oil long enough for it to go limp, a matter of seconds. Don't let the tortilla turn crisp. Drain the tortilla on paper towels, and repeat with the remaining tortillas.

Pour about ¼ cup of sauce evenly in the bottom of the baking dish. Arrange 6 tortillas over the sauce,

overlapping them if necessary. Spoon one-third of the remaining sauce over the tortillas, covering them entirely. Scatter one-third of the onion and cheese over the sauce. Repeat with two more layers of tortillas, sauce, onion, and cheese. Once assembled, the casserole can be left at room temperature for up to 30 minutes before baking. Bake the enchiladas for 20 to 25 minutes, until the cheese is melted throughout and a little bubbly on top.

Cut the casserole into individual portions and serve hot.

TECHNIQUE TIP: The red chile called for here is the pure, ripe, dried, and ground pod (minus stems and seeds), not commercial chili powder, which is a blend of chile and other seasonings. While spicy, the New Mexican chile is well short of incendiary, offering robust flavor to balance its piquancy. If you can get the incomparable and relatively scarce Chimayó red chile, from a northern New Mexican village of the same name, snap it up.

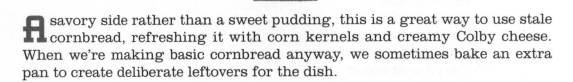

COLBY CHEESE AND CORNBREAD PUDDING

A savory side rather than a sweet pudding, this is a great way to use stale cornbread, refreshing it with corn kernels and creamy Colby cheese. When we're making basic cornbread anyway, we sometimes bake an extra pan to create deliberate leftovers for the dish.

SERVES 8

8-inch square pan of stale cornbread, crumbled
2 tablespoons butter
1 medium onion, chopped
1 cup corn kernels, fresh or frozen
1 teaspoon minced fresh marjoram or thyme, or
    ⅛ teaspoon dried marjoram or thyme
3 eggs, lightly beaten
1 cup evaporated milk
1 cup grated Colby cheese or mild cheddar cheese
Paprika

Preheat the oven to 350° F. Butter a large baking dish.

Place the cornbread in a large bowl.

Warm the butter in a small skillet over medium heat. Stir in the onion and sauté until translucent, about 5 minutes. Mix in the corn and marjoram and cook another minute. Spoon this mixture into the cornbread. Then stir in the eggs and milk, followed by the cheese. Pour the pudding into the prepared baking dish. (The pudding can be made ahead to this point and refrigerated. Let it sit for 30 minutes at room temperature before proceeding.) Dust the top of the pudding with paprika and bake 30 to 35 minutes, until lightly firm and golden.

Serve the pudding hot.

TECHNIQUE TIP: A moist, soft-textured form of mild cheddar first created in Colby, Wisconsin, Colby cheese melts especially well in this and other dishes because of its high moisture content. It's often marketed as "longhorn," a name derived from the cylindrical mold used to form the cheese rather than any association with rangy Texas steers.

MIXED BERRY CORNBREAD

The light sweetness in this cornbread comes from mixed dried berries, which plump up during baking from the moistness of the dough. Unlike fresh fruit, they keep their color instead of bleeding, maintaining the bread's rich, golden hue. We cook it in a cast-iron skillet to get the crispest crust, but a regular baking pan works fine, too.

SERVES 6 TO 8

- 1 tablespoon vegetable oil
- 1½ cups yellow cornmeal, preferably stone-ground
- ½ cup all-purpose flour
- 3 tablespoons sugar
- 1 tablespoon baking powder
- 1 teaspoon baking soda
- 1 teaspoon salt
- 1¼ cups buttermilk
- ¼ cup orange juice
- 3 eggs, lightly beaten
- ¼ cup butter, melted
- 1 cup mixed dried berries, such as cranberries, blueberries, strawberries, or cherries (use at least 3 varieties for best flavor)

Preheat the oven to 400° F. Grease a 10-inch cast-iron skillet with the oil and place it empty in the oven just before you begin mixing ingredients.

In a medium bowl, stir together the cornmeal, flour, sugar, baking powder, baking soda, and salt. Pour in the buttermilk, orange juice, and eggs, and gently mix by hand until the mixture is thoroughly blended. Stir in the melted butter and half of the berries.

Remove the skillet from the oven and pour the batter into the skillet. It will sizzle merrily. Scatter the rest of the berries over the batter. Return the skillet to the oven and bake the cornbread for 20 to 22 minutes, until it begins to brown on top and a toothpick inserted in the center comes out clean.

The cornbread is best served pip-

ing hot right from the skillet. It's still scrumptious, though, at room temperature. If that coordinates better with grilling, let the cornbread cool for about 10 minutes in the skillet to firm a bit, then turn it out of the skillet and onto a rack, where its surface will stay crisper. Cut into wedges just before serving.

INDEX

W

Z